The John Fraser-Robinson Direct Marketing Series

THE SECRETS OF EFFECTIVE DIRECT MAIL

The secrets of effective direct mail

John Fraser-Robinson

McGRAW-HILL BOOK COMPANY

London · New York · St Louis · San Francisco · Auckland · Bogotá
Caracas · Hamburg · Lisbon · Madrid · Mexico · Milan · Montreal · New Delhi
Panama · Paris · San Juan · São Paulo · Singapore · Sydney · Tokyo · Toronto

Published by
McGRAW-HILL Book Company (UK) Limited
Shoppenhangers Road, Maidenhead, Berkshire, SL6 2QL, England
Telephone 0628 23432
Fax 0628 35895

British Library Cataloguing in Publication Data

Fraser-Robinson, John
The secrets of effective direct mail. — (The John Fraser-Robinson
direct marketing series).
1. Direct-mail marketing
I. Title II. Series
658.8'72

ISBN 0–07–707085–2

Library of Congress Cataloging-in-Publication Data

Fraser-Robinson, John
The secrets of effective direct mail/John Fraser-/Robinson
p. cm. — (The John Fraser-Robinson direct marketing series)
Bibliography: p.
Includes index.
1. Direct marketing.   I. Title.   II. Series: Fraser-Robinson, John.
John Fraser-Robinson direct marketing series.
HF5415.126.F73 1989
658.8'4 — dc19 88–34876

ISBN 0–07–707085–2

234 CUP 910

Typeset by Kudos Graphics, Slinfold, Horsham, West Sussex
and printed and bound in Great Britain at the University Press,
Cambridge

This book is wholly dedicated to two 'life enhancers' —

To Julie, my wife, without whom . . . no book.
And to Thomas Bernard Robinson, OBE, without whom . . .

Contents

CHAPTER 10   THERE ARE ONLY **TEN** KINDS OF DIRECT MAIL — AND EACH HAS SOMETHING **CREATIVE** IN MIND. THEY ARE . . . WITH THE **READER** IN MIND, WITH **COPY** IN MIND, WITH **DESIGN** IN MIND, WITH **HUMAN NATURE** IN MIND, WITH **IDEAS** IN MIND, WITH A **PROPOSITION** IN MIND, WITH **LETTERS** IN MIND, WITH **PERSONALISATION** IN MIND, WITH **THE PACKAGE** IN MIND, WITH **RESPONSE** IN MIND   **295**

CHAPTER 11   THERE'S ONLY **ONE** KIND OF DIRECT MAIL AND THAT'S . . . **YOURS**   **339**

PART THREE: ASSISTANCE, CONTACTS, THE LAW, AND STANDARDS. LANGUAGE, AND WHERE YOU CAN READ SOME MORE

CHAPTER 12   CONTACTS AND ASSOCIATIONS   **343**

CHAPTER 13   LEGISLATION AND STANDARDS   **357**

Preface

This is a book about money and success. Not mine. Yours.

It is a book that will unlock, reveal and explain certain ways to make money, and to be successful.

Despite whatever else you read, or are told, there is no shortcut. Yet, in this book you can learn some of the fastest, surest, safest ways.

Not the ways of old, but the ways of new. Some born of old. Some not so old. Some entirely new. Some as yet unborn.

There's so much nonsense talked and written about the 'Simple Act of Selling'. Still more about advertising. And a whole myth built around the great god, marketing.

While there is, of course, some fundamental truth and value in much of what is taught on these subjects, too few have yet started to worship the new alternative and spread its gospel.

For in the last few years, what I describe as 'an alternative' has taken shape, formalised and grown so fast that many who should know, confidently predict it will take over.

It will certainly overtake. The alternative is already perceived as the ultimate process. It improves and sophisticates yet further as each day passes.

It uses the latest technology to knock the selling process back decades, to the days when quality of relationship between the producer or purveyor and the customer was caring, individual and vital.

This much-heralded and little understood process can bring out the best or the worst in your business and your organisation. Therefore you must control it.

It is both an art and a science. But above all else, it is the future.

You don't have to crave money and success to want this book. But it certainly helps. Inevitably though, the book will appeal mostly to those who find interest in one or more of the following:

people . . . truth . . . selling . . . profit . . .
effectiveness . . . advertising . . . business . . .
computers . . . learning . . . growth . . .
common sense . . . experimentation . . . analysis
. . . and perseverance.

This book is about your future. It is written for you whether you are a small business that wants to be a big business, or a big business that wants to stay that way — however sure you feel at the moment.

And there is much philosophy, ideology and information. Plus pure knowledge and experience for anything and anyone who falls anywhere in between, whatever your markets.

For beginners. For pro's. For sales people. For accountants or finance people. For DP people. For marketing people. And for managing directors and chairmen. Anyone sufficiently interested, involved and committed to the success of their mission to want to glimpse tomorrow today.

Some may be shocked or alienated. Others inspired. Some may find their thoughts confirmed or their eyes opened. Others still, will find it full of new and exciting ideas. While many will experience the extra confidence of feeling that all the 'jigsaw pieces' are dropping into place.

Welcome to the world I live in. The world of direct marketing.

John Fraser-Robinson

PS (of course!)   On a practical note, I have endeavoured to write a book that can be read from beginning to end, 'dipped' into for 'boning up' on bits and pieces, but which will also be a reference work in the truer sense. Therefore, you will find a thorough index. But more, to help you 'dip and bone', you'll find useful subject headers pulled out in **bold type** within the index itself. A sort of literary fast forward. In structure, much as you'd expect, you'll find chapters divided more or less into subjects: a chapter on Creative, a chapter on Production, and so on.

Acknowledgements

I should like to acknowledge the support and hard work of four people.

Mike Adams   I trust the resulting book merits a place in his collection which is surely the largest private direct marketing library in the country.

Tasmin Overstall   who researched this book so carefully for me (and seems to have 'discovered' direct marketing into the bargain!).

Linda Tuckwell   who sat down with my IBM PC, got straight to grips with Wordstar 4, and typed and typed and typed. And gave Bank Holiday weekends! Thank you so much, Linda.

And Julie Fraser-Robinson   who listened, talked, discussed, argued, encouraged and added. And constantly cared and supported. A very gifted, valued and valuable friend. A generous wife.

► PART ONE ◄

Direct marketing — The scene is set for a powerful story

Bob Geldof. Martin Luther King. Margaret Thatcher. David Ogilvy. They all have some things in common. For example, vision and conviction.

We could discuss the rights and wrongs of their visions and their convictions, and the merits of what such intensities drove or inspired them to do. In Ogilvy's case, of course, it was to found an advertising agency in which he was eventually to cultivate a unique difference. It understood the purpose of advertising. To sell.

The agency became firmly committed to this cause. Indeed, it believed in it. As Ogilvy himself said, 'Almost every product or service can be sold by direct response. From my own experience I know that direct response can be just as successful in fund-raising as in selling executive jet aircraft.'

Raymond Rubicam, co-founder of the huge multinational agency Young and Rubicam, like Ogilvy and unlike so many other classical advertising figures, was there too. He said, 'The object of advertising is to sell goods. It has no other justification worth mentioning.'

His team soon found themselves competing among a rapidly growing horde of strange, relatively unknown figures who cloaked themselves in something called, quite wrongly as it transpired, 'mass marketing'. Things have moved apace since

1

then. A Briton, in 1986, described what has become known as direct marketing thus: 'the slightly spotty adolescent of the marketing world'. He must, with hindsight, be feeling quite foolish. On the other hand, in the same year, a speaker at the International Direct Marketing and Mail Order Symposium more accurately predicted a complete marketing *volte-face*. His words are my next sub-head.

Within the next decade 90 per cent of all marketing will be direct marketing

Pathetic or prophetic? Let me tell you from my own experience and observation. The man is quite definitely a prophet. He exaggerates a little — but he's right. I'd hazard a guess at 65 to 75 per cent. I'm not sure that it will go the full 90 per cent.

Before we take a look at what direct marketing is, let me tell you what I've seen over the last few years. Should you work in advertising, marketing or selling, these next lines will be important to you if you wish to survive. If you position yourself, as I do, in the world of selling, and agree with Rubicam's sentiment that the object of advertising is indeed to sell goods — or anything else for that matter — then you will be cheered. For this is my guarantee, that all the money and success that I promised you will surely happen. You only have to get it right.

What I have observed over the immediate last few years is a phenomenal shift of advertising spend. Clients who until recently had never heard of direct marketing now assess it quite differently. One building society, for example, has moved from a level of about 5 per cent of total advertising budget on 'direct mail and other bits and pieces' to a formal direct marketing budget of equivalent to nearer 30 per cent. It is now the norm for many companies to seek three main sources of marketing supply — an advertising agency, a PR agency and a direct marketing agency.

Whole selling operations are moving over to the direct marketing process.

So we are dealing with revolution, not evolution. A massive upheaval of the status quo. Slaughter in the twinned worlds of advertising and marketing.

There are seven main reasons why this should be so. So let me run you through the seven 'A's of direct marketing.

The seven 'A's of direct marketing are also the seven 'ayes' of direct marketing

Each 'aye' offers a sound, powerful reason why you should choose the direct marketing approach to advertising:

It's accountable down to the last penny. You can see what works. What doesn't. What is cost-effective. What isn't.

It has the *added value* of the advertising effect, included at no extra cost, on top of the bankable business it will do for you.

It is answer-back advertising. We deal in dialogues, not monologues. As a result, we make contacts and create relationships.

Direct marketing is *allegiance advertising*. We command loyalty by creating friends as well as customers. We understand individual service. We give promises and we keep them. How do you know? Because we *always* guarantee it.

Direct marketing is *automated advertising*. You can draw in the latest technology to knock you back into the days when service, recognition and individual attention were the watchwords of success. And surprise! They still are. The more so, because they're all too rare these days.

Direct marketing is *appropriate advertising*, it yields the potential of tight, close targeting. You gather, hold, review and appraise — all *before* you approach the customer or prospect.

And lastly, direct marketing is *action advertising*. It goes for the ultimate. It sells. What better action is there? By putting across attractive propositions, it inspires the prospects into action.

To develop the points, let me ask you seven questions. I'll make the whole process less arduous by giving you the answers too! Well, at least *my* answers.

1 *Why spend your money on ordinary advertising when you can buy* **accountable advertising?** The fact is that the advertising you will buy as part of your *direct* marketing process has, or should have, a clear sales objective — whether you seek to generate sales *per se*, or stimulate leads for a sales force to follow-up. Whether you wish to build traffic for your retailers, agents, dealers or

distributors to convert to sales, you can know precisely what the sales result is.

Quite naturally, if you are advertising to achieve complete sales you have two perfect yardsticks:

(a) *The cost per reply*, that is, the cost of the advertising divided by the number of replies.
(b) *The cost per sale*, that is, the cost of the advertising divided by the number of sales.

Both of which can be readily related to a budget. Or better, to a marketing allowance per unit sale.

This is a discipline quite foreign to those who work in conventional advertising. Have Bounty ever explained to whoever writes their storyboard what it means to have that one extra shot requiring two more half-naked beauties sucking sensually on 'the product' as they wander nymph-like along the white tropical sand? It is actually going to require sales of a further million or so packs. My figures, not theirs, I hasten to add!

In contrast, the direct marketing creative director knows about such economics. He or she knows that the more that is spent on the advertising, the more their target responses move up in proportion. Moreover, no self-respecting creative in direct marketing will be happy working on a cost per enquiry. The sale is not complete yet. And therefore the job is not done.

One of the major influences that lies within the creative area is the quality of reply. I make this point since it is a quite common misconception that the creative is *the* major contributor to the quantity of replies. This is not so. Although it is difficult to assign direct proportion to the typical value of the creative contribution I would estimate it at 25 to 35 per cent.

I find that in terms of the cost per enquiry, creative is less influential in the overall mix of influences. Whereas, in terms of the cost per sale, its relevance is much heightened.

No matter whether your advertising seeks to sell in total, or to generate an initial response for follow up. No matter whether you intend to convert to sale by salesforce or by one or other of the marketing media, you will find it is generally the creative that most significantly affects the ratio of enquiry to sale. In other words, the conversion rate.

The point of this becomes clear when you consider the method of calculating the cost per sale. And this I commend as the most appropriate short-term (or single campaign) measure of your accountable advertising.

$$\text{Cost per sale} = \frac{\text{Cost of advertising} + \text{cost of conversion}}{\text{Number of ultimate sales*}}$$

It is vital that, as near as possible, a true 'cost of conversion' is entered. The true cost of your salesperson's time. The ten visits to get four sales that make your 40 per cent conversion rate. Or whatever.

The full cost of mailing out brochures and samples to all 1400 enquirers, even though only 350 will become cash-in-the-bank customers, and achieve your 25 per cent conversion rate.

The creative approach is in clear focus. Creative that over-excites, over-sells or promises the undeliverable will result in a high response, but a low conversion. It will thereby increase the proportion of sales calls or post-enquiry conversion packs, as well as the amount of front-end advertising required to achieve your sales targets. If ever there was a commonsense argument for honesty in advertising, this must be it. The economics reinforcing the ethics.

Is it any wonder that most direct response television seems to adopt creative requiring simple rostrum camera studio production? Anything more adventurous could add 35 per cent to the sales targets.

This accountability — the capability for certain knowledge as to the effects of your advertising, not by campaign, but by individual ad — forms part of my rationale. Indeed, a cornerstone.

2 *Why spend your money on ordinary advertising when you can have **added-value advertising**?* The last point takes care of the direct response part of direct response advertising. If you've got it right, it will already have paid for itself before you reap the added advantage of the pure advertising aspect.

In other words, as well as accountable advertising, it is also added-value advertising. After all, is it likely that those who responded are the only people who read, were influenced by, or simply noted your ad? Indeed not. Many more will have read the copy. Many, many more will have

---

*Ultimate sales are those that stick. After returns. After money-back guarantee claims. After any 'cooling-off' periods. In other words, when the money is safely and irrevocably in the bank.

5

scanned your pictures, caught your headline. Just as if it were an ordinary ad.

Direct marketing, including all aspects of direct response advertising, offers you accountable advertising with the added-value of the 'free' advertising beyond the sales you achieve.

Powerful stuff.

3 *Why spend your money on ordinary advertising when you can have **answer-back advertising**?* Direct marketing ads — whatever the media in which they appear — are designed to promote a dialogue. This means that they have clearly defined — but often quite different — tactical objectives to classical advertising. This is amply demonstrated by classical ads that incorporate, for instance, money-off coupons. I see a money-off coupon as a sales promotion device. It is clearly there to promote a single sale, quite often a trial of a new product or sampling of an existing product, in the hope that there is a long-term residual sales increase as a result of customer satisfaction with the product or service.

Yet often, the existence of the coupon is, from the copy platform, largely or totally ignored. In most cases (and somewhat cynically, I suspect by accident) the graphics team on the other hand get it right. The coupon stands out like a sore thumb.

Examine, if you will, how the desire to create answer-back advertising is different.

Monologue advertising has the simple objective of dealing with 'top of the mind' reactions from the consumer. Corporate image. Brand awareness. New product information. Image advertising.

Dialogue advertising is very different. Equally simple, but very different. It makes the advertiser approachable. It invites the reader to respond or participate. To visit, ring up, or drop a line.

This desire to create a dialogue radically affects creativity and choice of media. For example, direct response posters are a rarity. Careless copy or tempting graphics may promote graffiti, but rarely much other sort of dialogue. For it is a fact that posters are limited in the information they can successfully impart. Although there have been exceptions, it is accepted they are not a good direct response medium.

Direct marketing media selection and creativity tends towards those which, for example, can offer a response card or coupon. Or provide a Freefone or 800 number. And which lend themselves not only to offer the dialogue, but also to create the desire for it.

Monologues are a complete communication. They are a beginning and an end. Dialogues are potentially the beginnings of relationships, from which sales are a more certain result.

4   *Why spend your money on ordinary advertising when you can have* **allegiance advertising**?   It is very, very rare indeed for any direct marketer to be in business for a one-time quick buck. It is a fundamental of direct marketing that there is the *TEN-X factor* of the existing customer.

It is my experience that, as a rule, it is at least ten times more cost-effective to repeat sell to an existing customer than it is to seek out a new one.

That can be twice the order value at one fifth the advertising cost. Or perhaps five times the order value at twice the response. Or any combination of levels. The strange thing is that, whatever the ratio of cost to effectiveness, it is quite extraordinary just how frequently the resulting figures show a ten times more cost-effective result.

And, as many direct marketers have learned, the more repeat sales that are made with a customer, the more loyal, friendly and willing they become. Which is why the whole concept of RFM analysis is so important.

RFM stands for *recency*, *frequency* and *monetary* values.

Even as I write, I am aware that this topic is a whole new subject within a subject. Yet the relevance and value of RFM is such that it must be covered.

Direct marketing experience, particularly with mail order, indicates that RFM analysis can so greatly enhance targeting of both the audience and the message, that it can most dramatically improve cost-effectiveness.

Recency indicates the time when a customer last purchased. Frequency, as it more readily suggests, is the number of purchases across given timespans. And monetary value, the third indicator, where we look both at the total spend of the customer and spend per sale. And patterns thereof.

From such analysis, customers can be clustered together into common types, and the timing, sales value and nature of offer can be determined to find the most suitable future path. Moreover, the individual sales message, particularly in the case of telemarketing and direct mail, can be readily adapted in view of the historical experience.

None of this information is, after all, anything more than would be used, often subjectively or instinctively, by a good salesperson. But then I hold strong views that direct marketing is not, and never will be, anything more than the simple application of professional salesmanship. But in its purest sense. And without a visiting salesperson. A point which will re-emerge later, since direct marketing is also of quite exceptional power in the tactical support of a salesforce — not just for prospecting, but in the development of a long-term customer relationship.

Strive as I do to find fresh ways of presenting ideas to audiences at presentations around the world, there is one which constantly defies improvement. And I hope will position the TEN-X factor in your mind.

Let's climb the loyalty ladder

The loyalty ladder is the original concept of a salesman called Ray Consada. It was picked up and worked on by Murray Raphel and Ray Considine and is published in their book *The Great Brain Robbery*. Let's take a look at the loyalty ladder first and then I'll talk you through it.

The very articulate thoughts developed by Murray and Ray here explain that the world is made up of people who wander around blissfully unaware of your existence. The prospect was never more cruelly, yet accurately, depicted than when dauntingly immortalised in the ad for McGraw-Hill dubbed appropriately the 'Busy Man Ad'.

The ad makes a compelling case that sales start *before* a

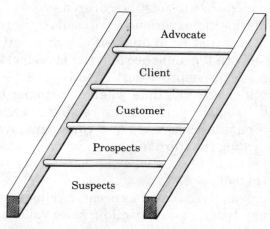

Figure 0.1
The loyalty ladder

Figure 0.2
The 'Busy Man Ad'

sales call and proposes business publication advertising with McGraw-Hill magazines.

> I don't know who you are.
> I don't know your company.
> I don't know your company's product.
> I don't know what your company stands for.
> I don't know your company's customers.
> I don't know your company's record.
> I don't know your company's reputation.
> Now — what was it you wanted to sell me?
>
> *Moral:* Sales start *before* your salesman calls — with business publication advertising.

The loyalty ladder theory acknowledges that your advertising — direct response or other — raises the knowledge and interest level of significant numbers of prospects who therefore become suspects.

Once the suspects have identified themselves, the unchained might of your sales effort is let loose on what I shall, in contradictory terms, describe as the unsuspecting suspect.

Who can challenge the unassailable wizardry of your sales team? Not many! So some of the suspects become customers.

It's a sad but accurate thought that so many at this point run around, leaping for joy, content that they have got a sale. What blind fools! The TEN-X factor confirms the increased ease with which a repeat sale will be forthcoming. And as success yields another sale, so too must we find a new league for the customer to belong to. And a more generous name to call them by. How about, clients, says Murray — his distinction of a multi-purchase customer.

And lastly, inevitably, the top of the pile. Advocates. So-called because they're so enraptured and enchanted with their relationship with you that they pay you the quite extraordinary and invaluable compliment of getting involved with your advertising. They do it by word-of-mouth. Not only the cheapest, but I suggest the most effective 'advertising' it is possible to buy — containing implicit and often actual endorsement of the product.

The snag, of course, is that you can't buy word-of-mouth. You have to earn it. The benefit is that not only does word-of-mouth carry the built-in testimonial value, it also depends on the satisfactory and very cost-effective result of the TEN-X philosophy. This recognizes that you have by now enjoyed a repeat-selling relationship with your customer, which should have been enormously profitable. Adequate compensation for the fact that no money on earth will buy word-of-mouth. You really have to earn it.

It is an indisputable process. A well-recognised feature of the sustained use of direct marketing is that it breeds an amazing level of loyalty from customers and thus truly deserves the description of *allegiance advertising*.

Lastly, having explained allegiance advertising, some underlining on its value. For this, a quote from the best-selling *In Search of Excellence*, by Tom Peters and Bob Waterman, published by Harper and Row in 1982:

> In observing the excellent companies and specifically the way they interact with customers, what we found most striking was the consistent presence of obsession. Service, quality, reliability are strategies aimed at loyalty and long term revenue stream growth and maintenance.

5 *Why spend your money on ordinary advertising when you can buy **automated advertising**?* Direct marketing flourishes in our hi-tech age. It lends itself so naturally to computers, laser printers, interactive electronic media, and the like. This is happening in parallel with the fact that what is hi-tech one day is comparatively low-tech the next. Take the laser printer, for example. Once, and not long ago, only the fodder of the rich and patient. Mechanically Heath Robinson in its paper-handling technology and with a base price of £250 000 or so. And what seems like only months later, more reliable, with less down-time, available desktop for less than £2500.

We only have to listen to the language of direct marketing to realise that it could only exist during, alongside or because of (I suspect it's equal doses of all three) the computer age. For example, database marketing, electronic media and telephone marketing too. Even an apparently innocent subject, off-the-page advertising, will undoubtedly reveal the value of computer-aided media selection and results analysis. So much to do with direct marketing benefits from the processing and number-crunching capabilities of the computer.

But I beg you to remember that each record processed, each number crunched, is at least a human being. But far more important still, a potential or existing customer. And therefore a god.

It's vital you understand that automated advertising is a real and immensely deep well of opportunity for you. Don't, for heaven's sake, see it as about cost-saving or productivity. If you do, you'll shrivel not grow. Then the most exciting sales opportunity to come along in the history of marketing will unceremoniously pass you by.

It's a major mistake to view automated advertising as a way of maintaining today's standards for less money. In fact, I suggest you let automated advertising set tomorrow's objectives on yesterday's standards at today's prices.

Let me explain about 'My Businesses'

Have you read the two *Excellence* books? They extol the virtues of an old-fashioned concept — that the customer is king. They suggest, among other philosophies, that success is assured if you dedicate yourself to customer service. I don't have a problem with this notion. In fact, I have always tried to live up to it. It's some of the places I go to that haven't read the books!

The philosophy of 'customer is king' requires the virtues of something we all already know. We know because we like it when it happens to us. And it's never often enough.

We all like to be remembered. We all like to be cared for. We all like recognition. We love good service. And bask in personal attention.

And when you feel this happening, you have found a 'My Business'. Take My London Hotel for example.

A few years back, I took a suite in a hotel on Park Lane. I was attending the British Direct Marketing Awards. It wasn't a good night for me. It was a *great* night. Probably a once in a lifetime.

I collected six or seven certificates, I think five trophies and the coveted Gold Award. For me, a real event, since it made me the only person to have received the 'Gold' twice in the entire history of the award.

The odd bottle of champagne was seen to pass the table. But most of it stayed right there. Around 4 a.m. I staggered into my hotel. I was showered with greetings and congratulations. There and then it seemed that everyone on night duty was joining in.

When I checked out around lunchtime I made a point of thanking the manager for his kind handwritten note which had been delivered on my breakfast tray.

Let a year pass. A year, I have to say, when I think I only used the hotel once between my 'Gold' night and today.

How do you think I felt when the front desk clerk greeted me with this:

'Mr Fraser-Robinson! We are so pleased to have you back with us again. We checked with your secretary, and she said it was

Awards night. So we've given you the same suite as last year. It seemed so lucky for you.'

And more along those lines.

How did I feel? Wouldn't you make that 'My Hotel'?

So what is this? Salesmanship? Professionalism? Excellence?

Yes, it is undoubtedly all of those things. It's also notetaking, record-keeping, and a great deal of belief in the very highest standards of relationships.

Have you noticed how people accolade professionals? You go to *the* grocer. You go to *the* supermarket. But you talk about '*my* accountant', '*my* solicitor'. Even the ones you don't like. '*My* bank manager'. You decide to 'own' these people because they are important to you. Or, rather, because they've made themselves important to you, or even influential in your life.

So I know I've made it when a client says, 'JFR is *my* direct marketing man!' — I still have a job to do when they say, 'I use JFR'. Personally, I 'use' a toilet.

My advice is to go for a 'my' position in the lives of your customers. No matter whether you're a (my) charity, a (my) jeweller or a (my) supermarket. They owe you when they own you. Because you've made yourself theirs.

There's nothing particularly new in this thought. Pendulums swing. And this one is on its way back. Ask IBM. Or. . . . (Can you write your name in here?)

A personal principle

Before I move on to my next topic, I should like to place before you a personal business principle. Link this principle to direct marketing and you will have all the money and success you seek. Probably more.

The object of a business is not to make money. The object of a business is to serve its customers. The result is to make money.

6 *Why spend money on ordinary advertising when you can buy* **appropriate advertising**? It was a well-made joke at the time that agency folk in direct marketing have never worried about being in the junk mail business. After all, look how well the burger chains have done with junk food!

What makes such mail 'junk' to its recipients is the lack of appropriateness to them, their lifestyles and their work, interests or pastimes.

So try this one out for size.

The more a communication relates to us, the more interesting we find it. The more interesting we find something, the more likely we are to read it.

The more we read of something, the more likely we are to be persuaded by it. The more we are persuaded by something, the more likely we are to want to adopt it. The more we want to adopt something, the more we want to . . .

You're right . . . we want to buy it.

Did you ever buy anything from junk mail? Of course you didn't. The stuff you didn't buy from — that's junk. But the ones that hit home, well — they were quite interesting. (Remember those 'I did get *one* the other day that . . .' conversations?) Junk isn't interesting. And the reverse is true. If it's interesting, it isn't junk. It's appropriate to you. Or put it another way: the advertiser got his targeting right. As more and more direct marketing becomes database-driven, so it increases the opportunity to improve the appropriateness of the advertising — its relevance — to the recipient.

The more you know about a customer or prospect, the more you can understand. The more you understand about people, the more closely you can relate to them. And the more successful the potential of that relationship will be.

As this book moves nearer its specialist subject, so you will notice that direct mail — far from being junk mail — can be, should be, must be, relevant and appropriate, or it will fail. People will vote with their rubbish bins.

On the other hand, it does pay to examine why so much direct mail will go that way. And why so many people claim that they throw it away. Why do they say that? Are they reluctant to admit that they are influenced, or worse, convinced by it?

I don't think so. They say they throw it away because they do. The fact is direct mail — like most direct marketing media — is a low-response medium. Far, far more people will reject than respond. I have had clients over the moon with ½ per cent response. So it make sense that you are likely to talk with perhaps up to 99 times more people who weren't interested enough than the one who was. And you'll recall that, if it's not interesting, it's junk. Not a lot in between.

Don't concern yourself with the fact that it's a rare, rare exception when you find more people who respond than those that don't. On the other hand, there's no reason why it shouldn't be a goal!

Direct marketing — information-based hi-tech advertising — enables you to make your advertising more appropriate. And, consistently, no more so than with direct mail. That's one reason why an ad in a national daily will be successful in pulling an order from 1 in 2000, when direct mail can be expected to pull at 20 or 30 times higher. The indisputable fact that it can, and will, says a lot about the power of direct mail. A point that will be looked at when we discover together why direct mail is the king of direct marketing.

It is a strength of most direct marketing media and messages that they so often provide you with the opportunity to be more appropriate. And therefore, more effective.

7 *Why spend your money on ordinary advertising when you can buy* **action advertising**? Direct marketing is about *action*. Action in the form of sales. Or action in the form of sales enquiries.

Direct marketing should therefore be provocative. It should provoke action. It must be powerful, persuasive and exciting enough to arouse desire in people. Not just to be aware of you. Merely to make you more prominent in their mind. Just to think well of you. Or recognise you.

Those simple tasks fall in the role of ordinary advertising. Direct marketing must be stronger still.

And here's one reason why it is so strong.

Understand the power of a proposition

Nearly all direct marketing ads include a proposition. After all, if you want to rouse someone to take the action you want, there is nothing like an attractive or acceptable proposition to do it.

We all need our bones to chew. But if you want response, then you must give me something to chew over, something to say 'yes' to.

Make me an offer. If it's a good one, I'll accept.

Compare this concept with ordinary advertising and you'll see that most ordinary advertising is passive. It may still be persuasive — but passive. It places the message in your head. But it isn't explicit enough. It arrogantly assumes that you'll react. You don't, of course, not usually.

Every advertising message should make an offer. It's the offer that suggests the action. And if the offer is put across thoughtfully, it will more than suggest action, it will close the sale.

Offer has, of course, two meanings. Offer in the sense of a proposition: Take my advice. Include one. But also, there is an offer in the sense of a 'special offer' available to you. And very potent it is too. We all like to receive something a little extra. Something for nothing. Something to reward us for placing our business with you.

The seven 'A's of direct marketing — there's a PS!

Because there's one more 'A'. Or one more 'Aye'. The compelling benefits that direct marketing offers its users are also making it *advancing advertising*. More and more people are learning about it. More and more people are realising that ordinary advertising is not enough. They get better value, do more, achieve greater things and improve their effectiveness through this powerful way of doing business.

So we arrive at the point where we need to know what direct marketing is. You wouldn't believe what a difficult definition this is to arrive at.

Searching for a definition

It's a subject I liken to the ceiling of the Sistine Chapel. In total, a wonder. But made up of a thousand wonders. Imagine a library of books. A library beyond compare, but only so because it is made up of individual masterworks.

Direct marketing is like that.

It appals me to admit this, but two of the most workable descriptions (as opposed to definitions) of direct marketing were found, not amongst the pearls in the Aladdin's cave that are the books of Ogilvy, Raphel and Stone, but in our own trade magazines. *Direct Response* to be precise. Stand up, Paul Rowney, and take a bow. Here comes the first:

> Direct marketing is the generic term for the use to which all media can be put to generate a direct communication with a potential or existing customer. Therefore any advertising medium has direct marketing potential.

And the second:

> The most successful Direct Marketers are those that have perfected the art and the science of communicating with their existing and potential customers in the most effective and economical way possible.

You see what I mean. OK, but not totally satisfactory. So let's go to the States and ask the Hoke Communication stable if they can chip in. Who are Hoke? They've cornered the market as *the* direct marketing magazine publishers and specialist booksellers in the US — and at an international level, they're all there is. After a lifetime in direct marketing, Hoke and the Hokees have written the following definition, which is published alongside their now famous direct marketing flowcharts. It's around page three of the magazine each month.

DIRECT MARKETING — WHAT IS IT?
An aspect of Total Marketing —
not a fancy term for mail order.

Marketing is the total of activities of moving goods and services from seller to buyer. Direct marketing has the same broad function except that direct marketing requires the existence and maintenance of a Database.

(a) to record names of customers, expires and prospects,
(b) to provide a vehicle for storing, then measuring, results of advertising, usually direct response advertising,
(c) to provide a vehicle for storing, then measuring, purchasing performance,
(d) to provide a vehicle for continuing direct communication by mail and/or phone.

That's one of those definitions that, while describing accurately, needs 'fleshing out' to be more explanatory. Let's seek the assistance of Joan Throckmorton, a US consultant and prominent member of the American Direct Marketing Association. In her book *Winning Direct Response Advertising: How to Recognise It, Evaluate It, Inspire It, Create It,* she makes this point and expands:

We may not be as original today as we think we are, and that leads us to a big problem. Everyone wants to try the 'newly discovered' marketing. It's future marketing. It's chic. But as we rush forward, some people are indeed forgetting the lessons of the past (if they ever learned them). And knowledgeable direct marketers are expressing concern.

Direct marketing has been exceeding its bounds while practitioners jostle to define the bulging bounds themselves. The expansionists want direct marketing to be all-encompassing, and often self-interest pushes them to stretch their definitions to any form of advertising that requires a measured response! Some of these expansionists also claim that it's impossible (or unnecessary) to test — that direct response should go into a vast national media mix, all of which must 'break' (or reach the market) in time and in tune with general advertising.

The purists (among whom I stand firmly), recognise direct marketing as measured response combined with the establishment (and use) of database — dialogue marketing. All the rest is whatever else you choose to call it — sales promotion or response advertising — it is *not* direct marketing.

What difference the definition, you ask? Here's the difference. With the lack of a clear, mutually acceptable definition, direct marketing will become diluted and diffuse. It will gradually lose its careful practitioners and stern requirements to test and implement and 'roll out', to measure and learn and improve and project. It will cease to work to define and acquire a customer, then to establish a dialogue and cultivate that customer.

It will go for the megabucks of packaged goods and mass sampling instead. And as it does, it will become *nothing* — nothing more than a promotional tool, a coupon that's counted, a 'vote' on a national toll-free number, a faceless wave of response or rejection, mass advertising's child. That's why it's important for you to understand what direct marketing is, and has been, and can continue to be — and to keep it pure.

Looking at the latest models

More graphically perhaps, we can steal the very explicit schematic models proffered by Vin Jenkins, as they appeared in an Australian Post Office-sponsored publication.

First, the classic marketing model:

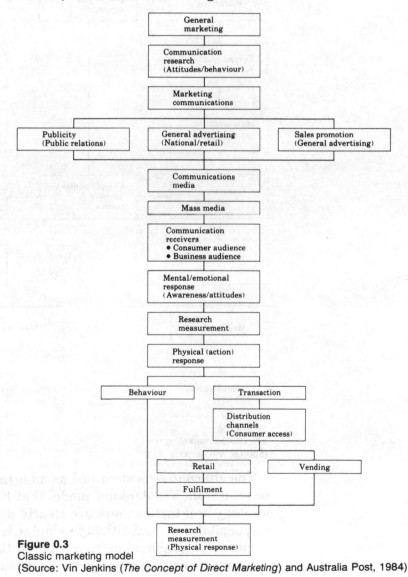

Figure 0.3
Classic marketing model
(Source: Vin Jenkins (*The Concept of Direct Marketing*) and Australia Post, 1984)

Vin then proceeds to demonstrate with what he describes as the 'Interrelated Marketing Model' that the two systems can not only coexist, they can actually help each other out. Running in parallel, but with different objectives. He also established, vitally, the need to ensure a cohesion between the two in terms of the positioning — corporate, brand or product — and the creative tactics.

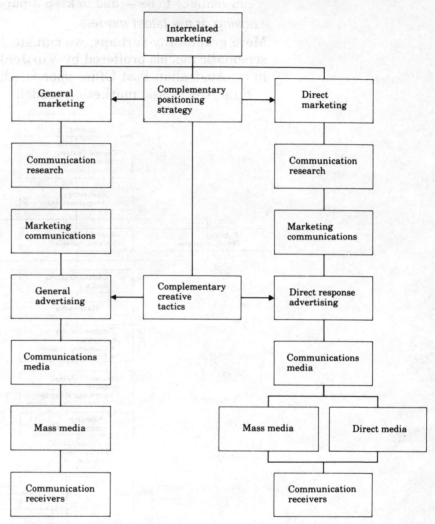

Figure 0.4
Interrelated marketing model
(Source: Vin Jenkins, ibid)

The alternative is identified as integrated marketing. It can be seen from Vin Jenkins' model that both in the matters of strategy and tactics there are clearly different but mutual responsibilities. And although similar is suggested at the media level, it should be remembered that there could be substantial overlap here where media such as TV, radio, press

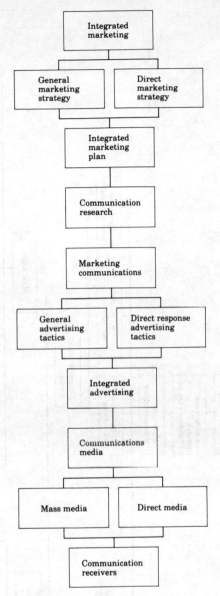

Figure 0.5
Integrated marketing model
(Source: Vin Jenkins, ibid)

and others provide attraction for both marketing streams. This will need thought and control.

For his specific model of direct marketing, Vin took as his base — and I'm sure he would wish me to acknowledge the fact — the original Direct Marketing Flowchart from the Hoke *Direct Marketing* magazine. The original, modified from time to time, appears each month in *Direct Marketing* alongside or near the definition we considered earlier.

Finally, the marketing model, or as I have re-captioned it,

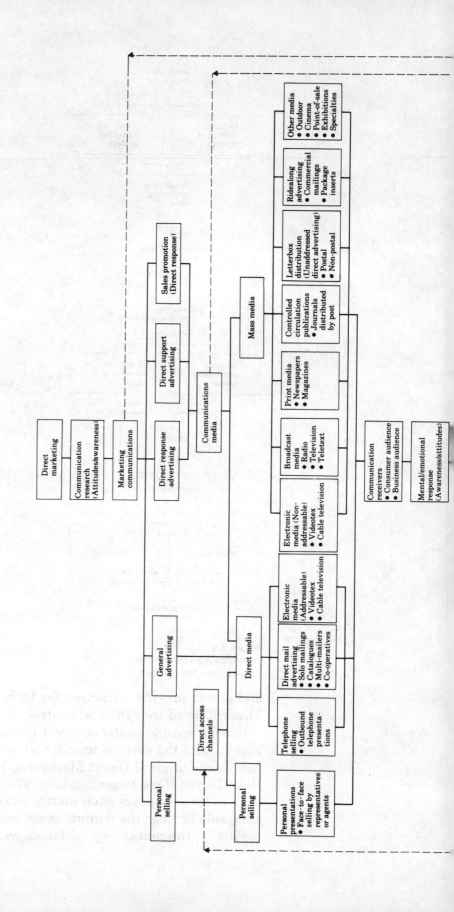

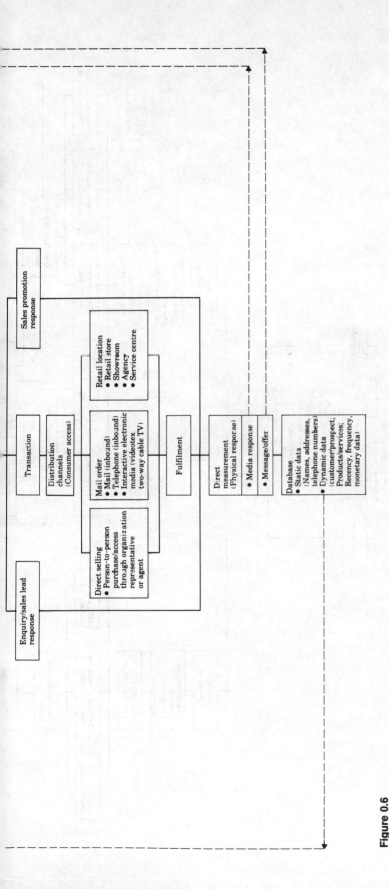

Figure 0.6
Direct marketing model
(Source: Vin Jenkins, ibid). Modified from the Direct Marketing Flow Chart, *The Magazine of Direct Marketing*, Hoke Communications Inc., New York

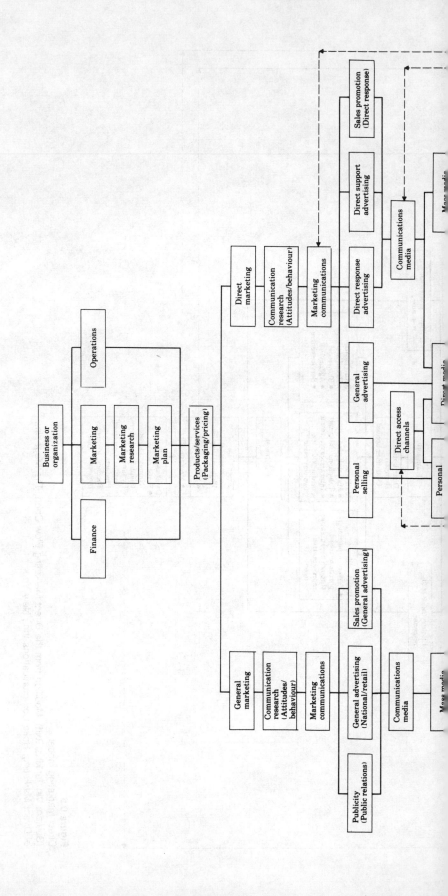

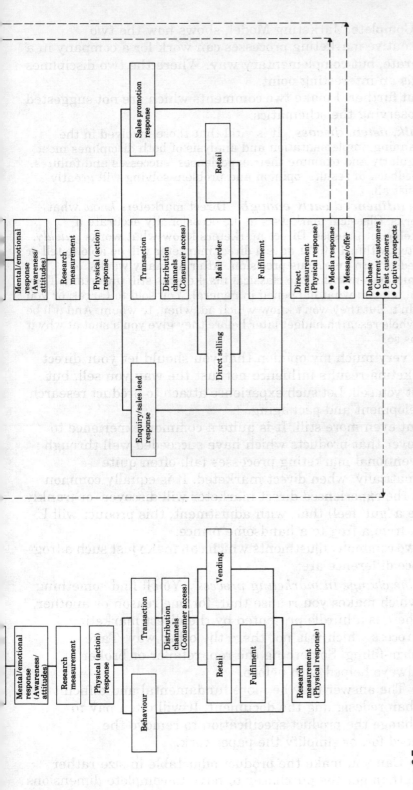

Figure 0.7
The complete marketing model
(Source: Vin Jenkins, ibid)

23

the Complete Marketing Model, shows how the two alternative marketing processes can work for a company in a separate, but complementary way. Where the two disciplines join is an interesting point.

But further, I make two comments which are not suggested in observing the schematics.

Talk, listen, discuss It is vital that those involved in the planning, implementation and analysis of both disciplines meet regularly and examine their experiences, successes and failures. Feedback of results, opinion and problem-solving will greatly assist all.

Be influenced early enough Direct marketers *know* what works. Classical marketers make occasionally accurate if intelligent guesses. Direct marketers know what works *quickly*. Often within 14 to 21 days a direct marketer will be able to tell or predict with enormous precision. After as many weeks, or sometimes months, the classical marketer is still uncertain. They can tell you what happened in general. You sold to target, or you didn't. But they won't know which ad, when, to whom. And it'll be a whole research budget later before they give you a shot at why it was so.

It is very much my opinion that you should let your direct marketing results influence not just the way you sell, but what you sell. Let such experience attach to product research, development and packaging.

But even more still. It is quite a common experience to discover that products which have succeeded well through conventional marketing processes fail, often quite dramatically, when direct marketed. It is equally common that the experienced direct marketer will discover (or frankly have a 'gut' feel) that, with adjustment, this product will U-turn from a frog to a handsome prince.

Two common adjustments which can make just such a frog–prince difference are:

1   *The change in marketing process* You'll find something which makes you realise that, for one reason or another, there is a hurdle presented by the direct marketing process which was not there the other way. Take form-filling. Something the rep, retailer or broker always helped with before.

    The answer may be more fundamental and difficult than redesigning the document. It will often pay to change the product specification to remove the need for, or simplify the paperwork.

    ● Can you make the product adjustable in size rather than get the purchaser to have to complete dimensions and measurements? This reduces return through error as well.

- How much information is *genuinely* needed? How much is asked for through habit?

The bureaucratic worlds of finance and insurance are making great steps here, although there is still far too much resistance from underwriters and actuaries.

It is however encouraging to see a new breed growing with the team. They carry the title 'marketing actuary'. Until recently (and possibly still!) a complete contradiction in terms.

2 *The change in marketing style* Irritatingly for those most concerned with image and positioning, hugely profitable pockets of new opportunity or niches of a market can open up with simple change. Like re-branding.

Thus, for example, a product which is just one of a stable on the classical side, can become a rip-roaring success when marketing direct.

This may have to do with the way the product is presented. Or it may, indeed, have to do with the way people involved in the two alternative systems perceive the product. After all, if you ask the manager of a department store how important a 'twinset and pearls' is to his sales figures, he will tell you, something less than 1 per cent. Ask the question of a catalogue specialising in twinsets and pearls, and the answer is predictable.

Taking an insurance example again, a plan dubbed 'Fifty Plus — The Senior Citizens' Whole of Life Low Cost Assurance Plan' will be necessary only for completeness sake to a typical broker. There's no way he'll get off his backside to sell it. Re-branded as the 'Maturity Funeral Expenses Plan' you've got a rip-roaring success to sell direct off-the-page in the national dailies. And other places too.

Also notice that frequently successful product names in direct marketing express a specific benefit and/or a specific link to the market. Classical marketers seem to like describing the product itself. And what is Cover Plus? Insurance, roofing material or paint?

'The simple act of selling'. I present that to you as *my* definition of direct marketing. It is only the medium through which the sale is achieved that differentiates direct marketing from other methods of selling. The word 'marketing' is what causes the confusion. Yet equally, it is more than selling. It is embellished at both ends. For the seller the complete marketing process is involved: research, product development, strategy and tactics, etc. But also the buyer's situation is different, too.

It pays to think a great deal about the buyer's situation in direct marketing. A point which I shall spend more time on when we reach our specialist topic of direct mail.

My point is, however, that we are not talking here about selling in isolation. Selling is one part — indeed the pivotal part — of the marketing process. We are looking quite clearly at the whole subject. Thus, as an academic or theoretical point, I take issue with the first part of the Hoke definition, because to my mind there are a number of activities left out from what I consider the marketing process — conventional or direct. As I've mentioned, product development is one. By definition before the 'process of moving the goods' can possibly have started. We don't have the goods yet!

There seems to me a rather dangerous inference in many textbooks. Marketing — direct or otherwise — is not about single transactions. It is about growing relationships. Growing in the sense of maturing. And growing, too, in the sense of developing.

Understandably — and correctly — the Hoke definition of direct marketing on one plane includes this by recognising the 'on-going' nature of the direct marketing business. But on the other plane, there is the product-line extension aspect of direct marketing. A high score there for the oldest direct marketers in the British market — the catalogue companies.

Let's examine their attitude to customer relationships. I break it down into three supreme factors.

1   They aim to be a 'My Business'.
2   They understand the loyalty ladder.
3   They know that in direct marketing, line extension is a way of life. But different.

So you see, they understand that what they set up with their catalogue holders is a transactional marketing distribution structure. You can pump an almost endless range of products down it, depending only on the basis of the relationship. And even that is a movable feast.

Think about it.

It's quite logical. The typical female catalogue buyer can shop from her catalogue just as she can shop in town. Better. Because the payments are spread and she can handle it within the 'housekeeping'.

And when she sells from that catalogue she gets commission. In turn, the commission adds to her ability to spend. It seems natural too, that if she — or her mum — buys a fridge, she can also buy extended warranty insurance. Indeed, since they sell insurance through the catalogue, it's very convenient to fix a home contents policy that way too. And so it goes on.

Here is a pattern of thought. It is logical, reasoned, practical and, as those that have tried will tell you, can be extremely profitable. It maximises the loyalty ladder, the concept of a 'My Business', but more important, wholly endorses the notion that direct marketing is a perfect, uncorrupted marketing distribution track.

So now we come to my direct marketing flowchart. It's sickening in its simplicity. And so ideological as — at first glance — to be wickedly dismissible. It won't take a second to absorb. So we'll discuss it in a second!

The simple act of selling — my flowchart

Here's the chart:

Seller
↓ ↑
Buyer

This, to me, represents a perfectly balanced and satisfactory negotiating position for both parties. But let's compare it with some of the other distribution channels.

A familiar one is this:

Seller
↓
Wholesaler
↓
Retailer
↓
Buyer

It doesn't look too bad until you think about how it gets extended — each extension pushing the buyer and the seller further apart:

Manufacturer
↓
UK importer
↓
Seller (Sole UK Supplier)
↓
Regional Sales Office
↓
Branch Sales Office
↓
Wholesaler (Head Office)
↓
Retailer (Central Buying)
↓
Retailer (Local Store)
↓
Buyer

Then there's the familiar business version of the earlier one:

Seller
↓
Sole Distributor
↓
Appointed Dealer
↓
Buyer

Or even the insurance and financial product system:

Carrier/Re-insurer
↓
Broker
↓
Policyholder

And what confusion these corrupted systems, as I call them, (meaning only that they are less than perfect!) cause. Take the insurance situation. let's start with the policyholder. Who do they think they're dealing with?

Well, when everything is going well, most think the broker. Some realise that their contract is actually with the underwriting company. You can imagine how confused they get with a serious claim when into the picture comes a loss adjuster!

I can't recall how many dithering insurance companies I've sat down with. They've researched the potential of the TEN-X concept and worked out that cross-selling products to their policyholders really would be a great idea.

It's surprising in this day and age that there are still some life offices that will write a without-profits life policy and expect simply to take the premiums throughout the term of the policy. Without ever contacting the client — the buyer — during the whole length of the term. Sometimes for as long as 25 years.

Now, as a customer, how would you feel about somebody who took your money for 25 years and never bothered to get in touch with you? Unless you missed a payment. In which case you receive a terse administrative document that tells you to pay up or else you'll find your cover withdrawn. Arrogance rules! Whether you like it or not!

So back to the ditherers who want to tap the TEN-X potential. What's the problem? The brokers!

'We don't want to bite the hand that feeds us. You see, brokers are responsible for the vast majority of our business. And well, they see the policyholders as their clients.'

There is an answer, of course. And those companies brave enough, forthright enough, and fair enough, have taken the profit rewards that result.

But all this paranoia and confusion develops because the relationship developed between the buyer and the seller — on an equal balance of power and responsibility — becomes distorted and corrupted.

A three-layer chain becomes an eternal triangle — as the insurance example. A four-layer chain becomes a wrestler's tag match. And so on.

I had a fascinating after-dinner conversation with the marketing manager of a well-known white goods manufacturer quite recently. We were discussing an opinion I had voiced that the next big direct marketing explosion will be in the white goods sector.

My host started to describe the power which multiple outlets hold over them. I was incensed. In effect the major multiples had achieved such major off-take levels that the company couldn't really afford to lose them. Thus, using this as a lever, the retail chains could threaten withdrawal of floorspace unless the manufacturer supplied at the price they demanded.

You can imagine how that little line works out! Brand owner advertises to persuade consumer to buy. Consumer visits large well known retailer on High Street.

'I'd like to buy a Chillo fridge.'
'We don't deal with Chillo any longer.'
'Why? What did they do wrong?'
'I don't know. But Head Office told us that they've been deleted from our list of authorised suppliers.'

Great. The situation described by this marketing manager seemed to my ethics to verge on commercial blackmail. A far cry from market forces.

'Well,' I said, posing a hypothetical question, 'why don't you appoint another retailer and write to all the purchasers over the last, say, five years and tell them that henceforth you have withdrawn stocks from Nasties National, and your new official supplier will be Nicer National?'

I should have known better, of course. Here comes the marketing manager's question.

'How could I possibly reach those customers? It's a lovely thought, John. But there's just no way.'

'Then you must do something about it,' I said, 'because apart from anything else you are letting those customers down. They decided to buy your product. They wanted Chillo. You are obliged to accept that as a responsibility beyond supplying the cabinet.

'People don't buy "cabinets". They buy benefits, satisfaction and trust. They reward the Suppliers with loyalty and with profit.'

Here's what lies behind these comments.

Retailers/brokers/agents with a clear conscience have nothing to fear. They *add* to the process of conventional marketing. The customer benefits. And the retailer benefits. Everybody's happy.

These retailers acccept that a manufacturer not only places his goods in their store. He vests an enormous responsibility in them. The responsibility for building a sound customer relationship on their behalf. That relationship must include service, confidence, courtesy and trust.

This means they must train their staff in human relationships, and importantly, not just to sell the product, but to know it. They must learn to listen to the customers, appreciate their needs, and with skill and experience match the right product to the right customer.

For now there exists an alternative distribution channel for most — not by any means all, but for most — manufacturers and suppliers. And indeed, significantly for most customers.

The alternative is direct marketing

For every tale of woe that exists about the pitfalls of shopping by post, I'll happily swap you a 'Disgusted of Tunbridge Wells' story about customer complaints and problems to do with the conventional marketing side. Neither is perfect.

But the comments from those who are 'sick of being jostled by the screaming hordes' in department stores (all of whom have de-stocked to improve profitability so that 'they didn't have the darn thing anyway') abound because they are abundant.

Satisfactory relationships of any kind have to be nurtured and fostered. They have to be worked at. For direct marketers that, too, is easier to achieve. The discipline of having to back up every offer with a guaranteed 'satisfaction or your money back' promise is often made (and kept) on a no-quibble basis. And therefore, the customers know they don't have to 'go through' any face-to-face confrontation to claim.

In direct marketing, the marketing department, whose responsibility is correctly to determine the tone, style and nature of the customer care policy, are in direct contact with the customers. When they create a communication its customer care aspects are transmitted precisely as they are. This means they have a pure and direct influence on the sale.

On the other side, the conventional marketing process has to make sure it happens down the line. Tight control and supervision is vital to ensure the theory and the practice are one and the same.

Whether you use one or both your marketing options — conventional or direct — here are four anecdotes which have a moral to them.

1 *Listen to the Real Customer*   A bad intermediary — retailer or whatever — is like a rotten apple in a basket. The rot spreads all ways — up and down the distribution channels. This story is a strangely British disease.

It's a product launch. The ad agency does a good job. The ads create a level of consumer demand. You want the product. Here comes the difficult part.

Getting it!

You visit shop after shop in search of the product. After five or six, you vent your frustration on the shop assistant. 'Sorry,' she says, 'we don't get any call for it.'

Finally, when she's dismissed 36 equally keen would-be purchasers, she mentions it to the manager. That provokes a memo to the buyer. Next time the rep is in, the buyer decides to take a supply of 'that stuff you said you were launching about three months ago'.

A few weeks later it's on display in the outlets. Normally that's just about two weeks after the consumer demand has dwindled to zero.

I blame both the supplier/manufacturer and the retailer. If you've got enough faith to invest in the manufacture of a new product line, then you should have enough faith to support the retailer too. A 'sale or return' deal will get the shelf-space to get distribution, inspire the outlets to have confidence in the product, and therefore meet the demand. Then, quite rightly, it's up to the product.

In direct marketing, we can test our markets with quite remarkable ease and comparatively small investment. The only people we have to motivate to sell the product are the agency we're using to launch it. And as for sale or return, we offer that — *always* — to the customer. It's a great way to do business!

2 *Desire is not enough — you have to make it happen*   There's a branch of a well-known DIY superstore near me. I personally wouldn't work for them — simply

because their name suggests you're not going to get a very fat pay packet. In fact, judging by their checkout staff that may well be the case. My experience is that I intrude inexcusably into their day-long, apparently very important, conversations with each other.

There's no contact whatsoever. However much I spend, whatever I've bought, I'm just another one in the line.

And on the rare occasions they look up, they can never work out why I'm laughing. It's the sticker on their till that says, 'SMILE — and give your customer a nice day.'

Perhaps that promotion is over now.

3 *Lead from the front* I rather enjoyed my Christmas last year. It may not be everyone's idea of Christmas, but I spent five days at what used to be called a health farm. It's a well-known place. But torn a little at the time. I left — I must say in many ways impressed — but none the less quite concerned that somehow, as an act, it didn't pull together. It seems that the market has changed. Nowadays there is a greater business opportunity from normal people with a natural health awareness, than the old market of the desperately overweight or stressed, plus the downright masochists.

Thus, they were in transformation, changing from a health *farm* to a health *resort*. Because of weak or ineffectual leadership, the result is somewhere between an old fashioned health farm and a failing four star hotel with added facilities.

My confusion remained until one day I opted to attend one of the principal's lectures on positive thinking.

The lecture was in most ways unremarkable, save for its lack of original thought. It was a well-presented, if ego-trippish digest of some personally chosen points from about eight books.

Sharing her experiences, the lady principal (I later heard the marketing director) then told two stories. The first was to do with staff discipline. 'Well,' she explained, 'I took . . . [the offending member of staff] on one side and asked, "If you had to handle that situation again, how do you think you could improve it?"'

I'm with the one-minute manager all the way. Criticize the act, not the person. But a company principal sets the standards and very often the methodology too. In such situations staff need to be told what you want, not be left to fathom it out.

In direct marketing we enjoy the luxury of automated advertising. With direct mail, for example, we can put the principal behind the sales policy in touch with the principal behind the buying policy. Or put another way, the chief executive in touch with the decision-maker.

I do so admire those senior executives who not only put their name to sales letters, but who, recognising the attendant responsibility, set aside or make time to deal with the individual correspondence that ensues.

Having got one foot well in the mire, our lady principal decided the other should keep it company.

She went on to explain how she had instructed her staff that the overall job was more important than the detail. 'Don't worry that you open the door of the restaurant five minutes late,' she said, 'they know they'll get fed.'

There's one for a book! I'll call it *In Search of Arrogance*.

4 *Nuggets go with prospecting. Customers get the bullion* Don't run the bath with the plug out. Ensure you spend enough time, effort and money keeping your customers alive, well and happy.

As the loyalty ladder demonstrates, this dedication is well worthwhile since the act of reselling successfully rekindles the strength and builds your customer relationships. And it's profitable into the bargain.

But in such dedication, fine words are not enough. You must recognise the value of the customer and demonstrate that value to them with your actions.

Thus, for example, if you're going to do something wonderful — like hold a competition with a fabulous prize — or even reduce your prices (don't panic, I mean hold a *sale*!), then make sure not only that you offer it to customers too, but that you do it first.

It was a long flight but I really warmed to the man in the next seat. What started our conversation was that he dropped his key ring. It was rather large. I couldn't help noticing it. It didn't go with the handmade leather shoes, the Gucci belt and subtly badged Hermes tie. Nor did his suit — but I later learned 'it's one of ours'.

The key ring. It was one of those plastic encapsulations. And there, encapsulated for all to see was — you'll never guess — a Habitat credit card!

It seemed a little incongruous. I ventured, 'You must be a particularly important person to Habitat. That's a hell of a big key fob!'

'The reverse,' he said, 'I carry it as a constant several times a day reminder that believing your customer is king is one thing, making it happen is something else.'

I invited him to continue.

'It may sound all a bit silly to you. It was on the surface a fairly trivial event, but it became of great significance to me.'

'Just about the same time I got married a new, brave company was born. We had scrimped and saved to buy a flat in Fulham. So this new store, on the way between work and home, was very handy. Conran's first Habitat was open for business. It offered design. A lifestyle. It appealed to us. And good prices, too.

'So we went there buying this, buying that. Furniture. Blinds. Crockery. Cutlery. Then my wife stopped work and we had three children. Somewhere along the way we'd got a bit better off. And we moved to out of town. By that time Habitat was there too.

'What better, brighter, budget way was there to deal with the furniture, fittings and fancies of three youngsters than our old friend Habitat! We opened a budget account and for five years or so, we went on pouring money into the Conran coffers. Every month the statement arrived — and once, maybe twice a year, a new catalogue.'

'This,' I interjected, 'is an important cardmember benefit. They'd given the catalogues a cover price of £1.50 by then.'

'OK, you've got the picture. I'd been a customer since virtually day one. I handed over sums of money that must have stacked up to — for me anyway, and at that time — a quite sizeable chunk of my disposable. Then one day we went to a sale. By two minutes past nine we were in. There was a table. At half price. Half, dammit. Slightly marked. One only. 50 per cent off. Susan looked for an assistant. I looked for the slight mark. And then I saw a sticker that said, quite clearly, "SOLD". Susan suggested that probably a very good, or regular, customer had nobbled it the day before.

'But the point is, I was a good and regular customer, and I bloody well had been for 15 years. We've never been back since. So now I always make sure that my good loyal customers are the ones who should get first crack.

'Anyway,' he continued, 'I got so angry I decided to write to Terence Conran, and tell him what I thought. And so I did.

'My reply was a letter from a secretary that said that my

letter had been passed to their marketing department. And that was followed by a duplicated note that arrived a week later. It thanked me for "bringing the matter to their attention".

'So I carry this Habitat credit card like this every day, I mean *every* day. It reminds me that in my stores the prospects get the nuggets, but the customers get the bullion.' He smiled.

'What do you think of that?'

'I think,' I replied — summoning up every ounce of my business, marketing and sales acumen — 'I think that Tel needs his bumps felt.'

The pendulum is swinging now

In its purest sense direct marketing represents a total and alternative distribution system. And I have demonstrated, I hope, that the shortness of the gap between the seller and the buyer is in many, many senses, a very positive advantage. We've looked together at some of those advantages and quite clearly seen how technology and communications developments are pulling together to make direct marketing very much more advantageous for very many more people.

All that in addition to the market and environmental shifts. So what is actually happening is a change in the Ph factor of marketing budgets.

Historically, while direct marketing was less important, the spend was less important. Now that the arena for direct marketing has changed, so too the pendulum is on the swing.

Ironically, two of the biggest hurdles in the way have probably been — or have been caused by — two of the largest users of direct marketing.

I speak of *Reader's Digest* and the catalogue companies. Two 'purist' users. The first with a reputation from the past for genuinely Jack-Russell-on-the-ankle techniques. The others for being — or rather being perceived to be — down-market.

Outside the UK, people might find this next point difficult to understand. Inside the UK, we'll probably all deny it. Too silly for words!

Many, many senior marketing people — especially professional and institutional — considered direct marketing (particularly direct mail) as beneath them. Or not quite 'the sort of thing one does'.

A friend of mine — I won't embarrass him — works on a charity account. They've used direct mail for years.

Powerful, heart-tugging, wallet-opening letters have gone out in their millions. And all signed by The Man in Charge. He had for years vetted every bit of copy personally.

Thankfully, although a jolly good 'old school' chap, he had the good grace to realise that the people such as him who they mailed were, on the list, in the vast *minority*. So since he knew what he wanted, his agency — indeed the friend of whom I speak — was charged with putting his message across 'to the public'. One day, the charity boss retired and another ex-high-ranking officer was recruited to take his place. Sure enough, as always, the appeal copy was placed before him for approval.

Days of persuasion followed. The agency assembled other charity mailings. The good, the bad and the ugly. Their own guardbook was brought out to demonstrate how extremely well what the New Man dubbed the *Coronation Street* style worked.

Finally he conceded. 'But,' he said emphatically, 'I'm certainly not putting *my* name to it!'

Out came the guardbook again.

'Sir, we've tested very other kind of signatory you can mention. TV personalities — we've tested male against female. Film stars — ditto. Celebrity sufferers of "our" disease. You name it. We've done it. From Sir Robin Day to Thora Hird to the Cabbage Patch Kids.'

'And?'

'And nothing, but nothing works so well and so consistently for us as the director's own signature.'

My friend leapt in quickly. 'Not to worry, sir,' he said, 'it's only going to existing donors.'

That did it. On went the signature. Out went the mail.

A few days later, the new man started to get letters — personal handwritten letters, some on regimental notepaper. Cheques for quite large sums were enclosed. Some with congratulatory or well-wishing encouragement. 'Splendid stuff. Keep up the good work. See you at the Reunion Ball.'

It is amazing who watches *Coronation Street*, isn't it, chaps!

As recently as the seventies, of course, most of the big agencies still curled their lip and turned up their nose when somebody mentioned direct mail or direct marketing. The inference of below-the-line, my deah, was that this was a fairground stall, whereas they were Aspreys and Mappin and Webb. Above the line.

Thank goodness somebody's rubbed out the bloody line.

So today, if you're old enough to remember 'the line' — above and below — you're obviously ready to be put out to grass.

And now, since the budget shift is under way, of course, direct marketing is a rather sexy little number.

Nowadays, if you want to show how trendy you are, you talk 'direct'. I swear somebody at Letraset has been making a fortune out of a rub-off sign that says 'Direct'. They've sold it all over the world. Saatchi's have bought a load. FCB have bought some. You name it, they're all at it.

Everybody's been taking books from the library

You'll remember a few thousand words back I described the complete, the alternative marketing process of direct marketing as being like a library. A world renowned library. But made up of individual books, of which each one was a masterwork.

The fact is that most people have been taking books from the library for years. In other words, most advertisers have been using elements of the direct marketing process for years. Find me a business-to-business marketer who hasn't used direct mail; a charity that hasn't tried house-to-house distribution; a language course that hasn't tried loose inserts; or a newspaper without telesales. But direct marketing (I suppose) being below-the-line, has historically been the province of the client.

It was the client who organised and controlled things. Now it's all changed. More and more ads carry coupons these days (which incidentally does nothing towards turning an ad into a direct response ad. It only makes it an ad with a coupon). More and more people realise that the coupon enquiry, the sales or telesales follow-up, or direct mail fulfilment pack follow-up — or any combination of these — is simply someone else taking more, different books from the library.

What's happened is that more and more people are taking direct marketing seriously, since they've already tried it and they know it works. They've got the figures, the costs, the results, the sales to prove it.

But will it ever make 90 per cent of all marketing?

I've already predicted that 65 or 75 per cent is more likely. And not then as a total of people who opt in full to choose direct marketing as the way they will distribute. I think by far the most will find uses for both.

And why not? There's plenty of room. Why does it have to be a one-or-other situation? It certainly does not. There will always be a place for classical marketing and advertising. There will always be a place for direct marketing and direct response advertising. And for PR and for sales promotion.

However, and mark my words, what is absolutely inevitable is that direct marketing will take over as the place where the majority of advertising money goes. More clients will look to have a direct marketing agency, a classical advertising agency and a PR agency as standard. In that order. And until the fusion comes.

So I don't envisage this causing huge withdrawals from television or the national dailies. Rather, that the use to which advertising is put — its objectives — will change.

The future, while we wait for the dust to settle, is going to be uncertain. The dust will surely not settle until some issues are proven.

To go for a lasting relationship, not one-off sales, here's how to make it happen

Being English, of course, the audience fell about when one Californian stood up and proclaimed, 'Matter of fact, we don't call it direct marketing any more, we call it relationship marketing.'

While we're going to move on to some fairly dry stuff I would simply counsel you that the twin thoughts of money and success I mentioned at the beginning will probably be influenced more by the next few pages than anything else we've yet discussed.

Computerised caring — the effective use of 'active database attack' to ensure powerful and fulfilling customer relationships

At first thought, it probably sounds unlikely. Even the very words 'computerised caring' seem almost contradictory. And 'active database attack' doesn't sound very caring, does it?

For a moment, let's put behind all thoughts of computers and consider these basic and proven concepts which add vital weight and emphasis to our beliefs and suggest a whole *raison d'être*.

1 The *nearer* you can get *to understanding and providing* what the buyer wants, *the more likely* you are *to make a sale*.
2 The *more* you get to *know* a customer's *needs* the more you can line up your commodities to provide a *second* sale thus leading to further *regular sales*.
3 The more in *parallel* to any single customer's *needs* you keep your commodity range — what you have to sell — the *longer* the relationship with that single customer is likely to be.

This is no smart theory. It's why all good salespeople 'work their book'. Often their 'little black book'.

Contacts, phone numbers, the age of their kids, birthdays. All sorts of useful information which the salesperson uses as a memory-jogger to the buyer's situation.

Thus recognising something that all effective salespeople know. Sales are made through achieving material and emotional satisfaction.

What does this mean? Simply that one may be able to define marketing as the 'process of moving goods from the seller to the buyer' but that won't work with selling. That 'simple act of selling' is a focus of the human interaction that is the bedrock of decision. The decision to purchase.

Selling is the reverse prism through which one feeds the whole spectrum of purchasing influences and out of the other side shines the pure white light of success.

So you can divide and examine the elements of influence on a sale by all means — quality, reliability, service, delivery, etc. But you must not forget — whichever marketing process you use — that selling is a social, human interaction.

Of equal importance to the achievement of sale are the emotional qualities. Confidence, truth, respect, and so on.

Two salesmen met in a pub. One had just got back from a holiday in Spain. 'It was a great holiday,' he said, 'and all thanks to this.' He tossed a black plastic pocket book onto the table. On the front he had written one word — 'CONTACTS'.

The second salesman smiled. 'I love Spain too. In fact I own a villa there. And I do agree with you. It's all thanks to this.' He placed his notebook carefully alongside the other. Clearly he had inscribed on its front cover one word — 'FRIENDS'.

I hate the whole misnomer of the phrase 'business-to-business'. The fact is one business does not buy from another. One business does not sell to another. *People* buy and sell.

I suggested earlier that the machinery of direct marketing — the qualities of automated advertising — enables it to shave decades off the way people buy and sell in today's environment.

By this I mean that the direct marketing store is close to the old corner store. It's personal and friendly. Which is great, because I observe the world getting less personal and less friendly. This might seem strange when, for example, you look at Vin Jenkins' direct marketing flowchart. Notice that this powerful alternative process — the one that is allegedly 'direct' — frequently involves not one single moment where two human beings — the seller and the buyer — actually meet.

We are selling at arm's length. Therefore, what I am talking about now is shortening the arm. This too involves the material and the emotional. When we look at the 'simple act of selling' and the resources available, we realise that if a third salesperson — a direct marketing salesperson — had joined the other two in the pub, he too could have placed a pocketbook on the table. And also on the cover of his book there would be inscribed one word. It would likewise be in large clear letters. It would say . . . 'DATABASE'.

What is a database? What is database marketing? And what is a marketing database?

In 1984, Henry Hoke commented in *Direct Marketing*, 'We're often asked, "What's the difference between marketing and direct marketing?" The shorthand answer is database, the existence of a database.'

I do like simple things. Simple statements. Simple concepts. Not just because they're easy to take in and remember. But because they are often so utterly provocative.

They provoke thought, discussions, speculation, enhancement. They give freedom for individual expansion and exploration. Hence my quite shamelessly simple direct marketing flowchart.

And now my equally simple and completely adequate definition of a database.

You'll remember, of course, the days of lists. Address lists. Customer lists. Prospect lists. Broked lists. Rented lists.

Well, what's a list? Answer: It's the whereabouts of people.

And what's a database? It's the *whereabouts and the whatabouts* of people.

I did say it was simple!

So what 'whatabouts' do you need to know about people? Exactly the same things that our salesmen wrote in their pocketbooks.

Don't be fooled by the apparent simplicity of these statements. For if you revert to my comment about 'arm's length', this is one of the ways you can best close the gap, shorten the arm.

Along with the technological media advances that direct marketing makes its friends, the existence and role of a database is the axis around which the mighty hub of direct marketing revolves.

It is the information that drives your product programme. It is the information that inspires your company development. It is the information that attracts new customers and builds repeat sales. And the self-same information that determines the appropriateness, relevance and appeal of your proposition to the individual human beings who are your market. It is the memory bank that selects for you the most effective ways to communicate with people. The methods they prefer. The products they prefer. The timing they prefer. It is the facility that enables you to close the distance between you and your market. It is the means by which — today and in the future — you will, through harnessing technology, be able to have the mutually satisfactory, personal and cost-effective sales relationship with as many multiples of one as you wish. But always see and be seen that you treat each as *the* one.

A database is what turns direct marketing into relationship marketing. It is today and tomorrow the single most important resource to a direct marketer apart from the existence of the product to be sold.

A marketing database is a resource as valuable to the life of a healthy company, as food and water is to a healthy human being. And as dangerous, if abused or unethically handled, as the most fateful, virulent virus you can imagine.

I quoted earlier from Joan Throckmorton's book *Winning Direct Response Advertising*. Here are some more *bons mots* from Joan on this very point. And in reproducing them, may I draw your attention to two matters.

The first is the Data Protection Act. Your responsibilities and the legal requirements placed upon you in relation to direct marketing are covered later. Heed them. First because it is right and proper that you should do so. Second because, in my view, it is correct that the Data Protection Act carries the full weight of *criminal* law. You, and those responsible to you in matters of your database and your direct marketing, should regard this as the very minimum of standards.

The other is the UK Mailing Preference Service. Again, there is reference to this scheme later. There are similar schemes in the US and other countries. Cooperate with them. Join them. Support them. Use them. But more. Run your own. You will make no friends of those you pester, and they will be ultimately the most expensive to sell to. Why? Because they won't buy until you find the method by which they prefer to buy from you. If they don't like you phoning them or writing to them, so be it. The customer's word is law.

Let's see what advice Joan Throckmorton has for us in relation to our database.

Beware the Privacy Issue

The more you know about your market, the more effective your advertising will be in those customer-driven forms of marketing. But there are bounds and limitations to how much any of us should know about the other guy (without the other guy's permission). There is such a thing as privacy — and if you overstep the bounds of good taste you risk offending and irritating your prospect. Just what these bounds should be, and what the individual has to say about it, is becoming a national issue with a capital P — Privacy.

The growing computer information network that helps Direct Marketers be personal and caring and highly service-oriented can also become a weapon to be used against them if it is abused. Be careful how, and to what extent, you use personal data. (You want to make friends but don't be impudent. It's still a customer/business relationship. You're not one of the family.)

It's the old story, if we don't police ourselves here, someone else steps in and does it for us. And Privacy looks like one cause that every state and federal legislator has his or her eye on. Keep your eye on it too.

The computer had done for direct marketing what the first successful splitting of the atom did for the nuclear industry. In this context the database is a vast, vast reactor. Abuse of it will make a Chernobyl for the direct marketing world.

How to plan a direct marketing relationship

The next part is for you to do. I can't do it for you. I know nothing of your business. And you have the better of me. I don't know who you are!

However, in order to close my introductory overview of direct marketing, I would like to do two last things.

The second of those is to place before you a brief review of the most common media through which direct marketing will make you money. Bring you success.

The first is to formalise and explain yet another facet of the 'simple act of selling' which a salesperson will do instinctively.

My wife reminds me that 'instinct' is often a misnomer. So often it is a word used to explain a process of the brain which creates almost instantaneous conscious and subconscious impressions. The drawing together of information, emotions, feelings and experiences in one single dimension. The dimension upon which often — if you truly listen to yourself — the best decisions of your life may come.

A professional salesperson gets to know as much about his customer — or potential customer — as possible. He or she will get as near 'climbing inside the mind' of the buyer as possible.

They do this to maintain not only the effectiveness of their communications, but also to ensure they're going in the right direction. Seeking to sustain the parallel, of which I wrote earlier, between the range of commodities and the range of customer needs. Timing has a great deal to do with this. And this moves a further point. A view that repeat-selling is not repetitive selling. One sells repeatedly, but the result is a development.

One can, to a large extent, plan that development logically. Feedback and modifications will fine-tune your plan to meet the very individual recognition of each customer's situation. This is never to be a rigid sequence. It must be flexible or it will fail. But it is a directional guide.

Here are some of the factors you will need to consider:

- Your product range
- The nature of your products
- Any gaps in the product rationale
- Any seasonal or 'phase' factors
- Any added value or affinity potential
- The spending (or buying) power of your market

Once you have a basic concept of what you are trying to achieve, you will realise there are a number of 'If only I knew when . . .'. For example, for a consumer this might be:

- When they were born
- When they got married
- When they retire
- When they last bought

An example. A famous motoring organisation was frustrated for many years in the development of its insurance business because it lacked two basic pieces of information which were vital to the marketing of its motor and life policies. By adding two simple questions to their membership and renewal forms they were able to change the face of their direct marketing operation, and, as a result, replan their whole relationship track.

Those two questions were:

Date of birth —/—/—
Date your motor insurance expires —/—/—

In an industrial or commercial situation this might be different:

- When the lease expires
- When the contract expires
- How long the contract lasts

Or again:

- Number of vans in fleet
- Mileage or age at replacement
- Number purchased, leased or rented

I'm sure you follow the thinking.

What's the fastest way to profit from direct marketing?

Peaches and cream. A twosome. Hearts, clubs, spades and diamonds. All four aces and you'll take some beating. But if you want to go, not just for money and success, but for *fast* money and success, there are but three things for you to concentrate on in direct marketing. And here they are:

The Media   *The Message*   *The Proposition*

By and large, you're going to be looking for varying combinations of these three that will provide you with optimum achievable results in short (sales), medium (more sales), and long (even more sales plus word of mouth!) terms.

Why not use my rapid media selection table?

There's no shortcircuit to a good, thoughtful and creatively searching review of everything available to you with a list of the pro's and con's of each — take a look at all of them in relation to their cost (total and unit); the quantities and geography of the coverage they deliver for you; and difficult as it may be to assess, their pulling power.

It will also be prudent to consider the opportunity for, and the likely effects of, any increases in cost by selecting media which require different, specially prepared or targeted creative or artwork.

With that introduction, here's the table. I'm sure you will find it useful in providing either an at-a-glance answer or, as I would counsel, a set of possibilities.

Table 1.1   Rapid media selection table

Objective	Media most likely to succeed	Helpful Hints
Lead/Enquiry generation	Direct Mail; Press (Off-the-page or Inserts); TV/Radio Also consider: – telephone marketing – take-ones, etc. – member-get-member – house-to-house distribution	You'll usually find not one perfect answer, but a mix is the best solution. Remember the added-value effect. Thus if you get similar cost-effectiveness from one or more, make your decision on which gives you best additional exposure.

Table 1.1 *(continued)*

Objective	Media most likely to succeed	Helpful Hints
A mail order or other completed sale [one- or two-stage]	Direct mail; Press (Off-the-page or Inserts); Catalogues — Telephone. Also consider: – TV. Inter-active electronic media will be of rapidly increasing significance. – member-get-member and bounce-backs are very powerful here.	The price and nature of your product may be of significance. Generally (and this applies above too) you will find this a balancing act between quantity and the tightness of targeting at the right price. *Beware* — despite the logic of the media selection some media are not found to be so responsible. Currently most evening dailies and local press suffer this reputation.
Store or exhibition traffic building	Radio (local to store); Handbills; posters; Press; TV. Also a must: Direct Mail and Telepone (see helpful hints).	Depending on the event and its duration PR (news) coverage of the preparation at early stages can build figures dramatically. Try to build in some kind of redemption item which involves people as well as — when key-coded — tells you what's working best.

Telephone

Identify key prospects and phone them. Include local media representatives and journalists too. Always give a contact name and try, but not obviously so, to establish the time of visit. Then be ready with appropriate VIP treatment.

Direct mail

1 Be sure to include your existing customers. They like to know what you've got up to locally and you want to repeat or cross-sell. Moreover, always go for 'bring a friend' or referral business here.
2 Do some deals! Approach non-competitive organisations with a similar market profile and get them (important way round!) to recommend to *their* customers that they visit your event. You trade them commission or a return favour with a comparable number of names from your customers. Better still, come up with a linked offer. Buy your twinset and pearls from us. Get your blue rinse at Pauline's.
3 Invite people. Don't announce, tell or inform them.
4 Include any unconverted names — previous enquirers, etc. — this is a great time to make them customers.

| Repeat sell; cross-sell; up-sell; loyalty; anti-lapse; re-recruitment (post-lapse) | Direct mail telephone; free rides (inserts/off-the-page in Newsletters, etc); Statement/Bill Stuffers. Also consider:
– any customer or member communication
– even deliveries, maintenance calls, etc. | Try direct mail first. Personalisation is often up cost-effective. Recognise existing relationship wherever possible in your communication. NB. Variety may prove to be the spice of life here. Don't constantly bombard with the same approach although you should provide something (like the corporate or branding) which serves to remind. Keep it subtle, but there. |

Use a long-term strategy — even behind short-term goals

Take it from me, even if you think you're after a quick buck, you won't be. Direct marketing is a bug that gets you. Don't worry, you'll love it. But it'll get you as sure as anything. There's nothing between the disillusioned (they thought it was easy) and the disciples (they thought it was worth the trouble). I find an increasing number of both. I have no sympathy with the disillusioned, who include by far the largest number of over-opportunist, fast-buck merchants. The disciples are where you will find the rank and file of the professionals. Caring and thoughtful. Constantly learning and improving. And fully appreciative that customers are forever. Forever is what you make it.

What I urge you to do here is examine very carefully and fix as accurately as possible a value on a customer. Once you have done it, communicate it. When you hear a casual or terse piece of payment-chasing in accounts, or a sloppy greeting from the switchboard, hit them with the facts. 'Do you realise each customer we get is worth £X over a typical seven-year period? Do you know how hard it is to replace a lost customer? And it costs £Y just to get them in the first place.' Well, maybe not quite like that! But let them know anyway.

When you establish the value of the full term of a sales relationship with a customer, you start to understand so much. The TEN-X factor, the loyalty ladder and 'My' Business will become three facets of a new way of life for you.

And you will see why a marketing database is vital. You can't achieve the ultimate direct marketing relationship without them.

And you will see why . . .

- *Which?* and other publishers will give you a long free subscription offer. It's heavy duty sampling (and habit-forming!).
- Charities take a loss on recruiting a new donor or member. The TEN-X factor works just as well — often better — for them. One charity I know will get on or near 40 per cent response from certain donor mailings and has for over 20 years. Their list is several hundred thousand strong!
- People offer you jewellery sets at £9.95; 27-piece luggage sets for £29.95; three books for 99 pence. Or an office beverage vending machine free as long as you buy the ingredients and supplies from the given supplier.
- Let you buy one type of insurance, get another — or a

first period of cover free or at a vastly reduced price. And the popular derivative of that, employment and sickness or redundancy cover free with finance plans or loans.

All of these offers are there because someone has sat down and established the value of the customer or organisation over the full or long term. This can come from carefully considered projections and what is called regression analysis. Looking back at the where, when, why, what and how often sales can be achieved. Remember RFM analysis? All to do with recency, frequency and monetary value. This whole sequence was triggered by the heading: 'What is the fastest way to profit from direct marketing?'

Let me tell you another.

This does not involve you in any further expense or effort. You are holding the answer. You are discovering — and are going to have revealed to you — the secrets of direct marketing's most powerful single weapon. The 'book from the library' that will become, almost certainly, the most cost-effective for you. In two words — direct mail.

The celebrity wrap-up to this introduction to direct marketing

There are still some important points to be made. To make them let's call upon some well-respected voices in the business.

Celebrity No. 1

Here are some thoughts from a man for whom I have a great deal of affection. A professional in so many senses of the word. Walter Schmid started out (and remains), a list management expert of international repute. In 1969, he co-founded the Montreux (Switzerland) International Direct Marketing Symposium. This event has become the acknowledged forum for the very highest level of direct marketing thinking and experience. The symposium is held towards the end of April each year. Details are available from the Zurich-based symposium office and their contact address is given at the end of this book.

The following are excerpts from a speech delivered by Walter. He was identifying and giving his views on seven areas of misunderstanding which exist about Direct Marketing. We shall listen in to some of them.

Direct marketing is not a medium but a concept which is benefiting all existing media

Sending a letter with impersonal content to a nebulous target group is not direct marketing; at best, it's a mass mailing, and has about as much to do with direct marketing as the weathercock on the church tower has to do with a weather satellite.

Direct marketing is gaining increasing acceptance because its interactivity makes any marketing activity more efficient in developing sales at lower cost.

Direct marketing poses a danger to image

It is taken for granted that an image can only be built up and nurtured through the mass media.

Image is a valuable asset; a positive image is indispensable for market acceptance. But image alone won't sell anything. Companies are making this bitter discovery every day. That's why it's foolish to create a dichotomy between image and active selling. Both are required, and each does its own job. Why should direct marketing be damaging to the image when it is in a position to address the prospect far more individually than would be possible by the mass media?

Much as I hate to interrupt someone in full flow, a recent article endorsed Walter's thinking. Let's just look at that:

Direct communications can contribute enormously to brand and image building. For example, the way in which telephone calls are answered by a company has an enormous impact on the way in which its image is perceived by customers.

We are using market research increasingly to learn more about the role and importance of every element in the company/customer relationship. Similarly, more traditional advertising media can be used to increase response to direct mail. For example, *Reader's Digest* uses television to raise awareness of its prize draw mailing, producing a significant uplift in response.

Back to Walter Schmid:

Direct marketing requires direct response campaigns that are ugly

Direct response advertising activities do not fulfil the strict aesthetic standards established by the advertising community. Provided there really are 'aesthetic standards' those who design direct response advertising drives abide by them. After all, the sophistication of design in all forms of advertising is determined by the product, not by the medium. Apart from outstanding achievements, direct marketing agencies also produce outstanding ideas. So in this respect, they certainly do not differ from classical agencies.

However, there is a clear distinction: the understandable passion of many creative people to produce *l'art pour l'art* is stifled because its effect is not measurable. What's more, clients don't want art. No medium — no matter how glorious it is — is made to wane away in beauty.

Paying attention to technical requirements kills creativity

True, anyone who deals in a direct marketing environment has to have a great deal of technical know-how. There are lots of reasons for this. It's not enough to limit your message to pretty pictures and snappy headlines. The seller will not succeed that way either. However, creativity is not triggered through expanded communications links. A prerequisite is a spirit of readiness to view technology not as an obstacle but as an expansion to creativity. Most important of all, however, is the willingness to cooperate.

Here we come up against a division of labour which imposes far greater demands on readiness to compromise than is usual in advertising. Creative people are offered an experience of success which is free of complacency. The number of campaigns guided by direct marketing concepts is rising every year. There is virtually no industry that remains untouched by these developments. The more the different industries behave in different ways, the more differently the possible applications of direct response advertising are viewed; we have either an exclusive application or the consideration of a marketing mix.

In both cases, advertising accounts are being lost. Capturing a market share is an important goal for every proven product. This applies equally to the agency itelf. Therefore if it doesn't want to lose its market position, it just cannot stand idly by as advertising accounts flow past its nose.

Celebrity No. 2

A direct marketing book from McGraw-Hill has received wide acclaim. Written by Stan Rapp and Tom Collins, founders of the US Agency Rapp and Collins, it's called *Maxi-Marketing*. Understandably it expands, expounds and effectively merchandises much of the successful philosophy of their agency.

The 1980's will be remembered in marketing history as the decade of transition. We are living through a shift from 'get a sale *now* at any cost,' to the building and management of customer databases that track the lifetime value of the relationship with the customer.

As the cost of accumulating and accessing data drops, the ability to talk directly to prospects and customers — and build one-to-one relationships with them — will continue to grow.

In this new era, there are two major opportunities for those marketers who are ready, willing and able to break out of the box of the past assumptions: (1) Add to what is already working well; (2) Expand into new territory.

Maximarketing is a continuum that turns likely prospects into lifetime customers. It facilitates targeting prospects who are clones of the best customers in a database.

The advertiser can appeal to them with whole brain advertising that invites a response. Sales promotion can be designed to deepen the relationship with prospects, not just make the sale. Prospects' names and addresses can be obtained by building linkage to advertising.

Double-duty advertising can reap a twofold reward. The marketer can build a relationship with the customer database, his company's private advertising medium. And through the database he can begin to develop additional sales of various kinds, with perhaps even different channels of distribution.

This continuum adds up to much more than the sum of its parts, because it makes possible a single unifying market strategy. The goodwill that has been established in a company's brand name over the years can be turned to new products sold directly to the customer database.

And lastly, a few words of great significance to you

I'm not a great one for hero-worship. Except when someone aims a dollop in my direction, of course.

But as near as I'll ever get to bestowing hero-worship in this business is reserved for only a handful of people.

No matter where I go to speak —Helsinki, Montreux at the symposium, or further, much further afield — he's there, he's just been there, or he's due shortly. I see him as the great disc jockey of direct marketing. He collects and plays for his audiences all the hits of good salesmanship and good communication. Between each hit, he tells stories, and adds his own experiences and philosophy. His energy is boundless. His enthusiasm irresistible.

I call him the motivator. His friends call him Murray Raphel. His words which I have chosen for you appear on the next page. They are a highway sign to success. They close Part One. And open the next.

DOLLAR FOR DOLLAR,

NO ADVERTISING MEDIUM

WILL RETURN MORE TO YOUR BUSINESS

THAN DIRECT MAIL

PART TWO

Direct mail: The surest, fastest way to money and success

Introduction

I'm not a great Woody Allen fan. Apart from the odd apposite insanity. Like this . . .

> If only God would give me some clear sign! Like making a large deposit in my name at a Swiss bank.

I seem to remember offering you money and success. This next section delivers. Unlikely, but if you haven't found enough advice, enough direction, enough sheer help yet — that's OK. So while I can't open a Swiss bank account in your name, let me do the next best thing and introduce the main event. The star of the show. The top of the bill.

As it always is: *direct mail*.

No other medium yet comes near to competing with direct mail as the major direct marketing force. This may change. But not until way past when you've had your chance at money and success. As I said at the opening. All you have to do is to make it happen.

The next eleven chapters are about just that. So let me explain what I'm going to do. I've divided the main direct mail section into ten chapters. Dealing with topics like lists and databases; creative; production; and so on. At the end of each topic you'll find 'JFR's box of tricks'. This is an unashamed collection of useful advice, tips, hints and experiences that have worked for me or taught me something. In some cases there is as much in the tricks box as there is in the main topic. And possibly even more when we think in terms of money and success!

Lastly, I've included things I thought would help smooth the way for your future in direct mail, if not the wider area of direct marketing: a glossary; a bibliography; some contact points and telephone numbers. All those sorts of helpful things.

As we set off together for the next, however long it takes, I feel I should wish you 'good luck'. But as you'll see, you tend to need less luck in direct mail than other kinds of advertising. So much is common sense. The rest comes of experience and knowledge. Here come ten chapters of experience and knowledge.

1 There's only **one** kind of direct mail—

It's ... **yours**

or

The vital importance of **positioning**

What is positioning? Why is it important? And how do you achieve it?

Well, I'll tell you. And when I have, then you will know how each envelope you despatch will contain — as near as it is humanly possible — far more than you would think. It will not just contain bits of paper. The recipients will receive the surprise of their life. They will reach inside the envelope expecting bits of paper. Instead, they will find — a proposition; a product or service enticement; the means to order and enquire. But more. They will find *you*. They will find *your company*. And they will know you both.

Only when they know you and the company can they decide upon two important aspects of the sales process. Do they like you? And do they like you enough to spend their money with you?

The importance of positioning is in direct proportion to the importance of your products to the prospective buyer. Offers, products, guarantees, price, timing, the message — these things are the bricks of a successful sale. Positioning is the cement that binds. And adds strength.

I remember seeing a public service TV commercial from the States of the late fifties or thereabouts. The tough but lardy star of the series *Highway Patrol,* Broderick Crawford, reminded us, 'It takes 4374 nuts to hold a car together. But only one to spread it across the road.'

It's the same with positioning. There are probably 4374 things you can do to position everything correctly in a mailing, and then one careless decision or forgotten action will 'spread it across the road'. All the way to the rubbish bin.

What is positioning?

There was a two-word headline in the nationals recently. Potentially it was a contradiction. Yet because the advertisers have very well positioned themselves, for me at least they could get away with it. The two word headline was simply this:

Harrods Sale

Did I read the ads, check the prices and reductions, make any decisions expecting anything other than I found? Was I looking for prices cheaper than Currys or Comet or Argos? Or the postal bargains page? No. I was looking not to pick up a bargain from Harrods, but a Harrods bargain.

Positioning needs more space than I can give it. Though I'm not through yet.

I would suggest that this is a subject so fundamental to success in any advertising or selling function that you would do well to read the well-known book on the subject, *POSITIONING — the Battle for your Mind* by Al Ries and Jack Trout. Again (happily for them) it's published by McGraw-Hill. It is an excellent and convincing book, if a little padded out, on a paramount and fundamentally essential advertising constituent.

Why is positioning important?

Let me tell you the parable of the PC salesman. It all started with a mailing. Not a brilliant one, but one with two huge advantages which will no doubt feature again. I wanted what they had to sell. And they'd got their timing right.

The product was a personal computer and a few bits of software.

I sent off the reply paid card. The rep phoned to make an appointment. He explained the process; he would personally demonstrate the equipment; he would then leave it with me for a few days; then ring to check, if he hadn't heard from me before, whether I wanted to keep it. The paperwork could all be done by post.

It *hung* right.

It was a proposition made simply, quickly and with confidence. It was easy and convenient. The price was fair. It meant I could play with and feel the product hands-on. He sounded a nice guy (very important to the emotional side). So I accepted.

You wouldn't believe the mess that turned up! From the stains on his tie, to the off-white shirt (it was only just off-white on its first day of wear), to the frayed cuffs. His suit was much shinier than his car.

So while he's de-boxing, I'm de-bunking. Whilst he's setting up, I'm climbing down. His appearance had destroyed the magic words, 'It hung right.' Now it was no longer hanging — it lay shattered on the floor. So here's why positioning is important. And long-term. Positioning is for life.

> You cannot remove your position from someone's mind. You can only change it.

And once in the negative hemisphere, it's a truly difficult task to get it back. Sinners *can* become saints. But it's a long hard slog.

Think about it. I wanted to buy what this man had to sell. Yet evidence had undone it all. Stupid, silly little things. The stained tie. The frayed cuffs. The tired, shiny suit. And the rest.

I suppose you could argue that he could have got round it by playing the absentminded professor type. I may not look great, but I know my stuff. You know the routine. But he thought he was a salesman.

So I saw frayed cuffs. I thought other things. What kind of company lets a man like this out on the road? And I knew, I mean, I *knew* the answers. A sloppy company. A company with low standards. A company with lousy back-up, extended response times, etc. And a lost sale.

Well, not quite true. He sold the PC. But for another company. I bought the same elsewhere.

How do you achieve correct positioning?

First you must decide what position you want to occupy inside the head of your prospects or customers. And even that distinction will make a difference. Second, you must live and breathe it.

Some people — even recent books on this self-same subject — will lie to you. I quote from one fellow guru.

> Positioning should be expressed through a short simple statement.

What utter, utter rubbish. As good a copywriter as the issuer of that nonsense is, I defy anyone to write the 'short simple statement' that could have recovered the sale for our PC salesman, other, perhaps, than 'I know I've lost the sale — so please accept this PC as a gift.' Positioning is not everything.

But it is as important to truly competent advertising, direct or otherwise, as oxygen is to life.

In direct mail you achieve positioning by careful attention to everything. The typefaces. The tone of the voice. The nature of the offer, the weight, colour and feel of the paper. The quality of the design and print. Everything.

Your market will ask, does it *hang* right? They'll piece together evidence like a jurist at a murder trial. Do they trust you? Do they believe you? Do they want you in their home or office? Do they want to make a *relationship* (remember that one) with you? And what type of relationship — long and happy? Or a one-off? Can they have faith in you? All these questions must be satisfied by your mailing.

I have noticed a preponderance of a particular type of business to get this aspect of positioning very, very right. I would like to flatter them and say it is through care, consideration and the intelligent application of knowledge.

It is not. In probably 99 per cent of cases it is for an entirely different reason.

Most of these businesses are small businesses. They tend to be run by a 'character'. Someone whose vision of the company — its *human* qualities and characteristics — is so clear that it positively erupts out of their advertising. Or the other kind, where the same 'character' is actually and wholly responsible for the advertising and it is them. Its character is their character. Its manner is their manner. Its style and tone is their style and tone. Metaphorically, this 'character' comes out of the page smiling and reaching to take your hand and lead you inside their store, shop, showroom, whatever.

So many of them get it right. Not the techniques or the skills, nor indeed the philosophy. It is the naive communication of their absolute sincerity and the resultant welding of thought, word and deed. They *want* to get it *right*, and *want* to *sell*.

In my box of tricks there are some stories. View them as stories with a moral. Parables, if you like. From these, and scrutiny of all shades of advertising, it is clear that the task of positioning gets more difficult as the advertisers get bigger. As the distance increases between the writer of the mission statement, those who have to communicate it, and those who have to deliver it, so positioning becomes paradoxically more essential and more difficult.

The effect is then similar to those pass-it-on stories. The sort of thing where the message starts out — 'Send reinforcements, we're going to advance', and becomes — 'Send three-and-fourpence, we're going to a dance.'

The relevance of this is that when recipients hold your mailing, they hold *you*, your company. When you think they hold your mailing in their hands, they don't. All their senses and instincts are at work. You are in their minds. They'll poke and prod and scavenge to find you out. To catch you false-footed. To disbelieve your claim. To establish the sneaky trick in your offer.

JFR's box of tricks

- *The parable of St George and Ambassador* This is a tale of two insurance companies. Both lived by the seaside. One, St George, in Brighton. The other, Ambassador, in Bournemouth. One was weaned and reared on direct marketing, the other on 'the old ways'. One was brash, middle-market and thrusting, the other a brigade of gentlemen. Both were professionals. Both the epitome of trust and customer care. Both with sound, attractive products and a good track record. Both had a clear position in the market. Both had customers who were comfortable with those positions. So comfortable, they had bought the product!

  And they were both in the business of repeat selling to strengthen and upgrade the relationship to go for the next position.

  Ambassador watched St George. Like an old lion sleepily watching a cub. They *knew* about direct marketing. They got it right. Funnily enough, St George also watched Ambassador. And strangely, they felt like an old lion too. And saw St George as the cub. But in a totally different way.

  What was going on at the time, you may recall. The vogue offer for the likes of Ambassador was 'Sign up today — get the first month free'. The next version of this was worthy of a mention too. It was 'Sign up today — get the first month for only £1'. The rationale for this development was an interesting one. I'll come back to it at the end of the story.

  Anyway, the lion St George had observed the success of the cub, Ambassador, and decided to do the same. A test. Head to head. Half: the mailing now offered: buy some more, we'll give you the first month free. The other half: buy some more, and no more. The old-fashioned way!

  Which worked best? Why, the old-fashioned way of course! St George's policyholders couldn't believe their eyes. They *never* got something for nothing. So what was wrong? Why were they resorting to this kind of nonsense?

St George, being the brigade of gentlemen, had used brigade methods to build a customer base of people who related to the brigade way of doing things. No nonsense. No frills. Good, old-fashioned 'you gets what you pays for'.

Ambassador had built, by 'direct' methods, a customer base of people who liked direct marketing, responded to the classic direct marketing ways, and expected all the bells and whistles. What worked for the lion did not work for the cub. Whichever was which.

St George had acted out of character. Out of keeping with the position their methods had carved for them.

Of course you can move position. But you have to move the mind of the market before you achieve the new position. And often the more successful you are in achieving one position, the more difficult it is for you to move to another, however logical, however sensible.

I said we'd go back to Ambassador's change from 'one month free' to 'one month for £1'.

The thought behind this was quite sound. And I do advise you to give it consideration. It is all about something which direct mail people understand: the correlation between quantity and quality. The more you hype, the more replies you'll get. But the lower the quality will be! It's all about what we call 'back-end performance'. How long will the client stay with you? And will they buy any more?

Many insurance companies have found that over-attractive offers bring insubstantial business in substantial numbers. That's to say people who cool off during the cooling-off period and therefore who do not ultimately go on the books. Or people who lapse very quickly. This is a pernicious difficulty to spot, and a costly problem. Are you going to ask for the gift back? And your marketing cost is normally calculated on the full or average spend achieved. So, unless you get the quantity and quality right, you'll be making losses before too long.

Corporately, just as personally, there's no substitute for knowing yourself. And thereby understanding what customers are buying along with the satisfaction in the product or service itself.

That's why you should create only one kind of direct mail — yours.

- *Project yourself consistently in line with your adopted corporate style*. But think practically about the expense of doing it.

One well-known company had made yellow their colour. But a particular yellow. It never worked too well out of four colour, so they usually ran it as an expensive fifth 'self' colour. Their letters were mainly black and blue — plus, of course, the yellow. When the agency pointed out that this was putting up the cost to no real effect (proven by testing) the client said it had to be done. When the agency pointed out that the logo ran in black in the press, they were fired! You decide who was right.

A large insurance broker mailed out to generate enquiries from the very wealthy for a single premium investment of £20 000 plus. The letter was printed on Bronco to 'photocopy' print standards. Their everyday heading was thermographed on heavyweight Conqueror. The managing director had decreed that the time to spend money on clients was 'when they were spending money on us'. Bloody fool. It looked like he needed your £20 000 to set up his business, or pay last month's bills.

Let's be quite clear about this. Your reader cannot see, feel and experience you or your business. The only evidence — from which they will position you — is the mailing which they hold. They should get a clear correct image when they see, feel and experience your mailing. Build your position to better or different than it is, and you will be found out — the PC salesman! Fail to project the full quality and substance of it and you won't get an enquiry, let alone a sale.

Illustrated in Figure 1.1 is a letter distributed by a friend of mine who was looking for new business from this spring promotion. Happily he was successful. He achieved his target.

But look at the letter. Then picture his store. I see an old-fashioned hardware store. The man behind the counter is short, has a brown knee-length overall, a flat cap and a moustache. There's a light brown pencil behind his ear. And an old-fashioned till. The counter is oak, worn by time like a butcher's (but dark varnished wood) and it has a brass yard-rule inset in its side. Do you agree?

It's nothing like my friend's store. Indeed the opposite. How much more business could have been achieved if he had positioned himself as the bright, modern, well-stocked wallpaper, paint, DIY self-service value-for-money store that he actually runs?

- *Your sins will find you out.* Occasionally the market will position you first! When British Airways came out with 'We'll take more care of you', the frequent travellers

WESTS

Proprietors: A.J. WILLIAMS., D.J. WILLIAMS., M.H. WILLIAMS., D.R. WILLIAMS

HARDWARE & GARDENING

1 SEA ROAD, EAST PRESTON, BN16 1JN Phone Rustington 3453
8 STATION PARADE, ANGMERING STN, BN16 3AE " " 2261
THE SQUARE, ANGMERING VILLAGE BN16 4EA " " 70649

VAT Registration No. 193 9747 06

Dear Sir/Madam,

It is with pleasure that we write to advise you of **WESTS of EAST PRESTON and ANGMERING DISCOUNT PLAN.**

This year we are introducing discounts on many of our Gardening and Hardware items. For example through the month of February and March we are offering 17½% discount on Fisons Mosskil, Evergreen 80 and Lawn Food in 500 & 300 sq. yd. sizes.
Other discounts on items such as Gro-Bags, Levington composts, Bos bags, Killasprays and Netlon are also available as are loose Growmore at keen prices [25kg. @ £5.15 = £1.00 off RRP] Bone Meal, etc.

On the Hardware side there are discounts of 10% - 15% on Pyrex goods, offers on Abru step ladders, Tefal ware, Plysu plastics and more.

To assist you quickly to see the bargains an **ORANGE SPOT** will be placed on all discounted items in the shops. Why not call and see us or give us a call on Rustington 3453 for East Preston or Rustington 70649 for our Angmering Branch.

We would like to thank those of you who have patronised us in the past, and welcome those who have yet to entrust us with their valued custom.

Looking forward to the favour of your call and assuring you of our very best attention.

We are,
Yours faithfully,
WESTS

Figure 1.1
The letter received from Wests

'womed' them to death (wom = word of mouth). Up the loyalty ladder, advocates do it for your benefit. Off the ladder, reverse advocates can kill. Remember — make a customer happy and they'll tell two or three people. Make them unhappy, and they'll tell fourteen!

BA were hoisted on their own petard. They set about solving the problem the right way. They started to live up to the slogan. Turned opinion round. Advocacy (and terrific PR) took over. And zap! Now they're the world's favourite airline. Not difficult when you're the world's largest airline! Verisimilitude appears to rule, OK.

In all things tell the truth. Be who and what you are.

- Years ago, Leyland teamed up with the AA to give 'Supercover' with a Leyland car purchase. The Supercover symbol was formed of a pair of cupped hands — the gentle giant protection. When Fiat did the same thing (or near enough) they pictured an AA man in the glove compartment, suggesting that a Fiat without an AA man was the same as a Fiat without wheels. Maybe they know something we don't?

- Beware the branches and agents! However innocent and well meaning the attempt, giving others the freedom to 'do their own thing' is fine — provided, of course, they know what they're doing. If not, it could well undermine your positioning from within.

  A lot of the workshops and training sessions which I do are designed to deal with just such a problem. As a result, you can give branches, agents, dealers, or even individual representatives, the satisfaction and motivation of participation and involvement — but still be confident that required corporate standards will be met.

  In these days of fax and electronic mail it's easy to build in, if necessary, a simple, fast approval system that assists rather than interferes — but none the less monitors quality standards.

Don't buck the trend. Some things just are.

- For a charity, we asked people, 'What colour is cancer?' Nine out of ten said 'Yellow'.

  For a holiday company, 'What colour is a holiday?' Eleven out of ten (I agreed) said 'Orange'. Every time I tell this story half say they think blue. But only after they know about the orange!

- Off direct mail — but still with positioning — *where you advertise and the size of your ad can contribute to your positioning too*. Ever seen Gucci in *Exchange and Mart* with 2 inch single? They know their place.

  Back on direct mail — some less informed people will tell you that their product is just not the thing that one can sell 'in a mailing'. Maybe. But the old London Bridge was sold that way. And I've been asked to sell a wide range of products by mail. In fact, from funerals (your own — Yuk!) to a million pound hotel site.

2 There are only **two** kinds of direct mail—

The **rubbish** and the **relevant**

or...

Does good taste give you bad breath?

Your task, naturally, is to improve the ratio of rubbish to relevant. For your own good primarily. But you won't be doing direct mail — indeed the industry — any harm if you join JFR's effort to upgrade things.

My view is that there is one and only one fundamental way to achieve this. And I know I'll get a few cries of complaint as I run through my thoughts on this concept. Here goes anyway.

Life loves the lowest common denominator

One of the pieces of advice that publishers give authors — mine included — is not to 'age' your work with time references. Disregarding this advice with utter, careless abandon, I'm going to share some revealing knowledge with you. Recently a long-running TV soap (to the great relief of some!) came to an end. Barring the too-dreadful-to-think-about prospect of repeats, the last episode of *Crossroads* scored on the ITV ratings top ten. It was fighting with the perennial *Coronation Street*. And over on BBC, *Neighbours*, *Eastenders* and even *Dallas* are all in the top ten. In fact, *Neighbours* and *Eastenders* almost make up the whole thing!

Some years ago I was on a training course for TV interview techniques. The idea was that the seven or eight of us who had been crazy enough to subject ourselves to this course had three interviews which were videoed in studio conditions. And then, led by the excellent course tutor — who was a well-known and very proficient current affairs presenter himself — as a group, we watched the interviews and discussed our feelings and views on each other's performance. It was actually a fascinating day. He interviewed us all in a sweetness-and-light style the first time round and lulled us unsuspecting into a superb sense of false security. Without warning, for the second interview he set about demolishing us, talking over us, ignoring answers, every kind of unfair, unkind and generally vicious technique you could think of. It wasn't an interview, it was a slaughter! He made Sir Robin Day at his most evil seem like a pussy cat! What took everybody's wind away was that the conniving rat had done his homework first. He'd worked out two or three contentious issues about our various businesses and set us up fair and square!

His topics with me — the standards of good taste and creativity and the junk mail and privacy issues. Why was I surprised?

Out of the interview came a really rather sad reflection on the human race, advertising, and things in general. I later came to describe it in discussions with media and at conferences as the lowest common denominator factor. And I hate to admit it, but it still looms large, even as the medium improves, gains in professionalism, and becomes more and more widely accepted and used.

I was so pleased with myself. Despite the grilling, I won! Which, as I learned, is about the most stupid thing you can do. Any 'real' interviewer would have chopped the interview before I had a chance, I was told!

Anyway, he laid into me saying that creative standards in direct mail were banal. I was able to move him away from being 'the people's friend' and position myself in that slot by getting him to admit that he didn't like *Coronation Street*. It wasn't *his* taste.

I then made the point that his taste and the prevailing taste of 15 million households didn't seem to have a lot in common. I rounded on him by asking why an industry that lives or dies on how many people respond — a good yardstick of how many people like it — would mail out what recipients thought was banal? We succeed by learning what people respond to not what they view as banal. Effectively, we send what public taste told us it liked by analysing what it actually responds to. By the end, of course, I had positioned myself with the viewer. He was the bad guy. Which was just as well because my argument was as reasonable as using a colander to tote water. And it had more holes in it.

It is a dreadful confession to make but my experience suggests that for a short-term response gain 'lowering the tone' nearly always wins. But in the medium and long term it can cause enormous damage. Remember, the advertising effect works on greater numbers than the response effect.

If Aspreys ever go with a sweepstake, it'll be the most dignified you've seen. Or for their closing down sale when everything must go. Including standards!!

Ways to avoid being **rubbish**

The best way, of course, is to cut out the rubbishers — those who don't like what we do, what we are, and probably the most vociferous, those who don't like what we send.

Easier said than done.

Some steps are possible. However the dilemma caused by the LCD factor is that sustaining peak performance and achieving the 'high fallutin' standards that might be set by those who claim to be the arbiters of good taste very often means, if not two ends of a spectrum, at least a very wide gap. Much easier for those in countries which have no taste, where this won't be an issue!

The answer to this for the vast majority will not be in their subjective judgement of what is in good or bad taste, but in what best suits the corporate and brand or product positioning as we discussed in Chapter 1. Do we, I wonder, expect to see the Salvation Army, who use direct mail extensively for fundraising, resorting to sweepstakes and prize draws? World Wildlife Fund, maybe. Oxfam, who can tell? The Sally Army, never. Would you mail the Jaguar cars guarantee cards to recruit members for the Jaguar Enthusiasts Club offering a personalised green sunstrip (Greg and Tracy where are you?) with, as a bonus for life membership, 'SUPER DOUBLE DOWNY FLUFFY DICE'?

What would we need to do, I wonder, to convert a package to suit yer average *Sun* reader? (These are not social — or anti-social — comments. They are not even, as they might appear to be, bald snobbery. They are facts.)

As I said in Part One, whether your mail is perceived as rubbish or not has far more to do with relevance than weight of paper or graphic style. Pomposity does not have a great role in the direct marketer's life. Realism does. Recognition that we are in the business of appreciating the finer aspects of human needs and how those needs relate to interaction. In matters of taste, subjectivity is largely irrelevant. Objectivity rules. We are in the business of providing — or rather producing and sending out — what works. People respond to what gets to them, not what experts think will do it. Or even more significantly, they respond to what convinces them they should, rather than what they say would convince them.

This is a phenomenon that the market research world is familiar with. Direct marketers have to live with it every day. The difference between what we say we like, and what we actually like.

Quite early in my career I was involved with an on-pack offer for a fast-moving consumer goods (FMCG) company. The offer was to be a set of dining-table place mats. Three designs had been narrowed down and were to be put to a market research company to evaluate. After (I think it was) focus panels up and down the country, a clear winner — absolutely way ahead — was established: a surprisingly tasteful set of 'The Cries of London'. Second came some pretty, but unexceptional, prints of roses.

Out went the product, onto the grocers' and supermarkets' shelves blasting the usual 'Collect four labels and send to PO Box X with a cheque or postal order for . . .'

It died a death. Quickly, a decision was made to change labelling plans and go as soon as possible with the roses. Redemption figures shot up. A second and then third production had to be made to meet demand.

What had happened? In the focus panel environment the women who had been interviewed had voiced the opinions that they thought they should. Choosing 'Cries' showed they had good taste to the others in the room. Others on the panel. And the researchers. But what they wanted (when nobody else was taking any notice or making judgements on their actions) were the comparatively style-less but pretty roses.

Each mailing is not only an exercise in ultimate democracy — let the people decide — it is also a postal ballot on whether you have summed up their tastes, attitudes and preferences right. And indeed the balance between these and your own image and positioning.

I would love to tell you that quality always wins. In terms of product, I'm sure that is correct; in terms of a promotion, it is a far different story. So we are only human after all!

There is a clear inference here that you should follow the LCD factor down. Which is not quite what I'm suggesting and indeed seems to contradict the heading of this piece — how to avoid being rubbish. The cynic would suggest that my advice indicates that the more like rubbish your mailings are, in terms of taste and style, the better they work. My point is that you can't — and never will — please everyone. Those that frown on your mailings, feel strongly enough about it to write and complain or ring you up, would in most cases have done so anyway however stylishly you had approached them.

Poor old *Reader's Digest* seem to have become both the yardstick and the whipping post. We're back to party conversation again!

I've always found three ways to clear people away and get myself some space at an overcrowded party. Undoubtedly the two most effective are:

'Well, actually I sell life assurance' or the upmarket version: 'I have a fascinating job. Tax planning. And personal pensions.'

Room empty! Method three, disconcertingly, is:

'I'm a direct mail writer.' Next, in response to an enquiry as to what exactly that is, and the ensuing enlightenment, come the immortal words 'Not all that *Reader's Digest* stuff?' Shame really, as I think we're a fascinating if somewhat self-opinionated bunch. But then it's a dreadful burden just living with the vast, but absolute knowledge we have of the human race. And what it likes!

My advice then. Be open-minded enough and self-effacing enough to learn and grow in the warmth of knowledge. Knowledge gained through experience which will show you how your market most likes to see you, and how it most likes to be sold to by you. This doesn't necessarily mean you are condemned to a future somewhere in the murky depths trying to live alongside the likes of Hemeling Lite. So . . .

Step One   Be brave and experiment. And if possible rely on some professional advice. Most professional direct marketing creatives have an almost instinctive feel for this. But categorically, establish what works best regardless of other aesthetic considerations.

Step Two   Look at the answers and decide what you want to do about it.

To those bulging with corporate pride — or arrogance! — don't panic. Doing it this way round you can make a sensible and informed commercial judgement. You know what, if any, your profit compromises are, and what they're costing you. That should send tremors down the spines of the chairmens' wives of a few banks and charities!

Most of the problems in this area will be caused by the creative department. And, indeed, most of the solutions will be found by them. The answer is normally somewhere near the middle ground. Mostly it will come from differentiating between the techniques and the way they are styled and communicated.

A lady delegate attended one of my JFR Masterclasses. She

joined in and was thoroughly enjoying herself. But as we reconvened after lunch she came out with her worry. 'I'm sorry,' she said, 'but despite the fact that I'm enjoying myself and I really feel I'm learning a lot, there's no way my company could even consider this sort of thing. We are a rather exclusive establishment and most of what you're describing would be totally out of keeping for us.'

Within five minutes we'd reshaped several proven techniques to do with gifts and incentives, and she had even realised that the idea she liked best was actually the ultimate in exclusive prize draws.

Well, do you know how to acquire Buckingham Palace garden party tickets on the black market? There's got to be a way.

The most predictable aspect of all this is human behaviour — the emotions and desires that drive us. Faithfully, I promise you, nothing changes. Except the level.

My wife and I recently entertained an old friend of mine and her husband. They came to stay for the weekend and a fairly fragile breakfast conversation was prompted by the quality of our towels. 'They were a wedding present,' I told her. 'Two were sent by a friend who runs a mail order business.'

'This is one mail order company I should know about,' she said. 'They're far better than the ones we got at Harrods. And they were real wallet-busters!'

The lady visitor is a senior graphic designer for a well-known Covent Garden classical agency. Her husband, also a designer, heads up a very trendy international design group. A chic pair! Her face contorted with disbelief when I told her the price of the towels.

'We were so impressed with the two gifts, we ordered six more with our thank-you letter,' I explained. 'I've got a copy of the catalogue in my "garrett"'.

I nipped up to my office and looked out the catalogue with impish glee. I knew she'd all but pass out. Monty Dare of Keys of Clacton is a bright fellow. He knows his market. He knows who buys. What they buy and why. He's as aware of those things when he selects his products as he is when he sells them.

I know Monty will agree with my earlier words. Product quality is paramount. But the word 'quality' is assessed very differently in relation to the actual promotional piece itself.

Our designer friend was mortified. Monty's catalogue actually shocked her. She was both incredulous and outraged. The catalogue challenged almost everything her career was founded on and through which her success had been achieved.

She held it like a father with soiled nappy. The conversation provoked by the catalogue took us through to lunch-time.

She could not grasp Monty's understanding of his marketplace. To her it was incongruous that the best quality towels she had come across for ages should be available at about one third of the price of Harrods from a catalogue that, and I quote, 'wouldn't even get hung on a string in our loo if we ran out of paper.' Absolutely. Monty's database, I am sure, does not contain such a huge quantity of trendies with a joint income that would probably equate to the income of half a dozen or more whole families of typical Keys of Clacton customers. Well, it's almost certainly got one now!

She would dismiss the catalogue as rubbish. Tens of thousands of similarly happy and delighted customers eagerly await it. What, I wonder, did she do with the one that Monty's despatch dept will correctly have included with her towels? I must take a look in her loo next time I'm there. If she's as smart as I think she is, she'll have framed it to give herself something to think about when at her most contemplative.

The big worry of all this is that direct mail may be its own worst enemy. Perversely, the very thing that gets it such a bad name is its sheer selling power. The economics of success.

Direct mail is successful as a low-response medium. So many of us are happy with responses from only two or three in every hundred. And even at that level we're contentedly profitable. So we don't worry much that even greater numbers see us as irrelevant junk!

It will change. Database and printing technologies will enable it to happen. As we progress, we shall improve the actual ability, as well as the desirability and the profitability, of mailing only to those to whom we are relevant. Never to an ultimate conclusion, but nearer with each step.

Two immediate actions to cut out the rubbishers

There are two things you can do right now to help yourself and the industry mutually.

Action 1: Mailing Preference Service
The first is currently only an option for the consumer mailer in the UK. It involves the Mailing Preference Service. This is a service inspired by the industry, to enable those who really don't like receiving direct mail to be excluded from mailings.

I do urge every UK direct mail advertiser to support and subscribe to the service, thereby cleaning their list of those people who don't like mail, whatever it's about. This will both stop you from upsetting them and it will save you the cost of mailing to them. Many leading list brokers, data processing suppliers and mailing operations subscribe to the service and will be able to remove the names from your list and others that you may be renting. Insist on it.

Details of the service are available on request from the Mailing Preference Service at the address listed in the Contact Addresses in Part Three.

On their application form you have the choice of requesting to be taken off or put on to mailing lists. Although you might think this a strange proposition, over time, experience has been that the 'fors' often outweigh the 'againsts'.

For the future, consumer advertisers should bear this in mind. Especially since applicants requesting more mail are asked to specify on what subjects they would like more and these names are available — for a fee! Since the scheme is a comparative infant in the UK, the numbers of those wanting more are still small. In the US both positive and negative requests run into several hundred thousands. It was, understandably, the negatives who built up to these quantities first. Also, the US experience was, in my opinion, handled much more as an opportunity than a weeping sore that needed attention.

Action 2: do it yourself

The second piece of advice is for both consumer and business-to-business advertisers. It is to implement and run your own mail preference service. It will produce three benefits.

1   You are seen — as you will be — to be Mr Clean!
2   As time passes, you will save time and money as well as keep your image shining bright.
3   You will be able to say to any complainants, 'Well, we did ask. But you didn't tell us. Never mind, we've taken care of it now!'

Not quite in those words, of course.

If you examine your next new membership card pack from Amex, you'll probably find a suitable adaptable form of words. If not, here's one:

As a part of our total responsibility and dedication to the well-being of our policyholders we occasionally send reminders, newsletters, and other such items which highlight particular financial and savings opportunities or market situations of which our clients may take advantage.

If for any reason you should prefer not to avail yourself of this free service, please indicate this on the enclosed form by placing a cross in the 'Mail Limitation' box. We will then endeavour to keep your mailing to the minimum but you will still naturally receive your two six-monthly statements and other necessary administrative items.

More ways to avoid being **rubbish** — and be more **relevant**

As I suggested earlier, progress is heading in this direction anyway. The days of mass mailing are over. Segmentation, selectivity and the use of database techniques to improve and tighten targeting are where tomorrow's direct mail lies. Quantities will decrease. Versions will increase.

Perversely, the Data Protection Act seems actively to apply a subtle pressure against this movement. Some of the very same data which might be construed as sensitive, if handled ethically, would do much to add to relevance. Unethically handled, it would simply prove the need for the Act. And damn us all to a bleak future. Which is why it is vitally important for every single user of direct mail to understand and be sensitive to the fears and dislikes of their present and future customers, and to treat them respectfully, honestly and with care.

That's relevant.

JFR's box of tricks

- MPS screening is generally becoming accepted as a wonderful thing to do at exit — that's to say when you draw lists off the computer. But you could screen on entry — yes, when you put the new customer *onto* your file in the first place. An economic special version 'welcome' pack could recognise the preferences of those who have already registered themselves with the MPS. For those that acquire customers through processes other than through the mail in the first place, but who have mail programmes after customer acquisition, I would suggest this as a very positive first communication topic, and a real relationship builder for the future. Don't deny yourself the opportunity to get people to grant you a place as the exception to the rule.
- When you are advising customers or prospects of your own MPS, flag the national service too. It's not going to involve

you in a great deal of cost to provide the name and address of the MPS. It will be seen as a caring and thoughtful action. It may also deflect a potential complaint. Offering the consumer the alternative of writing to apply for MPS registration details instead of writing to 'have a go at you'.

● Always make any MPS, or similar, a negative option. That's to say, the reader must put pen to paper — or at least take positive action — to implement their wishes.

● Don't get carried away! One of the oldest and probably most repeated stories in direct mail is that of the US airline which developed a special price package for the several thousand delegates attending a week-long conference in Hawaii. 'Book your flight with us,' their mailing proposed, 'and your wife goes FREE. Yes, two seats for the price of one.'

You'll agree this was a truly attractive offer. So attractive that many hundreds of delegates accepted. It was easy, therefore, a few weeks later, for the customer relations officer to implement her brilliant idea. She mailed the spouses of the delegates with a short but telling letter that achieved a huge response. It thanked the delegates' spouse for accepting the offer and travelling with that particular airline to the conference in Hawaii.

Brightly, it included another offer on a reduced price double booking complete with lowered hotel prices to enable travellers to explore further and enjoy Hawaii together, without the pressure of a 'work' environment. However, the whole thing backfired terribly when over half the respondents replied that they had not been taken on any trip in the first place and wanted more, far more information!

3 There are only **three** kinds of direct mail—

IT'S ● **RETURNED,**

● **RECEIVED**

OR

● **RESPONDED TO**

or:

the Three R's of direct mail

Why does mail get **returned**?

Normally because somebody didn't get it right. I hereby absolve all those who can put their hands on their hearts and say we do encourage, at every opportunity, the customer (prospect, member, etc.) to let us know when they've moved (died, run out of money, etc.).

There are two things that can be done to encourage returns:

1 Provide the means for information updating and addition at *every* opportunity.
2 Ensure that there is an address on the outer envelope or carrier thus encouraging the return of the undeliverables in as many cases as possible.

These amendments or deletions should be dealt with just as quickly as possible.

Mail gets returned for three principal reasons. Two of which you probably deal with quite regularly.

The first is 'gone away'. And they didn't tell you yet. There are many, many ways to 'hitch-hike' for new addresses or forthcoming address details. You've seen the credit card companies and so on using the backs of their bangtails, the overleaf of their order, the bound-in insert of their magazine.

The second is the 'undeliverable'. This occurs for a number of reasons.

- Sloppy input
- Handwritten and insufficiently validated input information leading to incorrect addresses
- The rats lied

The third is actually an extension of 'the rats lied'. It has become a quite widely used ploy put about by Citizens' Advice Bureaux and the like. When you write 'not known at this address' on a mailing and send it back, your level of mailings tends to diminish quite quickly.

I tried this one with my bank manager. But he rang up!

There are two great knocks that hit the inexperienced direct mail user right below the confidence belt at one of the weakest moments — the time lag-between the mailing going out and the replies coming in. A sort of post-natal depression. They are the 'funnies' and 'nixies'.

You'll get the funnies first. There's one from the seven years or so that I was running my conference series 'The Secrets of Effective Direct Mail'. I built up, as you can imagine, quite a good client list of delegates. Preaching the TEN-X factor, I was always careful (and gratified by the results) to mail these out, trawling for referrals. And it never ceased to amaze me how many people would come a second — or even a third time. Now that's loyalty!

Anyway, after the first year, two particular previous delegates took great delight in responding to my invitations. The first would simply scrunch up the mailed items, flatten them and force them into the reply paid envelope. He or she never identified him/herself, which was a shame. If they had, I could have taken them off the list. Then I would have stopped irritating them. And they would have stopped irritating me. We'd both have been happy.

The other wanted me to get out more and enjoy myself. Every time I mailed him (and I assume it was a him) he would simply enclose a leaflet for a night club in London into my reply paid envelope and pop it in the post. Nice of him. But since, and I quote the headline, 'Sophisticated Nights for Gay Guys' was never my scene, I didn't incline myself to accept.

One charity I worked on used to get a 'disgusted' reply fairly regularly from the 'rightful Queen of England'. Unfortunately, she assumed we knew where she lived — somewhere in Preston — and so we couldn't remove her. She probably decided in the end we were going for a 'By Appointment'.

The first reply to the first mailing I was involved with for Bradford and Bingley Building Society was opened with great ceremony. We were all praying for an application for at least the top product that the mailing contained. Far from it! The reply envelope contained one ordinary domestic colour snap of a delectable young lady adorned only in 'naughty' white underwear. Her pose was only marginally less tantalising to the society's marketing men than the challenge of tracking her through the database, given only a postmark and time of posting!!

The funnies come first. People vent their feelings in many ways. Some are funny. Some are obscene. Sensitive people may prefer not to open your mail for you.

Next come the genuine returns. What the trade calls the 'nixies'. These all have one thing in common. They're ten times larger coming back than when they went out. Or so it seems! They sit in a corner of the office, taking up space, and they can become a mountain. Strangely, when you come to count them, they shrink back to their normal size.

You should plan for nixies. They must be dealt with as soon as it is economically and logistically possible to do so. They will clean your list, or the lists you rent. Some brokers and suppliers will even give you a postage refund if the quantity exceeds a pre-set percentage.

And the rest get **received**

This is the great unknown. Those that receive the mailing, but don't respond.

The future will focus the white glare of its spotlights on these people in two ways.

First, to find ways to reduce them — response rates should go higher and higher. Not just because of increasingly sophisticated sales techniques, but more because technology and database marketing will give us an increasingly complete picture of those we are writing to. And what they want to buy from us.

One thing we already know. Targeting the audience is not enough. You have to target the message too.

In 1984 Prentice-Hall published Herschell Gordon Lewis's book *Direct Marketing Copy that SELLS!* In Chapter 15, a look to 1990 and beyond, Herschell predicted as follows:

Human nature being as cantankerous as it is, we have no laws of probability.

What we do have is an apparent disintegration of the unity we can call 'our society' only on Flag Days, Thanksgiving and Christmas. Groups splinter and then re-splinter. Minorities are black, female, old, young, educated, uneducated, of every religious persuasion, of nonreligious persuasion, residents of a particular subdivision, drivers of small cars, drivers of large cars, truck drivers, railroad passengers, thieves and scoundrels, recent immigrants, old-line native-borns, police, firemen, rapers and rapees, and those with only a black and white television in their cars.

As I've said throughout this book, a major advantage of direct response advertising is its ability to appeal to vertical interest groups within the fields of interest they represent. No other medium can do that. The late-night news can't do it. The daily paper can't do it. Even special interest magazines can do it only in part, and then only on a rigid and unyielding schedule in which no advertiser has dominance.

Can we see any trends?

How many times can a single person be astounded by the same lunacy? I'm constantly re-astounded at the most common circumstance I see in the most enlightened practitioners of the noble art of direct response selling:

A meeting of six people for half a day, results in the careful choice of lists and media. We choose this list because it has women 18 to 34; we choose that list because it has senior citizens who own cars that cost $12,000 or more; we choose the next list because the family has bought a Boy Scout uniform within the past two years. . . Then what do we do? We create a single direct mail package and mail it to all of them, figuring we'll sort out the winners from the losers by analysing the response.

On occasions, when we've dabbled with packages tailored to the supposed key interest of a particular group and tested that package against the 'standard' approach, the results have been encouraging. Why, then, don't we do it more often? Time and economics are sensible restraints, but as we approach 1990 economics probably (yup, I know I said we have no laws of probability) will swing around to favour greater attention to the demographic/psychographic differences that caused us to choose that market segment.

Of course, he was right. Today, we're varying copy just as Herschell suggested, a great deal. And yes, we find it works. Moreover, as the software, systems and database capabilities improve we're all working to achieve — within the somewhat smaller markets that many UK advertisers find themselves — the full benefits of exactly those psychographic, demographic and other data which increase our view of the individual — our customer. But will this tighter targeting get us read against the backcloth of the exciting new electronic and interactive media upcoming before 1990 and commonplace before the year 2000?

Back to Herschell Gordon Lewis:

Will the message recipients of 1990 spend more time or less time reading the mailings and space ads, and viewing the electronic bombardment, than they do now?

My opinion: more. As we increase penetration into specific-interest groups, we logically can expect greater attention from those we reach, because their interest in what we say should be greater.

The overlaid use of relatable geographic, demographic and psychographic knowledge and experiential data (such as recency, frequency and monetary values) will lead to smaller and smaller mailings of an increasingly relevant and desirable nature to the targeted recipient.

The unknown here — the foggy areas which will gradually clear as time passes — have to do, in part, with the cost of all this.

In the past, the discipline has followed a reverse pattern. Once you've got your pack, find as many names as you can, get the price in the post down. And maximise.

But as well as cost, as the segments get smaller we must consider the practicality. There will come a point where such tight segmentation, such narrow targeting may change the medium selected. To telephone, for example. And what of the interactive electronic media? Well, they are up and running, albeit with varying degrees of modesty and take-up.

The other spotlight which must stretch the intellectuals of the direct marketing industry is on the quantification of those who received but did not respond and the use to which they put our communication. For they will, I believe, always stay the vast majority for the vast majority.

To date, what do we know? Not a lot. Some say, why do you care? For this reason. Because they are the vast majority, the vast majority of the advertising spend is being cast at them. Advertisers will become increasingly demanding and not rest content for much longer with the simple argument I propounded earlier.

Let me restate that. I said that since direct marketers were achieving their volume and profit targets from those who do respond, the advertising effect on those who didn't respond is free.

Sure. Free. But what's it worth? We already know that direct mail gets readership levels way beyond the press. We know it gets recall way beyond television. We understand that it provides an intensity of sales message absorption beyond most things — often even a face-to-face sales call.

But what's it worth? Advertisers spending the vast majority of their money on these, the vast majority of people, will rightly demand answers. The industry must provide them.

What of them? What should your attitude be? In a word: *Worship.*

I made a mistake earlier. I fell in with a 'roll-off-the-tongue' cliché: the customer is king.

Now I say, when they've responded and come forward to you, that's not enough. The prospect is king. The customer is next to a god.

The big problem with direct marketing is often its biggest attraction. Its accountability. People see that as a way of controlling — no, too often reducing — costs. How can they get away with the minimum acceptable level of service at the minimum level of cost? My philosophy was stated earlier. I'll repeat it.

The object of a business is not to make money. The object is to serve its customers. The result is to make money.

An example. I often find myself at conferences, seminars and workshops extolling the virtues of speed. More precisely, using first class Business Reply or Freepost to get the orders or enquiries back. My advice is to let people know that you want to do business with them. Use first class. It has obvious extra benefits. In lead generation, it reduces the time between the enquiry and the follow-up. For a few pence you can cut the follow-up time by 20 to 30 per cent. Ask any sales people what is the most important thing about following up an enquiry, they'll tell you without a moment's hesitation — to follow up quickly. When you want to know, you want to know. The more interested you are, the more frustrated you get at delays, and the more likely you are to look around.

Ditto the mail order buyer. You can sit at home and wait. Or you can get in your car and get it today. That's the choice. The longer the delay, the more likely the prospective buyer is to return the goods, and pick one up in town in the meantime.

Let them enquire first class. Let them buy first class.

'Ahh. We've tested that. It makes no difference,' people tell me.

And you know, it never will make a difference if you don't count opinion, if you only look at the number of replies you get —not the ones you didn't get. And you constantly cost the short-term delivery of a promise, not the long-term satisfaction of a customer.

Our job, as direct marketers, is not just to serve the customer, but to serve the customer better. We all spend a lot of money getting enquiries and orders. The cost differential between servicing those adequately and servicing them well, often boils down to pennies.

Regularly, *Direct Response* magazine carries out a survey to see how well response handling measures up. The results are a disgrace to the marketing business. And believe me, as a result, someone else, somewhere, is picking up an order.

A colleague of mine carried out some research in Germany for a kitchen manufacturer. They established that a purchase decision normally extends over about 18 months. That's to say, from the moment the prospects start thinking about a new kitchen, to the time they buy. Fascinated by this snippet, I instigated a coupon-clipping exercise in the UK to establish how long it takes to get the information you've asked for; how many people assume that simply sending out a product information pack is enough; how many realise that once may not be enough; and how many are prepared to rent their enquirers to other people.

Here are the results, and as a professional marketer, I find them embarrassing.

1 *Response*
Actually responded in any way to a coupon
    enquiry — 63 per cent
(Can you believe that 37 per cent of coupon
    advertisers didn't actually respond at all?)
Responded within seven days — 32 per cent
Responded with a considered and
    professional selling pack — 34 per cent
Rented list to other appropriate advertiser — 34 per cent

2 *Follow-up*
Time delay of follow-up call (total 43 per cent)
    1–7 days — 12 per cent
    7–14 days — 22 per cent
    14 days — 9 per cent
    ───────────
    43 per cent
    ───────────
Followed up more than once — 12 per cent

I rest my case. Your best will never be enough. Unless you're prepared to put up with it. And if you are, you're on your way out.

JFR's box of tricks

- *Repeat mailings often outpull the first*
  When did you ever see a TV ad that only appeared once?
  Did you ever hear a radio commercial just the one time?
  When was the last time you saw a poster one-off on the
  underground?

  I know direct mail is so powerful that it very often
  achieves its goals in one go. But that's like bringing your
  trawler into port because its full, when you're sure there
  are more fish out there. Go back for more!

  There's nothing to stop you. In fact, even if you've got
  existing artwork with offer closing dates, you can still use
  it without too much expense by adding flashes which
  proclaim: OFFER EXTENDED — PLEASE APPLY BY
  (NEW DATE).

- *The quick, cheap way to test repeat mailings*
  Printing 10 000 for your first mailing? Run 11 000.
  Printing 19 000? Run 21 000. Then mail the balance to a
  random selection of non-respondents. Code the response
  items and that'll give you a cheap way of finding out what
  response a full-scale repeat could get. Run-on print
  produced at the same time as the original run is very cheap.
  You'll have to test over a period of one or two to determine
  the best gap between your first mailing and your repeat.
  My experience suggests that this will most likely fall
  within two to six weeks. Be careful you extract as many as
  possible of those who have already replied to the first
  mailing, otherwise you could antagonise and place those
  sales at risk.

  One way to get round that and to minimise this, is to pop
  in a short handwritten or typed note (obviously personal
  and slightly rushed!) that says:

  'Since I haven't heard from you yet, I am enclosing a copy
  of my recent letter, highlighting the benefits of . . .'
  and then close with a PS that includes:

  'Should this letter have crossed in the post with your
  reply, my sincere apologies.'

- *Acknowledge orders and enquiries*
  Many mail order companies choose not to go to the cost of
  acknowledging orders unless the price is high, or there's a
  stock or shipping problem.

  Often this exercise, as well as being beneficial to
  customer relations, can break even, or better make a profit.

How? Include another offer! List renters the world over will pay a premium for 'hot' names. This is as hot as you can get. Also it's a good time for a member-get-member (MGM) approach!

- *Try the 'star shell' and 'ghosting' techniques*
  Both for consumer advertisers.

  1 *Starshell*: When you get a response, mail your original offer to the respondents' nextdoor neighbours. One or two on both sides can build you a small but high response list since the neighbours, while they may not have precisely the same taste, will often have very similar lifestyles, standards and income levels.

  2 *Ghosting:* When you get a return, automatically despatch a pack addressed to 'The New Owners of . . .' As above, if you got your list selection right in the first place, you'll often find that the new owners are just as good prospects.

  For business to business: Ghosting also works for services and supplies. Office equipment, cleaning, linen hire, etc.

4 There are only **four** kinds of direct mail—

- **wanted**

- **wasted**

- **working**

and ● **wrecking**

The first three are to do with understanding who you are writing to. And who you are trying to convince. The fourth — wrecking — that's back to database again. And a little re-emphasis about positioning.

The technique of the **wanted,** the **wasted,** the **working**

Amongst all the clutter of information that's available — and there's more all the time — do you know who you're writing to? I mean, can you picture them?

Many, many direct response copywriters — often including myself — extol the technique of picturing one single prospective buyer or responder. We fantasise their characters. Choose their clothes. Decide their politics and opinions. Invent a person who we think typifies our audience. Right monsters they can be too!

Another writer tells me of his own variation of this where he writes to try to achieve a sale with his least-likely-to-buy relative. Whatever works for you!

But this sequence may help you to identify the scope of your task.

For it's a fact that on every mailing list — or even database! — whatever your selections, segmentations or profiling, there will still remain only three types of reader. The joy of this rationale is, as you will see, that you need to think about only one of them . . . it makes your job much easier. Sometimes!

Let's look at Reader Type No 1 — A reader for whom your mailing was *wanted*.

He likes you. He likes your company. He knows you. And he approves of you. He likes your product. He probably already has something of yours and he's happy with it.

He likes direct mail. He *reads* direct mail. He likes shopping for lots of things that way. He's comfortable with the whole process.

But more.

He is actually in the market for what you want to sell. Indeed, he had more or less decided to buy one. In fact your mailing arrived that very morning.

I wish there were more of these types around. The fact is, there are never enough of them on *any* mailing list.

So what do we have to say to th s person to get the sale?

Answer: next to nothing. As long as we make it easy enough — maybe provide a telephone Rapid Order Hotline and accept all major credit cards; or be sure to enclose a simple-to-complete order voucher and a first class reply-paid envelope — we should have us a sale. Like picking ripe plums!

Stand back from Type No 2: The *wasted*.

He *hates* you. Your company *stinks* They're cheats. Scoundrels and rapscallions. Everyone says so. Your products are the worst, I mean the WORST. He had something from you already. And it broke.

Direct mail? It's not junk. It's worse. He uses better than that for toilet paper. It invades his privacy. He gets at least one full postal van of it every week. And it's all the same — garbage. And as for shopping by post, you must be kidding. They're all crooks — or else they would do what every self-respecting person would do and open a shop.

But more.

Frankly, he wouldn't consider your ignorant suggestion even if he had the quite exorbitant sum you ask for it. And 'let me tell you', the very last thing he needs right now is you time-wasting, when he is trying to get to work, the car won't start and the dog's just thrown up on his shoes.

He doesn't approve of credit cards and knows precisely what part of your anatomy the phone was designed for.

Dear Reader, we may not pull this one! And when you think about it, we are not dealing just with someone who is going to be difficult to convince, we're looking at someone who is going to be *impossible* to convince. Whatever we say. Your approach is wasted.

Give up! There are, sad to record, always too many of these on any list you may use.

By a process of elimination — the next is the one for whom our message and our offer and our supporting evidence is *working*.

This is the reader you've got to be sure you are writing to. The one you have to convince. They may be interested. Maybe they will buy. They need persuading. They need evidence. They need reasons — good ones. They need to trust and believe in you. But you can do it. It is the number of these readers — the ones on whom we're working — that will make the difference between profit and loss. The difference between success and failure.

So let's spend some time together now thinking about how we can achieve the numbers you need.

We'll start with two copywriting formulae.

The first was, I think, invented just in front of selling itself. But it stands the test of time. And repetition.

It can also be applied effectively to almost any sales situation — mailing, press ads, face-to-face, telephone, whatever. It works equally well to make a sale or generate an enquiry. It's AIDA.

It stands for:

Attention Interest Desire Action

This formula requires that first you gain the prospect's **attention**. Some of the most effective ways to do this are:

- *Powerful use of envelopes* — copy and art. Or just copy. Rarely art alone. But this must then lead in to the letter headline and opening paragraphs.
- *Benefit-laden promises* — these command attention. Often they can be put across in a dramatic intriguing way, but they must always be credible. Even if astounding or outstanding, they must not be outlandish!
- *Get an offer into the headline.* But if you can get an offer and a benefit — great! If these are one and the same, even better!

  NB Check out the box of tricks for advice on length of headlines and the curiosity angle.
- *If your offer is attractive — illustrate it right alongside. Feature a human being for increased readership. But use a caption*

  This is a long one! So let's start from the top, literally!

  Part One: You still need a headline, of course, but if the deal includes a free offer of something that will illustrate well, then go ahead and illustrate it alongside.

  Part Two: Any picture of a human being will attract the eye.

Part Three: Since you've got the eye around, why not use the power of the one thing which gets readership levels second only to a headline — a photo caption.

Next you need to arouse **interest**. Probably the best way you can do this is to throw another piece of the same meat into the cage. That means — expand upon the self-same benefit — THE MAIN ONE — that you are already running with. Don't be scared to repeat it. And repeat it.

Next we go to **desire**. What a lovely word! You'll notice it's got two 'E's. The first is for *emotion*.

I don't know if you are involved in selling business to business, or consumer, whichever it is you'll find a section on how the postures and attitudes vary later. Meanwhile . . .

Let me tell you now that there are two ways to rationalise a sales case — the intellectual and the emotional. Nearly all my money goes on the emotional.

The second 'E' stands for *enthusiasm*. Here's where you get to work on the canvas of their mind, painting word pictures as you go. Every one a Rembrandt!

Now **action**. Every salesperson understands the need to ask for the order. And then, *Go for the Close*. That's why you'll see whole conferences entitled 'Close that Sale' and 'The Power Close'. This will feature again in the next formula. What happens when you are in a car showroom? You've expressed interest in the silver whatever with a blue interior.

'Ahhhah,' says the salesman. It just so happens that he has one of those in stock. Yes, yes, it has precisely the specification you want (he'll tell you later about the £230 extra for metallic paint) but there was someone else interested in the self-same model earlier today. *Fear* sets in.

Well, well, what a surprise. What's he up to? He's after your deposit. That's the kind of action he likes!

That's the first formula — AIDA = Attention, Interest, Desire, Action.

Next, courtesy of Bob Stone, the Seven Key Points.

I joined an audience of 500 or so direct marketing evangelists some years ago to hear Bob set out these seven key points. It just didn't occur to him that he was teaching Grandma to suck eggs because Bob *knows* the strength of this formula. His formula.

This is the one that has never failed me yet. Whenever I get stuck, whenever I can't find a way out, this is the routine I turn to. And it *always* works for me. What's more, it works equally well as the sales strategy for a single letter or a complete package. Often both, especially when they are working together.

Bob Stone's Seven Key Points

1 Put the *main* benefit first.
2 Enlarge upon the *main* benefit, and bring in the *secondary* benefits.
3 Tell the reader *precisely* what he will get.
4 Back up your story with case histories and endorsements.
5 Tell your reader what he might lose if he *doesn't* act.
6 Sum-up by *restating* the benefits — but in a *different* way.
7 Incite *immediate* action.

And lastly the mail that's wrecking

Avoid mail that wrecks. By that I mean wrecks your chances of the sale or the enquiry you seek. It has a lot to do with thoughtful preparation and good housekeeping.

There are five main contributors. Five main wreckers. The first is:

Inconsistent positioning, presentation or promotion

Let's look at how inconsistent positioning can make a wrecker. Successful companies go to an awful lot of trouble to ensure they present a consistent corporate front to the world. They prepare a detailed corporate manual for advertising, sales promotion, etc. They spend time, effort and money training sales people, branch managers, staff and telephone operators. All those who deal with customers. They ensure everyone understands corporate philosophy and policy. But what happens when you drop the egg of customer perception on the stone floor of inconsistency?

To present a sophisticated, suave and upmarket image to the world at branch level, for example, but send out brash, aggressive mailings to customers at the same time. That's the egg of customer perception fair and square with a resounding SPLAT on the stone floor of inconsistency.

Such wreckers can be found in headlines. Over-the-top promises. Have you ever been the envy of *ALL* your friends? Maybe once or twice in a new house or with a new car — nearly. But *all* of them? And because of a thimble collection. SPLAT.

Other wreckers can be found in the way you approach. A charity goes over the top on paper or production quality. SPLAT. Or uses four colour process. SPLAT. Or too much personalisation. SPLAT again.

Next on the list is:

Thoughtless or even insulting personalisation

I was once congratulated on being 'one of the forward thinking executives at Amherst'. As the MD and chairman at the time I wasn't too moved by this flattery.

About a month ago, I received a nice wrecker from the building society through which I have my mortgage. They went to the expense of sending me a personalised card to be a member of a club which I've spent 20 years working to leave. It was plainly aimed at the 'first-time buyer' level. In my experience, it's better to attach yourself to people's aspirations.

And there was no reason why they couldn't. They would have saved money and saved face too. They might not be able to select by property value. But I'll bet they can by mortgage level or balance outstanding. Or even monthly repayment. A cut-off halfway up the lending scale would have saved probably 25 per cent of their cost. And not altered the number of responses a jot.

Misspelling a name. Addressing a Mrs as Miss. All these things are gaping cracks in your credibility. As is the next real wrecker.

Duplication

Let's be clear. Duplication is a wonderful thing. The existence of it is a wonderful thing. Letting more than one of the little devils out, that's a crime.

The only circumstance where the existence of duplication is not wonderful is on your own file. It should be avoided at all costs, as doubtless you appreciate.

But the more duplication you find existing between your file and another, the more similarity there is in the type of customers you have. In other words, the more the two market profiles have in common. We'll consider this aspect further in Chapter 9.

Lastly, another wrecker often much resented — and I think understandably — by field salespeople. It's the one that arrives when they are right in the middle of a negotiation. Or worse yet, the mailing that arrives extolling your virtues whilst a complaint is being dealt with. Or the careless and thoughtless 'your letter is receiving attention' that goes out to a sweet old lady who's written to tell you that her husband died last week 'just three days after our Diamond Wedding'.

After years and years of devotion to fundraising by mail, let me tell you that there is nothing you can do that will cut out *all* complaints. But you can look at your systems to see first, that these things are dealt with as speedily as possible. And secondly, that your system — which is nearly always capable of great speed and flexibility in reacting to incoming payments or especially lack of them — is just as flexible in relation to your customers, or donors, as human beings. So, in the case of our recently widowed lady, it is so easy to de-stream such letters and deal with them more sympathetically, more humanly. Dare I suggest, personally?

The last wrecking item is doubt. Doubt in the customer or prospect's mind. Perhaps, shame on you, there's something not clear in the mailing. They need some more information, a clarification, or just plain reassurance. Encourage such calls. Let people know that as well as telephone orders you take telephone calls. And if you need them on different phone numbers, no problem. Say so. Of course you are bound to get the odd ones who confuse the two. So will you ask them to ring the other number? NO! Your enquiry staff should be able to (close sales and) take orders. The order staff, if you can't give them the basic training required to answer questions, should be able to *transfer* calls.

JFR's box of tricks

- *Long or curiosity headlines* It's quite a fascinating business writing a book. Like detective work, I suppose you can gradually start to piece together the past, see where others have been before you. Where they've sought guidance to plug gaps in their experience or just taken the lazy way out by adapting someone else's thinking, together with the odd story or two.

  With some things, there's no escaping repetition or even rip-etition. AIDA. The loyalty ladder. And so on. Thus, when my own experience differs from other authors, I feel beholden to tell you about it, with the proviso that it does differ.

  Long headlines are an example. I've had enormous success with headlines as long as two or three sentences. You do have to make absolutely certain that they're clear and understandable and digestible, but in my experience they work brilliantly. Although when you are tempted to run a long headline, do make sure the typography is of the most excellent quality. With no fancy bits! Fancy bits please designers and not readers. As do word-plays and puns.

  The other difference I wish to report that flies in the face of another often repeated doctrine is that of the 'curiosity' headline. Again, as long as the curiosity wraps around a clear benefit proposition these headlines have worked for me.

The keyword is benefit. As a wet-behind-the-ears copywriter myself in the very early seventies, I remember being so pleased with a headline for Hertz Truck Rental promoting their refrigerated vehicles. It proclaimed:

'From Hertz. The Coolest Deal Yet!'

First, as I learned from one complainant, it should have had a question mark after it to be legal, decent, honest and truthful! But I also know now that it would have worked much better as:

SAVE 25% WHEN YOU
RENT A REFRIGERATED TRUCK
FROM HERTZ TODAY

- *Some other wreckers*
  Incredible claims — even if they are true!
  Obviously 'written' testimonials — especially if they're true. Rewrite them badly!!
  And
  Using 'Private and Confidential' or 'Personal' on the envelope when it's obviously not. Some people claim success with this. I see it as cheating and deceitful. I understand the use of such terms to imply a 'privileged' communication. I cannot condone the abuse of such a privilege. I cannot admire the lack of creative thought that cannot find a better, honest answer.
- *More on complaints* I have already started to communicate to you the quite exceptional power of direct mail. There is a downside to this.

It is unavoidable, particularly in view of the very personal nature of our central communication device — the letter — that the more effective you are, the more people who will read what you have to say and respond to it.

That includes the negative responses as well as the positive. As you build response, so often you will build complaints. You can't cut them out, you *can* be prepared and deal pleasantly with them. This experience remains constant without any question of your mailing being provocative or contentious or offensive. It's obviously even worse if you are any one of those three.

It is also worth remembering that most charities reckon to 'turn' complaints, and receive (often very) large donations from such people. Now there's a gauntlet thrown down to your salesforce! But gently does it, eh?

And, lastly, since the subject is back —

- *Support the field sales position where possible.* When a complaint is being dealt with, any kind of advertising can get in the way. In other words, irritate the complainant. Again endorsing the power of direct mail, it is significant that whereas a TV ad or press ad might irritate, direct mail can make them blow a fuse.

With large purchases, or prolonged negotiations (particularly in business to business), the simple arrival of a mailing can become a hurdle. Not necessarily a big one, but a hurdle none the less.

'Your lot aren't very organised, look at what I got this morning. Do I get the 10 per cent discount as well as the deal we talked about?' You can just hear the clever blighter now, can't you? And if your salesperson is on incentive to clear old stock that will do the job perfectly well, when the prospect gets an exciting 'new product' announcement, you can see the problem.

Although obviously this is not always so, it is in many cases possible to build in a 'promotion stop' facility excluding those prospects or customers from mailings where sensitive negotiations are under way — and that includes complaint handling — for a given period of time.

5 There are only **five** kinds of direct mail—

MAIL WITH
- clear **objectives**
- calculated **costings**
- precision **timing**
- an understood **audience**
- a **compelling message**

or

The Famous Five go Selling

Here come the five essential planning topics of direct mail. All of which require a great deal of thought — sometimes soul-searching, sometimes mathematics, sometimes just a cool look at your fellow man.

Defining **clear objectives**

First, we need to decide whether you are seeking sales leads, referred sales leads, a completed sale — or what?

Will the leads be followed up by salespeople? If so, how good are they? If no salesforce, will you use a fulfilment package? As you will see, this will make a substantial difference to the strategy, tactics and economics of the job in hand.

Five popular direct marketing objectives

1 *To sell — one stage*
   — two stage
2 *To generate leads*
3 *To generate traffic*
4 *To modify a relationship with the ultimate aim of 1*

But what else is missing?
It's a classical advertising objective:

5 *To inform*

There are other ways of doing this. Direct mail is an expensive way to pass information, although it is an extremely effective one. There arc five classic reasons to use direct marketing, and a hundred within each five!

Lead or sale?

This is going to influence the amount you say. And what you cover. But also the basic objective of your creative approach.

No problem if you want a sale, you have to tell every aspect of the story. Include every single benefit you can think of — I mean *every single* benefit. And all the features you can muster. Lock, stock and barrel. You only stop when you run out.

Going for a lead — that's a very different story. Not just in how you tell, but what you tell. Many people set about devising lead-generation ads or mailings, misunderstanding the true objective. And if you haven't been down this logic path before, it can come as a bit of a shock to you.

No point beating about the bush! So let's out with it:

> *You will not achieve the optimum response by trying to SELL the product or service.*

Hmm. Let's think about that.

If you sell the product or service effectively you've gone too far. People will call you saying, 'I want one, I want one.'

There won't be many of them — not nearly enough to pay for the mailing. Well, if there are — fire the sales force! You should be in mail order.

What we're trying to do here is get a lead. The sales force, they have the job of converting to sale or telesales. Or the next mailing. Or whatever. But if you want a *lead* you want a *lead*.

So the first and prime objective of the mailing is NOT to sell the product or service.

The objective is to sell the use of the enquiry card

But to sell the use — the return — of the enquiry card *because* of the product or service.

If there's even a tiny thought in your head that's saying 'Come on, John, that's splitting hairs, just messing with words' abandon it.

This is crucial stuff. And if you don't believe me, tell me why nobody gets it right. Well, almost nobody. Quite often you'll find a simple, good letter, a reply card and an outer envelope is as much as you'll need.

Most people tell too much. They go beyond the benefits into the features.

Did *you* ever send out a mailing consisting of a letter, a product leaflet and a reply card? You did? Fine, and where in the product leaflet was the product specification? On the back? In the centre spread? In a feature panel?

Anywhere is wrong. In lead generation we look to communicate the benefits. Not the features. Since we want *enquiries* back, we leave our prospect panting for more. If you arouse curiosity (or interest) and satisfy it at the same time, you have a completed cycle.

If you arouse curiosity and interest and provide the *means* to satisfy at the same time, then you are channelling the reader towards the action you want. They send back the enquiry card to start the process of satisfying that curiosity. That interest.

What's more, your salesforce are happy because they've got lots to talk about rather than just rehash what the enquirer already knows.

If this sounds disappointingly basic that's because it is. It is also vital. And fundamental to achieving the maximum response.

But there's a little more to come yet. We need to look at:

Getting the right balance of quantity and quality

This is often a delicate balance to find. And that balance is nearly always different for every company. It depends on the nature, type and size of your salesforce. Or whatever the conversion process you employ.

For example, if you have a small, highly qualified and, therefore, perhaps expensive salesforce, you'll need a smaller quantity of high quality leads. If, on the other hand, you have a large dynamic and thrusting sales team, you'll need higher quantity and lower qualities. Even the remuneration package needs to be taken into account. High commission, low basic will give one set of economic dynamics; high basic, low or no commission another. You'll get a better feel as we pull these thoughts together with number two of the famous five essential planning topics.

How to calculate the **costings**

Since we are dealing with lead generation, let's look at that first and take a look at the mail order side later. I should say that these, and most of the forthcoming calculations, are based on one-off experiences and therefore include no long-term or development factors. Nor place any value on pure advertising effect.

The first and most important point I wish to make about costings is that you should *always* do them. Right. At the beginning.

For easy reference let's pull back two simple factors mentioned much earlier in the book.

$$Cost\ per\ Response = \frac{Cost\ of\ Mailing}{Number\ of\ Replies}$$

As I said before, this is an interesting yardstick, but not a definitive one.

$$Cost\ per\ Sale = \frac{Cost\ of\ Mailing + Cost\ of\ Conversion}{Number\ of\ Sales}$$

When calculating the cost of conversion be sure to include *all* the costs involved. That is the process as it extends to all those who enquired, not just the smaller quantity that bought. This ensures that if, for example, you achieve a high response rate but the quality is not up to standard, then the true economics will be reflected, including all the wasted sales costs.

A lot of advertisers wonder whether a small gift or premium as incentive to reply would help. There are four considerations:

1   *Image*   In my experience any anti-incentive feeling is usually a problem that lies mostly in the head of the advertiser. Not the recipient of the mailing. They like offers. We *all* like something extra or for nothing! Consider this in relation also to . . .
2   *Your market*   Most institutional, government, local authority and civil service personnel are actually forbidden from accepting these offers. A point that can be overcome by explaining, apologising and letting them opt out (see example) or by gathering and storing such information until the quantity justifies different 'split-run' approaches.
3   *The effect on conversion rates*   The concern of most advertisers thinking about such items is that they will attract insincere enquiries from respondents who will not convert to sale in sufficient numbers. Sometimes this happens. However, by relating the incentive to the subject of the sale, you will find that the mutuality of interest ensures that, even if the recipient is simply 'on the take', at

least you have identified an individual with a particular interest.

4 *The effect on the economics of the sale* The economics are not as easily dealt with, since there is no short answer. The best way to find out is to try it. My experiences, in relation to such incentive devices vary enormously. So test.

Try to get a span of experience in the test, remembering to test 'no incentive' alongside to get a true value measure. Also be sure that you are testing significant quantities. Often less than you think you will need (see next chapter).

Thus you might test equal quantities of:

- No offer
- Product-related offer (product information)
- Product-related offer (low-cost gift)
- Product-related offer (higher-cost gift)
- Offer not related to product
- The last offer used

The appeal of the offer is very important. As I suggested, it will (as well as the rest of your mailing) affect both quantity and quality. For a motor insurance advertiser, I remember testing no offer, a key ring (quite a natty one!), a pocket road map of Great Britain and a pen-style tyre pressure gauge. Everybody's money was on the tyre gauge. The indexed results were approximately as follows:

No offer   100
Key ring   80 (yes, *less* than no offer!)
Map   260
Tyre gauge   180

Fascinatingly the map out-pulled the tyre gauge (some 44 per cent better) and cost about one third of the price.

I urge you to ignore the *detail* of this particular experience. You must develop your own. All I can assure you is a set of results often bordering on the perverse! The logic of which I promise can only be understood or rationalised once you've unlocked the answer.

One further point.

How to test sample variants as economically as possible

The more any good incentive is 'bound in' to the sales message the better it will work. I don't use bound in to mean in the sense that it isn't emphasised and promoted up-front. If you want the benefit of a man with a red flag in front of the car, there's no point in allocating him a seat in the back. I mean woven into the sense, the logic, the compulsion of the sales story. It makes *sense* to accept. Yet, in order to test incentives, this very integration which so often enhances the effects of an offer, also makes it much more expensive and complex to test.

An offer should be built into the *headline*, the *body copy*, *illustrated* perhaps *on the envelope* and probably in *letter*, *leaflet, flyers* and on the *order slip*.

So to test several variants cheaply, one must test on the basis of a less integrated offer providing the opportunity to change it cheaply.

Where you have an established winner that is outpulling or equalling control (which can sustain levels even if it can't improve them), then you know that unless you do something wrong the integration will boost results still further.

Once you have established the value of the effect of the given incentive, then you need to make a judgement based upon conventional value/cost disciplines.

Where should you use incentives?

In a loud voice, I'm tempted to answer ALMOST ANYWHERE. The only warning bells are those of credibility (is this really a research questionnaire or are they setting me up for a sale?) and the conversion quality aspect discussed.

Test and find the answers! However, if you are involved in a two-stage sell (stage one: enquiry generator; stage two: one or more conversion steps) then an incentive which is added to, or completed as a set, by stage two is a good idea. The first must be valuable in its own right.

Example

Stage 1: Free kitchen utensil
Stage 2: Four more of the same

or

Stage 1: Pocket electronic thermometer
Stage 2: Home health kit and storage case

or

Stage 1: Booklet 'How to Protect Your Belongings'
Stage 2: Five more companion financial 'How to' books and gift box.

Just as you must include in your cost per sale calculation the cost of the incentives, so too you must include all the other costs of conversion. Whether they be sales visits, phone calls or mailing packs. Whatever. And picking up on my earlier, somewhat basic but necessary point, you must include the costs of all of them to get a true measure of their overall influences on the marketing costs of the completed sale.

Which leads us to the simple further calculation of the cost per sale as follows:

$$\text{Cost} = \frac{\text{Cost of Mailing} + \text{Cost of Conversion}}{\text{Number of Sales}}$$

How to cost lead generation to obtain budget figures or results targets?

The basic formula that I use is not mathematically very bright. But it involves the use of whole percentages, and is easily memorized. It is:

$$\frac{\text{Direct mail}}{\text{Cost per sale}} = \frac{\text{Mailing cost per 1000}}{\text{Response per cent}} \times \frac{10}{\text{Conversion rate per cent}}$$

Let's suppose we've targeted, or gathered experience that suggests we can achieve, 1.5 per cent response and convert 25 per cent of those to sale. We are trying to establish what the resulting cost per sale will be against a budget mailing cost of £500 per thousand. Therefore:

$$\text{CPS} = \frac{500}{1.5} \times \frac{10}{25}$$

Our direct mail cost per sale will be £133.33.

I am showing you the equation with 'per 1000' and 'per cent' (hence the 'silly' 10) because the business tends to bandy these figures. And, indeed, a lot of costs are organised this way. List rental is '£so much per 1000' as often are lettershop and processing costs.

If you prefer to go in units — no problem. Let's take the unit equation with the addition of a premium being used. And this time we'll look at total cost per sale. Again, this is a simple case, excluding, for example, overhead expenditure in answering sales calls.

Let's therefore start by calculating the cost of the conversion process which for this example will be a mailed conversion kit with a follow-up going to those who didn't convert after our first attempt.

Suppose we have, from each 1000 mailed, 15 replies. Each one will involve us in the cost of our first follow-up mailing and, of course, our gifts. Then one in five will buy, the remaining four-fifths will be re-mailed a full conversion kit with some changes. Again one fifth will buy. Our conversion or follow-up costs will look like this.

Per initial response		*Total*
	£	£
Conversion mailing	13.00	
Gift	4.00	
Subtotal		
	17.00	17.00
Plus second approach		
Conversion mailing 2		
to 4 out of $5 = \frac{4}{5} \times 15.00 =$		12.00
		29.00

This, plus the mailing cost per response, will give us a total cost per inquiry of (extending our first calculation):

Cost per response ($= 500 \div 15$)	33.33
Cost of conversion process	29.00
Total cost per sale	£62.33

Given the concept, you can start to play some 'what if' games. You'll be surprised to see just how little effect is required in ultimate sale terms to justify the extra costs. This remains true surprisingly even though in budget terms the cost of gifts and incentives can become significant. Of course, the reverse of the principle is that trimming out the incentive to cut cash can cripple sales. But at risk of upsetting accountants and penny-pinchers everywhere, by far the most rewarding experience I have had came through *adding* extra pieces. Improving the selling power increases the cost, although ultimately improves the overall *cost-effectiveness*.

To make significant cost savings, over and above those of repetition or longer runs, bulk purchasing, and so on, is normally only possible where the job was sloppily organised and managed in the first place.

On the other hand, the opportunity to boost cost-effectiveness given an already efficient and value-for-money vehicle is a much easier task. In other words, if the job is right in the first place. Think about the ways to add value, not cut costs.

Now we turn to a far more complex and diverse subject. It is my intention here to limit my coverage to the very fundamentals. By far the most succinct, that is economic but valid explanation, that I have seen written is by Nigel Swabey and appears as a short(ish!) article in *Benn's Direct Marketing Services Directory,* 1987.

How to cost for mail order sales

Rather than endeavour to reinvent Swabey's Wheel for Basic Mail Order Economics, and with grateful acknowledgement to both Nigel and Benn's, I have selected relevant extracts. Here they are:

Ask any direct marketing service company to name the one major complaint they would level against the majority of new clients, and the response you will get (after due mention of the fact that everyone seems to expect 90 days' credit these days) is likely to centre on the lack of preparation on the part of the client.

It is not just a question of preparing a comprehensive brief. We all know that an agency's advertising or service can only be as good as the brief it receives. The three-minute brief that ends with that time-honoured phrase 'you know the sort of thing' just will not do in direct marketing. No, it goes deeper than that. What every service company has a right to expect is that the direct marketing client should understand the concept of affordable promotion cost. If your list broker proposes a high-quality mailing list at £120 per 1000 for a one-time rental, you need to be able to calculate the impact of that cost on your breakeven point. If your advertising agency proposes a free prize draw costing £40 000 for your next mailing programme, you need to be able to calculate the additional response required to cover the cost of the promotion. In short, you need to understand basic mail order maths and the relationship between promotion costs, sales and profits on each new project.

It would be as well for such folk to remember that, for every fortune made in direct marketing, at least two are lost. It is a demanding and exacting business that holds many pitfalls for the unwary.

The real advantage of direct marketing is the sheer measurability of promotional expenditure. As a direct marketer, you enjoy the benefit of instant feedback on your efforts.

The real challenge of this business, however, is in measuring 'results' before the event, as well as after. Provided that you have identified the cost of the product or service being offered, and can predict order processing costs with a reasonable degree of accuracy, you can change any variable in the mix to establish the effect of that variable on your breakeven point. You can test the effect of alternative retail prices, alternative types of promotion and the effect of increasing or decreasing the scale of your promotion. When you have determined the optimum mix and are satisfied that the required level of response or sales for breakeven is achievable, then — and only then — are you ready to translate your assumptions into a budget and proceed with a test campaign.

It does not matter whether you express your affordable promotion cost as an advertising-to-sales ratio, a sales return on promotional investment, the affordable percentage promotion cost on sales, or as a cost per order. The meaning is the same. You have identified the level of orders or sales required to breakeven on a given promotion expenditure. Without this, you cannot provide an adequate brief to the various agencies you intend to use, and are not equipped to assess the viability of their proposals.

Stage one — setting the objectives

The starting point for any breakeven analysis on a new project is to establish the overall objective. In the case of a book club, a credit card organisation or a traditional agency mail order catalogue the object may be to limit the cost of recruitment to a maximum cost per member. This cost per member is a reflection of the worth of the member over his lifecycle, thus a member spending a total of £100 over an average lifecycle might yield a profit of £16 after all operational costs. In order to regenerate the member file, new members need to be recruited at a £6 cost to achieve a net profit of 10 per cent on sales.

The retailer's approach might be rather different. The primary objective of a mail order promotion may be to generate store traffic, and provided that the increase in store traffic can be measured in some way, the retailer may be prepared to tolerate a small loss on his mail order trading operation.

For those companies trading at the sharp end of direct response mail order with off-the-page advertising or catalogues, the twin objectives are to recruit new members and to generate a profit on the initial offer. The nature of direct response mail order is such that lifecycle income is by no means assured. In these cases, it may be imprudent to mortgage future profits on your customer file by accepting losses on the initial offer. The object is to achieve a true breakeven with no new member subsidy. Cost-per-order is of course inappropriate as a measure of success in this sector. CPO is a good yardstick where the character and value of the recruitment offer changes little and where average lifecycle income is well established. In direct response mail order trading, the value of the initial order varies with the price of the item on offer, and a more appropriate measurement is one which reflects both response and average order value — such as the advertising-to-sales ratio.

Stage two — simple breakeven analysis

At a very early stage in the development of your promotion, it is worth running a quick check on your assumptions, to make sure that the breakeven point is achievable. A great deal of time can be wasted if you proceed to a full costing without a rough breakeven analysis.

Figure 5.1 shows a simple breakeven calculation on given assumptions. The underlying assumption here is that you are in a position to estimate the gross profit contribution per sale, i.e. the residual profit after deduction of all variable costs of sales including order processing. If, as in the example, the gross contribution per sale is equivalent to 35 per cent of net sales revenue, breakeven is achieved where promotion costs are also equal to 35 per cent of sales. By taking promotion costs and

Simple breakeven formula

Assumptions:

Promotion costs:	£200 per 1000
Gross profit	35 per cent of net sales
contribution:	£40
Average order value:	5 per cent
Returns for refund:	

$$£200 \times \frac{100}{35} \times 1.15 \times \frac{100}{95} = \frac{£691.72}{£40} = 17.29 \text{ per '000 or 1.73 per cent B/E response}$$

$$\text{Promotion cost} \times \text{Reciprocal of profit contribution percentage} \times \text{Uplift for VAT} \times \text{Uplift for returns} = \frac{\text{£ gross sales per '000}}{\text{Averge order value}} = \text{Orders for B/E}$$

Formula for 10 per cent profit on net sales (target)

Same assumptions as above.

Promotion costs need to account for 25 per cent of net sales revenue.

$$£200 \times \frac{100}{25} \times 1.15 \times \frac{100}{95} = \frac{£968.42}{£40} = 24.21 \text{ per '000 or 2.42 per cent B/E response}$$

Source: *Benn's Direct Marketing Services Directory,* Autumn 1987

Figure 5.1
Simple breakeven calculation

multiplying by the reciprocal (100) divided by 35 you find the level of net sales necessary to sustain promotion costs. The resultant figure is then 'grossed up' by VAT and refunds to find the gross sales revenue required for breakeven. This is then divided by the assumed order value to find the breakeven response rate.

Stage three — construct a pro forma P & L account

Provided that your trial breakeven analysis shows a breakeven response rate (or advertising-to-sales ratio) which is realistically achievable, the next step is to draft a pro forma profit and loss account for the proposed campaign (Figure 5.2). This serves several purposes. First, it provides the financial accountants within your company with a model of the form in which you would like to see the results recorded. Second, it acts as a checklist of all overheads and expenses on the campaign. Although the example is shown in simplified form, even this pro forma draws attention to costs such as the stock provision. If you are taking an item into stock, this provision is needed to cover shrinkage, damage in warehouse and write-down on any excess stocks. Thirdly, it provides you with the basis of a formal budget for the campaign, and identifies the six anchor points for your calculations of campaign profitability: net sales, gross margin, fulfilment costs, gross contribution, promotion costs and net profit. All costs and expenses should be indexed to net sales to ensure valid comparison of cost ratios on different campaigns.

Pro forma profit and loss account cash with order campaign

For financial accounting purposes	£	%	Simplified for unit profitability analysis
Gross sales (product)			Selling price
Plus			*Plus*
Postage and packaging income			Postage and packaging charge
Gross sales revenue			Gross sales revenue
Less			*Less*
Refunds			
VAT			VAT
Net sales		100	Net sales
Less			*Less*
Cost of product (including packaging)			Product cost
Postage on despatch of goods			Postage on despatch
Credit card charges			Credit card charges
Provision for cost of returns			Returns allowance
Total cost of sales			Total cost of sales
Gross margin			Gross margin
Less			*Less*
Stock provision			Fulfilment cost
Variable cost of order processing			
Variable cost of warehousing/ despatch			
Gross contribution (to promotion costs, fixed overheads and profit)			Gross contribution
Promotion costs			Promotion costs
Operating profit			
Fixed overheads			
Net profit pre-tax			Net profit pre-tax

Source: *Benn's Direct Marketing Services Directory,* Autumn 1987

Figure 5.2
Pro forma profit and loss account

Stage four — record the assumptions

There are a number of detailed questions that need to be answered before you can proceed with a detailed costing of the project, i.e:

1 What is the delivered cost? The full cost of the goods or service delivered to your customer, including duties, royalties, service guarantees, packaging, etc.
2 What average order value will be achieved? A compound figure based on the gross selling price plus p & p income, and a units-per-order assumption.

3   What stock provision should be allowed? Based on conditions of purchase from supplier, fragility and value as distress sale.
4   What returns allowance? The amount of provision for the cost of returns, and the handling of returns is a compound figure (see Figure 5.3).
5   What contribution (if any) to fixed overheads? Arbitrary unless the campaign is part of the company's core of business, no contribution if activity is incremental (marginal).
6   VAT rate? Not forgetting that p & p charges attract VAT at full rate.
7   What allowance for lifecycle income? Any new member subsidy or tolerable loss serves to lower the threshold of response required.
8   What is the variable cost of order fulfilment? Including all computer charges, stationery, general correspondence, postage, management time, etc.
9   What is the variable despatch charge? If goods are warehoused, the labour cost on despatch plus storage charges amortised across forecast sales.
10 What credit card charges? A composite figure based on an assumed proportion of all customers settling by credit card.
11 What promotion cost? All creative and production charges, postage, list rental, advertising, print, etc. Postage liability on incoming business reply envelopes is often overlooked in budgeting.

Returns allowance — refunds and replacements	£ e.g.
Value write-down on goods or refurbishment cost (including any transport cost on returns to supplier)	7.00
Postage in × x per cent	1.10
Postage out	1.80
Order processing charge (in)	0.60
Order processing charge (out)	0.60
Warehouse charge goods inwards	0.30
Warehouse charge goods despatch	0.15
Correspondence charge	1.20
Telephone enquiry on x per cent	0.20
	12.95

Assume 6 per cent incidence of refund on replacement:
£12.95×6 per cent=£0.78 returns allowance per order=2.4 per cent of net sales on £40 average order value.

Source: *Benn's Direct Marketing Services Directory,* Autumn 1987

Figure 5.3
The cost of returns

Analysis of distribution, Media, Breakeven Points and Profitability				
Advertising medium/list indentifier	Blogg's Widget Buyers	Quorum Customer List	Insert in *Woman's Realm*	Advert in *Sunday Times*
Method of distribution	Mailing	Mailing	Insert	Advert.
Circulation/ distribution quantity	X,000	Y,000	Z,000	A,000
Forecast % response				
Average £ order value				
Gross sales £ yield per '000				
Net sales £ yield per '000				
Gross £ contribution per '000				
Promotion £ cost per '000				
Total £ cost				
Net profit £ per '000				
Breakeven £ yield per '000 (gross)				
Breakeven % response (gross)				
Total gross £ sales				
Total names recaptured				
Total new names				

Source: Benn's Direct Marketing Services Directory, Autumn 1987

Figure 5.4
Return on promotion investment (ROPI)

Stage five — produce ROPI summary for campaign

The ease with which different offers, different lists and different media can be tested in one direct marketing campaign is such that you need a single schedule which summarises budgeted activity, sales and profitability across the board. This schedule is likely to be the master document for pre-campaign planning and post-campaign analysis of results. The form that I currently use is shown in Figure 5.4. The advantage of this schedule is that it enables you to identify at a glance the activities which account for the greatest proportion of total profits. It also identifies the quantity of new customers captured by each activity.

Thank you, Nigel Swabey.

How to mail with **precision** timing

You can't! Not with finite precision. But you can do the best you can. And, of course, the Post Office has a role to play in that. Consumer mail is best *received* (not mailed) on Friday or Saturday. Next best is Thursday. My advice, aim for Friday.

Business-to-business is best received on a Wednesday. Tuesday and Thursday are next best. Monday and Friday are worst. Saturday for most businesses becomes Monday!

It will help you to have a basic understanding of the Post Office timings for the three main delivery services — first and second class and Mailsort. More about these when we get to explore the postal services available to you in Chapter 8. The 'you gets what you pay for' rule prevails — so the more precise you want the timing to be, the more the cost goes up. But you can get quantity discounts using Mailsort 1 or 2 which are the same delivery standards as normal first or second class.

Mail for all seasons

You need to know and understand little more for direct marketing about seasonality — its relationship to your product, and its effect on your sales — than you do for classical advertising.

The little you do need to know is this. In direct marketing we experience two response 'windows'. These are the two periods when responses will be markedly better than the rest. They are (give or take the odd week!) the second week of January until the first week of June. And the second week of September until the second week of November. Of course, they are not dead cut-offs. And you must overlay this experience against your own and any seasonal aspect to the products.

Creatives know that you can't get inside people's heads until you get inside their lives. That's why so many of us sit around, chisel in hand like constipated sculptors, trying to imagine what a typical prospect looks like, *feels* like.

No professional in the direct response business can create a winning package when he doesn't know EVERYTHING there is to know about the human being he's writing to.

That's utter bilge, of course, the words of an American freelance copywriter in the late seventies, but one of those fine sentences that while being rich in crap is also right in sentiment.

That whole concept is more achievable in today's database world. But I ask you, 'EVERYTHING' there is to know!!

However, it certainly will help, before we can decide that we understand enough about our audience (and that we can presume to set about telling them how our proposition will improve or enhance their lives) to know how and why they have been selected to receive it.

A plea here, that you should involve the creative team — at least the copywriter — in as much preparation as possible. The more they understand, and indeed contribute, to elements such as list selection, discussion on incentive choices, reviews of previous results, the better. And their involvement will always be better than hand-me-down memos and the seventh copy of a contact report. For this will contribute to the overall understanding, not only of what they have to do, but who they have to do it to. And, therefore, how they will do it.

How to find the best kind of direct marketing agency

Easy. It's a one-man band! It goes downhill from there. That's naturally going to mean that he or she will have to be a schizophrenic super hero, Superman or Wonderwoman in full regalia, knickers outside tights, the perfect account director/manager/executive *and* the world-beating creative genius. And that's only one half of their life. Next, the media — Clark Kent and then the production/traffic/print/laser/computer genius beavering away in the backroom proving that he really is Superman.

Gosh! All that and specialising in your business too. Of course, it sounds fine in theory. It is a theory! In practice, more people can add greater talent, greater knowledge, greater specialisation, more capacity. But what goes in the global understanding — the brain being the globe — of what it's all about, is the sheer fusion and integration of the marketing plan in *every* aspect.

What happens is the fusion dissipates as the communications chain gets longer on both sides, no matter how many meetings or memos, no matter how much participation and involvement the systems and procedures of the agency and client permit.

Stop any top-of-the-business direct marketing type and they'll have to agree, if they're honest. If they're running a big agency, of course, they'll no doubt argue the point. Strap them to a lie detector! So, in my very personal view, you need to balance it out. Look carefully at the structure and nature of the skills available on the client side and go for as near as possible the perfect dovetail.

Understanding what constitutes the audience, is a major fact of understanding what will make them buy.

Undeniable fact. Simply common sense. But making it happen is about information, the gathering, analysing, digesting of it. And then the interpretation of it and the way the interpretation affects the implementation. Then, and only then, can the communication effectively take place.

The days are long gone, of course, when we had to resort to an all embracing, single message to a whole market. That happened way back in the fifties. Advertisers found — surprise, surprise — that if you identified the message in some way with the reader, they liked it. And therefore the response went up.

So, simple plate changes saw the emergence of attempts to link with the particular segments (lists they were then!) that make up the mailing.

Dear Doctor
Dear Dentist
Dear Teacher
Dear Gardener
Dear Motorist

Fine. A little later on the next step emerged. What happens if we actually change or vary the message to suit the segment. Eureka! Bathwater everywhere! Letters had whole first paragraphs that identified with and adjusted main benefit statements to the doctor, dentist, teacher, gardener and motorist.

You know what happened. Responses went up.

Meanwhile, over in the business-to-business market they'd been fooling people for years. Given the much higher value of the sales — and therefore the money available — they'd been sending out automatically typed letters. Not produced by electronic equipment, of course. It was electro-mechanical. The text was held on a sort of 'pianola' roll of paper that only played one tune.

That was expensive. So a second-best was also available. This involved running the main body of the text on litho or facsimile printing machines and then 'matching in' the name, address, date and personal salutation. The world became more and more full of clever blighters who examined their mail in the morning by turning the letters over to see where the indentations of the typewriter stopped. If you ran your hands over the back of the top and it felt like Braille until about one third down, you knew it was a mailing. Drat!

The business mailer looked back over his shoulder to see what was happening over on the consumer side.

The curtain parts to reveal a huge box with winking lights. The computer is here. Direct mail and direct marketing are about to hit warp speed. Hyperspace is on its way.

That was the late sixties! Hyperspace is still on its way. It's just that somebody keeps moving it further back.

Back? You might think that a strange choice of word.

But back we go as sure as sure can be. Hyperspace exists with the perfection of one-to-one communication. Just the buyer and the seller. Not one to a 1 000 000 (the fifties). Not one to 100 000 (the sixties). Not one to 10 000 (the seventies). Not one to 1000 (the eighties). But one to one. Back to the corner store again. And back even beyond that. Accept today. Send no pelts now.

As we considered earlier, what makes the difference is information — knowing the customer or prospect; understanding their needs, desires and aspirations. Do they need a house? Well, they have a small one, perhaps they'd like a bigger one? How many children do they have? How old are they? How much money do they have to spend? Would they rather have a good holiday each year with the kids? Or acquire things? Like a second car? Or a new kitchen?

What kind of people are they? What do they read? What videos do they rent? What sort of clothes — sizes, colours, styles — do they like? What do they like to eat and drink?

How often do they go to the bank? How often do they use their credit cards? Where do they use them? WHO ARE THEY?

It's like the old village doctor mentality. You know, or you can find out, these things. You may never repeat them. You may only use them for the good of the patient. Understanding them. Treating them. Improving your interaction with them.

However, we have to be careful not to infringe the rights of an individual to choose whom they involve in their lives. We must protect and even advance this right.

The need to gather information in order to communicate better is one thing. The need to accept the full responsibilities of such a trust is another. They are, and must stay, inseparable.

Psychographics, demographics, geographics and lifestyle discriminators — all these things are indeed useful to communicate better — and more appropriately. And that is just as good for both sides of the fence. These data enable us to understand our audience. To enable us to be less and less junk, more and more relevant and interesting. The ultimate is that recipients, impressed by the compelling accuracy of our interpretation of their actions — the way we understand them as people — and thereby the way we approach them and what we say to them, may cease even to consider for a moment that we have intruded into their lives, or consider that we might breach their right to privacy.

In our quest to segment, introduce database manipulation techniques, improve cost-effectiveness, we must all play the village doctor. And remember that even doctors can prescribe the wrong medicine. The consumer has the right to throw it away, however it makes us feel.

There can be no doubt that an audience that is understood better — or even just feels understood better — responds better. While the whole thing remains controlled, honest and ethical, the trip to hyperspace and the planet Wuntowun is in no danger of abort. Or even self-destruct.

So let's just pull all that together. It is vital that, to get the message across in the most effective way possible, all those involved — advertisers, agencies, bureaux, whoever — know as much as possible about the database they own and the many different human beings that it represents. The more information that can be gathered and shared, the more 'briefed' the advertisers' creative team will be. And therefore the more appropriate and intelligent the resulting message will be. Overbriefing — the provision of too much information — is a luxury all creative people would prefer to the crime of 'you know the sort of thing', or worse, 'like the last time — but different!'

Next, the fifth kind of direct mail has a **compelling message**

Understanding the audience is naturally a major requirement of the brief. And compelling messages are the essential task of the creative team. Compelling messages are always the end-result of a compelling brief, a brief which more than gives the details, it *enthuses*.

I've spent so long working from briefs rather than working on them that I thought I'd catch up on some reading. I mean I know what a brief is. I've seen hundreds of them. Giving all the details, all the background, from which we start to create.

They describe the product. Tell you about the competition. Give you all manner of detail about the lists. Any other media involved. The objectives. And all that stuff about the client's logo. Product positioning. What to test. Follow-up procedures. There's masses of it!

So I read through the creative bits and pieces in other people's books. Because the list I've popped in above is short of at least one vital element.

Money.

How much is there? What have we got to play with? Ridiculous. Other people's books, all those Americans — Nash, Caples, Rapp and Collins, Raphel — they must all mention money. They're Americans!

Well, yes, they do. This thing called creative budget. But that's no help, is it?

Yes, yes, of course creative need to know how much they've got, to allocate correctly between copy, graphics, photography, finished art, etc. But that's not what I'm thinking about.

How much is there to spend? Not on creative. On the whole mailing.

I mentioned earlier when we were looking at the costings, economics and maths that you can play 'what if' games. And so you can. But you have to have a starting point. Creative, in 'playing' with different ideas, offers, personalisation techniques — the whole artist's pallet that they have at *their* disposal — will need to consider 'what if' they suggest this or that. But this or that — new offers, new gifts, die cuts, shapes, special gumming or perforations — will affect not just *their* costs but the overall production costs too. How will these in turn affect response? Up or down? And the quality? At the end of the day, it will inevitably come down to professional judgement. But it must be educated and, from the financial aspect, well informed.

So, apart from a thorough brief economically speaking, how else can we ensure we get the whole team off to a good start? How about this?

JFR's Briefing Document

1 THE OBJECTIVES
  1.1 *Sales objectives*
    — The precise targets

      ● Quantity per cent
      ● Quality per cent
      ● Cost per . . .

  1.2 *Business objectives*
    — The relevance of the sales objectives to the business as a whole
  1.3 *Timing required*

2 THE PRODUCT/SERVICE
  2.1 What is it?
    — What does it do, how does it work, how much does it cost, etc.?
    — Is it complete, or any on-going or after sales elements?
  2.2 *Is it any good?*
    — What's wrong with it (weaknesses)?
    — What's right with it (strengths)?
  2.3 *Who says so?*
    — And how do they know?
    — Can we quote them?
  2.4 *Is it unique?*
    — Or merely different
    — Specifically, how?
  2.5 *Any guarantees*
    — Or other added customer/service benefits?
  2.6 *Is it mail order — or how is it to be sold?*

3 THE MARKET
  3.1 *How big is it?*
    — Market shares?
    — Where do you 'sit' in the market?
  3.2 *What does a buyer 'look' like?*
    — Research and sources
    — Geographics/demographics/psychographics/RFM

3.3 *Who makes decisions and*
  — How many involved?
  — Any third parties or other considerations?

3.4 *Previous and latest experiences*
  — Samples
  — Any customer correspondence
  — Case histories

3.5 *Selections/segmentations/lists*
  — Exploitable affinity or intermediary links or involvement
  — Relevant endorsements
  — Other activities
    ● PR
    ● advertising
    ● sales promotion

3.6 *The competition*
  — Run through same list as above where possible

4 THE MEDIA

4.1 *Why direct mail?*

4.2 *And why not others?*

4.3 *How is audience data held?*
  — Customer or file record layout
  — Processing requirements
  — Processing times
  — Processing constraints, restrictions

4.4 *Any other media factors*
  — Codes of practice
  — Restrictions

5 THE BUDGET

5.1 *Total*
  — Any specific allocations

5.2 *How budget is calculated*
  — Mathematics of sale
  — Dynamics of financial success/failure
  — Breakeven point

5.3 *Highest cost/risk factors*
  — Of mailing
  — Of project

6 CREATIVE

6.1 *Corporate*
  — Positioning/image requirements
  — Brand/product positioning and image requirement

6.2 *Product/service*
— Benefit/feature analysis
— Offer/proposition rationale
— In-house or other products or services or resources available as enhancements
  ● old stock/supplies, etc.
  ● ancillary or consumable items

6.3 *Review of previous creative work*
— And results

6.4 *Systems/response handling/legal*
— Procedures
— Timing

6.5 *Specific test requirements*
— Statistical data/viability
— Variants identified
— Outline matrix

6.6 *Information gathering*
— Any data for future activity
— Repeat sales

6.7 *Buyer attitude statement*
— Before
— After

7 FOLLOW-UP PROCEDURES
7.1 *Methods/systems*
7.2 *Despatch or follow-up times*
7.3 *Capacity/constraints*
— Manpower
— Resources

8 RESULTS ANALYSIS
8.1 *Who and how?*
8.2 *Reporting and review disciplines*
— Short-term — when?
— Long-term — when?

9 EFFECTS ON FUTURE
9.1 *In event of*
— Success
— Failure
9.2 *Development/growth potential*
9.3 *Any 'if it works . . .' factors*

Given a comprehensive document like this — but most important, with a full, if long, meeting to discuss it — there is obviously no reason why your message shouldn't get through in a clear, articulate, informed and effective manner. A word of advice: make sure you have the briefing meeting with the documents already written. Don't be tempted to use it as a confirming document.

Or worse still, don't even think about trying to prepare it as the meeting proceeds. This will be a meeting of quite a few people and quite a few disciplines, and quite a few strong points of view. It should be for discussions not strategic decisions.

JFR's box of tricks

For some reason I have never been able to fathom out, the 'spring window' is generally better than the 'autumn window'. Must be the sunshine in prospect and the recession of SAD — Seasonal Affective Disorder.

Topicality can make or break a mailing. Breakers are anything from an election, to the threat of postal strike, to a run of good summer weather. Whether the things break or just dent will depend, oddly enough, less on the strength of the breaker, more on the resilience of the strong wall that is you, your product and your proposition. And the margin over breakeven at which you're operating.

If you are out trawling for names below or around breakeven — just as a charity might well be, for instance — a breaker will live up to its name. So when your director general is found to be up to something naughty with one of the Kenyan missionaries, who it transpires is the same sex and there's a small question mark over a missing £200 000. And *The People* are asking, where does the drug-crazed son of an insignificant Tory MP — the previous lover (of either!) — fit in to all this? Now you've got a breaker on your hands!

Here's how to handle it. Lie down. Roll over. Raise your legs and hands in the air. Feign death. Eventually the carrion PR types will sort it all out for you!

But if you're out there fishing in deep waters — way beyond breakeven, making 'very nice, thank you,' returns — then you can probably stand most breakers. You may experience quiet periods during and after the breaker. Your main fear is a tidal wave.

That's probably anything from the *Sun* deciding it didn't understand your mailing, to the *Daily Express* and Esther Rantzen getting together on a BBC 2 special to get nice, real, but broken people to boo a lot on a live show and blame you.

Then, there's the maker. That's when Neil Kinnock, Cliff Richard and Sue Lawley join the Archbishop of Canterbury's fight to have you banned.

Am I joking? You decide.

Makers are, for example, good press or other media coverage prior to or at the time of mailing. There's just no substitute for being in the right place at the right time. And a PR agency can fix that for you!

It's a standing joke in the business that as your mailing goes out you pray for rain. Probably why there's so much mail order in Britain!

6 There's only **six** kinds of direct mail—

- **selective**
- **creative**
- **personal, personalised** (or both)
- **reactive**
- **tried and tested**
- **easy to respond to**

or:

The six built-in benefits of direct mail — a unique and powerful combination

Now I'd like to address the unique benefits of the medium. Often these will make a case for using direct mail each in their own right. But surely the strongest and most convincing argument for the medium is that every single advertiser with every single advertising action can have most or all six benefits at the same time.

How many ways can you be **selective?**

About as many ways as the people on your list! That's a bit glib! Let's have a look at what this quality is all about. And how selectivity works.

Most people talk about selectivity as a general quality that direct mail has, to select groups or individuals in, or select them out for that matter, of the broader target market, so let's look first at this thought.

There are basically two sorts of media:

- Those that *select* the market
- Those *selected by* the market

Thus, for example, photographers will read amateur photographic magazines. Company directors will read *The Director*. What has actually happened here is that the media owner has identified a market and then sets about building up his readership.

Direct mail charges through the middle and enables us to mail company directors *or* photographers! But that's by-the-by for the moment.

Then there are those media that, in some ways, it can be argued, select their markets. But I prefer to think of this the other way round. The consumer decides. This has to do with range of choice, but also the style of the media. We choose which radio station we want to listen to. We choose which TV channel we want. And, I think, we choose which newspapers we read.

Those are the extremes, of course. The black and white. But there is plenty of grey.

This can be to do with the available lists of specific types of people. Perhaps by purchasing history — something you have subscribed to, given to, or bought from. Or it could be something that you have qualified as, visited or whatever. But, as in a very simple way we saw earlier, direct mail enables you to select the message for the market. A doctor's message for doctors. A photographer's message for photographers. And so on. Structural engineers. Book buyers. Record buyers. Car owners. Dog owners. People into horoscopes. Healthfoods. Take your pick. You can be very selective too: record buyers by type of music, car owners by type or make of car, dog owners by type of dog.

In fact, you can also select what message you would like to go to each and every list. By geographics. Or . . . the choices are apparently endless. Select by sex. Or job title. Tell that to the trade press!

'OK. *Factory Equipment Monthly*, you can put my ad in your magazine PROVIDED . . .

- It only goes to factories with 200 staff or more
- They are in either the engineering, food or paper businesses
- The ad is seen by their company secretaries, office services managers and telex supervisors
- In fact, if they haven't got a telex, leave them out
- Make sure I only get exposure in the area south of a line Severn to Humber
- And leave out large groups. Better make it private companies only
- And, I just want those with an issued share capital of . . .'

But unlike the other media, with direct mail you can go right on selecting and fine-tuning. Doctors in West Yorkshire? No problem. Photographers in Brighton? No problem.

And on. Doctors over the age of 40 in West Yorkshire? Photographers with their own processing in Brighton? Still no problem.

Meanwhile, the other media have long given up.

But direct mail hasn't finished yet. We can be selective in other ways still. All those inside a given catchment area of your store? Yes. All those outside the same area? Yes. We'll send them a catalogue! How about all those around your competitors' stores?

You only want the odd numbered houses? OK, well if that's what you want. Still no problem. As daft as it sounds, selecting only those with names not numbers has done quite well before now. Sales areas. TV areas. Counties. Towns. Suburbs. Single or computer-selected clusters of Enumeration Districts. You can have practically anything geographic you like.

Businesses. Consumers. Heads of businesses. Heads of households (if anyone still owns up to such a title!), purchasing directors. Sales managers. Etc., etc., etc. . . .

Still no problem for the mighty direct mail. It's so selective you can even select who *doesn't* see it.

OK, *Sunday Times*. It's your turn. *You* can have all my advertising *provided* I can run my ad in your colour supplement for six weeks before my competitor gets to even SEE it.

Again, no problem for direct mail. It's so discreet.

There are few media that can be anything near as selective for the advertiser as direct mail. And that's before we have started to look at all the extra good things you can do with those other words that must by now be indelibly engraved upon your grey matter. Demographic, psychographic and RFM segmentation! Caravan owners. Plumbers. Golfers. Zoos. Farmers with 100–500 acres of arable crops. Umbrella shops within ten miles of Walsall. The list goes on and on and on.

And, so too, does the ability to treat the different people differently. To vary the message. To put different propositions.

Direct mail is **creative**

Here I'd like you to take a look, not at the creative process itself, but more how that process can be exploited. And the benefit creativity brings to direct mail. The selling edge we get with direct mail if we use the creative differences wisely and thoughtfully to bind everything together.

You'll see how that thoughtful binding is used to do these things we identified together:

- To grab more *attention*
- To create more *interest*
- To stimulate more *desire*
- To provoke more *action*

Let's look at the four 'S'ential differences:

'S'ential No. 1

Here is direct mail's Singular Selling Strength:

It's SOLO

By using the selectivity you've managed to get yourself in front of the individual sales prospect with whom you want to communicate. And so the great news is that once you get there, you have that prospect's sole attention.

What a perfect opportunity. No salesperson could ask for more at this stage. No others around battling for attention. *You are it!*

So, in order to ensure you don't waste your golden moment, you need to have something clear in your head. It's *cost* a *lot* of *money* to get there. Direct mail is expensive. All that selectivity is at a price. You are paying to have the wastage cut away in great handfuls. But more, you are paying for the unbridled power too. Not to mention the wages of the postman or woman who transported and finally delivered your message for you. Hence, my advice here might seem strange. I urge you to develop a relaxed — not careless or sloppy — but relaxed attitude of 'in for a penny — in for a pound'.

This takes courage at first. But as you come to know the medium and know how it pays back, so this courage will surely turn to confidence.

To help you think it through, let me remind you of the point we made earlier that the base cost — the origination, the planning, the time spent, the lists, the materials, printing and the postage — will cost you a lot anyway.

Thus, to do the selling job professionally, thoroughly and in every way as best you can, will cost you very little difference. Think of it like this:

	Cost	Potential effect
Worst job	100	100
Best job	120	150

So do the job properly. Remember, at the end of the day, you always have the certain knowledge of measured, controllable cost-effectiveness — a luxury that conventional marketing rarely affords and classical advertising hardly ever.

I think I would ask you to interpret my advice two ways:

1 *At the creative outset go for the affordable best* If your affordable best doesn't work nothing less will. Once you've established the pulling power of your affordable best, then review the whole project. *Not* with a view to making it cheaper, *but* with an objective of making it work better.

In this review process — once the power of your work is proven — be sure that:

2 *Savings aren't made at the cost of sales* If in doubt, test it. This is not a suggestion that you irresponsibly chuck money at a project. If you are a 'bargain basement' advertiser and you suddenly mail to customers on the most wonderful die-stamped, thermographed handmade 200 gsm paper, it's not going to have any positive benefit for you. Probably the opposite. They'll think you've flipped, or sense that you've been taken over by Fortnum and Mason and are no longer for them!

Spend prudently. But don't penny-pinch. Because the penny you are pinching is quite possibly giving all the other pennies less chance to do their job. And you're spending — or sending — them away.

So remember. You're alone with your potential customer. Don't lose the sale because you didn't spend that last bit that would enable you to do the job effectively. To get that sale.

'S'ential No. 2

Direct mail tells the sales story sensibly. Because it's

STRUCTURED

One of the great, great advantages that direct mail has over other media is that you can enjoy the freedom of an almost infinite number of different formats, many with successful track records of pulling response for other people.

This brings you choice. To make that choice you need to look not only at the practicalities of the job, but also at the opportunity to tell your creative story — your sales pitch — in the way *you* want. Consider each format from this view.

Here's an example of each.

The practical If you need to get a cheque or paperwork back it will normally pay you, both in response and speed of that response, to choose a format that offers you a post-paid return addressed envelope. FACT!

The opportunist Even if you do have 11 000 clear plastic C4 size 'envelopes' in the stores, you should mail this package in good quality white C4 envelopes because it gives a truer picture of the company. But more important, you don't want these never-approached-before prospects to be frightened off by what the plastic envelope reveals to them before you have lost your chance to gain their attention and arouse their interest.

Choosing a format for your mailing

The word I used a few paragraphs back was 'infinite'. And so it is. However, given your objectives and economics, and looking at the best way to achieve them, it should be possible to make some basic decisions. To rule in or rule out certain possibilities. First, we need to look at the basic communications opportunity. Have you got a clean sweep at it? Or are you using, or taking advantage of, some other event or need to get in touch with your audience?

The clean sweep

If you have a clean sweep you have the widest choice. That can be good news or bad news. More to choose from can mean harder to decide on the right one or ones.

Let's run through a few of my most popular formats, the ones that I know work consistently well, and check out a few visual and verbal examples. This is nothing — I mean *nothing* — like a definitive list. Just a quick canter through some favourites.

The basic pack formula

Standing the test of time, the ever-logical, ever-present, ever-successful letter, leaflet, response device formula is a sound starting place. It's not quite that simple, of course. Because you will need an outer envelope. And possibly a return envelope too. In lead generation you could well often leave out a formal leaflet, using perhaps an illustrated letter in its place.

On the other hand, you could equally consider bolstering the interest level a little with a die-cut, pull tab or 'lift to reveal' device. Whatever! The point is that in my experience the direct mail equivalent of the staff of life is the outer envelope, letter, leaflet, response device (and if required) a reply envelope. More will appear about the role and function of these pieces separately when we take a more detailed look at creative.

Additional items you can add
Let's take a look at some:

Extra leaflets — be clear about the function of these but don't worry too much about 'cluttering' up the envelope. Multi-enclosure packs can work well in many situations. But nothing works well if it confuses, wastes time or is dull. If you have clear functions for pieces then it can help the reader to identify the function with the copy and art.

● Quotes from newspapers can print and fold like mini-newspapers.
● Stories can be told in handwriting underneath or even on the back of photos.
● Announcements, 'Hurry, Hurry' and 'Stop Press' items imply news, urgency or last-minute thoughts. As do telex or telegram style art, or a dummy release marked 'Embargo'.

Endorsements — can be anything from a fake (printed reproduction) rubber stamp (suggesting the institutional, such as a local authority or tourist office), a specially positioned label or sticker (such as a kite mark or Design Council logo) attached to a separate full size or mini-reproduction of the letter from the endorser.

Do ensure you have approvals from endorsing individuals or organisations. Or indeed, any third party you might want to use as a case history or testimonial. Most people are flattered to be asked and willing to help. And many like to see their names in print.

Involvement pieces — work well in both consumer and business mail. They can be used to highlight and even make choice easier to select. They can use the elements of surprise, curiosity or intrigue. For real, or just for emphasis. These include a myriad of permutations including prize draws, sweepstakes, games, stamps, competitions, etc.

Useful or interest features — will build retention of sales information and keep your name in front of prospects. These are particularly valuable when you have no control over the timing. For example, while working for Hertz on a mailing which sold instant availability of replacement vehicles in case of breakdown, I asked the chap when he wanted to mail.

'Two days before they break down,' he said helpfully.

When I asked Royal Mail about the timing of a mailing designed to invite sampling of the Datapost service they suggested much the same — 'So it's there for their next rush parcel?'

Of course, I couldn't provide either of these but the variation of the old telephone sticker — I built in a useful thermometer for the Royal Mail — proved a huge response puller and kept the free Datapost contact procedure right in front of the prospect until the right moment. It also served as a constant sales reminder.

Remember the third dimension

Something that few other media offer you is the opportunity to use the three-dimensional. Samples, gifts or gimmicks abound and can create quite a stir. They can also distract rather than add to the sales message, so I do urge careful consideration and testing wherever possible.

Very, very often they add tremendous cost. And to very little effect. Appropriately, three, three-dimensional examples come to mind. The first was:

The record player in a whole new sense! This must have been five or six years ago now. My friend Mike Adams also received this pack. He keeps it among his treasured samples and guards it with his life.

Innocent enough — but with the added intrigue of a slightly lumpy envelope (never a bad one that — remember how you used to shake, squeeze and poke the presents round the Christmas tree!). It arrived in a regular DL envelope. It consisted of a piece of board about A4 in size which, when folded into thirds, formed a triangular shape and made a small record player. To prove it — as the simple instructions explained — there was a plastic 'record' on the top of the base. And a stylus in the fold-over from the top. All that was needed was my finger — and a reasonable constant rotating speed! I placed the end of my finger into the recessed space and started to turn it. With great delight I listened as a wavering but none the less quite distinct voice started to sell me these mini-record players for my next 'record results' mailing.

Fantastic! I dashed from my office down to creative. The department came to a standstill. And the standstill spread like a bushfire. I calculated later that the record player had become just that — it broke all records for people playing in the office. I dread to think of the cost of the lost working hours. We worked it out to somewhere between 20 and 25!

I've met a lot of people who received this mailing. When I mention it even after all these years, everybody in the 'trade' remembers it. But sadly I haven't met one yet who responded, let alone bought.

The second was, after many, many years, abandoned, yet, like the record player, is fondly recalled by all those who were on its mailing list. The advertiser John Dickinson and Co., the makers of Croxley paper and envelopes, used to despatch a small posy of fresh primroses to selected customers every spring. It was a charming and perfectly underplayed customer relations exercise. We looked forward to it each year. Whether they were all gathered fro' the fields around the mill or not — who cared! As far as our business and many others like us were concerned, we didn't notice when the first cuckoo was reported in *The Times*, when the lambs started leaping, when the bluebells covered the woodlands like a poet's carpet. Spring wasn't spring until that little box of primroses arrived.

At which point, may I ask you to stop reading for a moment and write a list of all the other advertising media of which you are aware that offer you this kind of recall, this kind of loyalty and affection building. This kind of *sheer selling power*.

It won't be a very long list!

And last of the 3 D-mentionables, the heaviest I ever received, which arrived some weeks before Christmas. It was a dartboard and a good 'un. Now, I may not be a typical agency Chief, but I haven't played darts — enough to want a board, that is — since my student days. So I handed it on to our traffic manager and laser specialist. He didn't want a second one! So he passed it on to the lads in the group's printing company.

Around Christmas-time, the darts followed. Still in their box, complete with corporate flights. I got my secretary to pass them on to the print lads too.

I know it won't make me any friends, and I'm truly sorry, but you know I can't remember the name of the laser company. I can only think that despite this truly heavyweight advertising, they misunderstood the meaning of 'targeted' advertising. And the lads in the print department, grateful as they were, will never make a decision about the laser supplier we use. Probably, there's a keen darts player in the studio that dreamed it up. For me, it was a boring game.

So what's the point? Let's get back to relevance. And look at it from there.

The record player was relevant. It couldn't be more so. But, in the cold light of day, affectionate as I feel for it all this time later, I couldn't honestly have put it up to a client. It was costly. It was silly. It was badly planned. If they had included a reply card and enabled me to enquire about the prices, rather than quoting them, I still might not have bought in the end. But at least they would have got a lead. And when following up — with the record player as their opener — they might at least have scored with something else, another product.

And Dickinson's primroses? In pure direct response terms, difficult to assess. In customer relations terms, for this customer — 110 per cent. I can't say I ever gave them an order just because of the primroses. But now — even five, six or seven years after they stopped — I still think of them as a caring company. And even if I don't see the reps these days, they'll always get a friendly welcome from me. What price that after all this time?

And the dartboard! Zero out of ten. Whoever they are! And I suspect I'll never be allowed to forget after this book hits the streets!

As long ago as the primroses — maybe more — a case history appeared in a Royal Mail booklet promoting direct mail. It featured a mailing for a vehicle contract hire company. The mailing consisted of a pop-up 3-D replica of one of their vehicles. Sellotaped to the top was a coin. 'Use this to give us a ring' invited the message on the side of the van.

At exactly the same time, and probably why I remember it now, I was involved with one of their competitors. The campaign was a series of three straightforward sales letters and an enquiry card folded into a window envelope.

We were pulling over three times the response of the 'pop-up' truck at quite literally less than one tenth of the cost. That makes 30 times more effective use of the advertising money!

The pop-up truck advertiser was over the moon. According to the story, he had secured more than (and remember, this is a *long* time ago!) £1 000 000 of turnover. I know for a fact the campaign I worked on achieved nothing like that. But then we were concentrating on 400 prospects in Manchester. They had mailed over 20 000. Fifty times as many. The moral here is clear. Three-dimensional advertising is available with direct mail. And, looking back, particularly effective in business-to-business mail. My own past is littered with 3-D mailings, but never, I think, where the same result could be achieved for less or where there wasn't some real relevance of the gimmick to the objective or product.

I've mailed fresh (but muddy) carrots to promote incentives. Spent bullet cases. Old, and useless, foreign bank notes. Bottles of whisky (miniatures!). Enclosed gold labels in the shape — and stunningly realistic — of Kruger Rands. Pink feathers, red roses, backgammon sets. You name it. But each was because it had an *easily-linked, tangible, relevant* association with the objective of the mailing.

3-D is powerful. And costly. Used intelligently, it can be very cost-effective. Ask the MP who despatched buckets of cow dung to his colleagues on the opposite side of the House. And *Reader's Digest* who attached a five pence piece to their packs.

RSVP

Almost any event, exhibition, seminar or reception will benefit from an invitation. My experience suggests that the more that invitations look like invitations, the better they work. So start from an ideal of a gold-bordered heavy card hand-filled in with my name in a classic royal blue ink!

If it's an invitation to the local Spar to taste the new all-in-one Yugoslavian loo-cleaner, aperitif and aphid spray, that's going to be a little over the top.

So again a balance of corporate and event positioning and tone will no doubt sign your path for you. As will production details, the data, media and, inevitably, cost.

Never resist the urge to enclose a good letter with the invitation. And do think about the practicalities of the event: ease and convenience, timing, parking arrangements, refreshments, and so on! The more attractive, informative and useful, convenient and enjoyable the event sounds, the better.

I became very aware with my conference series that people attend for a whole gamut of reasons. From a day out, to a good lunch, to an expenses-paid trip to the other end of the country. It was quite startling to see how, when we were in Scotland, at least one third of delegates came from London and vice versa! When we printed the full lunch menu and mentioned the free wine, up went the response!

And then there's the 'free ride'

Many times you will not have the 'clean sweep'. You'll find you have an opportunity as we say, to 'free ride' along with some other communication. You'll be looking at a range of formats that tie in with the objectives or production circumstances that prevail from the individual opportunity.

Thus you might think about 'one-piece' mailers, and the more straightforward inserts or 'bill-stuffers' or even the 'pack within a pack'.

One-piece mailers and mechanised origami

There's a vast range of increasingly ambitious and clever devices available now. Most are formed from up to metre-length runs of paper printed from the reel. On-line finishing enables very varied perforating, folding and gluing to achieve anything from a multi-folded all-in-one, to a pack that 'bursts' on opening to reveal a separate letter, leaflet, response slip and return envelope. Such devices can include rub-off, scratch'n'sniff, sticky stamps and a range of other items. All at very economical rates when compared with 'proper' pack prices.

Despite their economies, they have not taken over the world! There is no doubt that the recipient often treats these formats less respectfully and with a lower perceived value than an individual solus mailing, in much the same way as most house-to-house distribution has a lower perceived value.

Thus, as I have found quite frequently, but with some spectacular contrary experiences, an identical pack differing only in its delivery method, and not being therefore in an addressed envelope, can pull as little as 10–20 per cent of its direct mailed equivalent.

It must also be said, returning to one-piece mailers, that some of them are too clever by half, and practically require a degree in origami for the recipient to gain the full benefit of your proposition. Therefore, one must also consider the complexity of the message you require to put across as an important factor in your choice of format.

It is interesting to see that, as the ingenuity of the manufacturers increases (in terms of the different shapes, sizes, and formats that can be developed), so too they are increasingly available with quite a degree of single and multiple personalisations, mainly through the ink-jet process.

Have you tried to turn the tables?

All too often the marketing department will find the restrictions placed upon it by the administration function (very frequently the accounting or financial departments) is equal to an opportunity to run in the London Marathon . . . as long as you wear deep sea diver's boots!

It sounds OK until you get the whole picture.

And internal departments don't always have the same ways of doing things as the marketing or sales side for example:

- They require you to run to their timing
- They don't worry about the quality of computer printing
- They don't care that unsightly codes appear, and it's upper case only

Fair enough. They just need the item to get there. Yet given time to talk and think and plan, there are two ways to solve this problem.

The first is a mutually satisfying process. It helps them and it helps you. Both benefit.

The second is a sneaky way for you to win out in the face of uncooperative opposition. We'll deal with these in the same order.

The friendly mutual way

Very often, what administration tries to achieve is, by marketing standards, somewhat lacking. Administratively sound, but not *your* way of communicating.

OK. So give a little, take a little. You're taking their communication opportunity — and basically you'd like to revamp the whole thing. Well go ahead. But make *your* gift to them a complete upgrading of their documentation. They give you the raw information they wish to communicate, complete with all the necessary words. You redesign and rewrite the whole lot out of your budget!

You take the raw data — preferably on a tape. You provide the whole facility. This way they get their administration procedure carried out to a standard they've not had the luxury of enjoying before. You get a complete, integrated, highly professional selling machine in place of the manila, foolscap, unsealed dichotomy that would have been.

You get the benefit of a low-cost mailing, they get a better deal. (You must ensure that they only pick up the costs they would have done before, doing it their way!) And, into the bargain, you take most of the hassle and involvement off their hands. Everybody wins.

The sneaky way to win and get your own way

To be honest, you may choose this because it's the sneaky way to win out. And that's fine. But you could choose this because it's the most powerful. It often proves itself to be.

I call it the pack-within-a-pack. Let's take the premise of the free ride and turn it on its head. Normally, admin are going to take a statement, a renewal, a reminder, or whatever, fold it the wrong way into an envelope that's far too small and cheap and nasty. But it gets the job done. All too often, to Accounts, these aren't customers. They're a combination of slow-paying, forgetful, lying, shifty no-goods. They take more credit than they're supposed to (in other words, you got that record-breaking order!). And anyway, credit is something *they* control but everybody else in the world ignores and abuses. So there! With this kind of partner the friendly mutual concept is going to fall on very stony ground.

So the conventional, free-ride premise won't work. That requires them to say 'OK, here's what we're going to do, provided what you want fits into our envelope and our time schedule we will be very generous and at little or no cost enclose your item.'

Counter-move. Suppose you give us your item already sealed up and ready to go and we take it and enclose into our mailing package which we promise to emblazon suitably so your document doesn't get overlooked. And *you do*.

Now, instead of suffering a huge compromise in sales power you can add 'IMPORTANT DOCUMENTS ENCLOSED' to your envelope, hike up your readership a notch or two, and again, everybody's happy.

Additional benefit will come if you can get them to change to — or agree to your providing — an envelope which enables their addressed item to show through a window which when enclosed with yours is perfectly in position to show through your window too. Double glazing comes to direct mail!

Although you can, of course, have envelopes specially made to achieve this, it's by no means vital. A standard DL window and a standard 'top pop' 120×235 mm window will do the trick, straight off the supplier's shelf.

Here's a tale which will get your next meeting with accounts off to a good start. I can't vouch for one grain of truth in the story which is just 'doing the rounds' at the moment. I *can* vouch for the two debt-collection ideas it includes. Several companies have experienced great success with them. And they go back years.

The psychologist's answer to debt collection

At an international convention of psychologists the subject of debt collection was tabled for discussion. A leading authority from a professional credit control and debt collection company was booked to speak. He delivered a 60-minute, highly technical and highly professional presentation, liberally sprinkled with multiple 'commercials' for his company, which by coincidence just happened to provide a full 'credit management, billing and collection service in most major countries'. As the questions began to thin out, one delegate, a smartly turned-out, rather short gentleman, rose to his feet. He removed his gold-rimmed spectacles. And turned to face his colleagues.

'I don't know about you,' he said, 'but I'm a professional psychologist. And I don't have a bad debt problem. About 60 per cent of my clients pay on or near to terms. The others I have a system for. I let it go two months. I just send the regular statements. Then I send nothing at all the next month. So they think I've forgotten. Then I do one of two things depending on whether they're male or female. To the males, I send a firm letter enclosing a statement for *double* the amount they owe. This gets the cheque for the correct amount together with either a demand for a credit note or an apology, sometimes both.

'To the females, I send a statement showing a mistake in *their* favour. Not a big one. But an obvious one. This gets the cheques in just before they think I will discover my error.' He sat down to loud applause.

I started out on this topic of formats by saying that one of the 'S'entials delivered by format is that it tells the *Sales Story Sensibly* because from the format should come the *Structure* to make it happen.

I suggest that before choosing the format — but particularly in relation to additional items — you should have a clear idea of the role and function of each piece.

I had previously indicated my own preference — given a clean sweep — for probably the most popular combination which can be used as a complete package, or at least a starting point to which you can add other items as the sales story extends or expands. The time-honoured

Letter — leaflet — response piece

One of the reasons that this pack is so effective is that readers are familiar with it. They accept it. They find it fits in with the normal way of doing things. And so it's comfortable. And easy to follow.

- They expect the *letter* to INTRODUCE AND SET THE SCENE, a bit like a good salesman does.

- They expect the *leaflet* to ADOPT A LESS PERSONAL STANCE AND PROVIDE MORE DETAILED INFORMATION AND PICTURES.
- They expect the *response piece* to GATHER ANY NECESSARY DETAILS AND CARRY THEIR ORDER OR ENQUIRY BACK TO YOU.

This suits them. And believe me, more than nine times out of ten, it should suit you too. So, when you're looking for formats, considering some of the one-piece devices, or negotiating with other departments, aim for a solution which, wherever possible, gets you as near to this winning format as can be.

'S'ential No. 3

Direct mail is sense-you-all. It gives you Smell — Sight — and Sound to play with.

I received a rather tasteless (thank heavens!) Christmas card a couple of years back. On the front was a light brown printed square, garlanded in a classic holly and berries design.

'SMELL THIS', read the front page. Of course, I did. Recoiling from a truly vile odour, I opened the card to find a cartoon reindeer smiling. 'IT'S GENUINE REINDEER CRAP,' it said. 'MERRY CHRISTMAS. NOW WASH YOUR HANDS.'

It's amazing what they can do these days.

And so, as you may have guessed, we arrive at what I believe printers refer to as 'micro-encapsulations'. You and I shall demean ourselves and call it 'scratch'n'sniff'.

To start with, avoid reindeer crap at all costs.

An interesting counterpart to that, I was fascinated to hear of the 'mailing' (it was actually delivered by courier service) used by an airline to launch their new route to Brussels from the UK. Novelty abounded — but no more so than to the top travel agents in Brussels, key prospects to sell their regular executive business service. The ingenious marketing team arranged to deliver a copy of that very morning's newspapers with the lead story replaced with a specially written 'story' covering their new service, along with suitable pictures. The paper was delivered with a piping hot cup of coffee, two warm croissants, and a note to explain. One sure way to get your message read. And what a great opener for the telephone follow-up!

A local coffee supplier mailed out businesses in West Sussex to sell the concept of fresh coffee in place of machine vending.

They enclosed a generous handful of coffee beans. 'Smell these when you sit down with your next cup of disappointment,' they invited, 'and then decide which you'd rather have.' They backed this up with some convincing cost arguments and followed through with a fascinating water analysis offer, explaining that they would individually blend, roast and grind the coffee to your exact preference, and to match the water in your area. Just as a good restaurant would insist. Once the analysis was completed, and your blend chosen, you could accept a week's supply free. Try and get your staff back to 'cups of disappointment' after that!

Years earlier, I had been engaged in a project with the opposite objective: to sell the convenience of vending machine coffee. Out went a postal tube containing coffee, sugar, cup, spoon, etc. The letter explained that a vending machine would deliver coffee at one cup every 23 seconds, and invited the production director of the factories mailed to time his secretary's efforts. 'We understand your need for productivity', it said, 'otherwise we wouldn't ask you to take coffee with us in such an old-fashioned time-wasting way. Please don't get cross with your secretary, she can't win.'

And then there is sound. Be careful with this one. For years, I've used good and bad examples in my conferences. One favourite 'baddy' is a mailing which consisted of a sturdy square envelope labelled with my office address on the outside. To this day, I don't know who sent it. Inside there was a 7-inch single record. The sleeve bears only their telephone numbers. And the record label the same. That was it. Nothing else.

For a bit of fun, whichever country I've been in, I've asked audiences to assess the wisdom of this undoubtedly ad agency-inspired gem, by raising their hands if they had a record player in their office. Across the last five years only two people raised their hands. One sold jukeboxes in Oslo. The other was a marketing manager at EMI Records in London.

Yet with cassette tapes — or even videos these days — you can be much safer, especially in the consumer field. Although I would counsel you to try the much cheaper alternative of a simple pack with the cassette or video as the offer, which has the added advantage of enticing response and thereby building you a list of luke warm prospects, as well as focusing these relatively expensive items where they will do the most good.

Then there's a touching moment Yes, there's no reason why you can't let your prospects actually touch too. Fabric, wallpaper, colour selection samples. Any number of options are yours to play with, to experiment and find what works best. They often work well. But the one sense that in my opinion works best is common sense.

And 'S'ential No. 4

The last of my 'S'entials recognises that direct mail *Sends a Sales Star* — and he's a *Spaceman*.

Space is a luxury in most advertising media. Literally so in the press. The more you buy, the more it costs. While to some extent that remains true in direct mail, it's a lot less so.

The first postal weight step goes up to 60 grams in the UK, and in many other places, 50 grams.

You can get a vast amount of selling done inside 50 or 60 grams weight.

We're on to a fairly difficult subject here. It's not difficult for me. I've proved this theory time after time, mailing after mailing. Year in, year out. It's as true now as it was ten years ago. And I have every confidence and every reason to believe it will still be so in ten years' time.

Nearly everyone in direct marketing accepts it, lives by it. All the books — yes, *all* the books — confirm it. Yet for some reason people — advertising people, marketing people, particularly non-direct marketing copy writers — still find it hard to accept. Or maybe just hard to achieve. But here we go, anyway.

Longer copy sells more

It's a really important point. And whereas I'm always conscious that generalisations can be huge pitfalls, I am going to repeat it one more time:

Longer copy sells more

In direct marketing you will always get found out because of the ability to test, because of the ability to determine absolute cost-effectiveness.

Yet, if you go to a direct marketing conference and listen to speakers (and heavens, I've done it enough times — something like 400 or so in the last ten years!) you'll notice one thing which almost all speakers have in common. They don't suggest an idea or two that might work — they *tell* you. And they tell you because they know.

Way back a million years ago — you can tell I'm about to quote Ogilvy again! — Mr O was quoted as follows, delivering the following message for the heads of ad agencies who hadn't started (or perhaps heard of!) direct marketing. Here's what he said:

Insist that all your people are trained in your direct response department. If you don't have one yet, make arrangements with a firm of direct marketing specialists to train your people. Make it a rule in your Agency that no copy is ever presented to Clients before it has been vetted by a direct response expert. The direct response expert *knows* what sells, the rest can only *guess*.

To many, hearing this display of what comes over as certain knowledge, it must seem intransigent. Or inflexible. Or even downright arrogant. I can understand that, because for him, like me, it comes born of irrefutable, incontrovertible experience. Not one experience, hundreds of experiences. Repeatedly tested and re-tested.

Of course we all accept that, if you flip a coin and 10, 20, or, seemingly impossibly, 30 times the coin comes down on the same side, you start to question the flipper, the coin, and then your sanity. But this is not a game of chance. If it is a game at all, it is a game of experience. And you know, at the end of the day, if you're still not convinced you can always test. But do be certain when you test that you test *good* long copy against *good* short copy.

How long does it take to make a sale?

Seems a valid question in this context. Well, what's the answer? Some wonderful cliché. Like as long as it takes? *Yes*, actually!

But imagine yourself holding a classic four-page direct marketer's letter. It's well paced. Easy to read. It has simple but effective layout. And the typography, basic as it is — with much of it typewritten — is next to perfect. Got the picture? You should have. This kind of letter is to be found in about 50 per cent of all consumer mailings. And nearer 95 per cent of all the successful ones!

How long will it take to read it? Five minutes perhaps. Well, certainly if it's cram-packed to bursting. But more typically, I would suggest somewhere between three and four minutes. Now let's add a product leaflet and order slip. Two envelopes — an inner for reply, an outer to get us there. One small 'Special Gift Announcement' flyer. And three sticky stamps.

What do you add that lot up to?

Let's pretend it's going your way and the reader is so wrapped up in it all that — most unusually — they decide to take in every word you write. Let's pretend! In which case, I estimate that we're looking at a total running time of maybe 10–13 minutes.

That may seem a great deal of time to a classical

advertising copywriter who's used to holding the attention in 30-second bursts or for the odd minute or two. But forget the advertising world. How does it measure up to a salesperson?

Not enough! That's how it measures up! But the world is a far more cruel place than that.

Only the most exceptional cases will invest a full 15 minutes or so of their time with you. And rarely will you, in practice, ask for it. The direct marketing creative works his spell in bite-size chunks. And can often achieve the more simple objectives in as little as two or three minutes.

By contrast, imagine yourself as the sales director of a company with a salesforce of 200 or so really good salespeople. You've got them together for the annual sales conference and you're going to present them with a totally new concept in selling. You're going to show them that they can treble or quadruple their sales — *at a stroke*.

The music blares. The flashing lights go crazy. A bank of 16 projectors click through the conference theme one last time. There's all the show-biz tinsel build-up that goes with the event. The room returns instantly to a split-second of absolute silence and black, black darkness. Almost before anyone of the 200 senses can catch up, the stabbing white probe of a spotlight targets a lectern left of stage.

Blinking, you smile. You are on.

> Ladies and gentlemen, and so we arrive at the very apex of this year's sales convention. You've seen the advertising for next year. You've seen the new product range. You've seen the new commission system. Now I am going to show you how to make it work. In just two or three minutes' time you will all be the proud owners of the potential to double or treble your sales figures. Because you will be able to make twice or even three times the number of calls.

The room is silent. They're hanging on your every word. What will it be? Some new sales presenter? Or the introduction of the 40 hour day? On you go.

'So, as of now, we have a new company policy that NO SALES CALL — I repeat — NO SALES CALL, will exceed ten minutes.' The figure 10 appears 4 metres high behind you. More silence. This time they are stunned. Slowly the awful realisation dawns on them. It can't possibly work. The quiet disbelieving whispers build to a chorus of rebellion.

Take my advice. Get off the rostrum, quickly! You've just blown your sales career.

The whole scenario is quite outrageous. Right! That's because I'm being outrageous. No salesman could achieve under such conditions. Yet to direct marketers it's a way of life. And when we run over from three minutes to five or six people call that long copy.

Long? Long? I can't quite see it that way.

But it *looks* long.

Bad layout.

But it *feels* long.

Bad writing.

But it *goes on* so long.

Bad rationale.

But . . . but it's . . . it's absolute rubbish.

That's different!

Bad targeting. Bad timing. Bad offer. Bad pitch. Bad luck.

Let's think about some other little pieces of evidence and pop them in alongside my thought that direct marketing copy is only long in advertising terms. In selling terms, it's quite ridiculously short. And anyway, who's timing it?

The real perception of length matters only inside the reader's head. Yes, of course, someone will flick idly through a 13-sheet letter and wonder whether they've got time for it. The very bulk suggests that to them. But one or two or even four pages? They'll give it a go. If it sounds or looks interesting. If they are interested in what you have to say. And what you have to sell. If not, you can't win anyway. And you don't want to. That's important.

As we realised some time ago, if they're not interested they'll vote with their rubbish bins. You're dismissed before you can even take a 'ready-steady' gulp of breath.

Think positive. Forget for a moment the numbers falling by the wayside. Concentrate on those who were intrigued by your envelope message. They had that intrigue built to an irresistible level by the headline of your letter. Wanted the special offer in the picture alongside. And have decided to explore a little further. It's your green light to proceed. But do fix in your mind that you're now in a *stronger* position. You have made them *want* to read.

Now it's a balancing act. You've got to keep that momentum, expand it if possible, *and* start to create the desire to respond or to buy.

Now *you* are in control. You'll only lose them if . . .

1 They're not *that* interested
2 You say something they disagree with or disapprove of
3 You fail to hold them
4 You confuse or make them work too hard in the circumstances
5 You're not fun, pleasant or good company to be with.

Don't look up. If you see that there are more people giving up than staying you'll get disheartened. You mustn't let that dent your confidence. Keep on. There's a hard nucleus who are absolutely riveted by you. And I can tell from their eyes, two or three have already decided in your favour. They're going to respond. They're reading now because it's confirming their inclination to accept. Keep going. Keep going. You're really going to win through. Give them all you've got. Every reason to accept.

Whew! Nearly done. Let them know there's not too much more to come. Repeat the offer. Summarise and round up with all the main goodies. Now tell them what they have to do next. Give them the offer one more time. Hand them the reply slip. Tell them about the reply envelope. You're nearly, nearly there. Reassure one more time. Well done, you got the offer in again. That was brilliant! OK, thank them. Shake hands. Say goodbye. Right. Now get out. Let them think about it.

Fantastic! Just one more thing to do. Use that PS to poke your head round the door, smile, and give them the offer again one last time.

It's over. Well done. Your first successful direct mail sales call. A thousand people out there. Maybe more. And you got 15 or 20 to respond. What do you need me for? Congratulations.

Oh, by the way. Elapsed time 3 minutes, 4 seconds. It didn't seem that long to them. You must have a smooth tongue!

Direct mail is expensive advertising. But it's *selective*. It gets you in front of the right people. The kind of people who will be more interested in what you have to say, and what you have to sell. It can give you their undivided attention. What you make of it is ultimately up to you.

If you press all the right buttons, they'll give you the time, and a proper hearing. Direct mail is also *creative*. It gives you more chances, more opportunity than any other advertising to hold their attention. You can include colour, smell, sound, texture, shape. You can fashion your communication more artfully, more convincingly than any, other than actually sitting down with them and talking it through.

Because apart from all these things you have the space to do it. Be confident. Your enthusiasm will show. Your conviction will prove infectious. The crunch is not whether it will, but for how many.

There are three more chapters on how to do it after this one. The money and success get nearer and nearer.

Direct mail is **personal**

I would like to be clear on this point. I do not mean personalised, though it can certainly be personalised. I mean *personal*.

This, in context, is an extension of the points we have just made — particularly about length of copy. In which explanation, the point was made a number of times that copy needs to be 'easy to read'.

It has also already started to emerge that a letter is a very effective, powerful and persuasive medium for communication. There are, as we have already learned, particular qualities that are at home in letters.

Indeed, if direct mail has a sneaky, underhand advantage over the other media, it is undoubtedly this. That it takes full advantage of what a letter is perceived to be by those who receive it. The unique regard in which it is held by us all.

Letters are friendly little things

Letters have a pleasant, almost disarming lack of formality. Yet without being pretentious, precocious or presumptive. They are also polite. They wait until you're ready for them. They don't shout over you like the radio and television. They're not inherently silly like posters and more and more press advertising.

They 'talk' — yes, that is the right word for they are normally very conversational — in an easy way. Most are lively and fun to read. Some stimulating. Some newsworthy. Some quite valuable. Some very moving.

Letters are intimate. For example, you read them to yourself. And if you decide to let someone else see your letter, then you do. Unusual for advertising that. Some of this intimacy has to do with the way they, as letters, are perceived. Some of it has to do with the fact that they are undoubtedly the only advertising message that starts 'Dear' and ends 'Yours'. A final pledge of faith, sincerity or truth.

Letters are undoubtedly the single most effective piece of paper you can create for a sales message. Unless, that is, they are very foolishly or insensitively written. Otherwise they will command attention, demand to be read.

You are, for many years yet, well advised — whatever else your creative or economic considerations — always to find a way, a *prominent* way, to get a good sales letter into whatever you do. And make as sure as you can that your reader gets it first.

The salesperson in an envelope

Lots of people seem to choose that analogy. That the letter is like the salesperson in the envelope. And it's a fair description.

The letter is the one that sets the scene and relates the subject of the mailing to the reader. It explains what it's all about, and what you need to do.

And of course, letters — well these sort of letters — are *never* bad news. People know that because they've never had one with *bad* news yet.

. . . and letters are safe

Unlike a human salesperson they can be ignored, put down or curled up into a ball and thrown on the fire.

Unlike a human salesperson, if a letter confronts you, you can't lose.

You don't feel as though you've offended anyone. You never feel guilty, or threatened or intimidated. Yes, with a letter the advantage stays with you. Even when — and we all dread this moment — the salesperson's got you. You've been saying 'yes' for the last 20 minutes. They haven't sold you anything, they've 'made' you talk yourself into it.

How *do* they do that? To get out of it you can't come up with a single sensible argument. They've dealt with the lot. You know you have to buy but you're not going to. Because you just don't want to!

Face-to-face, on the phone, in your home, at their office, branch or shop, you now feel slightly guilty and embarrassed. You're the one who is uneasy. That's why you're shifting from foot to foot and looking around and hoping maybe a fire will break out.

And what of the phone? What do most people feel when the average (not the best, the typical) telephone salesperson gets to work? Defensive. On guard. And therefore threatened.

People write articles about how to hang up on telephone sales people. They bandy techniques of how to dispense with people quickly and painlessly. They resent the often awkward and intrusive timing.

Over the top? Unfair? Maybe. For example, some say that few people like direct mail. True again. But how many actively dislike it? In one survey 70 per cent of retailers said they'd actually rather receive new product information via the mail than from reps. Ditto the majority of doctors. And apparently, only 6 per cent of direct mail gets thrown away unopened.

At least a part of the answer is the cosiness of direct mail.

With mail, the prospect is always in control. It's passive. Persuasive, certainly in most cases, but not threatening, intrusive or intimidating. And you are always, silently, alone with the reader.

Such things sound like clichés. And maybe they are. But if you're not convinced by this emotional reasoning, check out another. In 20 years and more in the business, I have not met one true direct marketing professional whose comments differ, certainly not any without an axe to grind.

So direct mail letters may be — well, are — personal. But they never go too far. They can only succeed because you've decided to let them.

And because of all these qualities — the intimacy, the lack of threat, no fear of confrontation — somehow they become even more convincing, because you're not on your guard. Thus, it follows that because they are so friendly, they talk more like friends. Conversational. In language and tone. Very me-to-you. And if that's not personal, what is?

Personal or personalised?

What is the distinction? It's substantial. For all direct mail should be personal. Some should be personalised.

First, let's look at the difference. It is definable. But we don't need to define it. We all already know. Some media, when you look at them, even when they beguile you, you know you're sharing with others. Direct mail has a position — which is part of its character — that is all its own.

Personal is descriptive of nature, tone and style. The approach is personal. The message is personal. And the ways that messages are communicated — most especially in letter — are personal. More personal than perhaps any other advertising medium can be. Posters, TV ads, even press ads, direct response or others, cannot possibly share the intimacy of direct mail. Letters were designed for one-to-one communication.

And what of personalisation?

A different matter altogether.

Personalisation can never make a mailing. Few, if any, mailings have succeeded simply because they were personalised. It can at best only make a mediocre mailing better. But by no means always.

Personalisation is still a thing to test. If a personalised approach is a by-product of some other process, or some other objective you are trying to achieve (such as sending out a statement, bonus notice, reminder or similar) and you can obtain the benefit of it for little or no extra cost, then use it. For I've only rarely known it to pull less replies.

Direct mail is **reactive**

It reacts to you and your market. You can readily adjust it, tailor-make it to your business, your capacity, the size, geography and capability of your salesforce.

You want more orders or more leads, you send out more. Easy.

You want less, or of higher quality, you tinker with it and it reacts. Easy.

You want the replies to come in at a certain rate. Fine. If you know what response you're going to get, then just release it in appropriate quantities. Easy.

And if you don't know the response, just pop a few out first and find out. Easy.

You want to do something to select a bunch of people, but quickly. Easy.

You want to stop it at short notice without penalties. Easy.

You only want to stop it in a particular sales territory because they are overstretched or you don't have any salesperson covering. Easy.

You want to change the timing, leave six particular people out, vary your message to 25 per cent of your market, make one offer to some, another to others. Easy.

Is there any other advertising medium which, at anything like the same price, can deliver such extraordinary flexibility and react so precisely to your needs?

In a word, *no*.

Direct mail is **tried and tested**

Now, I'm no statistician. Which is fine for this part of this book. But not if you need to cover this topic — testing — in detail. In this case you'll need some extra reading. You'll find help in the Bibliography at the back.

However, if you want to get a basic run-down of the ways you can profit through exploiting this particular and very valuable asset then, that's what the next few pages will give you.

The testability of direct mail, when you first realise just how powerful it is, the degree of certainty you can obtain, and its value to your business, is a very enticing and flirtatious quality. You can become quite obsessed by it.

There are plenty of stories of people who have used basic testing techniques to unlock response differentials of 100 per cent, 200 per cent, 300 per cent and more. Indeed, only recently, I put together a test programme that unlocked a variant offering a 1000 per cent increase to cost-effectiveness.

You can sense the attraction. So let's look at the concept, the things you need to do to ensure accurate and as near as possible repeatable results, and the kind of things you should test to get the maximum uplift.

Why should you test in direct mail?

Because it's there! In other words, because you can.

Let's look at some typical questions that people ask at my conferences and workshops.

- Does envelope printing work, especially to business markets where fewer people see it?
- Does personalisation work, and if so, what style or type should I use?
- How much higher response do you get in a business mailing when you rent a list with personal names on?
- How can I tell which gift will work best — and how many should I get into stock?
- Are you sure this long copy thing works?
- Is it better to put the address on the envelope, on the letter to personalise it, or somewhere else?
- Which of those three lists do you think will 'pull' best?

And of course, this little gem:

- What response do you think I'll get?

Much as I'd love to be able to answer those questions, my advice is always, 'Why not test and find out?'

I firmly believe that you should be testing something in every mailing you send out. Whether you mail in hundreds or in millions. Obviously, if you mail in millions, the need, the opportunity and the potential is far, far greater.

But if you mail in hundreds, wouldn't you still like to know which type of sales letter, which type of offer, which style of approach works best for you?

I know I couldn't resist!

Things to understand before you test

From the outset it needs to be said that testing is a curiously satisfying, illusion-shattering and yet in many ways insubstantial, intangible and frustrating process. And endless. Like the proverbial sands in the desert, but with the odd fixed point.

I think what I'm really trying to warn you about is that testing tends to establish three principal kinds of results.

1   *The constant* — items which are always worthy of testing and re-testing but which constantly, albeit at varying strengths, give a clear positive or negative result.
2   *The varying* — other issues, which are often surprising, that tend to give differences because they are specific to a situation, project or time. These confuse wonderfully because just when you think you've discovered something that has been increasing or depressing responses and which will yield a significant change, you test again and nothing. Or the opposite. These are the desert sands. Constantly shifting.
3   *The hugely trivial* — these are things that you would think would make a significant difference, but in the event don't.

The first of these you obviously need to know as much about, and as many of, as possible. That's fine, because, amongst other things, this book is full of them. And those are precisely the items which I referred to earlier when I said direct marketing speakers deliver them as facts from the rostrum. The very things which enable me to have emphasised statements in this book such as *'Longer copy sells more'*. It doesn't alter my view at all that you should go on testing them. Pendulums swing. Attitudes, markets, techniques, change and develop. Results from these tests will tend to appear as small clues, indistinct trends to start with, gaining momentum as time passes. The second type constantly leads me to give advice that test results are for *you*! And not necessarily for anyone else.

These are the things that provoke dangerous, ill-informed and unguarded comments on discussion panels. While they are honest comments, they are none the less misleading. For example, 'We've tried that, it doesn't work? Two words more would improve the statement. They are '. . . for us', thus removing the implication that if it doesn't work for 'us', it won't work for anybody.

And lastly, the hugely trivial. I am reluctant to list these and the reluctance is born of long and bitter experience leading to the realisation that what is trivial for one advertiser will not be so for another. And, most significantly, what is trivial for one advertiser in one specific situation can become far from trivial for that same advertiser in another.

I repeat, and be warned, what you discover works or does not work for you is just that. *For you.*

Bad testing is better than no testing

This is yet another dangerous statement and therefore you must understand precisely what I mean. Then decide its relevance to you.

Bad testing, as such, is going to yield bad results. A bad result is going to lead to bad decisions and bad responses in the future.

There are two ways and two ways only to test: scientifically, to give reliable (statistically valid) results; and unscientifically, to give an experience.

In both cases, the test, the analysis of the results, and the interpretation leading to decisions for the future are three inextricable activities.

With unscientific testing, you must proceed very cautiously. You have 'gut-feel' experience, instinct. All those senses to work with. And they are valuable. But you must keep a red light flashing in your head all the time.

With scientific testing, because you have quantifiable elements of probability and error, you have much more secure data to work on. You will still need all the instincts and experience I mentioned, to understand what you have discovered, which type of result it is, and what use you should make of it.

How to make your testing 'scientific'

As I wrote earlier, by scientific I mean statistically valid.

The most important starting point is that you test *enough* to make your test valid. In other words that the test sample is both a sufficient quantity and also wholly representative and unbiased. Three notes on this:

1 *Enough is not a lot — most people mail too many*

I often hear views that 10–15 per cent is a good sample size. It may be so. It depends. But it has absolutely *no statistical foundation.* It is a difficult (but imperative to understand) fact that whatever you've heard, whatever you felt right, whatever you've been given to understand — there is *no significant correlation* for our purposes *between the sample size and the total list or quantity of names to be mailed.*

Confusingly, it is still true that the more names you take, the more reliable your result becomes. But this is simply because it is a *wider* experience not because it is *necessary* experience.

Mathematically, it is accepted that over a given number the wider experience gives proportionately decreasing additional validity. Or, in other words, there is an optimum practical quantity to take.

I shall demonstrate and explain how to calculate this quantity after further notes. But you will find that many people are mailing more than they need at the 10–15 per cent level.

2   *You must mail the right type of recipient*

'Right', in this context, is categorically an *unbiased* type. Relax! You don't need to ring round everybody to check out their politics, religion, sexual preferences, colour, mental stability and emotional fabric. Exactly the opposite. Because it's not the individuals who must be representative, it's the sample. Put another way, we have to ensure the success of our test, equally to ensure that the sample chosen from the list is truly representative of the whole list.

This sounds difficult to achieve. In fact, it's probably the easiest part of the whole process. Yet I have observed, over the years, people going through the most amazing contortions to ensure the unbiased nature of their sample. Some favourites: taking an equal quantity from each county or TV area. Taking equal proportions of male and female. Taking equal quantities by surname for each letter of the alphabet (difficult when you get to Q or Z!).

These contortions, as I describe them, simply say that people understand the need to eradicate bias. But invariably the methods above will increase, not reduce it.

Happily, I repeat, in direct mail the solution is simplicity itself. This sets it apart from other kinds of sampling, opinion polls or market research, for example.

Here's what you do. Divide the total quantity to be tested by the number you have calculated as the sample size required. People call this process 'an Nth name selection'. What you will establish by this method is the value of N.

I'll go through that again. With a couple of additional tips.

To ensure the lack of bias, and thereby the true representative significance of your samples, you need only to ensure that it is a *random* sample. To take a random sample you decide the total quantity of the desired sample size and then take every Nth name from the list.

Example

Total quantity $= 100\,000$

Test required $= 5\,000$

$$\frac{100\,000}{5000} = 20$$

Take every 20th name in sequence (N=20).

The two tips. First, remember the sample size is not an absolute for *carte blanche* testing in itself. You can't test five different — or even two different — factors within the same quantity. You *must* have the full quantity for *each* variation. Second, if you are testing more than one factor, allocate the names in rotation. Thus, if you have decided to test four items in quantities that calculate to 5000 you will wish to take 20 000 from the list. Follow this method:

(a) Take the 20 000 as prescribed above — in the case of a 100 000 test every fifth name.

(b) Then allocate each name sequentially by variant so that, on the file, steps one and two will look like this.

Step one

Take every fifth name.

Original file

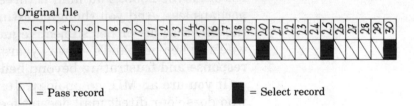

◨ = Pass record   ■ = Select record

Figure 6.1
Step one: Take every fifth name

Step two

Allocate sequentially.

Combines process of selection and sequential allocation followed by sortation into each sample.

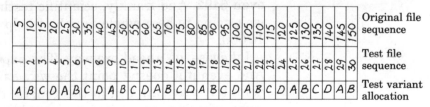

Figure 6.2
Step two: Allocate sequentially

147

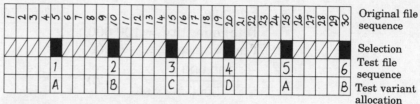

Figure 6.3
Combined process of selection and sequential allocation together with variant sortation

Fairly basic programming will achieve both processes simultaneously and enable off-take sortation into the respective four samples.

If you are restless, you are either: uncomfortable with figures or maybe computers — in which case, I do sympathise, I'm not a whizz with either; or you fall into the category described by my third and final point to do with making your test scientific.

3 *You've realised scientific testing is impossible for you*

I feel for you but there's nothing I can do, or for that matter that you can do, that will make your testing scientific.

You realised, I expect, with the sort of quantities I was using that you're going to have a real problem. You've got a list of maybe 2000. You mail it three or four times a year, perhaps less. And you thought testing was going to prove to the MD that his or her subjective judgement — or worse, his wife's or her husband's — was years out of date, killing response and frustrating beyond belief.

(If you are an MD, no apology. Just make sure the person who does your direct mail doesn't feel like this. I'm about to show them how to pull the wool over your eyes. So do yourself a favour — let them. It's in your own interest to do so. Take a surreptitious look!)

Here's what you do. Go ahead anyway. You see, only you know that what you're going to embark upon is not scientific. It still sounds very credible. The MD is blissfully unaware that you have calculated that (show you how next!) you need a sample size of 6492 and your list is just one tenth of that. Or even 6492. And frankly, scientific testing in this situation isn't going to be a whole bunch of help even if your list is 10 000.

Likewise, go ahead anyway. The experience is fantastic. And even if it doesn't point the way as clearly, it will definitely wave an arm in the general direction of what's right, what's wrong, what works, what doesn't, what's good and what's bad.

So if you've got a mailing of 500, go ahead. Test two letters. One short, one long(er!).

Go ahead. See what happens if you personalise on the word processor or just print them. Measure the result. Examine it against cost.

But keep reading — for, as you will see, both of these last two factors, measuring results, examining costs, have essential actions attached to them. And what's more, it may help you to use calculations and formulae to establish — by using them in other ways — just how *un*scientific your testing is. You could be surprised and reassured. If not, then at least you'll know the precise mathematical assessment of the risk you take with your testing.

Be advised — don't skip this next section!!

How ambitious should your testing be?

In direct mail you can test more widely and more precisely than with *any* other advertising medium. It is, as I noted in my opening, a flirtatious quality that the medium holds. You can read the advice in other books — and of direct marketing in general, it is sound advice — that you should only test one major factor (or variant) at a time. With direct mail you can do more. But in assessing how much of your mailing should be tests and how much should be the results of previous tests you must carefully consider the need for a control. And the advice of 'The Banker' which I'll explain in a few pages.

A single test or a matrix?

For reasons, mainly to do with press advertising which offers very limited testing scope, the single variant process has become known as the 'A/B' split. This is a simple head-to-head process where you divide your list in two, still on an Nth name basis (in this case every other name!), and mail half with each variant.

To test a greater quantity of items is possible, but more open to the results being misunderstood or misinterpreted.

Here's how it works. A matrix might look like this. Let's assume a sample size of 3000 has been calculated and the name allocation process already described is followed. Remember, each individual variant, in the example of Figure 6.4, 1A/2A/3A/1B/2B, etc. must mail the full sample size to remain statistically valid.

The matrix method evokes both focus analysis and tier analysis. Which, bearing in mind all that has gone before, can still be quite revealing.

Offers

Lists	1	2	3
A	1A	2A	3A
B	1B	2B	3B
C	1C	2C	3C
	9K	9K	9K

Figure 6.4
A simple test matrix

Focus analysis: A direct comparison of each variant. 1A against 1B against each of the remainder.

Tier analysis: The combined effect of the total type of variant:

Combined List A result against combined B Combined C

and

Combined offer 1 against combined offer 2 against combined offer 3.

However a matrix test is schematically drawn, analytically examine your results as above.

Production departments may prefer to express the above example as follows:

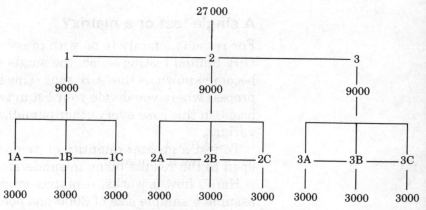

Figure 6.5
Alternative expression of matrix structure

What should you test?

Interesting question! The answer is the things that make the most difference to response. Sounds fairly natural, but it's a point often overlooked.

Favourite red herrings include testing:

- the signatory
- the second (or third or fourth) colour on the letter
- whether to stamp or frank
- the logo position

Take my tip — concentrate on tests to do with the things that will make the most difference. They remain — as they always will — in this order: *the list, the offer, the package*.

There are always exceptions, of course. Probably the most commonly overlooked of these is timing.

How to test

Basically, there needs to be nothing at all difficult or complex to testing. Unless you choose it to be that way. In other words, it's only as difficult as you make it.

There are five basic ways to assure the most fruitful and least misleading tests. Let's check them out.

1 *Code the variants*

It stands to reason that if you don't code the test variants to distinguish one from the other you could have problems. In fact, there are two reasons to code. The first is to ensure your mailing test variations go out correctly. The second is to enable you to tell which variations are doing what.

Contents codes Many people will be testing items which will change several items of print. Thus contents codes are printed on *all* items to ensure the right letter goes with the right leaflet goes with the right reply card. And they all get enclosed in the right envelope! Thus a typical coding system might look like this:

14/7–89/A/4/3
Here's how it made up.

14/	= Promotion code
7–89/	= Month and year of mailing
A/	= Offer A, B or C, etc.
4/	= List 1, 2, 3 or 4, etc.
3	= Component No. — 1 = Outer envelope

	2 = Letter
	3 = Reply slip
	4 = Gift voucher
	5 = Reply envelope

Response codes Whether you decide to have full contents codes or not, the item you really can't escape coding is the reply piece.

And if you're looking for a telephone response you'll have to find some ingenious way of measuring the difference. I guess the most common of all is the Jill Blake, Laura Good method. Phone and ask for Jill Blake, you're a Code A! Ask for Laura Good, you're a Code B!

2   *Minimise bias*

What we're trying to do is ensure the validity of result. And thereby improve the likelihood of achieving as near as possible the same result from roll-outs as we get from tests. We are also endeavouring not to handicap one variant, or possibly, give a head-start to another. All this seems terribly easy at the early planning stage when it's all theory.

Despite the production advice you'll get later on, you will find that lots of things can go wrong in the production of a mailing. Delays creep in. People let you down. Printers run late. I'm sure you know the story. So all of a sudden you're faced with a deadline. Test variant A is all set to go, but B is running behind. What should you do?

You have two choices — and *neither* of them is to mail A and let B go two weeks later when it's ready.

Choice 1 is to mail half of A. As soon as possible mail the second half of A together with the first half of B. And then, as a third release, the second half of B. What's important now is that you 'crisis code' the halves of A and B so that you can identify the two halves that went together from those that went separately! Crisis coding is quite easy — and there are some fast methods of achieving it. They will inevitably involve extra costs, but often these can be off-loaded onto the supplier who's let you down.

Here are some crisis coding ideas.

- A good old-fashioned rubber stamp.
- Trim the reply piece to be shorter or, more noticeable, cut a small piece off at the corner.
- Run them through a small litho or even letterpress machine and print a distinguishing mark such as an extra code letter or a colour dot or bar.
- Run them through addressing equipment again to print a distinguishing code letter.

This will enable you to distinguish to some degree whether you have introduced any bias into the test and give you some idea of what that bias may be. If necessary, you can weight your results to predict for the future. But be warned — nothing beats a good clean test. Which leads to your second choice.

Choice 2 — wait. And when you have all the pieces together proceed as originally planned.

With lists, there is not a great deal that can cause bias. You are after all testing the pulling power of that list or segment of the list. The only things likely to creep in to cause a skewed result might be the quality of the addressing itself. Poor or scruffy addressing particularly depresses response, one list being hand-addressed (hardly likely these days, but possible!). You are trying to get yourself as near as possible into the position of having the only difference between one variant and the other being the variant itself.

With creative that shouldn't be a problem, although a few design and copy headaches can be caused getting the balance right between merchandising gifts or offers to their best advantage while keeping the overall 'look' and 'feel' to the different packages.

For there is no doubt that weaving the gift into the creative approach — or the list characteristics, with visual and verbal links for that matter — can in themselves give you a response lift. But not usually such a great one as to make the difference between a real disaster and a huge success.

3 Calculate the correct sample size

Here comes some basic maths. Although it's tempting to go into great detail about the laws of probability and bell curves and whatever, I'm working to JFR's law of probability. That is: you probably don't need all the detail. So if you want to work out a sample size I'll tell you how (see also the record double-quick method at the end of the chapter). If you want to *understand* it, then you'll need further reading and you'll find plenty of suitable material in the Bibliography.

Here is the basic formula:

$$\frac{\text{Sample}}{\text{size}} = \frac{\text{CL} \times \text{Response per cent} \times \text{Non-response per cent}}{(\text{ET})^2}$$

CL stands for Confidence Level

You don't need me to tell you that there's nothing certain in this uncertain world. What is perhaps more surprising is that the oft-berated bunch known as statisticians and mathematicians are among the very first of us to recognise the inescapable truth of this statement.

Yet statistically one can calculate the confidence one can have in a given result or set of results. For us this means simply you can choose what confidence level is acceptable to you for response prediction.

The insertion of the CL figure in the formula is actually the application of a mathematical constant denoting one of the parameters you can set in calculating the sample size you require. Most of the industry works to a 'norm' of 95 per cent. At this level, the value of CL is 3.84.

Here are some other values in common use:

Confidence Level per cent	CL value
75	1.32
90	2.71
93	3.21
95	3.83
99	6.63

Don't worry, if you are still uncertain of what a confidence level is. We'll come back to that after we've looked at . . .

ET stands for *error tolerance*

Being the wickedly incisive observers of humanity that they are, S and M (statisticians and mathematicians) also know that even though one can make predictions with a certain degree of confidence, one cannot always be confident that the predicted result will be absolutely on the button. So, in order to meet the confidence levels (and to be a little more practical about things), we agree that we shall accept some tolerance of error in our prediction. And this error could be either plus or minus the response we want.

Response per cent stands for *Response per cent*. Not difficult! Drop in the response figure or estimated figure.

Non-response per cent is simply 100 less the figure above.

Now let's see what kind of statement can be made after we've used the formula. Then I'm sure the meaning and relevance of CL and ET will fall into place. We'll run through an example and then look at what our S and M friends would have to say about it.

Let's assume that we are happy with the 'norm' confidence level of 95 per cent and although we're looking for a 2 per cent response, we won't actually commit hari kari if we get 1.5 per cent.

Here goes:

$$\text{Sample size (SS)} = \frac{3.84 \times 3 \times 97}{(0.5)^2}$$

Therefore sample size = 4470.

Now what this means to the people in the S and M dept is that they can issue the following cautious, but optimistic statement:

In this example, all things being equal (which they never are, of course!) if you adopt a sample size of 4470 the response will fall between ±0.5 per cent of 2 per cent (i.e. between 1.5 and 2.5 per cent) 93 times in every 100 you mail.

How do you set the error tolerance?

That's for you to choose. There are a number of popular views on this. Here are two you could consider. For both of these we ignore — as most do — the 'plus' element since over-performance is not generally a problem, whereas the minus element is of concern.

Either set the level base on the differential between breakeven and the anticipated response or, if you are testing something you expect to give your response a lift, calculate the lift required to cost justify its use as the differential.

Let's do both of these as examples and you'll see how they work.

Example 1

Parameters — Confidence level 95 per cent (3.84)
— Error tolerance: Breakeven for mailing at 2.75 per cent
— Anticipated response 3 per cent, so say to ±0.25 per cent

Formula:

$$SS = \frac{3.84 \times 3 \times 97}{(0.25)^2}$$

$$SS = 17\,880$$

Example 2

Parameters — Confidence level 95 per cent (3.84)
— Error tolerance: Testing new flyer designed to lift response in line with or better than cost

Last result:	£20	cost per order at 2.64 per cent
Flyer cost:	£40	per 1000
Flyer target:	$\dfrac{40}{20}$	extra orders = 2 per 1000 mailed
Response rise required:		0.2 per cent (tolerance parameter)

Formula:

$$SS = \frac{3.84 \times 2.64 \times 97.36}{(0.2)^2}$$

$$SS = 24\,675$$

What happens if the sample size works out to be too large for practical use?

In this case, the formula is re-jigged to help us assess the degree of risk involved.

So it would become (at 95 per cent confidence)

$$ET = \frac{3.84 \times Response \times Non\text{-}response}{Sample\ size}$$

Suppose that we had just used the above formula and established our ET of ± 0.6 per cent on a 4 per cent response, then our friends in the S and M Dept would issue something along the lines of the following:

> All things being equal, your result indicates that if you use the particular sample size at a response rate of 4 per cent, you can be confident that 95 times out of 100 the response will fall somewhere between 3.4 and 4.6 per cent.

In assessing risk it may help you to gauge the range of ETs when you change the confidence levels in accordance with the options I gave earlier for CLs of 75 per cent up to 99 per cent.

One last thought on sample sizes

Be generous. It is always much better to pay a little extra to test a few more than you need, than it is to have a statistically invalid (in other words *unreliable*) test result.

Maybe, for you like so many others, the two most difficult things to fix in your head for the future are these:

1 there is no valid relationship between the sample and the universe from which it is chosen in relation to its size;
2 the higher the response, the *more* you need to test to maintain validity.

These two attack common sense. You would think that the bigger the test the bigger the sample that needs to be taken. The mythical 10 per cent seems sensible. Yet it has little bearing whatsoever.

Equally, you would think that the higher the response, the more you had 'got it right'. And therefore the need to take large samples would decrease. Whereas the opposite is true. Once they thought the world was flat!

4 *Make sure you've got a control in your test*

Where are you going? What are you trying to prove? And where are you coming from?

These hugely philosophical questions, if applied to our lives, could keep us going for hours. They even sound like something from an Open University programme made in the late seventies.

Seriously, what we are leading up to here is something well accepted by botanists, chemists, physicists and all experimentalists, the world over. The fact is that for your test to have any real significance or relevance to the status quo, you must include the status quo in your test.

The reason you need to do this is, as far as possible, to obliterate doubt, or at least quantify it! It follows that you must therefore place the status quo — in effect a control — in the same environment.

Thus it must mail at the same time, in the same conditions as your tests. Then you will be able to determine to some extent where you are, where you came from, and — if you've got your test priorities right — where you're going, and hopefully, what you should be testing next.

> We seek not that we shall find the answers
> — simply that we shall understand the questions.

An on-going mailing operation should accept this concept. At first, the 'test-and-learn' opportunities available to the direct marketer seem even more attractive and finite than they are.

Without doubt progress can be made. There are many paths open to us, but it is a *testing* process.

That means we shall discover losers as well as winners. It means things will be developed that are a waste of money. It means that prices will be higher because of extra database work, short runs and disproportionate creativity.

As well as a *testing* process, it can also be a *trying* process. For at the end of the day much of the experience, expertise and creative development can, in effect, become 'wasted' by the arrival of, for example, a new production process or list selection system. It should be viewed as an evolutionary process. At times this may seem to be a revolutionary process. A point which leads to:

5 *The concept of 'the banker'*

Testing is an inherently risky business. The overriding priority must be to protect the maximum amount of your investment from the unknown, untried and unproven.

It must be accepted that the overall policy should be to

change the minimum possible from the known. Indeed, something like 80–90 per cent should be on the same basis as the last, balanced against the results which were obtained.

The discovery of something that works is an exciting and tempting moment. Imagine, you've been doing things in a particular way for some time when along comes a better product, a new technique, a new creative approach, a list — anything — which seems to offer a significantly better result. 'Why', asks the manager, 'should you go again the old way when we can now offer this new one? It's got to be better.'

The answer is that although new ideas may seem to offer improvement, you can never know until you've tried them. Time after time in my career, I have watched things that everyone thought would prove not just better, but substantially better, go out on test and fail. Classics are:

- A new product feature or design that the manufacturer or supplier *knows* is better than the old. Yet the consumer likes the old. They're familiar with it. In fact, they are reluctant and resistant to change.
- A new gift or premium which seems to offer the prospective buyer temptation beyond delight. Whereas what they actually see is too good a deal and it makes them suspicious of the offer and destroys credibility.
- A price-cut or discount which equally destroys credibility. Or worse, shatters the perception of value for money. Or repositions the product so drastically (from, say, luxury to bargain) that they no longer want it.
- A new production process enables massive package cost savings but means that the existing creative and/or personalisation needs to be reshaped. Or worse, introduces more complex or time-consuming response mechanisms for the responder. Typically, these might be the switching from a full-blown direct mail package to an all-singing, all-dancing one-piece mailer. It may well slash in-the-mail costs by 20 per cent but the consumer now needs a week's course in origami to open, digest and respond to it!

So there is a constant need to search out and discover, to push progress and innovation. But each time you fall on a prospective candidate process or item — no matter how spectacular it seems — do view it with intense suspicion, until it's tested. For those with on-going programmes there is an answer. For those with continually changing programmes it is more difficult and requires the very best professional judgement in areas where, probably, the very best professional judges can make the biggest blunders. The consumer is both weird and wonderful. But also fickle.

However, if you have continuing programmes to develop, you can start to build a bank, or library, of ideas. And although the following thoughts appear to suggest that this is only for creative approaches, it is actually not so. As you will see.

The 'package library' concept

The major object of testing is to eliminate financial and actual risk.

The major risk, to be avoided at all costs, is one where an unproven idea is adopted each time thus effectively rolling from one unknown to another. Something that charities, financial and insurance organisations seem to do most often. 'We need another mailing . . .' starts the conversation. Thus, however good the brains at work for them, they throw out two most powerful allies: repetition and experience.

Moreover, the chance of creating a totally new approach with long-term potential and with high value is very limited. It will more likely develop through a future creative process or by this combined with a new market opportunity that has yet to arise.

Thus, I prefer to recommend the 'library' concept which enables packages to be pre-tested over one (occasionally two) previous periods.

In the first promotion four packs are tested:

Main mailing	Tests
Last control (X)	Packs A, B, C

Let's now suppose that pack B substantially beats the control and pack C beats control and nearly equates with pack B. Pack A is dropped. Thus promotion 2 comprises:

Main mailing	Tests
Pack B	Packs C (with improvements), D, E

Pack C with its improvements out-pulls the new control (pack B). Pack D is poor but pack E equates with the control. In promotion 3, therefore, the mailing is as follows:

Main mailing	Tests
Pack C	Packs E, F, G and X

The testing above now enables second-period tests to be carried out on Pack E, possibly incorporating enhancements. Two new packs — F and G — are tested for the first time, and pack X (the original control) returns to be tested again to see if it still pulls as well or better than before.

Thus, as this process continues, it can be seen how gradually, over the years, a 'library' of ideas can be built up, tested and used or kept for the future.

Having explained the theory, it is necessary to remember that occasionally the strongest ingredient can come from topicality. And topical mailings can provide excellent returns but with increased risk since testing is nearly always precluded by the very topicality.

Looking at results

Perhaps the first and indeed one of the most important things to keep in mind when you look at the results of tests is that you should never look at them in isolation. They will be one or more experiences in and among a set of other experiences. The learning — which is what you test to achieve — comes from consideration of the results set against two other perspectives. The last — what you have already learned; and the future — what you want to learn next. It is the application of these three tiers of knowledge that creates the most significant growth in you, your experience and thereby your success. You must also be quite sure to be precise about what your test has told you. This falls into two simple areas: what has changed and what has not. Results in either category are worthwhile.

Keep full records in a 'guardbook'

A guardbook is a simple thing of extraordinary value. At its simplest it is a record of what you have done and when. It contains samples of each and every type and variation of the work done and when, perhaps as a ring-binder, which enables those involved to look back and absorb what has happened before.

Keep a record of objectives, results strategy, suppliers and their costs, as well as the actual samples of each and every item, right down to what happened or was sent in response.

Many would be well advised to keep fuller records still, expanding the guardbook from a record of what was done to add the dimensions of why and how.

Many large companies keep a corporate guardbook which includes, not just samples and results of their ads and mailings, but also samples of their full set of corporate print and publications — from business cards, to invoices, memos and stock-sheets. This is often an unnecessary indulgence for a small company, but there's no such thing as a small sale. So I recommend the keeping of records as fully as can be achieved on a practical basis. But do ensure you keep all the relevant information.

Many record-keepers turn a guardbook into an historical set of samples. And so it should be. But you will gain enormous benefit from additional information alongside the physical samples.

So include four written reports on the following:

1 A general description of what happened. In others words a descriptive job history, brought to life.
2 A note of the surprises. Any problems or opportunities that arose during the project.
3 A note of how production, legal or other problems were overcome.
4 Often the most valuable — a hindsight report. What, if the job were tackled again (and therefore with the benefit of hindsight), would be changed, improved, avoided or remembered for the future?

Lastly, don't hide your guardbook away. It should not become an archival artefact. It must be an available working reference tool, something that creative, marketing and salespeople can read and refer to. Something the value of which will be determined by the intelligence and wisdom it adds to future developments.

Lies and damned lies

Test results are full of them, which is why experience and instinct are required for the most sensitive and perceptive interpretation of them.

If you know your business and trust your instincts you will occasionally come up against results that challenge both. In these cases always try to re-test. If that's *not* possible, go with your feelings. Treat the test results with absolute suspicion.

In any case, I have always worked to the rule that unless there was a differential of at least 15 per cent between one result and another, then I had learned nothing. And a re-test is advisable.

I remember being up on the conference rostrum one day with a friend who is very prominent in the insurance direct marketing fraternity. He recounted to a bemused audience, how he has used national daily morning papers to test testing! Apparently, he ran an A/B split (an opportunity to run an exact split of two alternative approaches offered by some newspapers) but the ad was identical in every respect save for a tiny almost indiscernible single digit code in the bottom of the response coupon. B OUTPULLED A BY NEARLY 15 PER CENT!

Just before you re-test on exactly the same basis it is worth bearing in mind a piece of advice that is as true for first tests as it is for re-tests. You should always aim to make test variations as different as possible:

● With or without — not with or with less!
● Long or short — not long or not so long!
● Four-colour or single colour — not four-colour or three-colour!

So just before you proceed with a re-test on exactly the same lines, take another look at what you did and see if you can't widen the gap between that and your control. A wider gap may give you the bigger differential. And therefore a more significant result.

Don't forget to project forward

What are you testing for? Normally it will be to determine one of two things:

1 Is this worth doing?

Or

2 How can I do this better?

To get a sound and reliable answer you must remember that testing costs money. If you load the future with the costs of the past, you may make a wrong decision. And you wouldn't be the first! It is a remarkably common mistake but a mistake none the less.

By this I mean simply that you must examine the economics of your test results against the costs of projecting forward *not* against the actual costs of the test. For example, if you carry out a basic viability test — an 'is this worth doing?' — you could quite easily spend, on a per 1000 basis, something like double or treble the costs that repeats in similar or larger quantities would incur.

If you set you results against the higher original costs, you could well mistakenly classify a project as not viable when it is actually perfectly profitable as a forward projection either in larger scale or simply without the start-up or additional costs that testing brings.

These additional costs will include creative work, small quantity or split-run buying, and possibly, extra charges for project management or more complex production.

Some favourite test subjects

As well as *Lists* and *Timing,*

Strategic
Mail order *v* salesforce (or retailers)
One-stage *v* two-stage sale[1]

Product
De-luxe *v* regular[2]

Offer
No gift incentive *v* discount *v* none
High price *v* low(er!)
Cash *v* credit *v* credit cards[3]

Creative
Hard sell *v* soft
Closing dates *v* early bird[4]
Full colour *v* selective colour
Photography *v* illustration
Personalisation — with *v* without
Copy length — short *v* long
Headlines[5]

Format
Reply paid *v* not[6]
Multi-piece package *v* self-mailer or one piece
Address placing[7]

Notes

1 *One-stage* v *two-stage sales* A lot of products need to be sold in two stages. Some just benefit from it. The first stage being the generation of enquiry, the second (following response to stage one) the conversion to sale.

  Although this certainly introduces another layer of cost into the proceedings, this can be more than offset by its two benefits:

(a) There is a substantial cost-saving in many cases since complex or expensive sales materials are directed only at those who have expressed a clear interest in what you have to sell and are, therefore, more likely to buy.

(b) It builds you a list of prospects for repeat approach on this product or fresh approaches on other products. Often providing you with useful additional information to make the future approaches on a much more timely, relevant and appropriate basis.

Example 1 Somebody applies to you for a free motor insurance quotation. In order to provide this, a host of information is supplied to you including perhaps whether they are married, whether they have children between 17–25, their insurance renewal date, etc.

The renewal date and car information gives you the opportunity to go back with perfect timing next year (if they don't buy from your quote, which the majority won't!). If you've been smart and collected the date of birth at stage one, a whole host of other insurance possibilities open up. Even if not, the other information you have gathered will enable you either to build a picture of prospects and segment them into types for product approaches, or to approach them with offers based on the specific details they have given you.

Along these lines, perhaps:

Dear Mr Smith,
Last October you asked us to quote for your motor insurance. From the information you gave us I noticed you have two children between the ages of 17 and 25.

Therefore, I thought you and your wife might be interested in the magnificent holiday opportunity now available from our Travel Department. Most of the delightful and sunny locations can easily be reached in the comfort of your Ford Sierra and they can naturally arrange Ferry and Hovercraft bookings for you and your family. Plus of course, our Gold Star comprehensive Travel and Holiday Insurance.

But first, let me take you round some of the exotic resorts and tell you all about . . .

You get the picture. You've probably had the mailing!

Example 2 You sell gas 'log' fires. The reply card in your mailing has the following tick boxes.

☐ Please send my FREE personal copy of 'How to put the Heart in your Hearth' including, without obligation, details and prices of the exciting range of 'Ha'penny an hour' gas fires.

Please provide the following information
My house has

central heating
☐ gas	☐ oil
☐ electricity	☐ other — please specify
☐ no central heating	

Insulation

double glazing	— partial	☐
	— full	☐
	— none	☐
loft insulation		☐
cavity wall insulation		☐

Fire location

I already have a hearth

with chimney	☐
without chimney	☐
with gas point	☐
without gas point	☐

---

2 *Regular or de-luxe — which do you sell first?* Do you offer the de-luxe as the main proposition with an economy option, or the regular as the main proposition with a de-luxe option? That's the test! It's worth noting that a de-luxe version will generally give you ±40 per cent of sales.

3 *Cash or credit or . . .* When testing cash *v* credit *v* credit cards, if you can't test all three, test both types of credit sale first. Then, whichever wins should be tested against the two cash versions (cash enclosed/bill me later). Remember, you're testing quantities and economics and fulfilment and money processing and credit costs as well with this test. Not just 'what pulls best'.

4 *The moral of the early bird* If you don't know what an early bird is, worm your way through to the creative sections in Chapter 10 where all is revealed! The best way to get there is keep reading.

5 *Headlines* Although the current trend (with which I agree, in the main) is to credit creative with a lot less influence than was previously thought, I have seen response improvements of 500 and 600 per cent from simple headline tests.

6 *Reply paid or not?* This one has more to do with the balance of quantity and quality than whether you come up with the cost of it. The whole subject is looked at in 'Direct Mail is easy to respond to' in just a few pages. But briefly, I think you should pay!

7 *Address placing* On the outer envelope? On the letter to look personalised? On the response device to make it

easier to return? This can make a world of difference to response. And is as much a cost decision as a creative format decision as it is a production decision bearing in mind how the data is held. More advice in both Production and Creative chapters.

The five most important things to remember when testing

1 *Concentrate* on testing the major items: these always centre on the list, the offer, the product, the timing, and the (creative) package. The most overrated of these is creative. The most underrated is timing.
2 *Test* big differences to get big differences. Two similar creative approaches will yield two similar results. Two similar lists will yield similar results. And so on.
3 *Act with speed and courage.* Test results age quickly. The faster you act the more validity and the likelihood there is of you pulling the same again. So don't wait until a whole campaign is complete. Develop a feel for early results and look at the predictive patterns to response. And make early, if brave, decisions.
4 *Don't do what others do.* Test results are invariably very individual. They tell *you*, at a given time, what *your* customers or prospects respond to from *you*. There are inevitably some general tactics and ideas that work well for the majority, but it only takes 51 per cent to be majority!
5 *Don't look for too much logic* behind test results. There's an awful lot of emotion in a purchase decision. The head may be logical and therefore more predictable, but the heart is a different matter. You'll gain some clues by watching what other people test, and then watching later what they use again.

Testing is not a finite act

Nor, whatever anybody or any book tells you, is it a science. To the advertiser, marketer or seller testing is an experience-builder, fine-tuner, a path-finder. And, of course, an extra. Something that classical advertisers don't have — at least in any such positive sense — but which, equally, direct marketers accept and revel in as a way of life. On the one hand, a vital benefit. On the other, a tangled misleading web of confusion.

Grasp its hand. Cautiously. Do not be beguiled by answers it cannot provide. Revel in those it can.

Are you wondering why I talk about testing this way? Seemingly shoving you firmly from behind into it, yet standing firmly in front of you like some traffic cop haltingly presenting his 'no entry' palm-up to you. I think what must seem like a dilemma may actually clarify with four last thoughts which I will run through.

Nothing stands still for long

People criticise testing but they can't resist it. The nub of the criticism has to do with the fact that almost as you learn something so its value starts to fade.

And it's true. All the odds are stacked against you. Speed and courage are the only antidotes. The market is changing. Technology is changing. The competition is changing. Inevitably, what works well in one season, one year to one market in one given situation may not have the same significance the next.

Again, we come back to the advice that says test the biggest, the most significant things, for these are the more solid, less susceptible to quick change. And make sure you include a control which gives you a yardstick to monitor the combined effect of those changing situations. You will never have enough time, money, or opportunity to test all that you would like to.

Throw away logic!

Testing is an eye-opening process! As you examine the results, you realise that the best thing you can do is throw away logic. If anything, I think one of the things I have learned over the years is the difference between a logical reason and a commonsense reason. Mostly, in my experience, it is the commonsense reason that will prevail.

Two examples: The first concerns a photocopier. It was some time ago but relevant none the less.

The particular copier was a Toshiba product. And one of the first sheet-fed plain paper copiers that shrugged off the old office equipment image. Suddenly, this new-generation machine, as well as being up-to-date, capable and affordable, looked good too. Indeed, it was the first to come in a range of pleasant colour schemes and had all manner of innovative gadgetry hitherto unavailable — self-diagnostic winking, LEDs, a digital touch-key pad, electronic readout display, being just some of them. The client noticed a common thread. Not only were his new machines bright colourful attractive machines, but the gadgetry was colourful too. So it seemed logical that it would benefit from being displayed and sold in colour. For the first time he briefed us to run his mailing using four-colour process showing the product off to its best advantage.

Not I! I've been caught that way before. Logical thinking! So I suggested a test. Not frightfully scientific, but a test none the less. We would divide the 40 000 mailing into two lots of 20 000, half using four-colour process, the other half exactly the same but replacing full-colour pics with ordinary black and whites. Reluctantly the client agreed to go ahead on this basis, although to his mind it was a foregone conclusion. A colourful product needed colourful selling.

The mailing went out. The replies came in. They were divided into piles. Four-colour process v two-colour. When all were in, the count took place. Exactly the same response! We would have to wait. A few months later when all the sales leads has been followed up we would be able to see if, although the response was the same, his logic was correct that those who had enjoyed the colourful presentation of the colourful copier would be more likely to buy.

We waited. Then, months later, the results were gathered and analysed.

Response, the same. Conversion, the same! There was absolutely no difference at all. Except a small lead in conversion rate for the black and white version. This, I determined, would have to be re-tested. No point said the client. By this time everybody's machines were just as colourful. It was no longer an issue. Let's go down and look at his new baby. Just in from Japan. Bristling with new features! And off we went again.

But don't write this experience off. A definite lesson was learned and a definite result achieved.

For the fact is that the two-colour mailings were substantially cheaper to produce. And they pulled the same response. So they provided a lower cost per response. And they converted as well, if anything slightly better than, the four-colour version. Ultimately then they were significantly more cost-effective.

The client did not have to go to the expense of full-colour mailings for some time until, interestingly, what changed was the noise level in the marketplace. Everyone else was using colour so the client felt obliged too! Designers and print salesmen have a lot to answer for!! Try it yourself.

My second example was to turn out to be a personal, pleasing and profitable experience. I went price testing. Again it was less than scientific, but more than worth it.

In the late seventies I launched my 'Secrets of Effective Direct Mail' conference series. My first test was to see whether I could do it — whether I could fill a room of people paying money to come and watch and listen to me doing it. I decided to hold a provincial dry-run.

I needn't have worried. 160 per cent of seats sold. And no one complained. In fact, I got several nice letters afterwards. I decided my dry-run had been a success. I would move to London. Commensurate with the new swish venue, sophisticated equipment and staffing levels, I doubled the seating capacity and, cheekily, doubled the price.

The response went up. Very nice too, I thought. But since the venue was working well and I was comfortable with the numbers, I decided to trim the response a little, stabilise audience levels and boost profits by upping the price. Never one to mess around I stuck another 50 per cent on and prayed I hadn't killed the goose that laid the proverbial.

The response went up.

Interesting that. But really quite a shame that now, less VAT, I had arrived at a psychological price barrier and I was beginning to look really quite pricey compared with other conferences.

So it was do or die. Stick it out. Or crash through the price barrier like Concorde through the sound barrier. Boom. On went another 25 per cent. Out went the mailings. Two or three conferences later, I couldn't believe it. The response was still climbing. But more fascinatingly, the quality of delegate was improving too. I was getting more and more senior management and director level. It surely couldn't last. On went another 20 per cent. Finally response started levelling out. Yet interestingly, that stacked up to a remarkable 400 per cent increase in price over a four-year period. An experience which has often led me to suggest clients test putting prices up as well as down. Often any decrease in numbers will be more than compensated for by the extra profits.

But you'll need to do your sums first. I believe my experience was exceptional both in timespan and volume. On the other hand, if you don't turn these stones over, you never see what's underneath.

All things being equal

Remember those words? I last used them to precede the statement from the S and M dept when we were calculating sample sizes together. 'And they never are' was my rather cynical bracketed remark. So I shall finish on testing with yet another cautionary set of thoughts. I do so not to put you off, but to make you aware of the realities.

The fact is you never get the same result twice. And for some reason, as yet unclear to me, response rates out of test always seem to under-pull.

In my experience this under-pull will give you a roll-out result of somewhere between 10 and 20 per cent below the test. I think any number of outside influences as well as timing may cause this deviation. What I can't figure out is why its always an *under*-pull! In Joan Throckmorton's *Mailing List Strategies*, discussing this same phenomenon she ends with this characteristically frank summation, 'A roll-out which is more than ten times the test quantity can be compared to shooting crap for very high stakes.'

So that's where the mythical 10 per cent sample size comes from! Get me the S and M dept right away.

Direct mail is **easy to respond to**

And so it is! You will recall my earlier advice that it is an indisputable fact that the easier still you make it to respond, the more people will do so.

Direct mail, again, has a unique edge. Not only is it easy to respond to, but it can collect orders with cheques or supporting documentation as required. And it can even supply the envelope — mostly pre-addressed and postage paid — as well.

A combination of convenience unmatched by other media even before you add the possibility for direct mail to include a response piece which in every case can have had a great deal, if not the majority, of the 'filling-in' already done.

I recall, in the *Post Office Direct Mail Handbook* (published by Exley Publications), recounting a case history which I shall repeat.

One leading motor insurance marketer obtained dramatically improved results by using the information gained in providing a motor quotation. That's to say about 30–40 per cent of the information needed to be put on the Motor Proposal Form for the motor insurance policy has already been completed at the earlier stage when the responder has asked for the quote, information such as name and address, postal code, type of car, size of engine, insurance renewal date, etc.

The computer was made to print out this information on to a proposal form which was sent back to the prospective buyer with his quotation. Thus, effectively, buying this particular insurance offer became at least 30–40 per cent easier than any other. Moreover, the potential buyer's perception of the proposal form was that it was shorter and less complicated than most — so much of the work had already been done.

For another insurance company I remember laser printing the application to the point where we had even completed, ready for signature, the direct debiting mandate including the applicant's bank account number, bank sort code and branch address. We all thought it was jolly clever! But response exceeded expectations in two ways: orders and complaints.

Of course, we had arrived at the bank information in an innocent enough way, from a previous policy held with the company. Hence such data being available in the first place.

Of course, after the panic, we realised what we had, or rather hadn't done. We hadn't explained.

A simple test in the next mailing confirmed our thinking. No need to spend much time working out the three test variants.

Variant 1 Personalise application omitting any information in the Direct Debit.

Variant 2 Personalise application exactly as before, but with explanation that the form had been completed, for the customer's convenience, from information already provided by them.

Variant 3 A control — exactly as previously.

The result: with variant 2 business levels stayed up where they had before. Complaints dropped off satisfactorily. QED!

Do you want all those replies?

We're back again to the balancing act, Quality *v* quantity, last discussed to do with offers and propositions. Let's just remember the context of quality — will the enquiry convert to a sale, or will the sale stick and not result in a cancellation or money-back claim?

Making the reply tempting will have a strong effect in both situations. Making it easy will too — but it will have more effect in lead generation, unless the mail order purchase is long and tedious, like the motor insurance example we looked at earlier where filling in the application for the prospective buyer cut down their work by possibly ten or more minutes and produced a massive increase in conversions.

The opposite is also true, but a dangerous tactic to tinker with. That's to say, you can decrease the number of replies and increase the quality of them by making it *harder* to reply.

As a general principle, I do advise you to come at this one as a last resort. So much of the profit or loss lies in the middle ground. Earlier we divided the recipients of direct mail into three and only three types — those on whom your mailing is either *wanted, wasted* or *working*. What I describe here as the 'middle ground' is precisely those we identified as the ones on whom our spell is working. We could win or we could fail. But because there are so many more of these than 'the wanteds' — those who want what we have to sell anyway — it stands to reason that their interest level is flimsier. Make it difficult to respond in any way and you will lose these in droves.

So do be very sure of your economics and targets before taking out response cards, special offers and other forms of incentives. And be wary of tales from the sales force that the replies are rotten quality. It's just as likely to be the salesperson who is rotten quality. Look at the figures right across the board.

As we draw to the end of Chapter 6, what have we learned?

As main topics we've looked at six distinctive qualities — some of them partially or entirely unique to direct mail. But remember the crunch. Most people do not choose direct mail because it offers any single one of these. Direct mail is rarely so weak. More usually, advertisers are obtaining a special power each and every time they use direct mail.

Every time they exploit and profit from the dynamic combination of *all* six. The benefits of being selective, reactive, creative, *and* that it is personal, can be tested and it's easy to respond to.

Unbeatable!

JFR's box of tricks

And they're all on testing:

- *Confidence levels*   If a sample size is looking a little hard to deal with, take this tip. In the testing section we discussed error tolerance as being a plus or minus factor and I made the point that few people worry about the plus part — more response than forecast!

   So let's go back to the statement issued by our friends in the S and M dept.

   In this example, all things being equal, if you adopt a sample size of 'X' the response will fall between ±Y per cent of Z per cent (say) *95 times in every 100*.

   There's the trick! 95 times in every 100.

Statistically, again we're dealing with a plus or minus. That's to say the remaining five should divide themselves equally — half under target, half over. Since we won't worry about over-performance we can assume that our 95 per cent confidence level is actually 97.5 per cent. Do you need it so high? To get 95 per cent on this basis you could scale down to 90 per cent and use the constant of 2.71 in your calculation. Every little helps!

- *Keeping testing costs down* When testing, it has been advised that the variants — whatever they are — will give their best results when woven into the package.

However, on a practical level with testing this isn't always possible. Thus a primary level of testing can be developed to give what one might describe as 'soundings', perhaps to rule out non-runners rather than precisely identify winners.

For this process, print changes should be kept to the minimum. Or even dropped in as 'over-prints', after a bulk run of common material.

Cheaper still, the test variants can be strapped to a standard package. It is common practice, for example, to merchandise a gift in all items — illustrated and sold throughout the package — on the envelope, letter, leaflet and response device, perhaps even in a separate gift flyer too.

To obtain 'soundings' one can scale this down. Perhaps the envelope generalising to 'FREE GIFT' details inside' or even 'MYSTERY GIFT — revealed inside'. Often you can refer to a 'gift' in other print items too. In this case my suggestion is in two parts. First, carry a full special gift flyer which thoroughly merchandises the different gifts on test. This will become an easy production task since all other items can be common, one simply encloses a different gift flyer into each package. A token or stamp to be lifted from the flyer and stuck to the response device will even enable that device to be standard too, and effectively codes it to provide your results data.

My second piece of advice is: bear with the costs of a changing *response device* anyway. I suggest this for two reasons — primarily because it's a very effective place to merchandise such offers, but also because it acts as a 'code' in itself.

Whatever you decide to do, if you are considering this very economical primary testing idea, beware that you don't overlook the need to maintain the 'randomness' of the sampling. The most sensible way to achieve this is to pre-sort the addressed items into the samples segments prior to enclosing. Otherwise you'll have the miserable task of enclosing one varying piece of each of the test alternatives in rotation. Not so easy or controllable!

The additional benefit to this 'economy sounding' method is that one can group varying print items onto a sheet as shown in the figure below thus economising on print too.

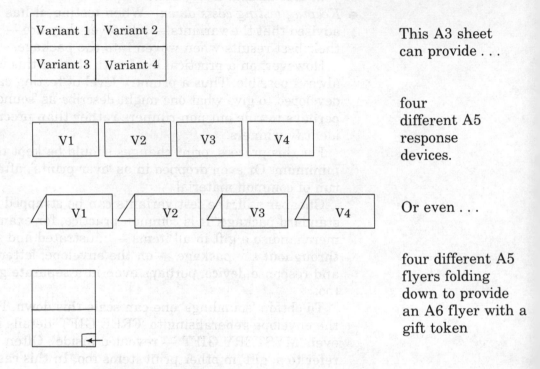

Variant 1	Variant 2
Variant 3	Variant 4

This A3 sheet can provide . . .

| V1 | V2 | V3 | V4 |

four different A5 response devices.

| V1 | V2 | V3 | V4 |

Or even . . .

four different A5 flyers folding down to provide an A6 flyer with a gift token

- *When you bring a new offer on test* go back and test an old one too. That means test all three — the new, the control and the one that was the previous control. You'll be surprised just how often 'oldies' can be goodies too.
- *Don't overdo your testing* Over-enthusiasm and over-ambitious test programmes are bad news! My experience suggests strongly that the thirst for knowledge is great until you get the hangover of confusion!

7 There are only **seven** kinds of direct mail—

It's either . . . .

Aimed at:

- **consumers**
- **businesses**
- **professions**

To achieve:

- **mail order**
- **lead generation**
- **response fulfilment**

or — not actually a mailing at all — it's . .

- **house-to-house distribution**

For many years I have advised that no major difference exists in creative strategy or tactics between direct mail, whether addressed to consumers, businesses or, indeed, the professions. As I have suggested in earlier chapters, by far the most common factor is that every mailing will be received (and if we've got it right) opened and acted upon, by a human being. Businesses or practices do not make decisions — people do.

It's a far more profitable experience to examine the few real differences that do exist. I shall identify these areas as follows: type and level of reader; environment; method of opening and handling; decision process; and buying process. In order for you to assess what effects this will have on your approach to mailing, we shall examine the difference between the three types of mail in the light of each of these areas.

To start with, let me introduce you to a short list I've been using in my conferences for some years. It was first published in the *Post Office Direct Mail Handbook*. It's really quite an interesting little resumé that's had a fair amount of exposure already but in case you haven't seen it before, you might like to check it out.

	Consumer Reader	Business Reader
Type	Human	Human
Failings	Human	Human
Weaknesses	Human	Human
Strengths	Human	Human
Motivations	Human (i.e. greed, lust, self-improvement)	Human (i.e. greed, lust, self-improvement)
Desires	Human	Human
Objectives	Human	Human
Sex	Select one of two	Male predominance decreasing
Language	Normal	Normal with added specialised or technical terms
Purchasing power	Major decisions shared with partner	Major decisions shared or discussed with colleagues or professional advisers
Posture	Generally homely and leisurely	Generally businesslike
Environment	Home	Work
Interests	Self, family and homely things	Self, business and company things

Now that's quite interesting, isn't it? It focuses mostly on those areas we identified earlier. Environment, decision process, etc.

How do **consumers** deal with their mail?

In all manner of ways. At all manner of times. In all manner of situations!

There's no way we can guess what's happening in their lives — who's in tears, whose father died last night, whose garage caved in. Or who's getting married today, starting a new job, celebrating their fortieth birthday.

But we can find some fixed points among this mass of people. Particularly in the way they actually open and set about devouring their mail. Impossible as it is to predict whether each household is a stacker or a sorter. Stackers tend to sit down with the post and plough through from top to bottom. Sorters divide their post into piles for the various family members. A very few couples choose to 'share' their mail and the first one there opens it!

At this point it should be said that millions of households do not get piles of mail. They get just one or two items a week. So one division they will make is to distinguish between The Bad and The Ugly. Because so much direct mail is bright and friendly, colourful and interesting, often with advice or stories or information that are quite a good 'read' anyway, you'd be surprised just how many people actually will categorise you as 'The Good'. Into the bargain, these people look forward to mail.

So we have identified one common point of the handling process.

The start.

You missed it? Were you paying attention?

It's the name and address block.

Who's it for? Me or one of the others? And, most important, have they spelt the name right? Have they got the address right?

That's why envelope overprinting is so popular in consumer mail. It's a great place to start the sales process. Or arouse curiosity! And think about it, imagine the space as a poster site and you have a choice — a site on Park Lane where lots of people go, or out in some backwoods spot. Which would you rather? Obviously, Park Lane. And that's what your envelope front is. Right around the name and address is somewhere we're all going to go. Park Lane!

The next step is pretty predictable too. Most people, again, once they're holding the envelope in their hands, behave predictably with it.

What do they do? They turn it over. After all, they know the way in is round the back. So there's your next high traffic poster site.

And both of these, strangely, have a quality in common with many posters. People won't dwell there. They're in the process of opening. Time and attention is limited. This is a place for short, simple messages. And as you will probably have observed, a great many creatives choose to use this space to tease, intrigue, or to whet the appetite.

Next comes the moment. When our potential reader is going to draw out the contents and, if we are successful, they'll start to part with their time. At first, often without even thinking about it. After all, there are no other ads fighting for attention. Just you. Solus. And, given a clear run, they'll stay with you until that one fatal milli-second when you bore them or simply cease to hold their attention. Then you've got a fight on your hands.

There are some things against which you just can't win.

Like the baby climbing out of the high chair. Something burning under the grill. The doorbell. I've never heard of anybody leaning out of their top window in response to the doorbell and shouting down 'Come back in ten minutes. I'm just reading this mailing — it's JFR's latest! All about a great new central heating system.'

Once again, we've just walked unsuspectingly past another really important point that's emerging from this short look at how consumers — people! — actually deal with their direct mail.

Here comes a clue — it's one of those luminous bumper stickers you can buy in all card shops these days . . .

Envelope stuffers do it backwards!

This is true. At least the 'professionals' do it backwards. Most people, I mean those responsible for filling envelopes, don't give it a second thought.

Yet since most recipients are going to open your envelope from the back, you'll profit from meeting them turned round to face them with a handshake and a smile.

There are two more common steps before this opening process becomes such a diverse and individual matter that we can no longer keep track of it. But we can still try to control it, as we'll see later. Indeed, building in a clear reading path is an important creative objective.

People don't dip into envelopes, they try to pull the contents out in one handful. This has most significance with larger envelopes. The point being that there is a distinct danger that small enclosures, such as reply cards, may get left inside and therefore overlooked and discarded. So it is best to find some way that small items in big envelopes are either clipped or 'spot-gummed' to a larger item to avoid this. However, it is often a temptation in this situation to build a response device into a large item, such as the last fold of a leaflet. This achieves the solution to being left behind or discarded. But it is well known that separate response devices tend to work better than those built in to other components.

While trying to avoid the temptation to produce an all-in-one style of package, one should ensure that what is there does come out of the envelope in one easy handful and that the more we can do to make that handful easy to manage, cope with and understand, the better. One 'school' tends to profit from the reverse of this advice. It is those — mostly mail order advertisers — who jam pack an envelope virtually to overflowing with a whole gamut of differing verbal and visual stimulations like a lucky dip tub filled to the brim with 'dips' and no wood chips or sawdust to pad it out!

Decisions, decisions! Yes, but whose?

We've seen how with consumer mailings the physical process of opening your mail is a fairly predictable process, normally dealt with by the individual addressee you have nominated. The One Person. However, very often, others in the family or household will get involved in the decision process and you must be sure to include them in the scope of your influence and recognise where this will happen. Therefore, for example, if you are mailing parents about a children's adventure holiday camp, remember to include something for the kids too. Something that will involve them preferably, as well as set out the splendours of the place.

More and more services and products, as the two sexes emancipate, are bought as a result of joint decisions. The days when the Man arranged the insurance and wrote to the bank, while the 'Little Woman' dealt with anything to do with the children's clothes, the vacuum cleaner and food, are mercifully well on their way past. Nowadays many women influence hitherto male decisions. And I'm sure we lads would all agree, the other way round.

There will no doubt remain some bastions of undiscussed decision-making, even about joint matters, but one must be conscious of the changes and how matters like this develop.

For example, it would be easy to assume that men were still the major influence over some purchases. I get about half a dozen or so wine mailings a year (don't ask me why — unless someone has started a new lifestyle database by sifting through dustbins. Now, there's a thought!). I get somewhere near half from those infamous German wine cellars who have just held — or will shortly be holding — a Mega-Mosel Sweepstake or a Tafel Raffle. Yet my wife, who buys over half (but drinks about a quarter!) of our wine, gets not one. Strange since, as a couple, we are fairly typical.

Over 70 per cent of wine decisions in supermarkets these days are made by women. It is, I believe, true that women generally make decisions based more on quality and value than men, but often achieve this by being less brand (or producer) loyal — in other words, more adventurous and less influenced by tradition or habit. They vote, as a recent article on this subject put it so succinctly, 'with their feet and their purses'.

I have decided that brain-death must have occurred deep inside the cellars (or sellers) of Peter Dominic who, for one reason or another over the past decade, must have had my name and address handed to them two or three times or more a year. The result has been not one single contact, at national or branch level, to make some attempt to influence our household's money back away from the increasingly skilfully bought temptations at the likes of Sainsbury's and Waitrose. Perhaps someone will, one day, explain the power of allegiance advertising to them. Or will Sainsbury's, like Marks and Spencer, get there first?

This may be an appropriate time to reveal that at least half the women executives I ask — and I ask a lot! — get infuriated enough to throw out, quite literally, letters that start 'Dear Sir'. Quite right too! One who had taken part in such an 'audience census' was kind enough a few weeks later to send me what she described as 'red rag to a cow!' I know what she means. It read:

> FOR THE ATTENTION OF THE SECRETARY TO THE MANAGING DIRECTOR
>
> Dear Sir,
>
> FEMALE SANITARY EQUIPMENT SUPPLIES

The answer is not, Dear Reader, to add 'or Madam'!!!

If you're reading this book as someone involved in the marketing functions for, say a large building society or an FMCG marketer, your researchers and analysts will already be way ahead of me — as, no doubt, will you! If perchance you are not so lucky to have that level of support and influence — or if you're simply a smaller company without the budget for such resources — then you still need to get it right. But you'll do so — as long as people like me remind you! — probably as much out of 'feel' as you will from hard information.

So I would ask you to mark two points from this to influence your thinking.

The first is to give consideration to who will be involved in the decision to respond to your proposition. The second, in many ways a much larger issue (although maybe not so for you particularly), is the consideration — highlighted by my note of brain death at Peter Dominic's — of the role that direct marketing can, and will, play even in the FMCG fields. This underlines a great deal to do with the changes you will witness and possibly take part in over the next decade plus.

Of all the things you consider, put consideration of the reader first

This statement is equally true of both the consumer and business and professional reader. But needs to be implemented very differently. We are, here, still thinking about the consumer.

I have urged you to think about them, quite literally, *in situ*. To think about their heads and their hearts as well as their wallets!

The last major area in which we need to give them so much consideration is one we have already touched upon. Making it easy to reply, be it by phone, visiting an outlet or branch, or by returning an enquiry card or order coupon you enclose. What do they actually have to do?

Your response to this advice will influence your decisions about design and copy certainly, but also about format, contents and the way in which you use any personalisation techniques.

For example, will you use their postal code to insert the address of your nearest branch or outlet as an option to a postal or telephone response? Quite easily done, and once the programme is prepared, you can use it any time for a multitude of reasons. There is nothing to stop you using laser technology to include even a simple digitised map, if you so choose.

You will need to make different decisions depending on whether you are asking for an order or an enquiry. Both purchasers and enquirers will demonstrate over time an amount of 'trouble' or effort they will go to for you. You need to assess this in order to balance what you ask of them. Will you ask them questions that will help you for the future? If you do, you have the opportunity to help them in the future by heeding their answers and therefore ensuring your communications achieve higher status as 'appropriate advertising'.

My advice is this. Do not cloud this issue — find out how much you can achieve without losing response. Do so all the time in the knowledge that this is a four-cornered fight.

The information you need now, and for the future, are the North and South Poles. The balance of quantity and quality of response discussed previously are the East and West.

The time and effort — or the 'trouble' — that a consumer will go to for you is, in general, a specific capacity. The capacity will increase as the relationship you have with them grows or matures. But it is definitive none the less. As you make things easier in some ways, so you can ask a little more in others. Develop as much of this capacity as possible.

One useful tip here is to put some friends or colleagues through the task of responding. Time them. Watch them. See what they do. Experience what they go through. In the early days of Freefone, for example, it was pretty much a joke that you could spend the same time trying to get through as you could responding twice by post, often including going out to the post-box! Happily it is a different situation these days!

When you have observed your 'trial responders', talk to them. Ask them questions. See if they understood what they were supposed to do, and attend to the problems. Then process their responses, and see whether your response handling system works as fast and efficiently as it should.

As your mailings go out, the continued observance of response handling will provide very useful information.

You will find places where responders 'trip up' because of ambiguous wording, insufficient (or too much) space, or perhaps that they 'miss' bits, often important bits, like their credit card expiry date or a much-needed signature. After each mailing a discussion with those that handle the response will pay enormous dividends. But do be wary of some of what they say.

Often systems or fulfilment teams will suggest things that make life easier or better for them. One I have come across many, many times is the desire to ensure all information for an insurance or finance application is available on one side of a sheet. The 'cost' of saving data input personnel the task of turning it over, is that the application becomes cramped, difficult to understand, let alone to complete. The result is always a drop in response.

How business mail is different

There is one radical difference. Business mail can nearly always be more fun! Not always — nearly always! I think there are two contributory reasons. First, the orders are bigger, ergo the budgets are bigger, ergo there is more scope to be adventurous. Second, with bigger businesses at least, people are not 'playing' with their own money.

I hope that doesn't sound cynical. I'm sure it's right. And the world of business mail is the richer for it. Which probably explains why the instant association with 'junk mail' is a domestic one. Business mail, referring to my comments in Part One may not always be as relevant as we would like, but it is frequently better quality, better produced, more interesting and often more fun too.

How do businesses and business people handle their mail?

In most medium size or small businesses — or even branches of big businesses — the mail is handled in a very similar way to the consumer we have just considered. Probably the single largest difference is that, in the main, the person who opens the envelope is not going to be the one who reads it. Or at least, whom we want to read it.

It is therefore understandable that, at my conferences and seminars, the business mail fraternity are less than impressed with my thoughts on the selling power of envelope messages. Yet test after test with both types proves, in most cases, that this is cost-effective in both areas. Let us consider why.

Undoubtedly, although I have experienced response lifts of up to 50 per cent through envelope messages alone, this is not everyday. They are not generally major response-builders. They are, however, usually extremely cost-efficient. The answer to this apparent conundrum lies in the very low additional cost of printing — or even overprinting — envelopes.

The distinction between those two descriptions is that printing refers to the addition of the message during the making (or actually before, albeit sometimes on the same machine) of the envelope. Over-printing is the action of printing onto made-up envelopes. Both are relatively low in cost compared with results obtainable. Printing, as distinct from over-printing, can cost as little as half to one tenth as much. The printing of envelopes, depending on the complexity of the desired image, when compared with the total cost of a mailing 'in the post' can represent less than a 1 per cent increase in cost. Yet its lifting power, when right, is far greater. And that, of course, is what cost-efficiency is about.

Tactically the envelope can be made to be very important. Yet as I have explained, it can cost as little as 1 per cent more of the total cost. Hence if an advertiser is expecting, say, a 1.5 per cent response to a mailing, and the envelope knocks that up to anything in excess of 1.515 per cent it has cost justified itself. Or put another way — if you have a mailing of 10 000 and you want 150 replies, an envelope message that secures just two more will be a winner. It is not surprising that it nearly always works. It is not surprising that I often describe an envelope message as one of the cheapest forms of advertising you can buy.

Finally on this point, there are other reasons for wanting to print on the envelope anyway. If you desire any of these, then it is entirely possible that all, or a portion of the printing of the message will effectively be free. And we can prefer nothing better in terms of cost justification! The reasons I refer to are:

● the need to put your name or identification on the outside
● the need to provide a return address such as 'If undelivered please return to . . .'
● the need to add a postal impression

The last two of these will be looked at again in the section on postal services in Chapter 8.

You will realise, after this small voyage of discovery into envelope messages, why my views are so clear and unequivocal. Whether you are mailing business or consumers you will, at least nine times out of ten, find a good or intelligently used envelope message will pay for itself. After all, it only has to flex a muscle to achieve your desired response increase.

More than once, even after such an explanation, I have been quizzed again on this by a business mail user. 'How', they ask, 'can this be so if no one but the secretary or the postroom get to see it?' My reply is that life is not quite so cut and dried. Nearly every mailing list comprises a mix of businesses. Large and small. Some have postrooms. Some do not. Some secretaries include the envelopes in the mail they pass through (especially if it looks part of it or is interesting or amusing). Some bosses ask for their mail unopened. The fact is enough get to see it for it to work. Even though that may be because enough is not very many!!

The fact, however, that there exists this 'extra step' in the opening process in so many cases is a major difference between the business and consumer direct mail.

The difference between business language, jargon and techno-speak

Now let's look at language, tone and style. Again, we should start from the same simple premise as earlier. Your mailing should be a warm and pleasant communication from one human being representing one company — that's you — to another human being representing another.

I'm a fairly traditional cove for someone with creative leanings. For example, I prefer to wear a suit and tie to the office or on business. Yet, I go for comfort at home. A more relaxed and casual style. Which is why my wardrobe contains,

like many people of my age and type, two or three pairs
of jeans, trainers and even (a confession!) a tee-shirt
or two!

When people call on me at home, we can talk about kids and
family and personal things for hours. Yet at work — although
personal or non-business subjects like these are often ice-
breakers or parting subjects — one finds the exchanges are
normally shorter. Yet they are still there.

So, similarly, I suggest you draw the distinction between
business mail and consumer mail. It should be more
businesslike. Less informal if you so choose. It, too, should
wear a suit and tie to work. But it should still be just as
personal and human and warm as a communication.

Be clear, however, that the individual to whom you are
writing is rarely different as a person at work than at home.
They may be more formal, adopt a more serious posture, even
puff themselves up a little — but scratch the surface, it's still
them! The same things make them laugh. Make them angry.
Make them despair. Make them take action. Make them
aggressive. Make them buy.

Now a lot of people interpret my thoughts here — about
being businesslike — in precisely the opposite way to the way
I mean.

For example, they assume — particularly for some reason
in relation to length of letters — that to make a letter
businesslike you must somehow shorten it. Or traditionalise
the typography. Or switch to their 'yours of 5th inst.' voice.

Absolutely not.

If you want to be seen as a business stuck in the postwar
forties, go ahead. That's what people will think of you when
you use that sort of style. It's OK to be sincere and true these
days. Faithful dates you a little!

'Oh, I'm long over that. Don't even get withdrawal
symptoms any more!' I hear you say. And yet maybe you will
still find it hard to accept that longer-than-one-page letters
are pretty much the norm these days too.

'Business people don't have time to read all that stuff,'
people tell me. And how right that is. But not because they
don't have the time. Simply because you haven't earned it. On
behalf of housewives and househusbands everywhere, I reject
the implication that someone in a domestic situation is more
easily convinced that they should give your material the time
you want. Indeed, I can see many business people parting
with the company's time more easily than their own. Broadly
speaking though, the yardstick is the same. If you bore them,
if you're not of interest to them, if you can't earn and then

hold their attention, you'll get rolled into a ball and tossed into the rubbish just the same at work and at home.

Send me a golf trolley offer, I'm not interested. Send me a mailing on bench-mounted centrifugal analysis parameter readers, ditto. Mail me anything to do with new database techniques, anything to do with communications equipment, or anything to do with making money and, as if by magic, you start with my attention. The rest is up to you. And it's not different at home with hi-fi equipment, anything vaguely gadgety, or to do with food or wine. I'm yours. To start with. The more you appeal to me, the more time I'll give you, wherever I am.

End of story.

Decisions, decisions. Yes — but how much for?

For the purposes of looking at business mail, I shall need to differentiate between mail order and lead generation. Indeed, many, far too many, assume that mail order doesn't apply to business mail. They'd be quite wrong these days. There are hundreds of companies in computer supplies, factory and office equipment, stationery supplies, etc., who sell very successfully through the traditional mail order vehicle — a catalogue. And many people who, for many articles and services, actually prefer to buy that way. As a secretary of mine put it some years ago: 'I like their stuff, hate their salesman. He's got bad breath, BO, a coarse sense of humour, and for some reason he always calls late in the afternoon when I'm hurrying to get the post ready to go.'

Consumers have been shopping by mail for some time, it's an accepted method. Those consumers who go to work don't seem to have a problem shopping that way for many work items. But more than that, a lot of things are sold by mail order that are not perceived to be so.

In the consumer field, insurance and financial products are the world's largest mail order product. Yet most insurance and financial sellers refuse to see themselves as a partially or wholly mail order business. Charities — who actually have the perfect mail order product — cannot see themselves in that business either. But they are. The direct marketing of an appeal is no different from any other campaign in mail order. The concept of the building of a relationship between the charity and its supporters is very much the same as that between any direct marketer and their customers. The economics are different. There's no product cost involved. The donation, less marketing costs to achieve it and systems costs to process and bank it, is all profit. That is why I describe a charity as having the perfect mail order product. There's no buying or warehousing. No despatch or shipping. No breakages or warranty claims. No money-back refunds or product exchanges or replacements. They are the envy of everyone else in mail order!

In business mail, equally, there are such 'hidden' mail order traders. Their products are books, travel and hotels, lower price consumables, insurance and service or maintenance contracts, conferences, seminars, and so on. In fact, the business of mail order to businesses has been going on for years!

How to decide when to sell by mail order and when to use the salesforce

Where do you draw the line? How do you decide when to sell by mail order and when to sell through a salesforce? And what mix, if you need to do both?

Trial, error and economics will provide the answers. But in both fields, as I mentioned in Part One, there are some surprises — even if they are exceptions to the rule. Christian Brann relates with obvious pride how he was involved in the sale of London Bridge to an American. It was only after the American had bought it, he realised it wasn't Tower Bridge! My own noteworthy almost–mail-order–sale was that £1 million hotel site in the Algarve. In most cases the average order value will be a little less than these two I suspect.

The complexity of the sale, the amount of money involved, and the number of decision-makers (and decision-influencers for that matter) will provide some guidelines. But be prepared for surprises. Mail order, by definition, an order taken by mail (but used with licence to include other non-face-to-face media such as the phone or fax), does not necessarily have to be supplied by mail. PCs, for example, can be, and are, sold through mailings and off-the-page. In this case the equipment can be installed by a local agent or dealer, or sent by carrier with set-up instructions for the buyer.

I remember being approached some years ago by a manufacturer of small hand-held scientific electronic instruments. Although this company made and sold a range of equipment up to bench-mounted, sophisticated hardware costing many thousands of pounds, they had uncovered a market for their hand-held compact items. These were much lower in price. Something around £100. Their salesforce was small and, while it offered national coverage, the sales teams were highly skilled engineers (and therefore expensive!) in their own right.

For the high-ticket sophisticated equipment this was a necessity to serve the market adequately, For the smaller low-ticket sales, it was an economic impossibility. In other words, they couldn't afford to send a sales engineer in to sell one of the smaller products. Their profit was gone before the engineer was more than a few miles down the road. Their problem was two-fold. Would scientists and lab technicians buy by mail order? And if so, would they buy this kind of product?

A programme of testing was developed and happily provided positive and profitable directions. It was fascinating to watch this client develop into the mail order business. Particularly to watch how, through testing, they discovered that the more they used classic consumer mail order techniques, the better it worked. But we learned quite clearly that although '14 days free trial' and 'send no money' coupled with 'no quibble guarantees' and other devices worked well, they had to wear their 'suit and ties' to work too. Pretty soon these mailings were strategically and tactically indistinguishable from consumer mail order packages. But they definitely looked well . . . more businesslike!

One more thought while I recall this experience, since it might be something you could try yourself — to businesses or consumers. The manufacturer arranged for a tele-sales call towards the end of the trial period. This was smart thinking since it enabled the tele-sales operator to:

- Answer any technical points or queries in using the equipment. This improved the 'stick' rate and cut returns by over 30 per cent.
- Go for a second sale. It was surprising how many other people in the same company wanted details or indeed wanted to order based on their colleague's purchase.
- Remind the buyer that there was shortly an invoice to be paid. And check that, if necessary to smooth payment, a purchase order was initiated by the buyer's company

Anyone for TEN-X?

Another interesting by-product emerged from the tele-sales follow-up. It transpired that many of the purchasers of the small equipment were also prospects for the more sophisticated bench-mounted expensive models too. By talking to the purchasers of the compact models, sales appointments could be made for the sales engineers to go in. This resulted in extremely high success rates — once again proving the Ten-X factor. It was much easier to sell to an existing customer. This manufacturer had unearthed a lead generation programme for higher-range models that was effectively better even than self-liquidating, it made a profit!

From your existing sales experience, you will know how many decision-makers and influencers are involved. How much money must be found for the purchase, and how necessary the face-to-face meeting is to the sale. In my experience, if you have not tried to sell direct, you will most likely have an exaggerated view of the need for a sales meeting. So, if you've even the first idea that your product or service could be sold through direct methods, go ahead and explore them. Although the 'strike' rate is lower, so are the costs. But be sure to turn back to the section on economics first of all and do your sums. You may well be very pleasantly surprised. See what breakevens are necessary. Determine how much you will need to spend to test. And don't penny-pinch. This kind of test could change your way of trading for years ahead. And become a huge source of profit.

Even if not, it is far, far better to spend out and obtain an answer you can trust, than to face re-testing because you don't think you got it right. Or find that a large investment in roll-outs, despatch packing and handling systems and staff, etc. is all to no avail. But my worst fear of all is that, through not having used a large enough shovel, you will not dig deep enough to find the gold!

One of the decision factors — that of the number of people who will be involved in a purchase — is something one must also consider in business mail lead generation too.

I made the point earlier that it is extraordinary just how much people expect of a mailing. It is equally extraordinary how often it delivers. Nobody would dream of putting their ad on TV or radio once. Few people display just one poster. Most people appreciate that ads should appear in consumer or trade journals more than once for maximum effect. Yet they send out one mailing! Equally, to sell a major piece of capital equipment which might have productivity, financial, quality control and environmental advantages for the buyer, they send out one mailing to get the salesperson in. Very often it will pay to adopt a multi-channel approach. Mailing to the financial executive with the financial advantages first, and including a brief run through of the others. To the production chief a mailing selling the quality and productivity and environmental benefits — and a brief run-through of the others. To the sales director, we run through the speed, quality and product cost benefits and mention all the others. And so on. Taking each individual potential influencer, reshuffling the benefits for the best priority for their individual interest.

This multi-channel approach accepts that different people in the different companies in your marketplace will buy for different reasons. Let them tell you what they are. So if you get replies from two people in the same company, do just one thing. Put them at the top of the pile! And get round there *fast*.

This system works most effectively. Yet often I see people assuming that one single mailing addressed to 'The Managing Director' will do the trick. It is true that in general things will travel 'down' a company quite easily, yet they find it very difficult to go up. In other words, an item passed down from above — the MD, chairman or their secretaries—rarely gets ignored. The same is not always true in reverse.

I do remember hearing of a US company which mailed junior management about a week in advance of board directors. With utter candour the accompanying letter explained: 'since we will be mailing the enclosed details in a few days to your Chief Executive and his fellow Directors, we felt you might like to return the enclosed enquiry card for advance details. That way you'll have all the data at your fingertips when that memo arrives, or more likely, you get that phone call from on high.' Good old-fashioned blackmail!

Ladies and Gentlemen

In direct marketing men enjoy the company, skills and effectiveness of many, many women. I am on record (well, video actually!) as telling the world that, in my view, women are better at direct marketing than men. Something about their mentality — a great deal of it to do with abundant common sense, sensitivity and intuitiveness. In these qualities alone (and speaking for all *man*kind as you will notice I like to from time to time!) we men can only stand in admiration and respect. No more so than in this world of direct marketing.

I remember in the early days of 'The Secrets of Effective Direct Mail' conference audiences would be 90 per cent men and 10 per cent women.

Nowadays, it's normally 60/40. At least in the UK. Occasionally it's 40/60. But it's not far off half and half. Are women more thirsty for knowledge, or are there more of them in this business? I suspect both! Certainly we have more female business leaders than most industries. I would guess at better than double the average. No wonder, as an industry, we frown on 'Dear Sir' letters! Which is actually my point to you. It's not just direct marketing. And strangely, it's not just men who forget how many businesswomen there are out there, secretaries do it too! And a female tele-sales caller once asked a female executive I know, to put her through to the print buyer, or if he was busy, her boss would do. The lady on the line, a head print buyer, responsible for some millions of pounds worth of print a year, hung up. And who could blame her!

It was, therefore, a relatively rare experience these days when I was able, at a Federation of Wholesalers annual conference a year or so ago, to greet my morning's audience of 150 delegates with complete accuracy and say, 'Lady and Gentlemen, good morning'.

Back to trouble and strife

There is no link to Cockney rhyming slang! By trouble and strife, I'm back to the trouble your reader has to go to in order that they can respond to your mailing.

If you're selling mail order, one difference may be that your customer will need to draw up a purchase order. It is for this reason, that the fax machine is already proving enormously successful. In one test I worked on for an industrial mail order catalogue a display panel about 40 mm deep and 50 mm across was used to provide details of his new 'Fax Orderline'. Over 40 per cent of the resulting orders came in by fax.

Whether for lead generation or mail order the advice I gave in relation to ease of reply is just as valid in a business-to-business context. Credit cards can prove a useful inclusion making payment of smaller sums easy — especially internationally.

Where does the **professional** fit in all this?

Something of a hybrid, with one or two oddities. Doctors, for example, are pretty odd! One of my most successful headlines selling insurance to doctors was 'Are Doctors the sickest people in the land?'!

Professionals as a group are much more difficult to gauge. Thus, the more you can do to encourage any field sales staff you have to feed back information, the better off you are. Here, on one mailing list you can range from names of one-man-bands, to huge practices with lots of staff. Accountants and architects are also good examples. Some published data are available to help you make assessments. Number of partners is one popular, if crude, yardstick.

And what of those who work from home? Doctors must be a prime example of this. Some — particularly urban practices — have clustered together in bright new health centres. Others still use the downstairs front room as the waiting room. And the one behind as their surgery. Ditto dentists, but the proportions are different.

Do we treat them as businesses or consumers?

I find that professional people enjoy being thought of as 'professional'. Most of them have studied hard and long to achieve their qualifications. And many, particularly the successful — and I believe this point to be most significant — are successful in their own name. If most others do well they do it with the spotlight on the company. If you're happy with a purchase, you think well of Boots, Sainsbury's, Marks and Sparks. Not the pleasant young man who served you. His name may have been on his badge, but a week, or even an hour, later you've forgotten it!

Hordes of professional people trade in their own name and are proud of it. So get their name right — but also get their qualifications right. Be aware of the professionals' quirks and ways. Even though consultants and surgeons are doctors to most of us, we insult them by addressing them that way. And be aware too — or maybe I should have said be wary too — of the systems and procedures they have. With the medical field that might be the 'supplies' chain. The buying procedures of the various health authorities and the bureaucracy. It is considered 'bad form', for example, to mail to hospital nursing officers without having first sent details to the supplies officers.

Over at the RIBA, to help architects handle and 'store and retrieve' all that product information, some bright spark invented a filing system which most of them use or refer to. SFB codes, as they're called, are applied to leaflets and product details. Which is why so many publications churned out by people who want architects to specify their goods, print what I would describe as a two-tier rectangular box, top right front of their material. Inside is the SFB code for their product, so it will be filed properly. That's fine if you want your information filed, of course. In direct marketing we tend, as a rule, not to like that very much. Too many of us have found ourselves tucked behind the clock, lost on top of the fridge-freezer and shoved in a drawer in the hall. We prefer action. Will putting on an SFB code get you filed *instead* of acted upon? Possibly even filtered out by some diligent soul before the prospect gets to see it?

You must think about what you want. Get to know the ins and outs of the professional life of a dentist, vet, solicitor and their colleagues before you will sell to them most effectively.

Through the last few pages we've been examining the differences between consumer and business mail. With the exception of the few, mainly practical, points I've made, it has, I hope, become clear that there is indeed very little difference between them,

To understand this point and to gain the fullest appreciation of how it affects and changes traditional thinking, will be of great comfort to those mailing the professions and, indeed, a strategic guide.

Things to know about selling **mail order**

So you've decided to go the whole hog! You want a complete sale. No problem. Indeed I hope you'll already have picked up quite a lot of helpful ideas, thoughts and experiences.

You'll know, for example, that few people go for a one-off sale. You'll have thought about this. You'll be excited at the thought of the TEN-X factor for repeat sales and this will temper your profit targets for the short term. You will appreciate that if you are going to start a long, satisfactory and happy relationship with great profit potential for your business you have to take it seriously. Invest to test.

You will know that what you are going to do is something people do, and have done to them, every day. You're going to sell. They're going to buy. You are aware that while you will sell to them at a distance, you must speak to them as if you were face-to-face.

You must remember that mail order wasn't dubbed 'convenience shopping' just for the fun of it. You have to be convenient and simple to buy from.

You must have the courage of your convictions, to tell the *whole* sales story. Down to the last nut and bolt. You must be warm and reassuring. Include not just every benefit and feature — the sizzle and the steak — but over and above all these, you must add the case histories and testimonials and guarantees that will convince. You must be honest, and make claims and promises you can deliver. If not you will lose money hand over fist.

You must become obsessed not just with the desires you wish to stimulate, but also with the problems, pressures and uncertainties you can cause. How do I pay? How can I find out whether it does this or that? Why can't they do it in blue? Will it fit on the shelf? Where will the money come from? Do they pack carefully? Am I medium or large? Will they change it? Is my money safe? What if I fail the medical? Do they *care*?

A nagging doubt in any one of these comfort zones will lose you a sale.

You will realise that while many so-called experts consider mail order to be a 'numbers' game, it is not. It is a *people business*.

That is one of those gloriously dismissible clichés. I know that. But clichés become clichés because they get used a lot. And that's mostly because of the truth that lies behind them. So when you're selling at arm's length and striving — as I put it earlier — to shorten the arm, there is no better method than a straightforward and open display of utter humanness. That can't fail to make your communication personal. It also has a disarming frankness, and if you can achieve it, a convincing charm. Selling by mail order is a truly fascinating business. Using direct mail in the process only serves to add to the fascination.

But I beg you not to dabble with it. If you're going to do it, do it properly. Take it seriously. Get it right. It will repay you handsomely. Equally, if you flirt with it, you will find it is the fruit machine that's been fixed never to pay out. And each time you pull the handle, the results will be so teasingly near, so eminently achievable next time. With those improvements — or changes — that you'll 'pop the next coin in'! Ultimately it will cost you a fortune.

Generating leads for your salesforce

When I said don't flirt with mail order, I did not mean you shouldn't use direct mail or direct marketing for other things. Indeed, even some of the most dedicated mail order companies are only using mail order as a part of their total business mix. None the less, the two principal uses of direct mail remain that of mail order and lead generation.

A third use, which follows close behind these, is traffic generation. That is the use of direct mail to increase store traffic. It is successful at both retail or wholesale levels but more evident in the retail arena. It is, in application, not so very different from lead generation, the most significant difference being, rather obviously, that the main objective will be to propose a store visit rather than the return of a product or service enquiry. However its mechanics are quite similar. If you are considering one or other of these, my advice is don't. Most times if you are proposing a store visit, it will pay you to offer the alternative of 'sending for details' — and it rarely does any harm to invite those thinking of returning an enquiry card, the alternative of calling in on you.

Like lead generation, you will often benefit from offering the prospect the ability to ring a given number rather than return a card. Certainly, those that are particularly keen or in a hurry will welcome this avenue. Both, naturally, are to be encouraged.

Why is direct mail so popular for lead generation?

The simple answer is — cost-effectiveness. Using a salesperson for what is called 'cold calling' is a very costly business.

Let's look at an example.

The first thing we need to recognise is just how costly a salesforce is. Research carried out some years ago confirmed this. I make this point, not to castigate salespeople as expensive or overpaid, simply to explain that if we can refocus their particular skills on what they are best at, then we shall get a better return on our investment.

The research I refer to analysed the way that salespeople spend their time. A dangerous notion! But anyway, it arrived at the following conclusion:

Analysis of Salesperson's Time

	%
In touch with office	18
Waiting	17
Breaks	10
Travel	30
Miscellaneous	8
Selling	17
	100

These figures as specifics are not important. Whether you, or your sales team, spend 17, 14 or 25 per cent of time in front of prospects and clients doesn't, for the purpose of this explanation, matter. The only thing we need to mark is that these people are only at the skill end — getting in, selling and taking orders — for the minority of their time. And what makes them expensive is their most valuable skill and this is only at work for a small part of their time — most often substantially less than a 25 per cent. It follows, therefore, that what I have described as 'refocusing' their skills at work, i.e. getting them in front of buyers, selling, has to be worth doing.

Subject to cost. Thus a process whereby you can achieve massive sales performance increases has to be worth examining in more detail. And that's what we'll do.

It always rains all day Monday ... and Friday afternoons

The weather obliges because it knows this is peak 'cold-calling' time! So our intrepid warriors of the salesforce set out to conquer the unknown. Trying to get past receptionists who've heard it all before, secretaries who have been trained not to let them in, notices that proclaim 'REPS ON THURSDAYS AND BY APPOINTMENT ONLY'. Disconsolately they leave a hopeless trail of business cards and brochures behind, until they stumble on the one potential buyer who is prepared to give them some time. Prepared, indeed, to see them.

In comparative terms, if we liken this to the loyalty ladder described in Part One, this meeting moves a prospect to a suspect. Albeit, because we've got face-to-face with the prospect our chances of making a sale are improved.

So, in the development of a warm 'suspect' our hero might have made, say five prospective calls, to get to see one on whom he can actually start to weave his spell.

Let's consider the costs of this process. We've had five wasted calls. And one successful one. The wasted calls, of course, since he didn't actually get to see the decision-maker, will be relatively short. Let's assume they have run up costs — salaries and other overheads included — of £50 each. For the successful call, they will spend more time with the prospect moving up their interest level, turning them into suspects, and they'll have more brochures to hand, use their sales aids, possibly try to get the prospect to see a demonstration, visit an installation, accept a trial offer. Whatever. We'll allow £75 for this visit. So it looks like this:

Cold Calling		£
Five 'wasted' calls at £50	=	250
One successful call at £75	=	75
Total		325

What happens next is what we call 'the conversion cycle', the process of calling again on the suspect to close the sale.

Again, these are far more likely to be the longer visit. Often the 'suspect' will start to reveal more information, introduce other people, and be prepared to talk in detail. And negotiations start. It is quite usual for this process to average two to three further visits. For the purpose of this example, I intend to average that out at two and a half visits, all at the figure of £75 that I allowed before.

	£
Costs so far:	325.00
Add:	
2½ further calls at £75.00	=187.50
Total	512.50

That's a lot of money. Yours may be more, may be less. You must do this sum yourself to see how it looks for you.

Next, you can take a look at how it works when you use direct mail to do the 'cold calling', refocusing the sales team on the conversion cycle. This will achieve an additional advantage for you. But we'll ignore that for my first demonstration.

I'm going to use a mailing that will cost £500 per thousand. That's to say we might have mailed 8000 prospects and it cost us £4000.

Our mailing pulls a response of 2 per cent which means 160 enquiries will have cost us £25 each. The salesforce go pounding after the business. They find it's not exactly a bed of roses. Contrary to what all the 'experts' said at the sales conference, not all of these people actually want to buy. Some of them, would you believe, only want a brochure! Let's say that, through sheer hard work, diligence, and genius of course, the salesforce average a one-in-three conversion to sale.

In other words, since we had a direct mail cost per reply (enquiry) of £25 we can reckon that we have a direct mail cost per sale of £75. But that's not all, we still have the sales calls to pay for. These will nearly always be the longer type. They will nearly always be the type that include plenty of free product literature, a demonstration . . . or whatever. In other words, the £75 call not the £50 one.

So let's add those in.

	£
Cost of mailing per sale:	75
(three leads required at £25)	
Now we have to call on the three	
(three calls at £75)	225
Total	300

So you can see that against the cold calling process we have already scored a tiny advantage — in fact, the direct mail method is about 8.5 per cent cheaper. Hardly worth all the fuss!

But we haven't really considered the major advantage yet.

Direct mail nearly always delivers you a substantially better quality of suspect than the cold-calling method. And it delivers this élite level of suspect for two important reasons that have a major influence on the conversion cycle. They make it shorter. More effective. Easier to achieve a sale. The reasons are understandable when you think about them.

1 *The prospect has taken the initiative* You haven't been knocking on the door brow-beating receptionists, secretaries and the like, leaving innocent bodies strewn in your wake as you try to convince everyone that they really should see you. You haven't called, called again, and called again until finally, just because you've got a winning smile and they're sorry for you, or flattered that they merit three calls, they convince someone to give you a minute or two. Which you, cunning fox that you are, get up to seven or eight.

What's happened is that this innocent, harmless, persuasive little number in an envelope has presented itself before the prospect. In the home or on their 'home' territory, they have made up their own mind in their own time — even if you did slide a few temptations in — that they want to get to know more. So you know, on one level or another, for whatever reason, they are interested in what you have to say or sell. So they've asked *you* to contact *them*. Naturally you will get more attention, a more interested and sympathetic hearing. They have demonstrated their interest.

2 *They know the basic facts before they express their interest* Very few people will send back a reply card asking for your 36-page colour brochure about 'water filtration equipment for fresh water fast-moving streams and rivers at under £100 000' unless first they've got such a river; second, it needs filtering; third, they have some influence over, or interest in, whether it gets filtered; and fourth, there's either £100 000 lying in a budget somewhere, or they think it's possible to get.

Very few people will ask you for full details in response to:

Accept your FREE FABRIC SAMPLES and a copy of *HOW TO RE-UPHOLSTER A THREE-PIECE SUITE IN JUST THREE WEEKENDS FOR UNDER £200* — INCLUDING ALL MATERIALS AND TOOLS unless they've got furniture that needs doing, some way of collecting £200 together (or the £17 a month you'll offer!) and the time and the inclination, or a friend or son-in-law, to do the work.

In either case, I suggest our cold-calling hero could make not six, but 60 calls to find such a pearl among the swine. Or needle in a haystack.

In most cases where the initiative has come from the suspect rather than from you, it's an easier sale. (For easier, read more likely to succeed. And with less effort.)

Hence it is not uncommon to see a comparable conversion cycle trimmed — to get back to the example — from three more visits to a mere one or two.

Let's place that scenario into our figures.

If you remember we'd allowed for a cost per suspect identification and first call of £300 against the cold calling £325. So:

	£
Cost of three leads at £25	75.00
Cost of three sales calls at £75	225.00
Cost of one and half calls at £75	112.50
Total	412.50

So in this example, we've a cost per sale of £412.50 when we use direct mail against £512.50 for cold calling. Cold calling costs a further £100!

This, in my experience, is a very modest example. I've often seen this work out and prove through experience to be £200 to £300. Often substantially more. I urge you to work it out with your own figures. And when you do, remember the all important by-product.

Cast your mind back to the Hoke Communications definition of direct marketing.

Remember these immortal words?

'to record names of customers, expires and prospects'

We're in danger here of confusing terminology. Suspects and prospects. So forget the loyalty ladder for a minute — in this context we'll consider a suspect, simply as a 'more interested' prospect.

There are only three kinds of customer in the land

The good news here is that direct mail is a great sales promoter for all of them.

Here are the three kinds:

- Existing Customers
- Lapsed Customers
- Prospective Customers

Your tasks are clear. And direct mail is all set to help.

It can turn prospects into suspects and — sometimes with and sometimes without your help — it can turn suspects into customers. It can go back to your lapsed customers and get them back into the fold with another sale.

And it can go to work on your existing customers either to repeat sell or with customer care and loyalty programmes. Most favour a blend of the two.

Nobody has a problem working out which is the best of the lists. The old TEN-X factor puts the customer list streaks ahead. For second place there's often a tussle — lapsed versus prospects.

And yet you'd be surprised how many throw away their list of lapsed customers. In the States there used to be a dealer who went round buying the old metal address plates and filing cabinets of record cards for scrap when companies went into liquidation. The receiver, looking at the scrap value would virtually pay the dealer to take them away. He took them right around to the competitor companies who cheerfully parted with up to a dollar a name, yielding the smarty-pants dealer often up to 1000 per cent profit.

So this is the by-product I referred to earlier. A name. Not any old name, but someone who at a given time, for a given reason, has 'put up their hand' — that is to say, placed an enquiry with you — and thereby effectively said to you, 'OK. Here I am. Come and get me. I'm interested in what you have to sell. I can probably afford it. And I want to know more.' Or even, put another way, 'I/we could use your stuff. Tell us about it'.

The number of times you will come across a list of people who have expressed an interest in what you have to sell *and* effectively, have shown a willingness to do business with you, is pretty rare. I suggest you take good care of every enquiry placed with you. Preferably go one step further.

Respecting the suspect

From my own personal experience I never cease to be — not amazed, but disappointed and despairing of the number of people who fail to recognise the value, or the cost, of a name. This failure manifests itself in two distinct ways. The first is apathy. Here I speak about the vast numbers of advertisers whose ads carry coupons, but who:

1   Either just don't bother to respond,
    or:
2   Shove the latest brochure in a big brown envelope with a
    compliments slip and a photocopied list of dealers or
    stockists. (Stockists in many cases is a misnomer. As I
    mentioned earlier, if it's a new product, the odds that you
    will actually find one in stock are tiny. This is, I pray, a
    solely British phenomenon. Mrs Thatcher will no doubt
    get round to it at some point.)
    And then:
3   They file the names away in an old shoe box. Of course, the
    cost of putting these onto a computer is astronomical.

People who behave like this fall into one of two types:

● The well-intentioned ignoramus
● The complacent toady

First of all, let's introduce the well-intentioned ignoramus.
    This person knows that couponed ads and mailings and
inserts pull enquiries. What they don't know is what to do
with them and how to handle them. Hence the brown
envelope, dealer list and compliments slip.
    You can toss a coin as to whether this individual will add
the name to a mailing list which will receive boring, trivial
garbage for the next two years (at which point they will give
up wondering why the list is so poor) or nothing will ever be
heard of again (in which case, rather than work out why their
compliments slips don't sell, they will abandon the whole
process as non-productive over the short, medium and long
term and decide this whole direct marketing thing is not up to
much).
    There are at least three well-intentioned ignoramuses at
Polaroid UK. When I enquired recently, I got three packages
in return. The first two about three days apart (national to
regional sales?) and the last about a week later (the dealer
support office?) and I'm waiting the arrival of my details from
the local dealer any day now. You can always tell the dealer's
package as distinct from the manufacturer's. Their idea of fair
play is to include all the competitors' details with yours!
    Now let's meet the complacent toady. This is a classical
advertising 'client'. Something desperately sad happened to
him at the annual sales conference. The new agency's highly
creative TV commercial and supporting campaign in the
national press (colour supps and women's glossies) didn't go
down terribly well, mostly because of that rather vocal

Glaswegian peasant of a distributor who stirred up so much trouble in the bar after.

Anyway, despite all the 'retro' graphics and the Bill Haley music ('We'll start another revival and give away loud check sports jackets, with the brand logo on the buttons!'), the poor old agency ('who took Jenny and I to Tahiti for the shoot') had a bit of a hard time.

That's why, as the conference closed, toady announced that the agency, since the slides for the conference had been made, had decided the ads ought to be couponed and the enquiries passed to the stockists (who, of course, filled the room).

Somewhere in the bowels of the marketing department of Armitage Shanks there's probably a toady. And I have some advice for him or her. Fire your agency.

My personal opinion that the ads stink is by the by. But an agency that is so brainless as to run a coupon across two pages (not even a centre spread — two *separate* pages!) is not only making a fool of itself. It's making a fool of its client. Still, at least they were facing pages.

Whether you like my opinions or not, they make a point. People are not placing enough value on the potential customer's interest in their product. And that is nothing better than an insult to the prospect. Experience tends to suggest this is not good for business. In the section on fulfilment we'll look at some ideas to deal with this. Now, we'll look at what's wrong.

I shall identify the problem thus:

1 Advertisers (and their agents) should realise that what they say might be good and therefore convincing. As a result it will stimulate interest. Hence a 'prospect' will become — in loyalty ladder terms — a 'suspect', potentially, what I am going to describe as a 'key suspect'.
2 Advertisers should make sure they foster readers' interest and move it towards a sale.
3 Advertisers (and their agents) should go to the next stage and let people express their interest (e.g. use a coupon). And return the compliment by treating it with respect.

Meaning that the expression of interest by a reader is the ultimate accolade for your advertising. It means it's working. It serves as recognition of your efforts. See it as such. Be grateful. This approach should help both with the well-intentioned ignoramus and the complacent toady. The ignoramus, being well-intentioned, can learn and therefore become well-intentioned and informed. The complacent toady will feel the benefit as his career flourishes from the re-

channelling of his toady-power on the source of all power —
the customer. Or potential customer. Those who, bless them,
ultimately pay us all.

Placing a value on a name

Let's stay with the complacent toady. You may have discerned
that this person (I use the term loosely!) and I are not best
friends.

They are complacent for two reasons. First, the ad was paid
for. So they didn't need coupons to justify anything. Second,
coupons are a pain. Bearing in mind the blood, sweat and
tears that went to getting the budget, making the ad and
getting into 'the majors', who needs these fiddly bits of paper
(or these two fiddly bits of paper if you're with Armitage
Shanks Agency!) landing on your desk causing problems? And
the cost! It could trigger a reprint of compliment slips. Not to
mention licking all those stamps. Punters just don't realise
the trouble and expense they put toady to when they send a
coupon back.

If you have even the first glimmerings of empathy with
either selling or direct marketing you'll probably feel heartily
sickened by the last few paragraphs. I can understand that.
You know that if young toady had been instructed to get those
coupons back it would have taken just as much time and effort
as it did to organise the other ads. But also, it would have cost
money. So much per name. And even talking about it in those
terms focuses the mind. £10 a name. £25 a name. It stacks up.
So for toady actually to be getting the names, effectively free
as a bonus to his advertising, makes us direct marketers
deadly envious of his cushy number.

So what is the value of a name? A prospective customer's
name. Well, you can look at it two ways as I see it. First you
can place a value on it in terms of what it has cost you to get.
Or you can look at it in terms of its *potential* value to you as a
new business contact. Let's look at that because, depending on
your product or service, it's quite possible that this could be
highly valuable. Maybe not the first time, but think of it in
comparison to all the other lists you might be tempted to rent
or even buy outright. What has this one got going for you?

1   These people are at least prepared to talk about doing
    business with you.
2   They've made that decision, not on a whim, but after your
    ad or mailing or whatever, has given them some basic
    information on the product(s) or service(s) that you offer.

3 The fact they've expressed such interest suggests:
   (a) they are in the market for some
   (b) they think they can afford it
   (c) they're prepared to think about it now. And therefore, maybe again in the future.
4 Even if they decide not to accept this first proposition from you — it will be much easier to sell something else to someone who knows a bit about you, and who you've already impressed.

So, in the context of lead generation, we start to sift these enquiries and grade them by level and likelihood of sales. This becomes a joint effort between the salesforce (often tele-sales can play a large part in this) and the direct marketing programme controlled by a KSI (Key Suspect Identification) database.

Whether you store the information on a database, a set of index cards or in a 'little black book' is up to you. A database has obvious advantages and can be as basic or sophisticated as you require.

What we are going to do is gather information, record it and use it to manage the sales process — triggering the action we want, noting our progress, monitoring changes or events.

We need the information not only to qualify the potential sale for us, but to give us some 'shape and feel' for the process we shall have to go through to achieve a sale, and the value and nature of what such an achievement might be.

Let's start with the basics of what we're trying to do.

A KSI campaign with regular follow-up mailings

Many companies have found success by dividing their direct mail into two phases. The first is a programme of mailings with the sole objective of identifying named key suspects (often several in the same company) in relation to all the different elements of their product range.

This is nothing more than a sophisticated data-gathering exercise, although some early sales will naturally accrue. Responses are then fed into a database which is used for highly specific and segmented mailings. Also, the list is used for calling purposes by the sales and tele-sales forces. The result is a well-integrated programme offering a valuable source of specific promotional opportunities.

Next we have to decide what to do with the data. Or rather, how we're going to use them and when.

I can't really help with this, other than suggest for you the scope of your thinking. What you must look at is the kind of process that creates a sale for you. What steps it goes through. Define the full task. If differences exist, identify them. Do big companies buy different things and differently? Do you have a product with after-sales potential? Can you reckon on a salesperson making the sale, and tele-sales tackling after-sales? What will that do to the relationship? How can you monitor success? How can you use the computer to identify purchasing patterns and inform you when they vary, up or down? Should there be a credit control function built in?

We want to combine the unique power of closely targeted direct mail in support of a well-informed salesforce, who have everything at their fingertips.

The essence of this system is that it recycles information normally forgotten, overlooked or ignored, but which is very useful commercially. The salesperson will only *rarely* make cold calls. The computer-based system will fully occupy his time with far more cost-effective and far more profitable work. Over and above that, it drastically cuts the overall paperwork and involvement.

You have to consider a number of variable factors in the equation which is used to determine the ultimately cost-effective use of your budgets and resources.

Identified, these are:

- Response rate
- Cost per response
- Conversion rate
- Cost of conversion
- Resulting cost per sale
- Repeat sales/after sales potential
- Length, depth and profitability of potential relationship

What you must discover is the optimum permutation or balance of those variable factors in your own particular case. You must consider these in the light of the size, nature and ability of your salesforce. You must reflect the (possibly changing) emphasis on the need to sell particular products or product ranges at any given time. You must remain flexible enough to cope with opportunities that arise from time to time in the marketplace (i.e. competitors going bust; competitors' new products coming on the market; your own product development or other changes in marketing objectives).

When you have a clear picture of all of these you can start to define responsibilities and tasks, who makes decisions and what the review and reporting procedures will be.

Let's clarify this whole concept with a typical — if simplified — example.

Step 1   KSI mailings go out inviting a response of two types. One on a specific product. We'll call these category 'A'. the other more general — 'please let me have more information about . . .' These are category 'B'.

Step 2   Response details go onto computer and enquiry is logged in by type.

Priority goes to those asking for specific product details. Tele-sales will make sales appointments using VDU diaries of sales reps' calls and times. Appointments are passed to reps. Computer logs that it needs a report within, say, 48 hours of visit.

Tele-sales now also follow up category 'B' aiming to convert some to 'A's in which case they make an appointment.

In either case tele-sales could ask for some supplementary information.

Step 3   Category 'A' are visited. The sales personnel are briefed and provided with a form (not to be completed in front of the suspect) upon which they record as much relevant detail as possible — size, number of employees, turnover, branch or subsidiary addresses, contacts and positions. Even, as I have seen in Sweden, down to details of how to get there. The computer will ask for a report within 48 hours of visit.

Category 'B' are mailed. Details are recorded of date despatched and material sent. Computer requires tele-sales follow-up report inside five working days.

Step 4   Data input and review. Sales supervisory level, having got the resulting data up on the machine, now run through the printout of *each* individual case to agree next step.

Action is decided — visit, call or mailing. Date is decided. Individual responsible is decided. And so on.

You can gather from this example how the database can now start to drive the sales effort.

Sales calls reminders are brought up weekly for the field force. Complete records provided together with the next report form. Tele-sales, likewise, get their list — complete with numbers, of course. A steady stream of category 'B' are re-approached.

Next the mailing programme can be shaped, now based on all the data you have gathered. So you won't send out any information they've already had recently. You won't approach them and tread on anybody else's toes. You'll be running a tight, organised, well-informed and highly effective sales effort. And this will be so because the KSI system of two-tier approaches — one to get the response, one to gather information and support the sales effort — provides the following clear benefits:

For sales personnel
1 Focused use of skills
2 Team spirit (achieved through highly integrated work)
3 Improved effectiveness and sales volumes
4 Improved organisation, efficiency, information and back-up
5 Simplified reporting

For sales supervisory
1 Improved application of resources, human and computer
2 Intelligent and informed tactical decision-making
3 Tight management
4 Simple, effective review procedures by suspect, by suspect type/area, or by sales person/group
5 Hitherto unequalled control of the team

For sales management
1 More accurate reporting, and (because much of it is machine-based) as frequently as required or on demand by individual group or region or suspect or sales force
2 Exceptional control
3 Improved decision-making
4 More accurate targeting and forecasting

Often visions of life where the computer rules develop when the mind starts to play with this concept. They should not. The other nightmare vision is of the sales team disappearing beneath a mountain of sprocket-holed, fan-folded paper spurting out of a crazed printer. Forget it. This process can actually *decrease* paperwork.

It would also be possible to conclude that suddenly the poor unsuspecting salesperson is going to become a 'Shoestring' type sleuth going round filling in forms and asking questions until the sun drops below the horizon each day. Of course, we know they'd never do it!

First you must remember that we gradually build up the information on file behind each suspect and customer record.

We don't suddenly issue the salesperson with a 24-page three-part NCR set to complete!

But there are times when they can make valuable and productive use of moments which are often wasted. For example they can gather information:

1 About names, branch details, telephone numbers, etc. in reception while waiting to see the suspect
2 While holding on the phone, switchboard operators love to chat. It is a great opportunity to ask 'How many people are working in your Slough building?' Or 'By the way, can you tell me the name of your purchasing manager/chief accountant/office manager?', etc.
3 Just after the visit, back in the car, is the perfect time to note details of follow-up action required, products discussed, date of next visit, etc.

So you see, it really is a question of training people to manage their time and opportunities effectively — by using *pre-filled documentation and input form design*.

It is possible to reduce radically the effort required by the salesperson in at least two ways:

1 The document generated by the computer will have as much information from the file as possible already computer printed on it.

    The salesperson will never need to dig out phone numbers, will rarely need to look up details of previous sales, will not need to search files to see if there is someone else in the same building worth a visit. They will be *given* all that information.

2 Intelligent form design will ensure that they have only the very minimum of writing to do. Rather than make them list, for example, the products that any given suspect is interested in, they need only tick the box or boxes from the printed list.

    Also it will not be necessary for them to provide complete name and address, etc., if the contact changes they would simply correct the computer-printed details on their call sheet.

    Note: One valuable benefit of this system is that you stand to suffer a lot less damage when a salesperson moves on to another job.

The role and type of direct mail to use in a key suspect identification project

As we have seen, the role of direct mail in this is dual. To reiterate:

1 To scan the marketplace, seek out those with a predetermined (by you!) level of interest in what you have to sell either immediately or in the future.
2 Once the key suspect has been identified, to maintain communication and keep them informed, but more important to re-approach and rescan this sector of your market to inspire, or to pick up the first tell-tale vibrations of a sale.

I have a suggestion or two. Based again on my own experiences. I write them so that you might consider them first. Not because they are, by any means, the only things to do to get people onto the database — the real task of Key Suspect Identification.

Try a mix of two approaches and vary them to find out which is best, if one or other, for you.

Approach 1   Have a series of general across-the-board mailings for use in the marketplace.

Approach 2   Have a series of specific product mailings which can be used as 'carrots' to pull in the leads — in this case leaving salespeople to expand the product range face-to-face with prospects.

The specific product mailings, while being comparatively more expensive, would mail only to selected segments of your market. These could promise higher responses and possibly better conversion rates too. Equally, they could also represent a more limited sales opportunity for your salesforce.

Once you've got your key suspects onto the database, I would suggest the following:

1 Encourage personality-based relationships, multi-level relationships — Jacqui for tele-sales, Elizabeth for visits and Jane for technical support is quite acceptable. Just as, at my local car dealers, it's Colin for sales, John for service and Chris for favours!
   However, the roles must be clearly defined. The suspect, while feeling they can approach any contact for help, should know who looks after what.
2 Extend those relationships across the media. If you're going to send a mailing to certain suspects on a technical aspect let the technical contact sign it (*not* write it!).
3 Go for variety — that's to say, don't let your mailings become too 'samey'. Add a bit of spice and pace into the programme. And now and again go for the throat. In other words, don't get so wrapped up in namby-pamby soft-sell 'human interactive communications', that you forget to

ask for the order. No single type of mailing pulls better in this situation than what I call 'The Flavour of the Month'.

Focus all the elements of marketing on a pre-matched set of suspects and products for a period of intense sales activity. Thus a particular product or part of the range is highlighted by:

(a) some exceptional offer or promotion — often a reduced price or introductory offer; coupled with
(b) a mailing to carefully identified sections of the market; coupled with
(c) an incentive-based motivational thrust by the salesforce to pull orders, concentrating on the chosen product(s).

Don't overstep the mark

Moving back to the more general topic of lead generation, I would like to pull back a thought. Underlining that there should be a quite distinct definition of the role of your direct mail and the role of your salesperson or device.

To generate an enquiry is about priming the suspect for the sale. Benefits achieve this, *not* features. Your job is to get the salesperson in front of a warm suspect. Someone who is interested and wants to buy. Their job is to get the sale. They are distinctly different objectives and will be achieved by different methods.

You need very much to experiment to find the right balance of quantity and quality. And to understand the long-term economics. For example, the key suspect identification concept is a long-term investment and pay-back. The reward is effectiveness. But if you've got 500 units on the shelf and they've all got to move in the next six weeks, it's not for you.

The other thing to ensure — whatever decisions you have made about methods, processes and approaches — is that they all move in the same direction and therefore pull together. This is as important in long-term strategy as it is in short-term implementation. Maximum benefit will accrue from your segmentation of the market, the propositions that you put to each segment, and the sales case that is put to the individuals that make up that segment.

I have spent some time with you on lead generation. I have done so because it is undervalued, misunderstood and worthy of a great deal of care and attention. It is my view that it is used far, far too often in a tactical rather than a strategic way. As a result its *true* potential is never uncovered.

How to make fulfilment achieve exactly that

Fulfilment is the term used to describe the action of responding to a response — fulfilling a request for information or, indeed, fulfilling an order.

For these next few pages we shall concentrate on the fulfilment of requests for more information, or fulfilment as the second stage of a two-stage sale.

First, some advice for those who have nothing, or apparently nothing, for a product! I think particularly of finance companies, building societies, insurance companies and to some extent charities with membership or subscription renewals. Those kinds of people whose 'product' is not in a box, three-dimensional, will not grace the home or office, be seen or felt or used regularly — but is still very often quite pricey or a major outlay. And who, equally often, send out as the result of an order — never mind an enquiry — the most appalling, flimsy and often incomprehensible set of worthless-looking scraps.

They've gone to enormous trouble and spent often sizeable sums of money to get a customer on the books. They've convinced some poor mortal to part with £15 a month for the next 20 years and what the new customer receives is a computer-printed piece of 'systems' paper telling them, very often, lots of negative things. What effect does this have on the recipient who has just parted with an amount that will ultimately stack up to a spend, at £15 a month for 20 years, of £3 600?

With many financial products and services there is a mandatory cooling-off period. Or, at least, an opportunity for the buyer to reconsider. It is, therefore, imperative in my view, that three things should happen:

1   The 'product pack' should confirm the wisdom of the decision. Not just to buy — but to buy from you. In other words, it should resell.
2   The 'product pack' should evoke confidence, but also look and feel worth the investment. It really does cost so very little in relative terms to make a policy, or savings plan or loan document look important and worth the money.
3   The 'product pack' should in some way be made useful and encourage the relationship. The best way to do that — encourage the relationship — is to start the next sale.

Now, back to fulfilling requests for information or fulfilling the second stage of a two-stage sell.

Most of what is said elsewhere — tactically, strategically and creatively — applies to fulfilment packages. They are, after all, only a mailing of a different sort. And the first, often overlooked, difference is that they are more important. Because, as we have come to recognise, they come after you have spent good advertising money stimulating the interest, and because they go to red-hot prospects. People who have taken action to demonstrate their interest in you by making contact with you. This is your big chance to make a sale or set one up for the future.

You must take as much time, trouble, effort over the fulfilment — in many ways more — as you did over the original advertising.

Here are the steps you should take:

1   Think about what they want   Yes, they want more information. But what else? Inspiration? Reassurance? Advice? Help?

Within the confines of what you can afford you must give them all of those things. But you must not stop there. You must offer them more. By phone. By mail. By visit.

Or at a nearby outlet.

You must be felt to be caring, interested, understanding, and above all, approachable.

2   You must think about what *you* want   But from the recipients' point of view. It's no good just plonking a confusing mass of information in front of them. Think about how to present it in a clear, logical, convincing way. Use your accompanying letter to lead people, not just through the sales story, but quite literally, to lead them through the materials you are sending.

Also, think about what you want in terms of their next response. And sell that idea to them. Make a proposition. Describe the action you want from them and justify it. Give them reasons to do it. And in terms of taking the action you want, achieve these four ideals:

● Make the action attractive
● Make the action sensible
● Make the action clear
● Make the action simple

And whatever else you do, don't forget to start by thanking them for contacting you!

House-to-house, door-to-door, there's another type of mail

The Royal Mail call it HDS — Household Delivery Service. Most of the other contractors call it either house-to-house or door-to-door distribution. It's a business that's changed a lot over the past few years. Although I'm bound to upset someone, let's divide the main sources into three types: the pro's, the pro-ams And the rest. Taking them in reverse order. The rest run from doing a deal with the local newsagent, Boy Scout troop, etc. and upwards from there. It's so often the cheapest. And notably, therefore, the least sophisticated and also the riskiest. You're probably way ahead of me on the risk. Dumping. The artful practice of 'losing' a few thousand leaflets, saving leg-wear and making a dishonest quid or two.

The next two categories have, with varying degrees of success, built-in fail-safes and guarantees for their clients. Mainly through back-checking and field supervision. The pro-ams won't like the title but in many cases it fits none the less. Not for all, but for many. These mostly comprise the publishers of freesheets and the rash of quasi-newspapers and property weeklies that are about.

I call them pro-ams because their primary concern is their publication. And distribution work is an add-on, quite a profitable one.

There is a movement among the larger and more established groups to consolidate and sophisticate this service. The problem being, for the larger non-local advertiser, that their spread is often patchy. And their workforce young — mostly very young — and therefore somewhat fluid.

At the top end are the pro's, mostly independent contractors. Some have their own field staff, whereas others contract staff as the workload requires. At 'crew' level — the crews are the actual distributors — one often finds the same crews making themselves available to different operators. However, as the quality is dictated by the planning and field management, having experienced crews is a bonus, but it is worth checking just how far down the scale the 'tied' management extend.

The larger national distribution companies now offer most of the targeting systems available to consumer mail users — Acorn, Mosaic, Pinpoint and the like.

Royal Mail's Household Delivery Service is unique in three ways. Whether that makes it good, bad or no different is something you should decide for yourself. Combine the results of testing and dealing with the people and networks concerned to see how it works for and with you.

The unique points in relation to the Royal Mail I wish to mention are, first, that it is for the main part delivered with your mail. Some advertisers have found this an advantage. Some even a creatively exploitable advantage.

Next, it is both discriminate and indiscriminate. It is bookable by postcode areas — and in some cases I have heard down to individual postman's walks. Although I would be surprised if this was something they wanted to encourage or, for that matter, required by many.

It is at the time of writing indiscriminate in that, if one is dealing with an area that includes business letterboxes as well as consumer letterboxes, both will be included. Most other contractors do not, as standard, include businesses. Depending on your product this may be worth considering when selecting either areas or contractors. Although naturally, house-to-house is regarded as a consumer medium, I know of some companies who have used the Royal Mail service to cover industrial estates, business parks and high-density business areas such as shopping precincts and town centres. And reportedly with success.

Lastly, and again at the time of writing, the Household Delivery Service does not surcharge for rural areas which other contractors may, if indeed they cover them at all. The Post Office, of course, maintains its service to cover all delivery points and therefore does not penalise those who wish their coverage to include outlying or extreme areas, or indeed those who simply wish their coverage to be complete.

Additionally, it has been found that mail order to such cut-off or far-out-of-touch areas is very effective.

The Royal Mail deliverers — postmen and women! — seem to have smaller bags or less capacity than the others. Their service has by far the tightest weight and size restrictions.

Which performs better — direct mail or house-to-house? And how do you find out?

In response quantity terms, direct mail nearly always out-pulls the household distribution method, although to some extent this performance may be affected by one other difference, as distinct from a straight media-to-media comparison. Distributed material, as the present Post Office Act stands, cannot be addressed. Many direct mail users actually put the recipient's address to good use, for example, using a window envelope which reveals the address on the outside when it is printed in an appropriate position on an inside piece. If this is being used on the reply card to make response easier, it can be expected to lift response. This in itself may provide some of the performance differential.

Generally, most regular users of both media seem to expect a response from distribution of anything between one-half and one-tenth of that which you would expect from direct mail.

Once and only once in my career, for a charity, have I been able to push the response level up in house-to-house beyond direct mail in a direct head-to-head test.

However, you must note that I make all of these remarks in terms of quantity of response. And quantity only.

Direct marketing and therefore direct mail and house-to-house too, as we have seen, is not a business that makes decisions on effect. It is effect in relation to cost. All of the various distribution methods I have described to you are substantially cheaper than the regular postal service — as little as one-tenth at cheapest, and a third at most expensive.

You therefore need substantially fewer orders or leads from house-to-house. Remember, however, to include the cost of the item in your calculations. Because the distribution is one-third doesn't mean you can tolerate a one-third response, since the one-third reduction on delivery cost may only make a one-sixth reduction overall. While considering costs, and when comparing this method against direct mail, you should remember that the delivery cost is not the only saving. You also save the addressing costs too!

Shares going cheap!

Another potential, not commonly available in direct mail, is that of sharing with other advertisers for a proportion of the cost. It's certainly worth enquiring about this since it is not unheard of — depending on the subject matter — for shared drops to pull as well, or occasionally better than the more expensive solus drops.

House-to-house can be used for most of the things for which people use mailing — plus two others: couponing and product sampling. Money-off coupons are very effectively distributed this way, with very high returns. And there really is nothing comparable, especially against cost and return figures — to achieve distribution of trial samples to the consumer — accompanied by a next purchase voucher, one can obtain effective measures from the redemption figures.

At enormous personal risk (someone in the industry will come after me, I expect), I must say that the common perception of house-to-house is downwards from direct mail. And just as direct mail has junk mail so house-to-house has doormat debris

Finding the best creative approach for house-to-house

Here we go again! You'll need to test to find out.

Often adapted versions of what works well in the mail will score highly here too. But if you only want to get a sample or a coupon into the consumers' hands there's no need to spend lavishly on the item. To achieve a charity donation, mail order sale or a sales lead, you will need to make many similar creative choices as with mailing.

The two most popular approaches are to follow the principles of direct mail on the one hand, or inserts (as in magazines) on the other. If you are going for a sale or donation, you have the problem of providing a response envelope which for many people dictates 'the direct mail' style. As an alternative, the one-piece mailer can provide the necessary envelope and also do a great job in this medium.

JFR's box of tricks

- *Getting fulfilment packages taken more seriously* Here's an idea that works extremely well — and will hardly set you back anything. No need to test it! Just do it. Depending on the quantities you're dealing with, it can be achieved for no more than the cost of having a rubber stamp made. Or some labels printed. Or even just a small piece of artwork to add to your existing envelope message.

  What you're going to achieve is an instant lift in the prospect's eyes. You'll be better than just another old mailing. People will pant to get inside! You can obviously put a little creative thought into how you do it. But these are the basic magic words that will achieve this extra effect on those who've requested details from you.

  'HERE IS THE INFORMATION YOU REQUESTED.'

- *A lead generation format that works a treat* Although I'm not comfortable with formula-produced creative work, I'm going to pass on one that works most effectively. It achieves the huge benefit of presenting the recipient with a simple package to handle and understand, presents itself in a logical and sensible order, saves money *and* is easy to respond to! All such good plus points that it has a lot going for it.

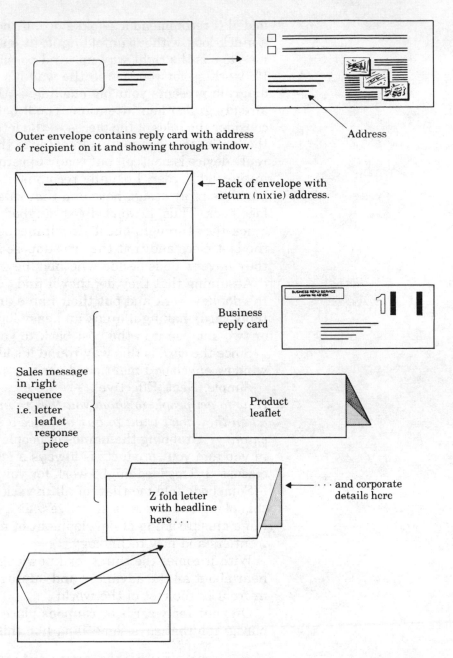

Outer envelope contains reply card with address
of recipient on it and showing through window.

Address

Back of envelope with
return (nixie) address.

BUSINESS REPLY SERVICE
Licence No AB1234

Business
reply card

Sales message
in right
sequence

i.e. letter
leaflet
response
piece

Product
leaflet

... and corporate
details here

Z fold letter
with headline
here ...

Figure 7.1
A simple lead generation format

So you see what happens. The recipients see the message
alongside the window with their name and address
showing through. They turn over (another message if you
want) and open. As they take the contents out, the letter

217

folded (I recommend a Z-fold since, if they do flip it to have a quick look without unfolding it, at least the sales message is the right way up. And possibly there's a strong PS working for you there!) the way it's shown in the diagram presents your big opening — the headline — and already grabs their attention. You'll notice also that, if we consider the roles of the pieces — the letter is the salesman, the leaflet tells you more and extends the information. The reply device is next, all but ready to return — everything is in the right order. I usually recommend a straightforward business reply design here and that side of the card should face back. Thus, it won't divert anybody who's having a quick flick through, but it simultaneously flags that it is the last piece and that they're supposed to reply. Now all they have to do is decide whether they want to.

Assuming that they do, they'll find you've already done the donkey-work and put their name and address on the reply card, making it quick and easy for them to tick a box or two and pop it in the post back to you.

Since the card is this way round it's ideally suited for the window envelope I mentioned earlier.

Simple. Neat. Effective!

● *How to get people to show you they're interested — even when they don't want to buy or place a specific enquiry* Grabbing the names of people who are interested in you and your products is always a good idea as we've discussed. This idea might work for you in this hi-tech age.

Somebody told me that, of all the scientists ever born on this planet, 90 per cent are alive today. This highlights the huge mushrooming of development of new ideas, new frontiers and new technology.

With it comes the thirst for knowledge, and the need to hear about all the advances and improvements. Preferably in front of the rest of the world.

On your reply cards or coupons place a tick box and a paragraph that says something like this:

FREE TECHNOLOGY UPDATE SERVICE:
ADVANCE INFORMATION FOR YOU

As you know, our products and their capabilities are constantly changing and improving to include the very latest technology and design features.

To receive FREE and without obligation a copy of our regular ADVANCE PRODUCT INFORMATION SHEETS, please tick this box.

I recommend you check out the provisions of the Data Protection Act in relation to this, but you're on to a winner if you get it right.

- *One product or more?* A good question and one often asked of me by those planning a mailing. My advice is the same whether you are mailing business-to-business or consumer, lead generation, traffic building or mail order.

    Let's first take out the obvious. I mean you wouldn't have a single product catalogue. And if you've got 1049 electronic gadgets to sell, you're a catalogue whether you like it or not. Let's also take out essentially or near-essentially linked products — in effect a multi-product purchase such as a PC, screen and printer. Or a stereo and speakers!

    I'm thinking more of the people such as an insurance broker — 'Shall I sell life, household and motor? Or everything I do? Should I go *one product more?*' Or an office equipment dealer — 'Shall I hit them with the new compact fax machine, and the colour copier, *and* the new software packages? Should I go *one product or more?*'

    The answer: More. But one at a time!

    Generally my experience has been that it's better to put one clear proposition across. Thus, I would define a motor policy and a household policy as two propositions. Each needs to be sold fully, not one confused with the other. Similarly, the fax and copier, supplies, materials, maintenance contracts, etc., I see as 'bolt-on's' — it's the same sale, just as long as things don't get over-complicated.

    Lastly on that — don't give up on the bolt-on's! Just because people don't buy at the time doesn't mean they won't in the future. So, taking maintenance or service contracts as our example again, those who didn't buy with the original purchase could well find their minds focused and be prompted into action by a reminder 11 months later when the warranty is about to expire.

8 There are only **eight** kinds of direct mail—

You have now arrived at the first of two consecutive chapters where my knowledge and the assistance I can give you is to be used in a particular way. To supplement everything you can discover for yourself. But also to guide and help with the relationships you develop with your collaborators and suppliers. This should assure a greater understanding of your objectives. Your practical production objectives, of course, but also your business and campaign objectives.

You should view each of your supplier's skills, resources and capabilities as a craftsman's toolbox. Whereas you are an architect — the visionary — they are the builders. So the first and most important advice I can give you is to show them the 'models, sketches and building plans'.

The successful production of mailings is only partly about the 'bricks and mortar'. It is also about money. And, setting aside the materials, it is about cooperation, communication and teamwork.

Direct mail is complicated. It involves a whole gamut of skills and many technologies: research, copywriting, graphics, photography and photographic reproduction, typesetting, printing, envelope manufacture, paper manufacturing, computer work and data processing, database or list management and broking, addressing, labelling — manual or mechanical, enclosing, postal sorting, and so on.

It's also still a developing industry. Worse than that, it is a very rapidly developing industry. When you are sourcing and buying direct mail services of any sort, you should recognise this as a risk and proceed accordingly.

You must explain your needs in minute detail and allow plenty of time in your schedules to cope with all the awkward formats and processing involved.

The very first thing a good professional production person will tell you is that it is vital that a production team doesn't control anything other than production.

In my view, it is therefore better for you, as the architect, to stand back a little from the process. By all means understand the production. But don't try to do it.

The business of providing for and supplying the direct mail industry is increasingly big business. And, like the very markets we are approaching, it is de-massing. More and more one is bringing together the skills of highly accomplished, technologically fast-advancing suppliers who, rather than move slowly forward on all fronts, are specialising. And because the business is expanding so fast, they are finding plenty of work in their own niches.

This causes something of a dilemma.

Fifteen or even ten years ago, before we got into this whirlpool of technological progress, I would have counselled you differently. Find a good supplier who is helpful, thoughtful, offers good value for money, the appropriate quality and delivery standards and stick with them. At the pace things went then, that was fine. And common practice.

These days, since the spread of electronic technology is not just fast but across so many fields, suppliers and subcontractors are having problems coping with it themselves. And you know the reason. Write-offs are at the limits. No sooner is a piece of equipment delivered, set-up, tested and running, then ZAP! Not only is it out of date but their competitors now have something that does it twice as fast, and better too!

My advice is spread yourself round a little more. Where you used to have one supplier find two or three. Where you used to have two, now use three or four. Don't worry about them! There's plenty of work around. Your first responsibility is to stay on top. And that means using *all* the technology which is so suited to direct marketing. And to which direct marketing is so perfectly suited.

For those who cannot, or even who just don't like the sound of standing back and not being so involved in doing it, I understand that it's not always possible. For example, if you have a large in-house database operation, they may have to be involved. And if you have in-house print, finishing or lettershop then the same may be true. But with some notable exceptions, these departments will have other demands on their capacity and, more important, other demands upon the company's capital investment.

To take advantage of the latest technology — whether it be for speed, price or a new technique — I suggest you identify not only suppliers and contractors with the flair and initiative to pioneer and develop, but those who are prepared to experiment with you. Whether you are mailing 500 now and again or several hundred thousand fairly regularly.

If you use an agency and delegate your production to them, this last advice is not for you. As an agency client, unless you are huge, I encourage you to place *all* your work through them. Give them freedom *and* the responsibility. Be demanding. Demand results. Demand standards. Demand service. Demand value. Demand dedication. But leave the work to them. They can only do their job properly when they are in total control. If they don't, fire them. But be sure you gave them enough space to perform. That you gave them support, encouragement and thanks, not interference, intolerance and inconsistency.

Making your **plans**

Despite all this talk of technology and pioneering, one part of the production process has remained a stalwart for producers for years. I am referring to an old and tested friend, the reverse timetable. I don't know whose idea it was. I do know that almost everybody uses it. So now we'll run through it together and comment on a few things as we go.

Time, and the management of it, is a perennial problem for anyone organising a mailing. There's never enough of it. And even if you lay your plans well, building in plenty of 'spare' for slippage and proofing, and all the other things that cause delay and discussion and re-thinking and re-organisation — and often invite unnecessary comment, change and procrastination — somehow it nearly always seems to end up with a breakneck deadline or two for someone or something along the way. It's normally the poor old lettershop at the end of the chain that is left with the daunting task of achieving the impossible. They have a very stressful way of working and living!

There are some wrinkles to cope with late mailing panics,

but still maintain a 'landing' or 'drop' date. That's the day(s) you want the mail to be received by the addressees.

For example, you could upgrade from second to first class mail, or from Mailsort 3 to one of the discounted standard class services equivalent to first or second class mail (Mailsort 1 or 2). No problem if the envelopes are going to be stamped or franked. You can even stamp over a previously printed postage mark. It doesn't look so good, but it gets there on time! Failing that, you've a fast label printing job to organise and then arrange to affix them, placing the postal impression label for the newly selected faster service over the impression that was originally printed on the envelope.

The trusty reverse timetable

It would be very nice to be able to sit down, look at today's date, ring everybody up or have a meeting, and then add all the times up and work out when you can get the mail out. Life is all too rarely like that. Nobody wants a potential, or tested and proven, sales boosting idea in three to four months' time, they want it now. Or tomorrow. Or failing that, ASAP, which is adspeak for yesterday! The job of the production team — inside or out — is to do it for you, to achieve the impossible each and every day of their working lives!

Thus we turn conventional timekeeping on its head. And start from the other end.

1 The arrival ('drop' or 'landing') dates

When all is well with the postal service these dates are fairly predictable. Reference to the UK timings for the delivery of the different classes of mail follows shortly.

I'll remind you that business mail is generally best received on a Wednesday, second best Tuesday and Thursday, and worst Monday and Friday. Anyone who mails first class on a Friday is wasting their money — unless they want to get to a business open on a Saturday or arrive on the worst day of the week.

Consumer best days are Friday and Saturday. The rest of the week is pretty much the same. In terms of months, again with some exceptions, the industry seems agreed that the two best periods of the year are mid-January through to the first week of June, and the second week of September through to the second week of November. You will need to overlay onto that your own seasonal aspects.

If you're in mail order, as I commented earlier, short daylight periods or rain, indeed any kind of moderate inclemency weatherwise will help. But just take it as a bonus!

No need for a hotline to the Met Office. Bank Holiday weekends are something of a problem. Some report excellent results, others catastrophes.

If you are a charity, you will probably already know that Christmas and, in Britain anyway, Easter lift responses. But you need to link, creatively or in theme of appeal, to get the best out of it. This seems to remain the same despite the fact that everybody's doing it. Possibly the sheer weight of fund-raising mail at these peak times has a bludgeoning effect on the marketplace, sufficient to provide the response lift it does, regardless of the fact that the 'kitty' is being shared between so many more.

2 The mailing date

No need to explain this! But what should you have taken care of by the time this all important day arrives?

First, you need to have taken care of the postage bill. Lettershops, unless you have an account with the Post Office, will normally have asked you to pay for the postage in advance. If you haven't they are perfectly within their rights not to release your mail.

By now your response procedures must be ready to happen. Whatever they are. Tele-sales must be briefed, rehearsed and standing by. Fulfilment packages must be printed, prepared and ready to go. The analysis procedures must be set up. Samples must have been taken out and placed on file. Advance copies must have been sent to any parties requiring them.

3 Finish enclosing date

My own preference is always to aim to make this at least 24 hours in front the release date — which effectively should mean, in working day terms, that it's two days prior to the date of mailing (i.e. mail 25th, finish enclosing by close of play 23rd). If you are using a new supplier or if there's anything tricky or unusual about your requirements, you can avoid potential disaster by visiting the lettershop on the intervening day and taking some random samples from the finished job, just to be double safe. I warn you now, nothing creates a faster, deeper sinking feeling or is more stomach-churning for client or supplier than to find a problem at this stage!

4 Enclosing start date

Some time during the 48 hours before this date, you must have gone through the coding details, quantity and counts expected and required. And also by this time have notified the lettershop of any special requirements. Such as stop lists (those you want taken out at the last minute). It is not always possible to deal with at this stage, really these are much better dealt with at the time of list preparation.

Often, specials, perhaps for your salesforce or dealers and distributors, are to be included in the mailing. Again, for preference these are better dealt with and inserted into the main listings as a part of the list preparation. But if you want a different letter, or extra or different enclosures inserted, they will need to be kept separate until after enclosing and then merged with the main mailing.

Naturally all your materials will also need to be printed, finished and delivered by this date. If you can arrange for these to be in a good 24 hours in advance, it will enable the lettershop to check properly that all deliveries are full and complete, perform check counts against delivery notes, and assemble and group any variants or segments together. If you have a complicated test structure, allow 48 hours. It is always true that the less time there is, the more errors occur.

The batching and grouping of materials prior to manual or mechanical enclosing is always considerably less risky if codes run throughout the components, enabling the lettershop to check quickly, simply and accurately that given pieces are actually supposed to be with each other and are going into the right envelopes.

Labelling is often carried out in advance of enclosing and if this is the case your label carrier — usually the response coupon, or outer envelope or letter — will be required earlier.

I am a great advocate of pre-production meetings involving as many suppliers as possible, but this cannot always happen. Whatever the case, always make sure that enclosing samples are received from the lettershop for you to check. If you have time, my best advice is to visit them the day before the enclosing starts to 'sign off' an enclosing sample or samples for each and every variant of the mailing. These should be prepared by the lettershop in accordance with their initial written job instructions which in turn should be prepared from dummies which you will have sent to them earlier.

It is too late at this stage to be sitting down with them and showing them what you want. The method I have suggested actually 'proves' their own internal translation of your dummy and instructions. When sending dummies to them, whether printed, made up from proofs, or 'dummied up' from photocopies of the artwork, always send *two* sets of each variation. Use a highlighter pen to indicate variations and notable codes. The first set should be made up as required but left unsealed. The second set arranged to protrude about halfway out of the envelope and should be stapled through each corner effectively holding everything in place.

This gives them one sample to play with and examine, and another which demonstrates the precise enclosing order and pattern that you want. The stapled sample is free from the hazard of some well-intentioned person trying to 'improve' your wishes or just failing to note every detail exactly as they take apart the sample to see what's what and what's how. At an earlier stage you will have agreed with the lettershop what 'overs' they need. To remove any misunderstandings later, it will pay you to ensure that you have given them clear instructions as to your requirements for any surplus materials prior to the enclosing getting underway.

5 Print completion date(s)

One leading lettershop has produced a whole set of clear instructions to assist with packaging of print. How very wise this is! So often printers, realising that the print is moving from one 'trade' shop to another, skimp on the packaging and, because the client will never see it, they are rarely found out. To avoid this happening be sure you have given them clear instructions for the packing just as you will have done for the printing. Otherwise to meet the quantities, your mailing house will have to resort to enclosing dog-eared, damaged, torn and crumpled pieces. Badly packed and damaged enclosures may also slow down or make mechanical enclosing impossible. This will result in extra cost and delay.

Your printers should be instructed to supply you with finished samples as soon as they come off the machine so that you can prepare 'live' samples for the lettershop.

And one last thing. Make sure your printers understand what you mean by a completion date. Is it the date you want the printing complete, or the delivery complete? You know what you mean. And, probably, they know what you mean. But the comparison can nearly always buy them a couple of days and nobody quite knows who's to blame. Except the lettershop, who receive your phone call to ask if they can trim a couple of days. That's the problem with being last in line!

6 Machine proofing start/finish

Machine proofing is unnecessary for straightforward items or reprints. However, if you have four-colour process items, anything vaguely tricky, different or unusual, be sure to build in both the time and the costs. Duo-tones, for example, can lead to bitter disappointment or outright success. But not much in the middle.

Do understand what this proof stage is about. It is to proof the technical side of the printing and whether the 'process work', the designers' bright ideas, have worked. It is *not* for checking copy or whether the label position fits the envelope window. All these things should have been done long, long ago. Moreover, others, such as sponsors, third parties or any colleagues in your own company who see these proofs, should have been made very aware that they cannot make detail changes at this stage.

This means that you must have told them at the artwork approval stage that it was their last chance. Many on the other hand seem happy to delegate colour proofing to their agencies or sometimes for expediency to the printers themselves. This I cannot recommend for any reason.

7 Artwork handover date

It really does all have to be 100 per cent by now. Which is why I recommend scheduling at least one amendment stage. And although it may have to be used for other things eventually, I propose you should originally schedule two.

8 Second amendment stage

This is essentially a double checking stage. None the less I propose that you go through an exact repeat of the stage I'm going to describe next. You'll remember, this being a reverse timetable, it will actually precede!

9 First amendment stage

Allow enough time. Although, naturally, other parties can check the artwork, photocopies are often sufficient. But if it's necessary that they see illustrations you could get colour photocopies rather than risk coffee stains or worse on the originals. Or as I have seen more than once, people actually marking comment or opinions on the original drawings.

Don't pass transparencies round, have colour prints made from them, otherwise they'll get scratched, damaged or lost. It is essential for your budget and your sanity that you coordinate and merge all the different changes and comments before going back to the studio with them. And if necessary pass these round for confirmation too. Otherwise, in order to keep to scheduled commitments, you will be tempted or obliged to pass corrections through in waves. It is frustrating and infuriating for the studio to have to reset or lay out something which they have just re-set and re-laid out earlier that day. For you it is expensive. And unnecessary.

Occasionally, you will also find that one person's or department's amendments or changes impact on another's. This is deadly to timing, thus if you can merge all amendments, gather all those whose approvals are required, and then run through everything with the studio or agency in attendance. This can save an awful lot of heart and budget ache.

I would like to add a word of explanation here for those who are surprised to see, at amendment stages, that their agency or copy and art teams want to change things too. 'I paid you to get it right, I didn't expect to get to look at the proofs with *your* amendments marked on it,' was a comment once fired at me. Personally, I like to work with people who think while they work. So if when they look over the job they spot mistakes, or want to make some suggestions for making improvements, I think they should be welcomed. More than that, few writers, however good they are, don't pick up work they've written a few days or weeks later and decide something would be 'just that bit better if only . . .'.

Things look different typeset as opposed to typewritten. Things look different as artwork as opposed to roughs or visuals. Although part of the advertising writers' and designers' task is to be able to envisage the item in print *when they create it*, that is not something one can always do well, even with years of experience.

10 Finished artwork completion date

Make sure in advance whether artwork will be camera-ready or not. If not, your printer or process house will require extra time to make plates. This can add substantially to the costs. So if the studio have quoted 'camera-ready' hold them to it. This means either they take the job back to finish out or they must meet the charges for doing it.

In order to provide the best finished result, a lot of processes and requirements might be better or more accurately carried out 'on camera'.

11 Finished artwork start date

In the same way that a lettershop will need all the finished print before they can start enclosing into envelopes, so you should work to provide *all* the materials for the studio.

This includes giving them the visual or finished colour rough to work from. They cannot do their job properly without it. If the MD wants to show it to the nextdoor neighbour, the sales director wants to show it to the sales managers and one of your third-party intermediaries or co-sponsors for another reason, give colour copies or have slides made for the sales conference. Give the originals back to the studio. And make sure anybody wanting to indicate changes does so on the photocopies not on the original. Otherwise confusion will abound.

In relation to copy, you should always maintain a master, dated and with an issue number, as you and other parties make changes. Days before handing it over to the studio, circulate the final consolidated clean typescript punctuated and emphasised exactly as you want the set type to be.

Make sure everybody understands that this is their last chance. Be rigid about this and eventually everyone will realise it's for a good reason. Life will instantly become a lot less hassle further on down the production line when time is running out.

12   Copy and visuals completion and production

Don't ever accept original creative work any way other than face-to-face at a meeting or presentation. Don't judge your supplier's work by committee. Endeavour to make their first run-through fairly intimate, preferably just you; possibly one other key influence, but no more. In my experience, if you get more, the weaker, less senior or personally insecure individuals will feel the need to criticise to justify their presence at the meeting. The more noise they make and the more problems they can create, the more they see themselves demonstrating their need to be involved for the future. And everybody of this type always prefers their own ideas to everybody else's!

I once had a client who, when my agency handed over any artwork, attached a sticker to it with no less than 13 spaces for approval signatures. It effectively invited 13 opinions.

This happened whether or not the individuals concerned had any need to see, influences over, or responsibility for the creative item. It was crazy and cost the company a fortune in time and money. What made it worse was that the boss's position was No. 13! So 12 executives used this to demonstrate to their boss their eagle-eye, marketing ability, legal prowess, sales flair and heaven knows what else. You won't need a schedule if you let this happen. You'll need another time round on planet Earth. So keep it down to a minumum. And make sure the most senior people see it first!

13 Creative briefing

In an earlier chapter I have given my own preference for a creative brief. It is wide-ranging in scope and gives lots of detail.

However in the same way as a meeting is required to receive the creative work, I recommend that you organise one to get it started. Creatives need to be motivated, enthused and excited. You'll never do that over the phone or in the post. Don't hurry these meetings. Encourage banter, humour and informality. Encourage your agency or studio to involve directly the team doing the job rather than let an account executive or account manager translate the brief on. It never passes on well.

14 Written brief ready

I said earlier that the brief should be written. It must also be agreed. It will help you to ensure that your brief does not contain any surprises for anyone. My advice is to get a 'sign off' of the brief itself from anyone and everyone who will later sign off copy and visuals or even artwork.

There are lots more production tips and points to come. Many of them to do with scheduling and planning. All of them will help you to stick to a schedule. But none of them, not even all together, will actually enable you to keep to the schedule you wrote on Day One.

You'll see why this is such an unlikely achievement under the next heading. If you've already faced this task, you'll know how true this is.

Scheduling is a repetitive exercise. You need to keep rescheduling and reissuing copies to *all* parties. However, two dates should be treated as sacrosanct from the beginning — the landing date and the mailing date. In all others, be flexible for your own benefit. Flexible, but strict.

And above all else, encourage teamwork and team spirit. Don't tolerate suppliers jostling with each other to score points. They'll work best for you when they're concentrating on the job, not on poking each other in the eye. And whether you succeed or fail, share the ups and downs with the team. Make them sweat when you do. Treat them when you've won.

Be **prepared**

To be prepared, you need to understand what's going to happen. Let me show you, step by step. This is a workflow plan which will give you some idea of all the different stages, steps and pitfalls.

1.0 Mailing production

1.1 Preliminary discussion

1.2 Method of approach developed — strategy prepared

1.3 Strategy discussed, amended, approved

1.4 Brief prepared, circulated, discussed, amended, approved

1.5 Briefing meeting — creatives and as many others involved as possible. Discussion to cover all aspects but **must** include budgets and lists/database capabilities and timing (go to 3.0 personalisation/addressing)

1.6 Mailing concepts developed, formats agreed, outline production specification prepared

1.7 Production specification passed to suppliers for estimating with outline timing requirements

1.8 Estimates received

1.9 Creative concepts reviewed against prices and any discrepancies or specification or cost problems considered and resolved

1.10 First timing schedule issued

1.11 Creative given go ahead

1.12 Copy and visuals presented

1.13 Photocopies and full specification passed to suppliers for submission of first written estimates

1.14 Copy and visuals processed to full approval, materials gathered, studio briefed to proceed to finished artwork

1.15 Schedule reviewed and reissued if appropriate

1.16 List or database specification finalised (go to 2.0 List/database)

1.17 Finished artwork received. Photocopies to all appropriate parties

1.18 Amendments gathered, merged and consolidated

1.19 Final changes and amends recirculated

1.20 Studio briefed for amends. Schedule reviewed and reissued if appropriate

1.21 As 17–20 until approval received from all parties

1.22 **Signed** proofs obtained as appropriate

1.23 Meeting to pass finished artwork for printing. Prices and timing checked and problems resolved

1.24 Revised photocopies, coding instructions and any other 'special treatments' or requirements re-instructed to suppliers

1.25 Process work carried out and completed

1.26 Machine and or proofs prepared, circulated and signed off

1.27 If any amends — review and re-issue schedule if appropriate. Postage payment checked

1.28 Final samples prepared for lettershop from machine proofs and or photocopies

1.29 Print complete, finished samples checked and circulated. Lettershop instructions re-checked. Deliveries confirmed. Quantities and coding details re-verified. Made-up samples signed off

1.30 Lettershop commenced, mailing dates and response handling details rechecked

1.31 Lettershop complete. Counts completed and checked. Spot check on finished items. Release sanctioned

1.32 Release confirmed. Postal dockets received. Response handling alerted

1.33 Invoices received, verified, and passed

1.34 Cost discrepancies analysed and noted

1.35 Guardbook entries, with job history and log entered

1.36 Responses processed. Surplus material arrangements checked and confirmed

1.37 Response pattern logged and reports prepared

1.38 One month from mailing: interim figures reviewed and reports passed

1.39 First debriefing: all suppliers attend — report on response to date and feedback. Financials circulated.

1.40 Two months after: final figures reviewed, responses and financials circulated

1.41 Final debriefing with computer analysis and review and reports circulated and discussed

1.42 Nixies dealt with

1.43 Guardbook entry finalised

2.0 List/database (from 1.16)

2.1 List and data specification agreed

2.2 All segmentation, availability, coding and costs drawn up

2.3 List owners circulated with copy and visuals for approval

2.4 List details, segmentation, codings, prices and dates finalised. Addressing or tapes ordered

2.5 If approprite, mag tape dump and record formats checked, details passed to computer print bureau

2.6 Go ahead to bureau with instructions issued **per tape** including coding details.

3.0 Personalisation/addressing (from 1.5)

3.1 Requirement feasibility checked and costs estimated

3.2	Bureau confirmed all details of selections, formats, codes, mail preference and samples (copies of copy and visuals at the least) agreed
3.3	Bureau estimate, timing, provisos received and verified.
3.4	List security requirements reviewed and instigated
3.5	Bureau receive copies of finished artwork for addressed/personalised items, production details checked thoroughly
3.6	Format proofs received, reviewed and approved
3.7	Live proofs on actual printed stocks prepared, reviewed and approved. Timing checked if amends required
3.8	OK to run
3.9	Run computer, counts and samples provided, checked and verified
3.10	Finished production delivered to lettershop
3.11	Deliveries checked for quality and against quantity counts

Sixty steps to follow. So you see there's a lot to do. A lot to get right. Don't let the apparent complexity of the task worry you. It's a system you need. Once you develop one and you discipline yourself not to skip the safety steps you'll find it's all easy and most of it's fun too!

Get in some **practice**

You know what they say! It makes perfect. So the few pearls I have for you here are about some practices that will check out both your mailing and your people.

The first kind of practice I suggest is to practise constructing and deconstructing your mailing.

To do this you need to use dummies, that is, fabricated mock-ups of the mailing. Do this at every possible stage. Use photocopies of the proofs, backed-up machine proofs (that means stick 'em together if the printer has produced one-side-only proofs, which are often cheaper!). Grab actual samples as soon as you can and check again. Look to see that the address panel falls in the correct window position. That there isn't too much floating — that's caused by pieces being too short and so the address moves and is not properly revealed through the window.

And check, by the way, the envelope manufacturer's tolerances. Windows can move during a production run, as can address positions through knife draw (guillotines cut in a slight arc, not straight down as you would think). You often see a wish by creative not to reveal the advertiser's identity on the outside of an envelope completely spoilt by the order coupon or donation slip floating to reveal odd lines of copy through the window. So if it's 'Please make cheques payable to World Wildlife Fund', that's a dead giveaway!

Check that the folds or reveals work, that headlines across folds position correctly, that cut-outs are where they're supposed to be — and cut them out. I've known studios make a cut-out on one side and forget what it does to the other. Check what's coming back to you when people tear something off. Lots of people put terms and conditions in 'harmless' out-of-the-way places and inadvertently contravene codes of practice because these items should stay with the consumer, not wing their way back into your hands on the back of the response!

So actually try the mailing when you make up the dummies. Fill in the response card. Hand samples to other people. See how they handle it. See if they open leaflets the way they're 'supposed' to. Get *other* people to decipher your instructions, see if they explain sufficiently how to do them, how to choose or select, whether they have enough room to get their details in comfortably. Does the reply coupon fit in the reply envelope?

But don't let your 'practices' end there. As soon as possible prove your response systems. Get a neighbour to send a card in. Make a phone call using your other voice. Ask awkward questions. See how long the follow-up letter takes to arrive.

Everybody accepts the need to proof. 'Dummying up' and practising are just as important. And certainly easy to build in to your systems. Cutting up and taping or gluing all the bits to make your dummies is time-consuming but you can probably browbeat someone else into that!! It will be an enormously worthwhile investment and a great failsafe. And don't forget to make a dummy in the process. One prepared using actual materials. And then weigh it! A couple of grams over a postal weight limit can cost a lot of unbudgeted money.

How to obtain the best prices

Shop around? Well maybe. But be clear about what you're shopping for. Do you really want the best price? Or do you want quality and reliability too?

Here's an interesting little game you can play. I call it JFR's trading triangle.

First, an equilateral triangle:

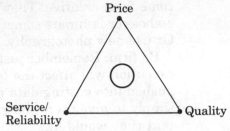

JFR's trading triangle — Choose the qualities you want to assess them against and place a large circle in the middle as a 'no go' area.

In fact, you can vary the angle position qualities to suit the situation. What you are about to do is to get your potential suppliers to 'self-assess' themselves. You will already have assessed your own requirements.

To make the assessment, simply pick up your pen and place a dot in any *off-centre* position (the middle is *verboten*!). The dot position will show your own 'mix' of the three qualities.

Next, it's the suppliers' turn. Once they have 'played', you reveal the results and discuss them. But keep their chosen slot on file and regularly measure them against it. In real life, these qualities don't necessarily conflict. But playing 'JFR's trading triangles' is an interesting way of talking with your suppliers or potential suppliers and 'forcing them off the fence', so to speak, to position the priorities of the company.

What you are actually doing is stimulating a necessary discussion to cover important ground for both sides. You are clarifying your own buying criteria against the suppliers' avowed intentions or claims.

Your needs may well change from item to item, or project to project. If you've assessed your suppliers correctly, my experience suggests that there is no need to obtain more than two, but maximum three, estimates on any single job. And when you are totalling them to establish a campaign cost, don't forget to budget for 'amends' stages. They are often left out of the pricing process.

One of the most contentious stages in the process is quite inconspicuous in the job step programme on pages 231–33. It was

1.9 CREATIVE CONCEPTS REVIEWED AGAINST PRICES AND ANY DISCREPANCIES OR SPECIFICATION OR COST PROBLEMS CONSIDERED AND RESOLVED

It's an innocent enough *looking* sentence. But it describes an awkward, often passionate and occasionally tempestuous round of discussions, negotiations and, finally, arbitrations, to come up with the perfect balance for the use of your budget.

The most passionate pleas, tantrums and foot stamps will come from creative. They'll want to add an adhesive, or emboss or laminate something. Or die-cut or go to four colour. Or use new photography.

Be firm. Remember just how little the creative idea or execution will affect the total outcome. Why should you be pushed into cutting data processing corners or print quality, simply to give them the glue flap, tricky fold or whatever, that they would like?

Such discussions will wander into the realms of fierce hypothesis. And they must do so. For as long as experience and knowledge — as opposed to personal preference, bias or manoeuvring — is creating the hypothesis it will still be useful. And don't fall for that 'Well, you might at least test it!' routine. Stand your ground. Be ruthless even. It is *not* a designer's job to come up with first-class designs. It is a designer's job to come up with first-class designs that come within the budget. That includes *their* part of the budget *and* the total.

Very occasionally, the creative idea is bigger than the other factors. It is rarely bigger than the budget. Lists and offers will generally be far more influential than creative. But lists and budget people are not normally as voluble and articulate as the creatives.

One of the devices I have found useful for many purposes is the budget planning table. It sets parameters and facilitates the kind of negotiations I'm suggesting.

Budget planning table based on £100 direct mail cost per sale

(The figures in **bold** are the most commonly acceptable, but you must calculate your own economics to be sure.)

Example

Suppose you can afford a £200 direct mail cost and your sales force regularly convert 40 per cent.

Note: This table is formulated on a £100 Direct Mail cost so you've got twice that budget to play with.

You can see that

 @ 1 per cent you can spend twice £400=£800
 @ 1.5 per cent 2×£600=£1200
 @ 2 per cent 2×£800=£1600
 @ 3 per cent, if you only achieved a 10 per cent conversion, you can spend £600 per 1000.

	Conversion rate					
	10% £	20% £	30% £	40% £	50% £	60% £
Response rate 0.50%	50	100	150	200	250	300
0.75%	75	150	225	300	375	450
1.00%	100	200	300	400	500	600
1.50%	150	300	450	600	750	900
2.00%	200	400	600	800	1000	1200
3.00%	300	600	900	1200	1500	1800
4.00%	400	800	1200	1600	2000	2400
5.00%	500	1000	1500	2000	2500	3000
7.50%	750	1500	2250	3000	3750	4500
10.00%	1000	2000	3000	4000	5000	6000
12.50%	1250	2500	3750	5000	6250	7500

You can look at this and get a feel for budget.

Choosing the methods of **printing**

Let's divide this into printing proper — you know, what printers do! — and computer printing. Conventional printing first.

I don't feel it falls within the remit of this book to turn you into a Grade 1 print expert. And there's no need to. What I would like to do is give you four things to think about.

1 *Get to understand your printer's machinery, capabilities and sheet sizes* There's no substitute for stimulating ingenuity, solving problems and getting value for money. All of which are important factors in the successful realisation of a good mailing. Moreover, an enormous number of the problems that you will face at that tricky Step 1.9 will be solved by knowing precisely what capabilities your printers have.

More important still, you should ensure whoever is responsible for the concepts and formats of your mailings, *and* whoever is responsible for producing the finished artwork, also get to know your printers just as intimately as I am suggesting that you do.

You will quickly get to 'milk' the best combination of

237

value-for-money print and practical creativity (something with which the world is not always overflowing!).

You will know what they can do easily, cheaply and quickly. What processes need to be 'put out'. What folds they can handle quickly. What goes out. And so on.

You will learn all the different suitable permutations available from their machinery. Although I encourage standardisation of sizes (it avoids wastage) as a rule, there

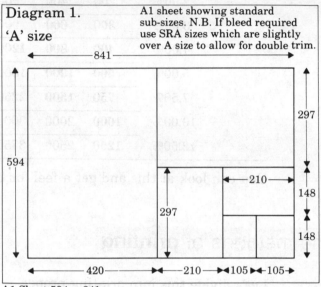

Diagram 1.

'A' size

A1 sheet showing standard sub-sizes. N.B. If bleed required use SRA sizes which are slightly over A size to allow for double trim.

A1 Sheet 594 × 841
All measurements in millimetres.

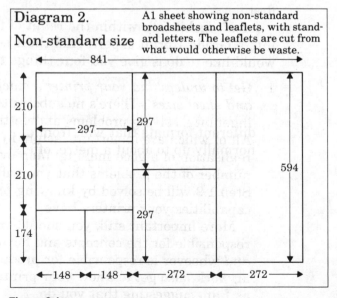

Diagram 2.

Non-standard size

A1 sheet showing non-standard broadsheets and leaflets, with standard letters. The leaflets are cut from what would otherwise be waste.

Figure 8.1
Standard and alternative formats

238

are some alternative ways to use flat paper, effectively 'grouping' components out of the same flat sheet rather than printing them separately (see Figure 8.1). And if you can't avoid paper wastage, rather than just cut it off and lose it, see what else can be done. Need any compliments slips or memos, or remittance advices? If not, gum and pad them. Or give suitably-sized offcuts to local schools or charities — they are always welcome.

2 *Get to know your printer's range of finishing equipment and its capabilities* Again, this also applies to your creative team. If your printer has good contacts with trade finishing houses, visit them and get to know what their capabilities are. Encourage both to keep you up-to-date with things new and different that they're doing. If possible get them to send you samples regularly.

3 *Become a sample 'squirrel' and hoard samples* Keep masses of samples — yours and other people's. Examine the mail you get at home and at work. Don't think twice about using other people's good ideas, or at least testing them to see how they work for you. Go through them from time to time and remind yourself of what can be done. And, most important, encourage others to raid your hoard. Don't let them take the samples away, only the ideas.

If you see something good and you can't think how it was done, or who did it, ring the marketing team or print buyers at the advertiser concerned and ask. Most will be flattered and delighted to oblige with information and advice. They'll often tell you the snags as well. And whether it worked or not. So be prepared (pleased even!) to be as open and helpful yourself.

4 *Discover the world of one-piece mailers and in-line origami* There has been a huge amount of development — principally for longer runs — in the area of reel-fed printing and finishing to produce a mass of different devices which can be folded and glued in a wealth of different formats that will, from one length of paper normally up to about a metre, offer a fascinating and very usable range of all-in-one formats.

Devices which can be torn down one perforation releasing separate items — such as a letter, booklet, order coupon and reply envelope. Many of these make excellent inserts and house-to-house pieces since the components do not get separated and lost. Equally, many can be addressed and personalised to provide very low-cost and quite effective direct mail packages.

You'll be amazed at the huge array of capabilities

available from scratch'n'reveal, numbered or adhesive items (stamps, stickers, game pieces, etc.), and little gimmicks and gadgets that modern adhesive technologies and modern paper processing equipment can provide.

And then there's computer printing

With some subjects these days, one is hesitant almost to put pen to paper with any positive statement. Or place anything on record as fact. The whole database and computer field provokes such feelings. But, there are some basics which it will be helpful for you to know. Let's start with the laser printer.

Laser printers

They are high-resolution (therefore high-quality) printers, relatively cheap in production, and certainly the bigger machines are fast.

There are principally two kinds of process — 'hot' and 'cold'. They come either as sheet-fed or continuous stationery. The hot process is aptly described since the fusion of the image to the paper takes place under the influence of over 200 degrees Celsius. This had led to some problems, technically speaking, with conventional printing inks and papers but, if in doubt, one can run on extra proofs prior to printing for a test. With the 'cold' process the fusion is caused chemically.

The laser process uses an electrostatically-charged drum which, as it revolves, collects a toner powder as directed by the laser beam. The toner is then transferred to the paper and the image is fixed or 'fused' to the paper. If you think of it as a damned clever photocopier which copies the computer-generated 'image' you won't be far off!

Probably the biggest drawback is the limitation in paper stock that can be fed through. Paper and inks need to be tested, but folds, creases or perforations can cause problems.

Sheet-fed machines will cope with standard letterheads and also can handle 'duplex' printing where the items are personalised on both sides of the sheet.

Dot-matrix printers

At the time of writing, I generally don't regard dot-matrix printer quality as suitable. This may change with developments. Certainly they are cheap, but the finished print looks it!

Daisywheel printers

They are slow and therefore expensive. Yet they provide the very highest quality. However, modern laser printing is not far off the quality, with the benefits of speed and price.

Impact printers

In direct mail production the day of the impact printer is drawing to a close. Just about the only saving grace is that they are cheap. And quality wise, there are only two things worse: dot matrix and my handwriting.

Ink jet printers

Ink jet and laser have for some time been battling for supremacy as the mainline. In the seventies, in-car entertainment was making up its mind between eight-track and cassette. In the eighties, video had VHS and BETA. In direct marketing it's ink jet versus laser.

Ink jet is lower quality but the highest speed. And yet ink jet will probably be the first to bring us colour as an option. The process has already been used to produce full colour out of three, not four colours. And it's impressive.

The process is actually the most definitive and controlled piece of spraying you've ever seen. The ink is literally 'fired' at the paper by an 'ink gun' which is, mercifully, controlled by the computer.

The game of the name is personalisation

I remember inventing a term to describe my attitude towards personalisation or rather what it should achieve. The term is 'techno-creativity'.

Personalisation, in my book (sic), is not about sticking somebody's name and address on the top of a letter. Together with a personal salutation. That's 'matching in'. A process which modern computer printing has made easy and cheap and fast. But it's *not* personalisation.

In an earlier chapter, I referred to days gone by when one of the services on offer from direct mail producers was a litho-printed letter with the name, address and personal salutation 'matched in' on the top. For short runs of prestige letters typomatic machines were used. These were extraordinary contraptions, driven by a master machine with a pianola-type roll of paper with holes punched in it. Air was forced up against the roll and, when it met a hole, was released through. This triggered a group of up to four slave typewriters which, with the hole position linked to the key positions of the typewriters, would produce, to all intents and purposes, four 'individually' typed duplicates of the original.

Downstairs, in my home, is a PC which, coupled with a software package, drives a desktop laser printer. At something more than ten times the speed, it provides perfect 'top copy' letters. Instead of the operator feeding in the paper, positioning the carriage and typing in the name, address and salutation and then switching to automatic, a simple merge printing facility takes sheets from the hopper and does the whole job. It's like comparing ABS braking in a car with using your feet to slow down a scooter. But I still call that process, sweet old-fashioned thing that I am, matching in.

What's happening is that we're trying to give the readers the impression that each one of them has had someone sit down and type a letter to them. I wonder how many are fooled today? I wonder how many will be fooled in five years' time, or even ten?

Why does 'personalisation' work?

Let's track that one through time. Up to the mid-seventies or thereabouts, it was all about making people believe they'd had a one-off letter. So, as the computer develops to give us impact-printed personalisation with its appalling quality, we found we could drop in names like tossing coins in a fountain. Clumsily, maybe, but often.

Slowly things became more sophisticated and variable text printing came along. By typesetting the letter using the computer printer, it was found that one could get a match or near-match. So again, no one could see the join. It was about that time that a major international direct marketing organisation carried out a few tests. Having spent, as the rest of the industry had, huge sums of money trying to get the machinery to provide as near as possible an acceptable 'match' of computer fill-in to printed text, they found that the old clumsy way, where the named fill-in and the printed text didn't match, were pulling better.

Eureka! Something had changed. Those worldly Citizens of Life that we call consumers, had fallen in! That competition with 2000 prizes accompanied by the one-off personal letter from the managing director of a huge international company? One of them was a fake. Direct mail was about to move out of the Stone Age and into the Iron Age.

It didn't take many million dollars' worth of research for the next stage of direct marketing man to understand. It wasn't the fact they were fooled by the match-in. They liked to see us play games with their name. Boy, did we kill that particular goose in the next ten years! We gave them names until they were sick of them. In panels, highlighted on flaps. You name it!

Next came the secondary in-fill. Other information which we had on file could be used. This unearthed a problem that was to have huge repercussions, eventually leading to the need for the database marketing concept. The vast majority of list owners couldn't actually retrieve their data. It was all there for statistical, and analytical reporting functions. But to pull back and *use*, that wasn't on. While the system's boffins grappled with that one, the hardware boffins had come up with new types of printing kit. Laser and ink-jet were born.

This was great. Now we could do anything we liked with the names. Stretch them tall or long. Turn them upside down. Use them pretty well any way we could dream up.

As laser and ink-jet caught on, so their uses became more inventive, and their users more skilled. As well as for selectivity, simple file information could be regurgitated in text matter. Age. Sex. Job title. Business activity. Make of car. And so on.

The change-over to Appropriate Advertising had, in a very modest way, started. Readers observed that letters from direct mailers were no longer just written at them. In some pioneering way they were beginning to be written *about* them.

For example:

Dear Mr Pilkington,
    As a houseowner with a mortgage of £65 000 in the price-spiralling South East, you will likely already have noticed the problem I am writing about.
    And, as a Company Director aged between 40 and 50, let me tell you that the solution, for you, is perhaps easier to find.
    When you applied for your mortgage two years ago, the value of your home was £250 000. Since that time, given our knowledge of the Mayford area of Woking you must, in some ways, be very pleased about what your property would fetch on the market today.
            But the thought of selling Southdown
            House after two years may not appeal.

What's more, you would probably have to . . .

You can see what I mean.

So what had started out as a desire to make letters that looked original, evolved to the present where they are original. Again.

Not only is *my* letter appropriate to *me,* it is appropriate to *me* only. If someone else received it, they could only be interested out of sheer nosiness!

During that evolution the objective of personalisation changed. Originally it was used so that a mailing wouldn't look like a mailing. It still is.

Then, as it all started to look like that, personalisation was used to grab attention. It still is.

Then, as it all started to look like that, personalisation was used to make replying and buying easier. It still is.

Nowadays, with the parallel development of database marketing, we are on the brink of *individualisation*. As markets fragment, so the front ends of those who wish to communicate with them must fragment too. The size and reach of the fragments will be determined by two criteria. The intensity of the relationship and the desired effectiveness of the communications within the relationship.

Hence the very careful need to understand, manage, control and develop the technology of the communications. For it is this that will enable us to understand the needs of each market fragment, and to respond to those needs.

Now let's see what relevance that has to the production of personalised mailings. First, it will determine marketing and sales objectives. This guides what you have to do. Next you have to decide how you will achieve your objectives, and how you will use the resources available to you. From this will develop a communications strategy. And from that strategy, it will become clear to what use you will put the resource of information. Will it be to segment the market? What are the common aspects of the segments? And are they completely or partially common? What is the most effective way to relate the exclusively tailored proposition to the segments?

You will be endeavouring, using the media at your disposal, to cluster groups of individuals together. This makes the communication process more economical. You will be trying to develop an acceptable proposition (and here I use the word acceptable in its most literal sense). Next comes the task of putting that proposition across in the most acceptable way. And after that we have to make the act of accepting as acceptable as possible too!

From all of this will come the conclusions that are necessary to decide whether you will use some form of personalisation and what you want to achieve. The effects it can create are, remember:

1 To make the letter personal in varying degrees
2 To grab attention and stimulate interest
3 To transmit information (often administrative data)

4   To tailor, communicate, enhance and relate the proposition
5   To facilitate acceptance of the proposition

Now we have knowledge about how many people we shall be going to, how that quantity is structured and grouped, and what the segment quantities are. We have decisions, too, on the complexity of the production task — from simple address labels through to all-singing, all-dancing computer letters and documents. A set of creative options will be developing now and the major items that will narrow the options down are the processes, formats, speeds, prices, quality, capability and timings that are available. These are all the very stuff of production. And this is the stage where production performs its most inspirational and creative tasks. The expertise to select the best potential formats and methods for creative to perform.

Not just ideas. *Workable* ideas. *Affordable* ideas. And the more the merrier!

Next must come a method of producing the finished result followed by planning and scheduling. All production have to do next is make it happen!

Direct mail has to be carefully produced

I must confess, I'm as guilty as the rest. Maybe more so. At dropping production people in it. Sometimes up to their necks. Sometimes over their heads. The most frequent subjects of this nasty and addictive habit will know who they are. And therefore they'll know just how much I appreciate their efforts over the years.

The reason for this little personal glimpse into my guilt barrel is because I'm not the only one. Production people perform a vital, often highly stressful, and in many cases, under-rewarded job. Now I don't think we'll change the world here. So let me underline the importance of their role.

Often in life the 'front-end team' get the garlands, the awards, the dinners at The Dorchester. And so often, the people who breathe life into our creations seem to be just 'doing their job'. Yet every time sales, account handling or creative score a win, it was the production people who actually made it happen!

The reason I mention this is because of the sheer amount of production effort that is required in direct mail. Proportionately, it has to be more than any other major advertising medium. Because it *is* a complex business. You will have seen over the last few pages just how much so. Attention to every detail is not something one does to polish up and fine-tune the odd job. Every single job requires endless care and thought. And I can't think of any other advertising medium where the need to involve the production team is so crucial, at such an early stage. My experience has been that the production team can, if involved sufficiently, become a vast bank of creative solutions. And this goes for the industry's suppliers too. They are always looking for the next horizon.

My suggestion is to make good friends with the production team. Encourage and support and listen to them. In most cases you or I will be the cause of their headaches and heart attacks.

Not the work we give them. But the task we give them.

Here are a few tips to help your jobs go through a little more smoothly.

Avoid stupid four-colour process demands

Designers are notorious for pushing the aesthetic through, not just in front of the practical or functional, often at the cost of it. Resist this.

Watch particularly for choices of tints and background colours that are difficult and slow for printers to get right. Four-colour processors and printers need to concentrate on getting the people and the products looking good. Flesh tones not too pale or blushed. If they're trying to get a delicate and difficult shade of off-pink grey to hold to the match specified as well, you'll end up with a compromise. Encourage your designers, when a complex job comes along, to go to the process house or department and see it through.

Don't let designers force through white-out text in four-colour process areas where the background is busy, varying in contrast, or just not strong enough to 'hold out' the copy. On top of this, they often seem to choose fine, 'thin' typefaces which, with the slightest movement of register, start to fill in and blur.

All of these things — and many more, which are nothing more than designers' whims — simply make reading the copy more difficult. You will have enough trouble getting enough people to read enough of your copy without anyone making it more difficult, I promise! The art team's job is to make it an easier, more desirable thing to do. Making it pretty is going to do some of that. Making it pretty difficult is not.

Never check anything

Get out of the habit of checking things. Make your standard double-checking. Involve those who aren't involved. Get their opinions as well as their corrections. I'm sure you have experienced the feeling of complete disbelief when somebody points at a wrong word or spelling in something you know you read and checked not once, not twice, but half a dozen times. You can't do anything about that, your brain is picking up what it knows should be there. But others don't know. They read with a critical innocence you can never have.

These matters are important, not just to get the job right, but also to save lives! The responsibility for artwork being correct always lies with the client. Not with the studio. Not with the typesetters. Not even with the agency. It's down to the client. So if there's a reprint, that's down to the client too. It's a responsibility not to be shirked, made light of or even delegated. And a responsibility that makes double-checking instead of checking well worth while.

Does the response device work, fit the return envelope and is it as easy as you can possibly make it to complete?

Can recipients clearly see what they have to do to buy or enquire from you? And is it easy for them to do? Always give them plenty of room for their name, address and other details.

When using boxed spaces for the recipient to complete, allow a minimum of 5 mm in box depth and, ideally, 6 mm or 7 mm. A millimetre is only small, but it can make a difference to the number of replies.

And does it fit the reply envelope? You might think these little things are too silly to clutter up a book. I've seen them all and disagree!

I remember a beautiful example of an A5 (that's half A4) response card, printed on heavy weight board. Together with a D/L (or one-third A4) reply paid envelope!

And if you think that's bad, how about the really bright insurance company that recently asked me to reply on a standard business reply card . . . and *enclose* a cheque!! Nice one.

Just as bad, the vast numbers — even pro's who should know better — who produce response pieces on high gloss-finish card. So my Pentel or ballpoint smudges. And if you think I'm being hypercritical, let me tell you that no one likes to look stupid! So if we smudge or spoil a reply, more often than not we don't bother sending it in. After all we know you'll mail us again. Mailings are like London buses, aren't they?

A buyer or responder needs to feel safe, relaxed and in control. That's most of what the need for simplicity and clarity is about. So the next time a studio or agency submits a reply device that gives the applicant an inch and a half to fill in their full names, the same for their company name, four inches for their telephone number and another four inches for their postal code, you know what to tell them!

Make sure everyone is aware of the codes and their meanings
Use scratch coding, it's cheaper than plate changes. Make sure the code only alters in one colour. Make sure that every single piece of the package carries the code. This cuts down the risk of incorrect pieces being included in incorrect packages.

Here is an example of a cheap coding system for the lithoprinting process. To get ten different codes the printer merely has to stop the machine at the required quantities, and delete one numeral from the plate.

Scratch coding	
0123456789	Code 9
012345678	Code 8
01234567	Code 7
0123456	Code 6
012345	Code 5

The list of typical, stupid mistakes is also the list of common stupid mistakes
Perversely, the very qualities that make the best mailings — the *human* qualities — are also the same failings — the *human* failings — that make the last heading true. So, if I list a few typical mistakes, you'll probably recognise them as common mistakes.

- Spelling errors or literals spotted *after* the job is printed
- Poor quality print through wrong or badly chosen paper and materials
- Devices that don't pop up, appear, release or unfold correctly, because nobody made up working dummies
- Mini-cab, bike and courier bills to cover late delivery of proofs, separations or plates (often due to one of the first three above)

These are the types of mistake I mean. I've no doubt that they will be with us until IBM come up with a software suite that writes the brief, creates the job, proofs it and produces the mailing for us. On which day they probably also bring out one that writes books making the likes of me redundant. And knocking me off my hobby-horse!

But there is still one last piece of advice.

Check through the bills

This procedure is not to check you've been charged correctly. You should be doing that anyway. It's to draw up a list of expenses incurred over budget — extras, corrections or errors — or to improve quality or pull back lost time.

Don't use this list as the agenda for a mud-slinging meeting with suppliers. Use it as the agenda for 'How can we do it better next time?'

Such meetings tend to start along with all the enthusiasm of a new client agency or supplier relationship and dwindle to nothing as time passes. Make it a regular procedure and you'll feel the benefit. Either because it'll start to eradicate the causes or because the agents and suppliers will run out of excuses. Eventually.

Direct mail has to get **posted**

Now we come to matters postal. And I should thank the Bearded One-der for his input. Seemingly he's been banging the direct mail and direct marketing drum at Royal Mail since the Penny Black. I speak of Les Andrews, who, when I've finished this section, will no doubt correct it for me, remind me of the meaning of tact and diplomacy, and then hold out an empty glass. Cheers, Les!

Actually, since we're talking about Les Andrews and his colleagues above (grovel!) and below him, I might just share an opinion with you. Over the years I've come to know and work with these postal people quite a lot. From the trade union convenor at Worthing who turned a blind eye while I climbed a mountain of mail to search out a bag with a wrongly enclosed section of a mailing that we discovered at the last moment, to the equally rare, but rather more delicate, luncheon in the Directors' Dining Room.

What's more, while they weren't looking, I've actually been comparing our lot with other Post Offices round the world. And I've come to a remarkable conclusion, which, somewhat reluctantly for someone like myself who has a reputation for not suffering fools gladly and finding it difficult to resist flinging the odd killer-whimsy, I'll tell you.

The Brits are OK. Our chaps compare very favourably. Moreover, and here I slide dangerously near the slippery slope of sounding approving, I think it will be more by their judgement than luck, that you'll find yourself agreeing with me. Of course, they've got their share of clowns, bureaucrats and wallies, but then you can hardly be that big and not end up with a few. Ask Payless! And they're nothing like the size. Two of the good things they've done are worthy of particular mention. Since they'll affect whether you're new to Direct Mail, a seasoned user, or anything in between.

Good Thing No. 1
They've learned about direct marketing and then tried not just to supply the demand, but stimulate it. Now that for a Post Office — judging by most of the others worldwide — is a remarkable feat. But the particular benefit has been that they chose to stimulate direct marketing by encouraging education and understanding, as well as going the commercially justifiable route of selling it. As a result they have cooperated and shared the growing pains. And to some extent helped the industry to bear the pressure.

Good Thing No. 2
If you're just getting into direct mail you'll find them helpful and encouraging to talk to. I'd feel inclined to keep the conversation to postal services. That's only because their sales team are so switched on to direct mail that they tend to go a little over the top and come across like Solomon. It's a great energy and commitment that's been developed and nurtured. It was a visionary process started by Nigel Walmsley, now Managing Director of Capital Radio, when he was Marketing Director of the Post Office. His successors and those in whom the ideas were propagated 'picked it up and ran with it'. Thank heavens.

And here's the bottom line of this particular little eulogy. In the UK we're lucky, and we should recognise it. Every sign is that it will continue. Plus at times, minus at others, no doubt.

To Post Offices in other countries, save one or two, let me reveal the hidden truth. All of this was not to be nice to the direct marketing industry. It was a simple, old-fashioned profit motive. And it's paid off.

So if you want to know more, talk to the Royal Mail. You'll help yourselves, your nation's direct marketing industry and your nation's economy.

Postal services for the direct mailer

This is mainly for British readers. And notice the heading says 'for direct mailers' not direct marketers. That means that I'm going to give you an overview of the services that relate to direct mail not those, for example, to do with the mail order business such as parcels.

You'll need to know what's on offer for your outgoing direct mail. The main letter services are:

First class post

In their own sponsored book — *The Direct Mail Handbook* (see Bibliography) published by Exley — the Royal Mail bit its lip, crossed its fingers and agreed to leave in my comments about first class mail. I said that if you use it you'd got to be one of three things. Rich, late or crazy! And my view hasn't modified since.

There is, however, a discounted equivalent to first class post which you can read about under the heading 'Mailsort'. The delivery standard is 'next day' and they aim for 90 per cent within that time.

Second class post

This is the 'norm' for small quantities and its discounted equivalent, again explained under Mailsort, is favourite for picking up time if there's a panic to maintain a landing date. The standard the Royal Mail looks to provide is 96 per cent on the third day after collection.

Mailsort

This is a combined 'branding' for three Royal Mail discount services for large users. While the Royal Mail gives you discounts, it makes you earn them. However, with computerisation of lists and the onset of database marketing this is not such a problem. There is a requirement to postcode your addresses, and they do offer some help in this direction at the present time. It will be worth enquiring, if you are mailing, or thinking about mailing, large quantities. You should enquire through the nearest main Royal Mail office, or through one of the 'approved' computer bureaux, many of whom proudly advertise this status in the trade press.

Apart from requiring certain levels of postcoding (which is both understandable and sensible), there is also a requirement with Mailsort to pre-sort the mail into specified areas and 'prepare' the mail in a particular way. This is not the place to go into more detail. But you should note that the requirements are quite demanding.

So much so that when the Royal Mail gave birth to the infant Mailsort there was an unprecedented revolt by many mailing houses and large users who claimed that, although the Royal Mail had improved the discounts to some extent, the increased demands for pre-sorting were so stringent as to more than rule out the benefit, effectively therefore increasing costs.

It was also felt that the 'Mark 1' system would penalise small mailers with its complexities. However, Mailsort was reconsidered after some trials and hopefully will be the success the Royal Mail wish it to be both for them and their customers.

It is structured in three layers and is available if you are mailing over 4000 letters or 1000 packets in one single despatch.

- *Mailsort 1* — this provides first class delivery standards at discounts currently up to 15 per cent including the bonus for posting early in the day.
- *Mailsort 2* — works to second class mail delivery standards and offers discounts from 8 to 13 per cent.
- *Mailsort 3* — has a delivery standard which is markedly longer — within seven *working* days after posting. So this time must be built in to your reverse timetable. However, the discounts are also much greater, offering between 15 and 32 per cent.

Despite its fairly inauspicious first appearance there is an element of rationalisation in the Mailsort scheme and certainly it is far more geared to the future than the schemes which preceded it.

Overseas direct mail

As well as paying the full normal tariff for air or surface mail to reach foreign parts, there are two contractual services (not to mention the pricey, but speedy and thorough, Datapost system) which will be of interest.

- *Airstream*. This divides into two. First, a service for regular consignments which, as a mailing, weigh in excess of 2 kg. It's a worldwide delivery service which includes collection from you — and you don't even have to stamp or frank your mail.
- *Airstream Print* is the discount version which requires pre-sorting to the Royal Mail's specification and is available for printed (but non-personalised) matter.
- *Accelerated Surface Post* is for countries outside Europe and provides (for printed matter) a faster delivery than Surface Mail but at a considerably cheaper rate than air mail.

Now we turn to those all important services to handle the incoming responses. Let's start with the UK.

Business reply

Available as first or second class, the main difference between the two is the readers' perception — that is, their view of how highly you value them and their response. Plus, for you, speed and price.

I believe the perception element is important but in other respects it's a matter of choice. Except, that is, in lead generation, where the tendency for the first class replies to be

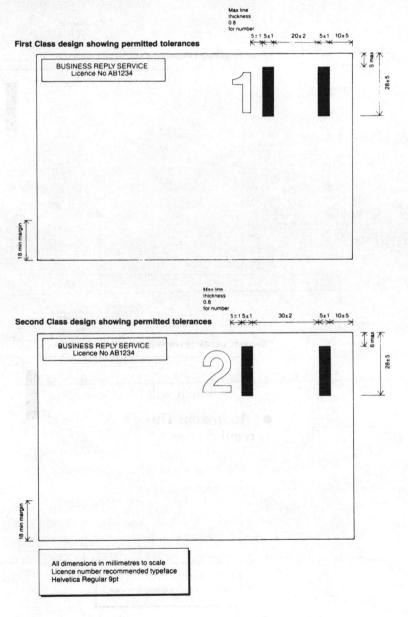

Figure 8.2
Sample Business Reply design
(Courtesy of The Post Office)

delivered with the first class post and at least one day quicker can be very valuable.

Leads cool off from the day the enquiry is posted. Therefore, the faster you can get back to the responder the better. In fact, you can organise with your local Head Royal Mail Office first delivery service for first and second class response pieces for a quite moderate fee.

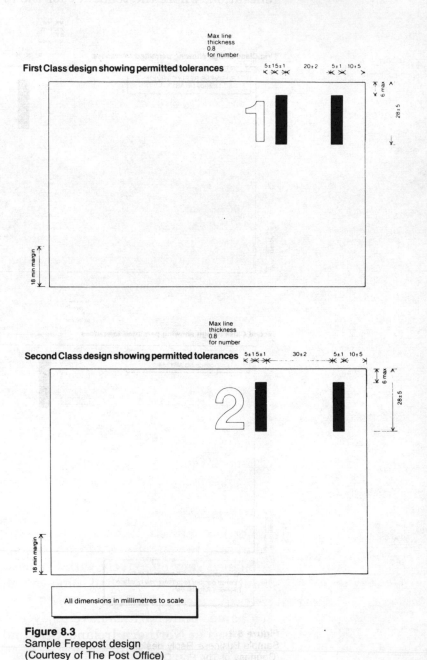

Figure 8.3
Sample Freepost design
(Courtesy of The Post Office)

254

Freepost

Originally Freepost was invented to provide a free (or rather post paid!) service for responders and enquirers to those media where it was difficult (or impossible) to provide a business reply opportunity such as a card or envelope.

That use remains. But it has also widened to provide an alternative service to Business Reply, again at first and second class levels when you pre-print the design. One important distinction between the pre-printed service and when you give out your Freepost address on ads, coupons, labels or the radio or TV, is that the latter service is second class only.

For all these (and the overseas) reply services you'll need a licence and to obtain the design 'patterns' from your local Head Royal Mail Office. The Royal Mail will also need to check proofs. And watch out! You'll be given a different postal code!

Overseas reply service

The service operates on very similar lines to the UK but on one class of service only. At the time of going to press, sadly without Germany, it covers these countries:

Belgium	Netherlands
Cyprus	Norway
Denmark	Portugal
Finland	Republic of Ireland
France	Spain
Iceland	Sweden
Luxembourg	United Arab Emirates
Monaco	

Admail

Lastly, in terms of the major response services, there is Admail.

This is a redirection service enabling you to give a local address in advertising of any kind. The replies are re-addressed to you, or the address you specify. Admail can be combined very effectively with Freepost.

Interestingly, I have had some valuable experiences in this particular area, I can tell you that a number of *English* companies and charities have enjoyed substantially better responses in Northern Ireland, Scotland and Wales when a local — as opposed to English — address is used.

Frank talk about stamping

There's more choice to stamping a mailing than you might think. You have basically three choices, stamping it, franking it or pre-printing it. As far as stamping is concerned, experiences vary. In the consumer and business-to-business field, it is, often forgotten that while stamping may serve to add the benefit of making your mailing look as though it's not a mailing, it can make people feel that the letter is from a small, insubstantial business. This can be an advantage or disadvantage.

You can frank your own mail or arrange for the Post Office to do it. They also offer a pre-franking service for bulky items where the address labels or envelopes are franked before enclosing. If you frank your own mail, you can add a message in the space next to the franking mark.

Alternatively there are a range of designs available. These are called PPI's — Printed Postage Impressions — and are for use with mailings in excess of 4000. There is a leaflet available from the Royal Mail which shows the designs and they will also supply high-quality reproductions from which your studio can 'lift' the reference for artwork. PPI is another facility which requires a licence and your licensed impression will have its own unique serial number which your studio should add to the artwork.

If you are printing or overprinting your envelopes, I heartily recommend the use of PPIs and, of preference, suggest that the nearer in looks that you can get to a classic franking or cancellation the better.

One particular advantage of PPI is that you will not get any angry letters from anyone whose stamps didn't get stuck on or whose envelope wasn't franked. Nobody likes to pay the postman for the dubious pleasure of being sold to by you. This is particularly true of charity appeals.

JFR's box of tricks

Some tips for personalisation

● Do all you can to make sure that whoever is creating your mailing understands the production and computer desciplines. This will ensure that their ideas are practical and should, if they are truly creative people, still mean that their ideas are stimulating and challenging in every way.

- Think carefully about pioneering. Remember the risks increase at the same time as the potential rewards. But the latter — the rewards — don't always follow.
- You may ultimately feel forced to use personalisation for the wrong reason. An awful lot of advertisers produce full-colour leaflets simply because the noise level is so high. In other words, their competitors all use four-colour so they feel obliged to as well.

I know a number of advertisers feel this way about personalisation. I do sympathise with the feeling. If you decide to do it for the same (wrong) reason, that doesn't mean you should be slap-dash. It's important to get it right. At least it then stands a chance of paying you back with a profit.

- The more heavily that you use personalisation, the harder you will fall (measured on a scale of indignant complaint letters!) if you get even the slightest detail wrong, inaccurate or misspelt.

Personalised or not, it is a fact that the higher the response, usually the higher the complaints. This, while regrettable, usually indicates the higher levels of readership and is therefore a sorry side-effect of success.

Whatever you do, however legal, decent, honest and truthful, somebody will dislike it enough to complain!

Three more postal points

- Think about first day covers! As you probably know, Royal Mail has an annual programme of stamp issues. It is published well in advance. There's no reason why you can't use these together with the optional enhancement of a special first day cover cancellation (franking mark). If you so choose, the mailing can be despatched in the special first day cover envelopes or you can have your own designed.

I remember one advertiser who tied into this for an extended period, always finding some inventive way to link his service to the theme of the issue. Thus creating mailings that were in themselves collectables — an idea so strong that people used to find the most devious ways to get on his list. And would even ring up and plead with him, if for any reason he decided to take their name off the list!

First day covers are very usable for overseas mailings since they can arouse a great deal of interest. Particularly in some Latin American countries where they have the distinction of being so valuable that they never reach their intended destination!

- Print your 'returns' address on the envelope. This will ensure that you recover the maximum number of 'gone aways' or nixies as they are known. If you don't really want to give the game away by revealing your full details, use a box number or your lettershop's address. Favourite place for this 'If undelivered please return to . . .' line is the back flap of the envelope.
- Postcoding is wise, worth the money and very usable. If your files are on computer they can have the postcodes added automatically for a very reasonable cost. These will be useful in securing the maximum price advantages from the postal authority — but also they are very useful in personalisation where they can be keyed to 'look up' tables for highlighting the names of local dealers, stockists or reps. They are also invaluable for a whole host of marketing functions including, as we shall see in the next chapter, for list profiling and de-duplication and merge/ purge operations.

And lastly to close the box of tricks for this chapter, some general production wrinkles.

- Be aware of forthcoming price increases on paper and envelopes. Sometimes it pays to buy early. If you have standard stationery or print items which you use all the year round, try to order them at the same time as ordering items for your Direct Mail campaign. Volume purchasing can cut costs dramatically.
- Try to make copy timeless. It's expensive to change artwork and printing plates every time you want to mail. Of course, dated material such as closing dates or special offers, etc., are used as a device to increase response, but you should try to use them in situations where they can be changed inexpensively from one mailing to the next. Such as adhesive stickers, and letterpress overprints. Avoid them appearing reversed out of four-colour process — meaning one simple date change lets you in for all four new plates.
- Ensure reply envelopes or cards meet the Royal Mail requirements. Check that all printing on envelopes is within the Royal Mail regulations. The regulations are there for good reasons. The minimum weight and size ensure your replies don't get trapped in others' mail or get mangled in franking machines!
- For personalisation the paper must be of the right weight — normally 80–90 gsm. Also it must be delivered several

days before it is required to allow time for it to acclimatise or 'cure' in the atmosphere in which it is to be printed.

- If your letter is more than one side, the reverse must be pre-printed unless you are duplex printing. Normally the laser bureau will typeset the reverse side for you to ensure a matched typeface with the personalised side.
- Perforations, gummed stamps and the like, all favourites with the big mailers, must be within certain areas and sizes for the laser process to work properly. These should be carefully checked.
- Because the cost of reel-fed computer printing is often calculated by the foot, length is important. Think about how you use this advice! Because the greater the length, the more economical printing becomes!
- If you're using personalisation on more than one piece which will become separated before or during enclosing, make sure that all pieces carry a code number which will enable a visual or mechanical match to be made. It's the only way to be absolutely certain they are twinned correctly in quality control checks or if something gets out of sequence. How can this be done mechanically? With OCR (Optical Character Recognition) equipment or bar codes. Such codes should be in a position that is discreet to the recipient but discernible for the production team.
- Deciding on a format can be a difficult task. Here is a simple routine which will help you decide on number, shape, and size of your components.

1 *What am I trying to achieve?*
   (a) Why should they want to do it?
   (b) What will convince them?
   (c) What will make them do it now?

2 *How can I achieve it?*
   (a) What is the logic to my sales story?
   (b) What natural steps or stages does it fall into?
   (c) How much space will I need?

3 *Are there any practical or functional aspects relevant to the format?*
   (a) Do I need to get cash back or is the reply sensitive or confidential in any way?
   (b) Is there any other reason for mailing? If so, what are the requirements (such as a bonus notice, statement, invoice, membership details, etc.) and can they be used in any way to relate, enclose or support my primary objective?
   (c) Is there anything which requires, or is worthy of, particular highlighting or emphasis?

(d) Will the recipient need any help handling the documentation? If so, how and where should I give them that help and advice?

4 *Which of the options open to me*

(a) Will make the most sense if handled as I plan, but still work best if, dropped, misunderstood or mishandled?

(b) Will work hardest to dramatise the sales story and be interesting for the reader?

(c) Will work out best from production, timing and budget points of view?

And then to review your decision.

5 *As a cohesive selling machine*

(a) Does it work?

(b) Is it logical, clear, and simple to assimilate?

And lastly,

6 Is there anything I can do to improve it, make it more interesting, useful, or simple to handle and respond?

Remember! It is quite possible that, in achieving as many as possible of the above you may fall upon a pretty basic format. There is nothing wrong with that. You can still use materials — paper, texture, and three-dimensional objects — to add an extra lift!

9 There are only **nine** kinds of direct mail—

They go to lists that are:

- **internal**
- **external**
- **customers**
- **enquirers**
- **business**
- **consumers**
- **compiled**
- **computerised**
- **rented**

Don't mess around with lists without a computer

Because 'messing around' is all you can do in comparison with achieving the full management and benefit of a list and thereby reaping the full rewards of its potential. You can use a non-computer medium to hold data, but it can't process it in anything like comparable times.

There remain no other practical cost-efficient or sensible media upon which to put a new list these days, whatever anyone tells you, unless you are trying to avoid the grips of the Data Protection Act, which for some reason excludes the likes of index card and other 'manually' held systems. Now why would you want to do that?

Lists? Or databases?

You'll remember that I have already given you my simple descriptions. A list is the whereabouts of people. A database is the whereabouts and the whatabouts. To be successful in direct mail in the future you will have to adopt a database mentality. That means you have to start adding 'the whatabouts' to the name and address information as early as you can in your selling process. But there are some limiting factors to that. They are the individual's basic right to privacy and the one legal enforcement of that which adds the individual's right to accuracy. It's called the Data Protection Act.

I unswervingly support both.

Personally I don't think you can legislate for an individual's right to privacy in quite the same way as you can in relation to other data. I believe the interpretation of that right is fundamentally the individual's too. It's up to them to decide whether they regard as an invasion of privacy being mailed by anybody at any time, being mailed by certain people or about certain subjects or even at certain times, or whether they really don't give a damn. Having said that, equally I don't believe that an envelope plonking through the letterbox — which you can ignore or not as you choose — constitutes an invasion of privacy. The recipient is, after all, at liberty to dispose of the envelope unopened, or opened and disregarded, as they so choose.

There is in most of these matters an acceptable common-sense answer. Most reasonable advertisers know that if they abuse people's rights or offend in any way, they will not achieve their objective. Thus the pressure to succeed will keep reasonable people on the straight and narrow. Public feeling, together with the Data Protection Act, will, in the main, take care of the rats. The great thing is that you and I, as non-rats, do everything we can to uphold standards and everything we can do to dispose of the rats. Otherwise they'll spoil it for the rest of us. And turn public opinion against us.

Ironically, whereas I think many extreme consumerists would claim that the age of the database constitutes a real threat of more junk, a veritable tidal wave even, I believe I have already demonstrated that the reverse is more likely. That we move nearer and nearer getting acceptable propositions to people that are interested by them, with the very minimum of wastage and the very minimum of upset.

Thus, your job is to start adding information about people as soon as possible to ensure the *minimum* of intrusion, the *maximum* of acceptance and acceptability. However, it is unlikely that you will ever reach a stage where that information is totally purchasable without you acquiring the company that owns it. Things are improving. That's to say the amount of information that you can obtain is improving. The amount of assessed information, or indeed, given information is expanding. Thus the list business is shaping up to the more sophisticated needs of the market.

And there will always be a need for lists. The continued search for new prospects and new markets will ensure this. Sometimes direct marketing media will be used to scan the marketplace looking for people whom we want to add to the database, and sometimes to make contact with those whom we have already identified or added. The search for names goes on!

How much time and effort should you spend on lists?

There is one extraordinary fact about lists. A situation that has existed as long as I can remember, and which still exists today. I urge you to think about it. And then do something about it. Hopefully it will change your thinking. And also, perhaps, your approach.

It is a fact that everybody accepts the list to be the single most important factor in achieving success. However good the offer, the creative, the production and personalisation, if you are mailing to people that can't, don't want to or just won't buy, you are on a hiding to nothing. Yet lists have been the most underdeveloped, underrated, undervalued part of the industry. It is improving. But slowly. Advertisers blow astronomical sums of money on creative, but baulk at the costs of de-duplication. They'll test one simple change of offer, and dash headlong into lists because they 'feel' right.

A 'good' list is worth its weight in gold

But what does 'good' mean?

Undoubtedly, for most of us, good means responsive. But the factors that affect response go beyond simple 'appropriateness'. Sure, it's a good idea to mail Eskimos about igloos. But do they want *our* igloos? Not if we spell their name wrong, mail them at an igloo they bought yesterday, or for that matter, mail the igloo they left yesterday!

So there are other things we can do to a list, or make sure that others are doing, to ensure it is 'good'. We shall certainly look at some of those things together, but before we can knock the names into shape we need to find them.

The two principal sources of names

I'll sound rather foolish if I tell you that names come from two sources and two sources only. They are internal and external. That's to say names that you can access within your company or names you have to go outside for. Now the reason I am being so basic and 'obvious' is because so many people overlook the full range of internal sources that are available to them.

I remember one large electrical retailer, a multiple,

explaining with great delight and pride that their staff were instructed to issue an invoice in triplicate to all customers in all stores spending more than £25. One copy of the invoice was returned to Head Office where a 'thank you' letter together with some special offers were mailed to the customer. Over 300 000 such invoices were received each year.

However, it transpired that, in order to save money, to address the outgoing envelope they simply cut off the name and address from the invoice and stuck it to the envelope.

So 300 000+ names came in and, because they didn't make any note of them, 300 000+ went out again!

So let's assume that you have been given the task of formally putting together a mailing list of customers and prospective customers and other contacts for your business. The obvious first place to start is with accounts, the sales ledger. Remember, with all these records the further back you go, the greater will be the need to verify the information. Since you will undoubtedly want to build a database in the future, take a good look at all the information you have and make some basic decisions as to what you will wish to store. You will need to consider whether, and if so, for what purpose, you might wish to retrieve it.

Next, the same process with any sales, customer relations or marketing records that are available, going right down to the individuals involved, such as reps or consultants and PR people.

Next look at any agents, outlets or intermediaries and see what you can glean from there. Now it's the turn of administration and service or maintenance teams. 'Hoover' out all you can. Examine service and maintenance paperwork and guarantee cards if you have them.

Remember in all this that you must set up a line of communication to ensure that these things will be automatically fed through to you for the future. Think about the ways that outlets or reception areas and maintenance or service teams — anyone exposed to customers or potential customers — can gather names, addresses and as much other useful information as possible.

Regard every contact as a potential for future direct marketing. Just as you will consider every contact when they are customers, as an opportunity to repeat sell.

Make sure in your search for names that you include telephonists, counter clerks, everyone. Even include the customers themselves. With them you can implement all sorts of fun and games to get them to join in and tell you more about themselves and to introduce you to other people they select as being suitable to do business with you. And you'll be surprised just how good (and willing) they are at it. So try member-get-member or customer-get-customer devices. Leave them space to recommend friends or colleagues on order coupons. Mail them questionnaires to find out their views and feelings. If you can't get 10–40 per cent response from a questionnaire or survey mailing you've got something drastically wrong.

And lastly, for the future, don't forget to make the gathering of names, and then the sifting, grading and classifying of them, a way of life.

I can think of only one or two reasons why anyone would want to advertise without a coupon. So why not consider that all your advertising should be couponed? The direct response advertising, naturally — but what about all the *other* advertising too? And if you're going to include a coupon, maybe you can devise something a little stronger than just 'further information' to offer!

Adopt a 'gathering' attitude to all events, activities and functions. Go to exhibitions, for instance, not just to give out information, but to gather as many names of prospects as you can, and as much relevant knowledge about them as you can. Your own lists, constructed, cleaned and massaged properly should always give you the best response. With one possible exception.

From time to time, I have seen even the best customer lists outpulled in what direct marketers call 'affinity' mailings. This is where the advertiser approaches another list owner and mails out, in the best cases, effectively coupling the power of their own proposition, message and market position together with that of the chosen affinity list owner. Generally speaking, the stronger the endorsement of the third party or affinity organisation the stronger the concept works. Having said that, I must also say that there should be some common ground between the two collaborators. Or at least one should be creatable.

Affinity group marketing is big direct marketing business. To the point where whole organisations in travel, publishing and social activities have been created, originally not to be in the travel, publishing or social activities business, but to create a group of identified lifestyle people with the bond of some kind of customer relationship and thereby some marketing information available.

I suppose, as we move on to consider external sources, you could suggest that affinity groups are not really internal, but external.

Technically, you are right. But I suggest that the more *you*,

265

as the list owner, present these opportunities, and the more you think about them as 'your own', the more successful you will be.

Step inside — and let's look for lists

What are we looking at external list sources for? Are you thinking of buying or renting one? Or building yourself one?

Building a mailing list is a specialist and skilled business. Building a database, the same but more so. If you are typical you will need outside help to build a database — computer *and* list people. To build a list you don't *need* outside help — but there are so many skilled people around, and so many and various sources of information, my advice would generally be to subcontract the list-building and concentrate on being clear what you need, and establishing how to check that *you have got it before* you pay for it!

However, you might also like to pose yourself these questions as a discipline before you decide.

1   Is the computer facility adequate?

You will run through with me in a few paragraphs some ways to decide whether you should or should not use existing facilities. If not, you have two options open to you.

The first is to create your own new file. Taken from the main file this would be, in effect, a marketing file or database, dedicated to your own activities. The second is to take the same information and place it in the hands of a bureau who are capable of providing full list management facilities. If you choose the right bureau this particular course should bring the dual benefits of expertise and experience.

Expertise in that, if your DP department's main activities are not those of direct marketing but perhaps more concerned with accounting and administration, the bureau will without doubt spend more time concentrating on new ideas, techniques and technology. All these highly specialist developments to do with the business of lists and looking after them and getting the best out of them.

And experience. You would expect this. Naturally, it will be one of the major considerations in choosing your bureau. But I raise it to highlight the benefit of not having to obtain a DP department that is already busy, and perhaps even set in its ways, in the new, demanding and apparently baffling world of direct marketing. To get the best out of them they too need to be totally involved in and aware of the business, what you are doing and your preferred methods.

I give this advice knowing that, having taken the step to start by putting the computer side out to an outside supplier, it is very difficult later to bring it in. Because it will get bigger and more specialised as time progresses.

This advice is for those where direct marketing is not the only activity — it's a new or additional or secondary one, at least as far as the computer team are concerned. This being so, you may find the ultimate solution performs better than most in-house facilities anyway.

The ultimate in my view, in the majority of cases where the level merits it, is to have specialist outside list management facilities with in-house on-line access.

Many bureaux now offer such facilities and it works extremely well, avoiding a mass of problems and securing in many ways, the best of both in-house/out-house options.

2 Are the available hardware and software adequate?

Most so-called mailing list or list management packages are criminally basic. They have as much right to use those descriptions as most classical agencies have to include direct mail amongst their capabilities. Both are doing it because they know it will sell, not because they can come up with the goods. In relation to hardware, if you are not already aware of the special demands of direct marketing business, you will, by the end of this chapter, appreciate my point. One could extend this comment to include programming too.

3 Is the computer facility available and does it have the capability?

Not only must you have access, you must have priority. Second in a pecking order is not good enough. Timing is one of the biggest benefits of direct mail, and speed of response to market developments another.

Moreover, you will undoubtedly want a higher quality of everything, so don't start out thinking you can get by on what they do, or use.

Not for you the systems that:

● Leave unsightly codes in address areas
● Will not provide perfect personalisation and addressing
● Use upper case (capital) letters and abbreviations or incomplete addresses

4 Can you do all the things necessary to keep a list in prime condition?

Let's look at some:

- Sort mail to Post Office requirements to qualify for lower rates and discounts
- Update, amend and delete, preferably daily or weekly, but at a minimum monthly
- Find and add new names — a list starts to deteriorate as it's built
- Mail frequently — most high-response lists have frequent use as an advantage not a disadvantage. Lists generally become more responsive through use, not less, and it aids the cleansing process through removal of nixies
- You must be able to select by any number of criteria and segment into small groups of high appeal for particular product services or situations
- You must be able to merge and purge with other lists, to remove duplication, and more. A topic we'll look at in more detail later

5 Do you have the time and resources personally or departmentally to take on the responsibility of a list once it is built, as well as during the building?

List maintenance is detailed, time-consuming and challenging. It is also vital. And unless your list gets the devotion it requires, it will waste away in both quantity and value.

6 What shortcuts are available to help you start up?

Access to qualified names in good condition (preferably with some reasonable history or activity behind them) will make a tremendous difference. These can come from external as well as internal sources, and as long as they are available outright (to buy as opposed to rent, often substantially more expensive) and are in a usable form (i.e. computerised and clean), they will be worth considering.

Favourite sources will include:

- Lists from competitors that have gone into liquidation or whom you have acquired
- Lists of exhibition attendees or conference delegates
- Members of trade or professional associations or institutes
- Lists of responders to suitable promotional activities, on-pack offers, competitions, etc.

- Lists acquired through exchanges with non-competing but comparably profiled marketers

If you have positive answers to all or most of these questions, you are probably right to press on with building your own. But the two most important things you will need are time and know-how. Which is why I suggest that a professional will probably do the job better, and ultimately quicker and cheaper too.

Perhaps one of the most sobering thoughts in this direction is the true cost of wastage. Whether that wastage is simply the inclusion or purchase of an undeliverable name and address, or much more likely, and in the long run far more wasteful and expensive, the inclusion of someone who is unlikely to respond. This will cost you a fortune in wasted mail — but, as well as that, may harden prospects against you with the course of time.

Where can you get lists outside your own business, if you don't want to build?

There are four principal sources: list owners, list managers, list brokers and list compilers

In evaluating which of these is the best external source of names for you, I would like you to bear in mind — the very front of your mind — their motivations. Who calls their tune. Why they are in business. And to whom their first responsibility lies.

List owners

There are two kinds — those who own a list built through their own trading process, and those who own a list that they have compiled for the purpose of renting and selling. They are distinctly separate types as a rule. Bearing in mind — as I have urged you to throughout this book — how many exceptions there are to how many rules!

You have very few problems with the list owners. Apart from checking out their reputation, you need only ask the right questions and then find which offers nearest to the specification you require and which works best for you. Be prepared for the answer to be both or all. One of the differences, for example, may be one list offers a high degree of information selectivity and qualification, another offers little of these but a wider spread of names. Both may work well and the answer may be to vary or alternate your rental of both. On the other hand, it may be to start with a special purchase deal from them both, to merge these with your own lists and then do a deal for the future with them on their new names and their nixies.

Enlightened list owners will not have a problem with this. They may even seek a reciprocal arrangement with you if your market is that close, or your activity level high.

But as far as these owners are concerned, their motivation is to seek maximum sales of their list, to do all they can to keep the list in peak condition, and to keep their customers coming back for more.

I shall now separate those who compile lists for a living and come back to them at the end because I do basically regard them as a distinct category.

The motivations of those who have compiled their list through trading will have one fundamentally different aspect. That is their own future trading potential beyond list rentals. Most owners — particularly publishers and mail order companies — will have built up their list through their own profitable selling to their market. They will have elected, when their list got to a reasonable size, to make it a marketable commodity, and to go into this as an additional profit source. This means two things to you. First, you will never be able to mail anything that competes with their own product range. And, secondly, that their own activities will always take precedence over yours. These two may be so strong as to preclude either of you wanting to do business together, or alternatively, never be a problem at all.

List managers

List managers are employed by list owners to look after their lists for them. That may simply be to do so for the list owner's private use or, more commonly, when a manager is involved, to keep the list in prime condition for the owner's use as well as to take care of its sale to the marketplace. This will often include the selling and marketing of the list (for which they may go direct or through brokers or both) together with all the administration, handling and processing involved. The involvement of the list owner, where they are employing a list manager, should be limited to demanding their own requirements, monitoring the performance of the manager as he trades their list for them and little else apart from decision-making from time to time. And banking the proceeds, of course.

List owners should find that a successful manager will not only keep the list in the optimum condition, but effectively return a profit over and above the costs of working the list. Thus, they get the twin benefits of 'free' list maintenance and management for themselves, and an extra bottom-line contribution into the bargain.

You might be thinking how this could work for you. We'll look at it in a few pages.

So, to sum up on list managers, they work for list owners. Their prime concern is the satisfaction of the list owner. You can only ever come, at best, second to that.

List brokers

If you want to rent lists, as opposed to have anything done to or for your own list, this is where you should turn. And I would urge you to seek out those who belong to the appropriate associations nationally and perhaps internationally. In Britain, that will be the British List Brokers Association (details in Part Three). The importance of this association is that its members operate within a basic code of conduct. Which is, hopefully, a commercial safety net for you.

The 'honest broker' will be the one who understands which side his bread is buttered. Like most direct marketers he will not be after the quick buck. He will want your business. Not once. Not to organise a few tests for you. But for the long term. He will need to understand your business, as well as your direct marketing. Particularly, with a good reliable broker, you should be prepared to disclose your results, your problems and opportunities and your short, medium and long-term direct marketing objectives.

As well as advice and knowledge, your broker should guide you through the maze of list rentals and take care of the arrangements for you. At worst you should be supplying sample packs for clearance, checking and signing rental agreements, checking deliveries and paying the bills.

So those are three of the four basic types. More on compiled lists when we look at business names. We'll spend some more time on how to deal effectively with all four of them elsewhere in this chapter, but I suppose the burning question has to be — are the rumours true? Do list people deserve the somewhat mysterious and shady reputation that they have certainly had in the past? Although, on their behalf, I must say the act has been cleaned up a lot over the last decade.

Undoubtedly, there are some sharpish characters in the list business. I'm not convinced, however, that the proportion is greater than that in any booming market. Unfortunately, just as we have also seen happen at various times with second-hand cars, copiers, double glazing, solar panels, time-share etc., these things happen, but at least they are problems that fade as the industry becomes strong enough to realise that the rogues are spoiling it for everybody else and deal with them.

Probably the two favourite 'routines' of the rogue are 'making up' and 'weighting'. Making up is the process of making up quantities. It will be done for three reasons. First, to oversell. If you can take as many names as they can supply, rather than tell you that's the lot, more names will be found. Second, if names are required elsewhere at the same time as your demand is required — by the list owner, for example — you may find that some 'enquirers' get fed into what you thought was a list of buyers. Third, if the quantities were 'guestimated' in the first case and run out short, 'making up' may occur again. It's a difficult problem to spot. And equally difficult to prove.

'Weighting' is about biasing lists in test to get you to rent again in larger quantities. It is well known, for example, that a list of mail order buyers is better than a list of buyers through other sources (such as via a salesforce or retail outlets). Equally, it is well known that 'hot names' (those that have been recently acquired or activated, probably recent purchasers) will out-perform others; that multiple purchasers will out-perform single purchasers; that cash buyers will out-perform credit card buyers. And so on. Thus our rogue can weight test samples to be sure that you get the optimum as opposed to a true and typical test result which indicates how the list will perform. Again, this is equally difficult to spot. But 'grid coding' can help.

Grid coding is achieved by asking the list owner what selections are available prior to rental and for the relevant quantities. Then you ask for 'grid codes' — codes denoting the selections — to be applied to the response device, and for counts to be supplied.

You can thereby check the proportions of the various code counts to see if they bear any relation to the figures given originally. You can also cross-check the counts you've been given with the finished addressed items. It's not foolproof but it's about all you've got, other than expensive telephone research.

There is another tendency for list owners and managers to find cute descriptions. One I recall was a list of 'lapsed charity donors'. Most charities who saw this list couldn't believe their eyes. This, for them, is next best to cash!!

'Lapsed charity donors' turned out to be a few hundred thousand people who had taken part in a ten-pence-a-week scratch'n'reveal football game that happened to be sponsored by a charity. Thus these people didn't actually feel they had participated or given to the charity as the major conscious action on their part. Most of them felt they had played a ten-pence-a-week football game. But described as it should have been, the rental attraction was next to nil.

Often imitated but never duplicated

I think that slogan is from the fifties or early sixties but I can't remember whose it was! I use it to subhead my last but by no means least important thought on external list sources.

Let's talk about duplication for a little.

Everybody shrinks at the thought of duplication and I can understand that. A list that duplicates with yours is going to cost a fortune in wastage unless, of course, you can remove the duplication. Another reason for the beloved computer with high-capability software!

Yet, ironically, in 95 per cent of cases the single most likely pointer to a good list is a high degree of duplication with yours. It tells you that there is a greater similarity between the prospective list and your own. And there is generally no reason in my experience to doubt that a list that contains a greater number of actual customers will not equally contain a greater number of potential customers. Having identified that high levels of duplication exist, you then have both to remove it *and* avoid paying for it. Why, after all, should you pay for names you already own? Most list owners, managers and brokers will be open to suggestions. List compilers, in general, haven't got there yet!

Most direct mail goes to existing **customer** lists

If you go back to my TEN-X factor in Part One, you'll understand why! I have been given to understand that the figure is 70–80 per cent of all direct mail. That's a lot! So I think the first point I would like to make about customer lists should be about the security of them. Not so much the 'backing up' procedures — but the responsibility for the list and the planting of sleepers.

First, in terms of security, it is worth noting that the Data Protection Act is a piece of criminal legislation. Therefore this raises the need for list security above and beyond a simple commercial responsibility. If your company fails to comply with the legislation the *individuals* concerned face the possibility of criminal proceedings and possibly prison sentences! This means that those to whom you give such responsibility must be aware of their responsibilities and the penalties they face — or you face — for contravening the dictates of the Act. Although I am not aware, at the time of writing, of any proceedings under the Act that have resulted in those responsible for lists finding themselves incarcerated courtesy of Her Majesty, it is still a fact that they could be. In truth, the legislation is, from a judicial point of view, not yet 'proved', and I am not aware of any precedents being set. None the less, you should make yourself very familiar with the Act and what you should and should not do to comply with it.

Bearing in mind the extraordinary value of a customer list as a usable — and therefore stealable — commodity, I would suggest to any list owner, however modest the quantity involved, that they should plant sleepers in the list. There are two sorts. Static and variable. A sleeper is a person, indiscernible from typical names on the list, included to report back to you all mail they receive.

It is important that some distinguishing feature is decided upon which differentiates the mail they receive from your list as apart from the mail they receive generally. Perhaps a particular set of initials or the way the address is styled or presented.

This should remain constant for a proportion of the sleepers. For the remainder, the distinguishing feature should vary for each use of the list and a log should be kept of the changes.

To enjoy the full deterrent value of this system you must make sure that all your own staff and suppliers know you are operating such a system, even down to marking all files and tapes with a warning that sleepers are included. Additionally, I would suggest you ensure that, if you are renting your own list, any renter should accept that this process exists as a condition of rental. Do make sure that lists/tapes or whatever are signed in and out at each stage of any journey. Be sure to ask about the security arrangements at any transit point and destination.

On top of that, you should ensure that:

1 Out-of-office-hours processing should always be supervised and catalogued
2 You run efficient password and library systems
3 Tape movements are always sent by recorded delivery means — and that they are adequately insured

Although we've talked about RFM frequently, we haven't recently. And we haven't discussed how you can make money at it!

Unless you have a reasonable quantity of names, and at least a first or second-generation database operating, the next four paragraphs may not be a great help to you — other, perhaps than to point out where you should be headed. Also, it is mainly for those involved in mail order.

We're going to take a wander briefly through the whole concept of RFM analysis and to enter the world of 'discriminates'. What all of this is about is a predictive or discriminating attitude, to name segmentation in order to 'fine-tune' the targeting of your mailings. I single out mail order as the field where this will be of best use, not only because it is where the concept is most proven but because it is also a field where the sale is made by a common factor. The catalogue or package. Perhaps another way of saying this would be an unhuman (as opposed to inhuman) sales device.

The 'birth' of RFM

Going back as far as the late forties and early fifties in the States it was discovered that there were some common elements to profitable repeat orders at the higher volume ranges. These were, as I have already pointed out, the recency of the last purchase, the frequency at which people purchase, and value of orders placed within certain time spans (such as a catalogue life or sales season).

In Rose Harper's fascinating book *Mailing List Strategies* (see bibliography) these are quoted broadly as:

Frequency: 50–90 per cent
Recency: 35–90 per cent
Monetary value: 15–90 per cent

By examining purchasing histories against such criteria it is possible to predict which segments of a list will be the most profitable for future use, or even to exclude those who, although they might order, will not return a profitable group of transactions against the cost that will be incurred by running the promotional programme. This method has enabled mail order companies to limit or control circulation of their material. They have learned to identify those who have demonstrated through performance (measured on a revenue to sales cost basis) that they are most likely to return the higher profit levels. Experience will show you where to draw the lines. In basic form, this is the theory of RFM analysis.

As computer technology and consumer profiling developed, so it has become possible to overlay other discernible discriminating factors on top of the RFM analysis. One can take, for example, deciles of those who show up best in RFM analysis and look at what other common features there are.

The most obvious for review will be geographic, demographic and psychographic (or social). Rose Harper's book is one which I commend to all those in serious or volume direct marketing and everybody in any kind of mail order, consumer or business-to-business.

Rose identifies the other major discriminators as: sex, address, date of entry on file, type(s) of product purchased, source (of name/type of test or media through which recruited), seasonality of purchasing, method of payment, recency of last transaction, other geographics and length of time on file. By examining the additional kinds of data that I suggest in the following pages, you might add to or sophisticate this list.

In this whole area the British and many of the other European markets have had the disadvantage of smaller size. It has often been overheard ln the bars of Montreux during the International Symposium gathering that 'It's OK for the Americans. They've got the numbers to play with.'

From 1992, we Europeans run out of excuses!

And what of our lists of **enquirers**?

Where, in performance terms, do these fit in? Let's run through the grades again:

Best list potential — customers
Next list potential — lapsed customers
Next list potential — enquiries

I should add to this in two ways. First it is quite likely that the most recent enquiries will out-pull lapsed customers. Second, that the most recent lapsed customers will still out-pull them! Work that out!

Having explained the original and updated concepts of RFM analysis to a workshop of delegates recently, I had to hand it to the one who came out with the next topic we need to consider. He asked, 'That's all very well for customers — but can you expand it to prospects (or suspects) too?'

Well, in some ways, you can. The concept we have been looking at is historically based. Therefore mathematically and actually it can provide you with some important data which can be used to select segments of customers who will perform better than others. The warning light is that the historical data relate, in mass or segment form, to those upon whom they are being used. So RFM as such is out. However some of the common factors may well provide you with some clues as to which segments of the prospect or suspect list will convert most easily. More interesting, perhaps, would be to identify which, almost regardless of the ease with which they will convert, will perform best after conversion, and therefore which you should most spend your time, effort and investment converting.

At this stage I suggest, if you are dealing in appropriate or reasonable numbers, that you consider putting together the thoughts we looked at together under key suspect identification and the last few pages.

The business of **business** lists

Another resounding factor in support of the key suspect identification approach to business markets is the singular lack of in-depth information available, unless you acquire it yourself, plus the florists, ladies' hairdressers and company managing director syndrome. Earlier in the book we identified these groups as exemplifying the higher rates of change experienced with business lists.

The clue to this particular puzzle lies in the fact that although the individuals change, the jobs, functions and tasks remain. Restaurants, snack bars, hotels, etc. may change style or cuisine or ownership. But they tend to say what they are, which is why many business mailers will report that names do not out-pull simple designations. I have to say that experience here differs enormously and there is absolutely no substitute for your own experience.

I don't mean so much that one person says one works best and the next person another. Indeed, my own experience has differed enormously.

If I were to try to pin-point what I think will make the biggest difference, it is probably the use to which you will put the name. In other words, only testing will tell you whether, if using external sources for lists, you should pay extra for named lists. Given a name, it may make no difference whatsoever if you don't really use it. For example, in many business situations, if you only use it on the outer envelope, how many will actually get to see it anyway? On the other hand, if you use it for matching in, personalisation of the letter, a flyer or order device, it may make a lot of difference.

On which point, incidentally, as well as personalising, in business-to-business mail you can 'corporatise' just as well, by using the company name on vouchers, letters, flyers, etc:

> This voucher is for the exclusive use of Hardcastle Engineering Ltd

Or both personalised and 'corporatised' as:

> and so we have extended this invitation not only to you, Mr Smith, but to any other colleagues at Hardcastle Engineering who you feel would benefit by attending.

What information should you store on a business direct mail/marketing database?

In this, and the following section relating to consumer lists, I am going to provide a checklist of the kind of data that you can consider storing on your database. You may take one look and decide that it's far more than you need. Or, indeed, doesn't go far enough. But it is current state of the art. You must additionally consider the items not included that make such a checklist relevant to you. For example, if you are selling retail/supermarket shelving, details of store area by square metre may be useful. Or whether they have central buying. Or whether any given outlet has their own bakery/fresh produce/butchery, etc. Or number of car parking spaces. Or number of checkouts. Whatever.

In each case, business and consumer, the checklist will be followed by some explanatory notes (see pages 280–81).

Corporate data
- Unique ID number/trans-data link (1)
- Company name
- Street/zone/town or city/state, county or department/country
- Postal or zip code
- Telephone number(s)/fax number(s)/telex number(s)
- Business or industry classification/SIC (2) code
- Preferred distribution channelling (3) codes
- Preferred ordering channel (4) codes
- Key contact trans-data (5) codes to personal data/by individual
- Business turnover/number of employees
- Count of duplicate incidence with other files — (6) buyer/enquirer — trans-data link to current employees
- Viewdata/cable subscriber

Operational data

- Direct/indirect customer
- Acquisition date
- Operational/area code
- Sales/branch/outlet code
- Salesperson/broker/agent codes
- Product or service purchase/enquiry codes
- Fee/commission/credit for sale due/to whom codes
- Business priority level code
- Supply codes . . . equipment/services/maintenance/literature/other
- Media coverage
- Computer system/make/language codes
- Credit control status/limits/excess procedures

Corporate relationship data by individual

- Trans-data link to corporate data (7)
- Acquisition source/method/media codes
- Acquisition offer/promotion code
- Recency of last offer/promotion — success/fail
- Business analysis by product/service
- Recency of last order
- Value of last order
- Last complaint date/reason/resolution codes
- Preferred payment method — bank instruction/credit/cheque/cash
- Business patterns — 15 month-review by quarters — frequency/value/product (service)
- Recommendations/referrals — mgm/name donor/other
- Count of duplicate incidence with other files — buyer/enquirer (8)

Personal data by individual

- Trans-data link to corporate data (7)
- Trans-data link to representative database (9)
- Surname
- Title
- Professional qualifications
- Nature of influence — buyer/specifier/finance/other
- Degree of influence on sale(s) — score 1 high/10 low
- Introduction date/employment started/previous job title (10)
- First/second names
- Sex
- Date of birth

- Marital status — married/single/single parent
- Name of spouse
- Occupation of spouse
- Children — number/sexes/ages/first names
- Residential postal/zip code + demographics/acorn/mosaic/ pin/point

Cumulative previous data from former employees
- Acquisition sources — method/media/offer/promotion

Notes
1 Trans-data codes are used to link corresponding data between organisations and the individuals involved.
2 SIC codes: Standard Industrial Classification is a standard method of identifying the business/trade or profession. Some business lists are selectable by SIC code, others are held by SIC order.
3 Distribution channelling codes denote what distribution system(s) or network(s) is used to supply this customer, e.g. via a particular wholesale/retailer, distributor/ dealer or even transport systems — own/Federal Express, etc.
4 Ordering channel codes denote the route(s) through which this organisation likes to order. For instance, via the local representatives, tele-sales, direct or a particular dealer, distributor, retailer, etc.
5 This is an interim code between the levels at 1 and 7 — provides shortform identification of key contacts (often limited to major purchase decision influencers). Although it can provide more, often used for name, title, and professional qualifications only.
6 Every time a new file is merged and purged with your own, a count is kept of the incidence of duplication. This is used as an indicator to help in assessing business priority Also used for targeting.
7 See 1.
8 As an alternative or addition to 6. Next level of sophistication lowers duplication check success count to individual level where named lists are being merged.
9 Trans-data link code string enables two-way patching for file updates, amends and analysis between main file and personal database details held by representative (the computerised little black book!) — this supplements main file with on-screen or statistical

reporting to include calling information, meeting resumés and agendas.

10 Information to denote service record and whether promoted up or taken on for job.

11 Statistical, historical count, recording success/failure history of additional cumulative information as individuals are deleted from records.

In many ways business list developments have lagged behind even the underdeveloped and underinvested consumer lists field.

This is an even greater irony — since in business mail the order levels at stake are substantially higher, and therefore the rewards greater still.

I suggest the invalid, but none the less true reason has to do with the much smaller quantities involved. Which in fact makes it easier to achieve!

However, for anyone about to make decisions on whether large-scale or up-scale budget allocations for a database are a good idea — and whether the database should be anything near as sophisticated as my checklists suggest, let me give you another list. A list of clues to help you make the decision.

- Lists represent the single largest criteria that will contribute to the degree of mailing success or failure.
- No other area of direct marketing has been so wickedly, foolishly and unprofessionally under-regarded. Only the US can claim anything like sufficient progress. But then we excuse ourselves by noting, of course, they've got the numbers.

And so my last clue.

- 1992.

May I suggest one more line to include under 'Personal data by individual'. . .

- First language/other's spoken codes

The all-consuming topic of **consumer** lists

Let's get straight to the consumer database checklist.

Operational data
- Unique ID number
- Trans-data link code to other data (1)
- Direct/indirect customer

- Operational/area code
- Sales/branch/outlet code
- Salesperson/broker/agent codes
- Product or service purchase/enquiry codes
- Fee/commission due/to whom codes
- Business priority level code
- Supply codes — equipment/service/literature/other
- TV area/satellite receiver/cable subscriber/viewdata codes
- Media coverage
- Home PC ownership/make/language codes

Relationship data

- Acquisition source/method/media codes
- Acquisition offer/promotion code
- Recency of last offer/promotion — success/fail
- Business analysis by product/service
- Value of last order
- Date of last order
- Last complaint date/reason/resolution codes
- Preferred payment method — bank instruction/credit card/cheque/cash
- Business patterns — 15-month review by quarters — frequency/value/product (service)
- Credit/payment/debt record
- Recommendations/referrals — mgm/name donor/other

Personal data

- Surname
- Title
- Professional qualifications
- Trans-data link (2) to representative or tele-sales personal database information
- First/second names
- Sex
- Date of birth
- Marital status — married/single/single parent
- Household or number/street/town or city/state, county or department/country
- Postal/zip code
- Telephone numbers — home/work
- Job status/business or industry/retired codes
- Date of last address change/previous postal code
- Date of last employment change
- Home owned + value/rented/other
- Occupation of spouse
- Children — number/sexes/ages/first names

- Family income band
- Credit/charge/store cards held
- Health record — standard/special (if special, life policy/medical underwriting)
- Residential demographics/Acorn/Mosaic/Pinpoint
- Count of duplicate incidence with other files — buyer/enquirer

Notes

1 Trans-data link code to other data — such as individual, partial or complete transaction data or files.
2 Trans-data link code enables two-way patching for file updates, amends and analysis between main file and personal database details held by representative. This supplements main file data with on-screen or statistical reporting to include calling information, appointment resumés and agendas.

Again, as I pointed out with the business-to-business checklist, you will need to look at other data you require to store. It might be residential data, when white goods were purchased, car and motoring information, whether the house is double-glazed etc. You may wish to have other supplementary lifestyle or psychographic information to assist you in understanding the customer or suspect's needs.

What are geographic, demographic and psychographic information? And should you bother?

Let's take the second question first — should you bother? The answer will depend to some degree on the scale and commitment you are making to consumer direct marketing. But most likely my answer, unless you are dealing exclusively with small local markets, is 'yes'.

Let's talk now for the benefit of those involved in European markets. 1992 is going to increase the need to use such targeting systems. But there are other pressures. For as market potential expands globally — and as manufacturers and service organisations look more seriously at the benefits of international branding — so too, simultaneously, markets are demassing or fragmenting. For the future the need will be to understand more about smaller groups of consumers within a larger total population.

The targeting opportunities available through geographic, demographic and psychographic data will be enormously valuable for this and will at least see us through the 1990s into the age of interactive view-data, home terminals and on into the videophone and home total communication module eras, no doubt. But while we wait for the technocrats to decide our communications fate, let's see what these systems offer for us in the shorter term.

Geographic/demographic systems

In the UK we've got Acorn, Mosaic, Pinpoint, Superprofiles, Homescan, Finpin, Spectra to start with! In the States Acorn again, Prizm, Vision and more. And more! If someone could come out with a DIN-type standard, that would be great. Although the thought of DIN-FIN-PIN does send shivers down the spine!

For many years in the UK, the conventional advertising industry has relied on the most ludicrously out-of-date socio-economic classification. You'll probably have come across them — A, B, C1, C2, D, E. Apart from being barely postwar in their classification of the consumer, they are socially embarrassing!

In order to find something more suitable, more selective and more effective mainly for direct marketing purposes, a number of suppliers to the industry have invented systems which relate Census data to the postal code system. Essentially these differ in that instead of socio-economically defining the individual, they more rigorously analyse the neighbourhood in which a household exists. The British Census works in units of about 150-ish households being what is known as an Enumeration District. These bear no direct correlation to the postcode areas but the different systems have achieved, by different methods, ways of achieving workable correlations.

Having done so they have 'profiled' the areas using the Census data, grading postcode areas into a number of neighbourhood types. Some operate 40 or so different types, others up to 150.

I am reluctant to advise you which is the best, as I am not sure that there is a best. Certainly some have performed better than others for me, but I have enjoyed successes and suffered failures with most of them.

Again, in terms of response uplift, there is no clear winner. I have had one conference delegate assuring me of a 500 per cent + response uplift. I would suggest — knowing the naturally exuberant type! — we divide that by two and even then I would suggest this says more about the mistakes he was making before than the strength of the targeting system! I have experienced, typically, anything from nil uplift (even one depression of response) to a 45 per cent uplift.

Psychograpic information is essentially behavioural data. Generally established through historical or acquired knowledge. It is often confused but not quite the same, I feel, as lifestyle data which are usually gathered by the circulation of questionnaires or surveys (or trading). The difference I note most in the terminology, as applied by practitioners of such data manipulation, is that the psychographic school base their work on what consumers do, whereas the lifestyle school base it on what consumers say they do. You may consider this a fine point.

However, it is certain that there is an expanding use of all of these techniques. And in the face of the de-massification of markets and increasing internationalism amongst marketers, I have little doubt that all these activities will flourish and become even more widely accepted and adopted.

All the systems tend to work by 'profiling' the whole, or segments, of your existing databank and ranking the units to which they relate (most often postal code areas) by their similarity of discriminants to your own file or subject segments.

The systems also have something to offer in the list rental field where they can similarly be used to overlay onto a single prospective file, or pre-merged files, to select the most likely respondents. Again, these are taken against the profile revealed by your own file or selections of it.

Let's suppose I know where you live or where you are in relation to one of my outlets (geographic data), I know the type of neighbourhood in which you live (demographic data) and the fact that you take two holidays abroad each year, both in Europe, one with your kids and one without (psychographic data). And eminently sensible, too, if you don't mind me saying so!

What about **compiled** lists?

In this section I am going to run through those lists that are compiled, not generally through trading, but largely from published sources such as directories. The vast majority of these are available for the business and professional markets. Occasionally, you have a choice between, say, magazine subscribers or readers as well, but equally often you will find yourself drawn to the professional list compilers. In the UK we have some noteworthy names.

The Business Database   or in other words, the contents of the British Telecom Yellow Pages on computer. Available with telephone numbers too. Each entry verified by telephone before going on the system for rental. Updated on a daily basis, although they do not offer names — other than if it's an individual's trading style. This particular list had its problems in its previous existence but is fast carving a name for itself as value for money and offering wider coverage of some hitherto poorly documented areas (such as retailers).

Dun and Bradstreet a large database of companies with a comparative wealth of data behind the names. For example, turnover, date of foundation, number of staff, SIC code, named chief executive, etc.

Key Postal Advertising the pre-eminent general supplier of off-the-shelf compiled lists. And a company whose principles (and indeed principals) are respected and admired throughout the industry. High-quality lists covering many hundreds of business classifications and a very usable industrial database with many named executives available.

Market Location Ltd a database loaded with information obtained through field visits. Can be linked through to site/location data for sales follow-up and combines a great deal of selectable site data as well as executive managerial and SIC coding.

I have chosen to mention just four (and in alphabetical order!), there are many more. And a host of publishers' files available. Also there are many specialist areas such as medical and farming. If you are anxious to track down a shortlist of suitable compiled list suppliers, you would be best advised to contact one of the trade associations whose details appear in Part Three.

The snag with many completed lists is that they are built from directories or other published sources. This is a decreasing problem since the more enlightened directory publishers will make the information available on tape or disk on an ongoing basis. You are not therefore so reliant on information that is out-of-date (in direct mail terms) when it is published. Moreover, even when this is not the case, the advent of computer technology in publishing has shortened the timespan between the deadline for information-gathering and publication itself. Hence they are still relatively out-of-date, but not so much so!

Lastly in this topic, relating as it does predominantly to business mail users of compiled lists, I would urge you to avoid the apparent 'easy way out'. There are some, notably the 'Times Top Thousand', for example, which are very rarely the right answer. This, as a case in point, is so riddled with holding companies, city-type head offices or registered offices, that it is probably not the best answer to market your new shredding machine.

On second thoughts . . .

More and more (and for the future probably even more) lists are being **rented**

Here we shall examine three things. Some thoughts and ideas for you in connection with the renting of lists. Then we shall pose the question to see if your list would benefit (yes, I said benefit!) from being rented. And finally we'll explore the concept of merging and purging lists, and how that relates to renting them.

First, what you should know about renting lists for your mailings

Here follows a checklist of questions you should ask *before* you rent a list. There are, of course, more. Specifically you will need to know about costs, timing, availability, how the list is supplied, to whom they are prepred to release it, what other mailings especially for competitors have preceded you (although this had been known to be an advantage rather than otherwise!), and what limitations apply. I suggest that before you place an order, verbal or written, that you examine the rental contract in detail.

Mistakes on either side will cause anger, embarrassment and a huge waste of money.

Much of what you need to know about selecting a good broked list is just old-fashioned common sense, i.e. a list of factory managers supplied by a publisher of a trade magazine with a subscription of £25 per annum will usually be more accurate and more qualified than a similar list from a *free* controlled circulation journal.

Here are some items to consider when you have found a list that sounds promising for you.

The first question we need to ask then is, where did the names come from? Even in these sophisticated days you can still see the odd red face when you ask this simple and basic question.

I'll give you an example. I had a client who was thrilled with a list of people who had obtained tickets for a large business exhibition. Forty thousand of them. For this he paid a 'trivial' £25 per thousand.

It included his fellow exhibitors and their salesforce and their stand-fitters and their suppliers. It contained every large competitor he'd got, their salesforce and their stand-fitters and their suppliers. Thirty per cent of the list was outside his existing sales coverage. Seven per cent were overseas visitors. It included every free-loader. Everybody who wanted a day out in London. *And* it undoubtedly included some great prospects for him. But what was the real price of this list? As an estimate, probably only 50 per cent were potential buyers. Your first instinct might be to reckon that instead of £25 per 1000, it's really costing £50 per 1000. Not so.

Twenty thousand rotten names means more than £2500 of wasted postage, probably another £4000 to £6000 worth of wasted mail — let's say for the sake of argument, £7500 in wasted money. Divide by the 20 000 good addresses, add to the £25 per 1000, now the price is around £400 per thousand! An expensive list by any standards!!

More questions to ask:

When was the list compiled or created — is it an ongoing process — and how is the file updated? Lists are living entities, they start to deteriorate *while* they are being built. They need new names added to keep them fresh and a constant or very regular updating process to keep them clean. Does the list owner, for example, mail first class from time to time to flush out nixies? Do they use, and encourage others to use, an 'if undelivered' request on the envelope? When they mail do they ask for and facilitate replies that seek new address and other data changes?

How often is the list mailed? What responses are obtained? Remember here that lists most usually become more responsive with use, *not* less. But ask what sort of responses others have obtained, in what situation and with what products or services. Don't necessarily be satisfied with the answers you get and, if you're in any doubt or suspicious, ring the advertisers and ask them. Ask, also, whose tests have failed lately — and why.

Ask whether it is a list of purchasers (or subscribers) or responders or enquirers. Purchasers (or subscribers who have paid) will usually be better than those who haven't. Or those who have simply enquired and not converted to sale. All can work, but generally the buyers are best. Cash buyers better than credit. And it is worth asking whether any RFM information is available. If so, whether selections can be made or test segments identified. List owners are usually smart enough to know they can charge a premium for 'hot names'. This is a term used to describe the most recent 'actives' or purchasers. But the top performers in the FM of RFM might also be interesting. That's to say, the most frequent buyers and the higher value transactions.

Is the list geo-demographically or psychographically profiled, or is there any lifestyle information? Even the less sophisticated lists sometimes offer (here comes the *oldest* gag in direct marketing) lists of purchasers broken down by age and sex! What else can they be broken down by(!)?

What quantities or assessments of deliverability are given, and is there any rebate or refund for nixies? Although few list owners will guarantee a percentage of deliverability, they should be prepared to give you some assessment. The most conscientious will offer to refund all or part of the postage to get the gone-aways back. Some will only offer this if nixies exceed the assessed level — and often they will only refund the excess.

After testing, what is the mailable universe and are there any discounts for multiple or volume use? You will generally be happier to have discovered success with a large volume universe than a small, since the volume lowers roll-out production costs and possibly lowers product or service provision costs too.

Do also check whether they can 'flag' the names you have tested, either for further analysis after the mailing, or so that, if you choose, you can leave them out of the roll-out. Again, I must place myself on the fence here and say that both have and haven't worked for me in the past. The time between test and roll-out might serve to influence your decision.

Can any other information be supplied that might be useful? One obvious potential Nice One might be telephone numbers.

In what form can the list be supplied, is it available for merge/purge? Can a 'net' name agreement be negotiated? Obviously, if you are considering any kind of data manipulation or personalisation you will be looking at computerised lists. Since we shall be looking at merge/purge in a few moments let's not say any more now other than it means the 'butting up' of one file to others (one is normally yours) to remove the duplication. By negotiating a 'net name' rental agreement, you will effectively only pay for the net off-take from any single list so avoiding buying names you already own, and buying the same prospective name twice.

Most list owners and managers will accept 'net name' against a minimum percentage guaranteed off-take. There are formulae developed to ensure everyone gets a fair deal in these situations but if you can duck that one, head for a deal that lets you merge in order of the least expensive name first. That way you, at least in theory, will add the maximum of cheap names and the minimum of expensive ones. The sting in the tail is that you sometimes get hit with the guaranteed minimum on the most expensive list!

Lastly, you need to know what their minimum test quantities are and what the costs will be for two activities. The test and a roll-out if successful.

Remember you will evaluate your test against roll-out cost projections not test costs. But you will still need to know the test costs!

What are the advantages of renting out your list?

Sex and money! Interested?

OK. I'll confess the sex bit is that it could make your list perform better!

Seriously, this aspect, so long as your list is a desirable commodity, could make you some good straight-to-the-bottom-line profits. And as I have suggested, the extra use could quite easily rev it up as far as you are concerned.

It has been suggested that a list can be rented up to 24 times a year without affecting peformance, although one would hesitate to rent it out as much if you are already mailing it 24 times yourself!

Some of the largest list owners refuse point blank to discuss renting their list. I believe *Reader's Digest* are one. American Express another. And there are others. One can still gain access to some of them, but it is tightly controlled and generally achieved through the affinity approach I explained earlier.

To be suitable for rental your list needs to offer an attractive audience, perhaps difficult to reach other ways, or simply a closely targeted group with good information behind the names. If it is a list of mail order buyers or purchasers of any kind, it will attract interest. In fact, if you run through the list of questions I suggested you ask before renting and score your own list, you'll probably get an idea of its saleability. And talk to some list brokers.

Unless it is something very special or rare, or desirable, I wouldn't hold up too much hope if it's less than about 10 000. And it should, naturally, be computerised.

What will you make out of it? You should be able to clear a *net profit* contribution (after all costs, overheads and broker commissions) of at least £40 per 1000. Possibly more. Thus, someone with a list of 100 000 names who achieves full rental, say nine times a year, should clear £36 000 net profit.

Not a lot? Think of the order value you would normally have to achieve to secure a *net* profit of £36 000. Probably in excess of £300 000. Correct?

If you are going to enjoy benefits of enhanced performance, you should be quite pleased with the extra profit as a bonus! On top of all this, your list will become cleaner through being mailed more often. So if you only mail it a couple of times a year, renting will definitely improve the quality of the list and probably keep it warm for you.

I repeat, my advice is to talk to a selection of brokers and see what they have to say. And while you're at it, talk to some list owners too. No doubt they'll run you through the ups and the downs.

And so we emerge at merge/purge

Merge/purge has got woefully complicated these days, but is admirably advancing.

Let's start with the basic need. You have a list of customers. You want to increase it by mailing out, achieving orders and adding new names to your file. To do this you are going to mail two lists which you've already tested, plus three lists you want to test.

You also want those you mail to receive only one mailing. And you want to exclude those on the Mail Preference Service list and a few others who, for any number of reasons — complaints, bad debts, recent nixies, etc. — you have on your 'stop list'. On the face of it, no problem. There are a number of bureaux who can do it, a number of systems and methods that they will offer, and a number of 'added value' things that can be done at the same time.

But basically (very basically!), the whole lot gets 'butted up to each other' on computer and out the other end spurts your clean list, sorted for postal requirement, free of duplication, everything in apple-pie order — plus, of course, the endless pages of counts and reports.

What has happened is that specialist software has been used to compare the records from all the different sources, and eliminate any multiple occurrences. The process is usually achieved through four distinct steps.

Step 1   Format and Edit — records are converted to standard formats, any unwanted or invalid data stripped out, the postcode is checked (and sometimes corrected) and any oddities rejected for scrutiny, exclusion or re-inclusion.

Step 2 Duplicate Identification — exactly what its name suggests, having subjected records to a number of logic-based tests the 'dupes' are found.

Step 3 Divide and Code — at this stage the good, the bad (stop list) and the ugly (duplicates) are grouped, and the cleaned and approved records are key coded to denote source (and any other required codings).

Step 4 Sort — The combined, clean list is ordered to meet the postal requirements for bulk mail price advantages.

The complications I referred to come in two areas, deciding the 'pecking order' of lists being the first. I gave you my thoughts — take the cheapest first. Others will tell you take the biggest list first. Others still not to take any of them first, but apportion the duplication throughout so they all share and share the pain alike. Personally, I organise the whole lot through one good broker and take their advice (which may differ based on the whims and wishes of the list owners involved).

The next confusion is that of the 'bolt-on-goodies'. One tempting one is to pre-decline the input lists using one of the consumer selection systems (Acorn, Pinpoint, Mosaic, etc.) and take by descending order of appeal. The top decile from each list first, then the second, and so on. Some 'results predictions' claim to be able to identify the best lists for you and to be able to grade them in order of predicted results. It's all done with glue, paper clips, *papier mâché* and some complicated frilly bits that take several different profiles of your list and compare the others for similarities. On the basis of its work, it looks into its crystal ball and makes its recommendations. The point of the whole message being to determine your 'pecking order' making sure you therefore take the maximum from the predicted high response lists.

Yet again, I have to report different successes. On the one hand, the predictions were totally laughable, so much so I wondered if I was holding the sheet upside down. On the other hand, out of ten predictions it got two transposed, I think the first and the third. The conclusion I came to was that the predictions were more interesting as a computer exercise to determine for large mailings which lists should be shortlisted for testing. But in terms of setting the 'pecking order' priorities even a misprediction as apparently innocent as transposing third for first and vice versa — however good the score out of ten — could cost more than it could make. It will get better!

Incidentally, the first idea — selecting against your profile — works well. But list owners are not so keen to play!

JFR's box of tricks

- Merge/purge. What I would give priority to when choosing my pecking order is the lists on test. Leave them until later and you run the risk of depleting the sample and damaging its statistical validity.
- How many times can you mail your list? Sneaky little question to feed into the bits and bobs section! And it's one that somebody asks in nearly every conference audience. And I can't answer! I can tell you a few Things to help you find the answer — the rest as they say is up to you!

Thing No. 1 I've not met anyone who has approached the problem intelligently who has actually found a ceiling — beyond common sense that is.

Thing No. 2 By common sense, I mean somewhere between 15 to 20. If you want to. And few do.

Thing No. 3 Whether you rent your list can make a difference.

Thing No. 4 A variety of packages, styles and products will help to stretch the tolerance and maintain response rates as you increase. If you are considering sending the same package or the same product all the time forget 15 to 20. Monitor responses, you'll soon see when they are bored.

Thing No. 5 Remember that as you build up the people who like you and buy from you, so too you will build up those you irritate. The response is always a minority. So too are the nearly offended or nearly irritated. If you let them boil over, some of them will erupt in your direction. Some will reap their revenge in other ways. Like moving bank account from your bank, not using your credit card, avoiding your shops. Or worse, much worse, anti-woming you. We talked earlier about the power of word-of-mouth — it works against you too when people are wandering around with such pent-up frustrations. Flush them out and save yourself some money. Use your own mail preference service to get them off the list.

- Building or creating a list of customers is not the whole story. Getting your customer list into shape is not the simple answer to money and success. You need to get it active. It will gradually get more responsive and more profitable as you contact people more often and they get used to mail (which they like!) coming from you. I say this despite the fact I belong to the AA and despite the fact that 75 mailings ago (not long!) I purchased 4057 Rock 'n' Roll Greats from *Reader's Digest*.

- Some people adore responding to mailings. And spending money. The industry has for a long time recognised the value of multi-buyers. These are people who are 'hooked' on mail order and responding generally.

  You can build a cumulative record into your file to add a notch to your customer records each time they appear as a duplicate on other people's lists that you are running against yours in merge/purge operations. It is very likely that this group will buy even those things which do not sell well to your whole list. There may not be many hundreds of them — but now you know what to do with that surplus from that mailing you were going to throw because you barely hit breakeven!

  Rumour has it that Franklin Mint have a small file of 2000 or so 'Franklin Freaks' across the world. Rumour also has it that if they came out with a limited edition porcelain cow-pat, these people would buy it. Is there any truth in it, I ask!

- Think about the answers you get to the list rental questions. One well-respected source of business lists compiles them predominantly through information it gathers while writing to companies asking for details in order to give them a credit rating. They are quite open about it and will happily discuss the process with you. Twice, earlier in my career, I had cause to question whether the selection called for had been carried out properly, since a check had revealed that companies with a lower turnover and with lower numbers of employees than we had asked for had been included.

  In transpired that, as people knew the information was being used to prepare a credit rating, they had a tendency to, let's say, exaggerate a little. No problem as long as you know. So you can 'exaggerate a little' when you write the selection criteria!

10 There are only **ten** kinds of direct mail—

and each has something *creative* in mind. They are:

- with the **reader** in mind
- with **copy** in mind
- with **design** in mind
- with **human nature** in mind
- with **ideas** in mind
- with a **proposition** in mind
- with **letters** in mind
- with **personalisation** in mind
- with the **package** in mind
- with **response** in mind

All the way through this book I have intimated, indeed a couple of times stated, that creativity is less important than people like to think. Particularly creative people! Among whom I proudly count myself.

Now, coming from someone who has been a creative director for nearer two decades than I would care to think about, some will ask if I am a traitor to my cause. Well, I don't think so. And I'll tell you why.

It is undoutedly true that on average (if there ever exists such a thing in its own right!) creative can be calculated to influence results, as conventional wisdom suggests, by somewhere between 25 and 35 per cent. Plus or minus a third. That's the assessment of the pure creative contribution.

But what a 25–35 per cent!!

In earlier years of my 'Secrets' conference series I used the example of a tripod to illustrate my view of the three key factors — the list, the offer and the package. Like a tripod, I said, take any one of the legs away and crash! A fairly crude example but it made a point. But to be self-critical, as you move the discussion to the next level up, it is not strictly accurate. It has been my experience that you can get away with a one-legged, or one-and-a-half or even two-legged tripod.

The one-legged tripod is where the only thing you got right was the list. Surprisingly, even with the product/offer leg limping and walking disaster for creative, you can still get a response if you are talking to the right people. Thinking about it, about 80 per cent of charity mailings fall into this category!

The one-and-a-half/two-legged version is where you have a half-good product/offer and a half-good creative and a damn good list. Or even a stunning product, a moderate package and a moderate list.

Plainly the list — the people, in other words — is the most important. What we communicate and how we communicate it are less important. But the sum of them — the two together — is just as important.

The concept of three-phase creativity

I believe most written advertising — direct response or other — is tackled by its readers in three distinct phases. They are the **glance**, the **scan**, the **read**.

There are two important points about this theory. First, that readers have a gearbox in their head that has only three positions, a bit like the old Daf cars — forward, neutral and reverse. Or even, Yes, Maybe and No.

Second, it clarifies the true role of creative in the wider process. And why you must put your proposition up front. It makes sense that if you're going to ask people to give their time to you, they should at least know what it's about. Most often, this has two ways of happening and it is an interesting analysis of the advertisers' confidence. Those with a strong offer come out with it fast. Those with a weak offer build up to it slowly!

Thus, we arrive at the conclusion that the function of creative is to *present* your proposition (in non-direct marketing, your message) and to *persuade* as many readers as possible to accept it.

There are, of course, many techniques to achieve these two functions. But the most important part is to recognise that we must achieve success not once, not twice, but three times, as our readers go through the stages of reading. We must succeed as they **glance** at it. To get them to move on. We must succeed when they **scan** it. To get them to move on. And we must succeed when they **read** it. To get them to absorb, accept and act.

The numbers will decrease at each stage. But you have to

make sure that, as the numbers dwindle, your effort increases in its influence on those that remain.

Over the course of this chapter, we shall take a look at some of the ways you can set about this task. In one section, for example, we shall see how our understanding of human nature can be used. How we react to certain stimuli can be used. And also what emotions and desires will drive us to act.

Now, however, I would like to present you with three personal methods that have helped me over the years. These three plus the age-old but still perfect AIDA formula (see page 85) plus Bob Stone's Seven Key Points (see page 87) are the only five I carry with me. They should enable you to crack any direct mail problem and can be adopted for most other direct response situations too.

Now buy!

Noticed Opened Wanted Believed Understood Yes'd

Noticed

Will you get noticed when you arrive on the mat? Or, if you think your envelope might not get seen, how can you get yourself to stand out or be placed on the top of the pile? Why not try to win both situations?

Opened

What have you done to *ensure* that you will be? And then what single thing will attract or impress above all else at the opening moment?

This latter question is a vital one often overlooked or ignored, but more often still totally misunderstood by both copywriters and designers alike (as you will see later in the section dealing with human nature).

Wanted

You need to approach 'wanted' two ways. First, what can you do to make your mailing wanted? If they want to read, there's much more chance they'll want to respond.

Second, have you done everything in your power to make the product or service wanted?

Believed

Avoid the incredible. Back up your sales story with undeniable fact. In place of opinion and rhetoric, give evidence. Testimonials and case histories, for example.

Understood

You must be. Your proposition must be. What to do must be. Clear, simple, jargon-free conversational language. Clean, easy-to-follow layouts that make your message easy to absorb.

Yes'd

What have you given people to say 'yes' to? Have you phrased your proposition so that 'yes' is the obvious, attractive and desirable thing to do?

If you have, you've 'yes'd 'em'.

The golden strategy

Grab attention   Open strongly   Lead logically
Demand action   Encourage response   Need it now

Grab attention

What can you do to grab attention — and *hold* it?

Open strongly

Maybe you can solve that problem by doing this. But, do this one anyway. The biggest possible benefit to the reader is probably the strongest opener at your disposal.

Lead logically

A sound sales case generally has a logical sequence to it. Find it and follow it. But more, make sure the composition of your mailing package follows it. This is one of the main pitfalls of taking a general product leaflet and simply strapping on a letter and reply card and making do with it as a mailing. I bet if you look at 95 per cent of these sort of packs the letter and the leaflet present different product rationales in different sequences. One has to be right. Or at least better! They may be in harmony, but what you need is unison.

Demand action

Just no getting away from it, the need to demand action from the reader, to spell out what you want, to make it attractive, desirable and urgent, crops up in nearly every worthwhile formula, checklist and for that matter textbook!

You *know* why.

Encourage response

There are so many ways to nudge, push, prompt, cajole, tease or urge a reply. A gift or incentive. A special offer, discount or saving. And, on top of that, you will encourage more to reply by making the physical act of replying simple in every way. Do they have to respond by mail? Maybe by phone? Or local branch or outlet? Will you take a credit card payment? Can a business respond by fax? All of these can only happen if you provide the information. And forget which one is best for you. Organise your response handling to which one is best for them.

Need it now

That's the level of excitement, enthusiasm and desire you've got to aim for. You've got to make them say, 'I need it now.' Can you use a time-close? Will you make some extra or bonus available if they act within the time limit?

And lastly on this aspect, if you've got somebody to say 'I need it now', at least pay them the courtesy of a prompt efficient delivery or response. Otherwise all the hard work you've done will drive them elsewhere to satisfy the need. Like your competitors. Or other sources.

Let's take a creative approach!

And now my own preferred *aide-mémoire*.

Arrive Propose Persuade Reassure Orchestrate an **o**pportune opportunity **Ask** for the order (or response) **Clarify Help**

Arrive

Have you done all you can to ensure that you've arrived in the right hands at the right time? And what steps have you taken to make the right impression — not just of your mailing, but of your company, and what you have to say? Do you look important enough to merit their investment of time and energy and attention?

Propose

Let them know *fast* what's in it for them. There is no single bigger turn-on for the reader than for them to ask, 'What's in it for me?' which they will *all* do immediately, and for you to come out with a strong, credible and wantable answer.

Persuade

Now set about a confirming process for those in Yes gear and a convincing process for those in Maybe or neutral gear. As we saw earlier in the book, your success with this group will make or break your mailing. Each one counts. So assess your benefits in the right order and set them out one by one. Cover them *all*, and have the courage of your convictions. It's cost you a lot of money to get in front of the reader, so put your mouth (or pen!) where your money is. Remember benefits never *bore*. Benefits never put people off. Just as long as they are real, believable, desirable . . . and at the end of the day, you can deliver.

Reassure

If you were in the reader's situation what would worry you? Small print? The thought of a medical? Whether you could afford it? Whether a salesperson will call? If the product is new, does it really work, will I get maintenance problems, or teething troubles? If it's old, how soon will it be replaced with the new model? If it's far away — like a distant holiday — who'll look after us, handle languages, etc.? If it's complicated — that it's worth the trouble and paperwork? Whatever the potential worries, address them, reassure your readers that you understand, you have the answers and that they won't be intimidated, embarrassed, regretful or let down.

Guarantees are very reassuring. So are free trials (with other benefits too!).

Orchestrate an opportune opportunity

To get people to act, they need reasons. One reason should be your proposition. But we want people to act now. Therefore we have to make it opportune (well-timed) for them to do so. Now will be the moment to orchestrate an opportunity for them — in other words, to add an extra level to your proposition which makes the whole concept a good one, but even better if taken now. An opportunity is by definition 'especially favourable'. Probably the direct marketing stalwarts here are the bonus offer, the time-close and the limited edition. They are very powerful but all too easily dismissed as 'mail order techniques'. Which they certainly are, but there are so many ways of devising all three of these for situations at all levels of society, and whether consumer, professional or business-to-business. For one thing is certain, we all hate to lose. And we all like to win. Here your task is to lubricate these desires.

Ask for the order (or response)

Talk about response as if you expect it, not as if it will surprise you! It's a small point, but the number of times I see this:

'If you return the reply paid card enclosed . . .'

The very use of the word 'if' unravels almost everything you've done so far. It suggests there is another course other than response. It suggests *you* believe they might not want to accept your proposition. It suggests that really it might not be all that it's cracked up to be. Have you been lying? What does this say?

'*When* you return the enclosed reply paid card . . .'

It's an entirely different set of implications. More confident. More positive.

Closing dates are normally good for response. There is nearly always a genuine need for one. Sometimes, because it contains a special offer or terms, sometimes because you are using incentives where supplies are limited. However, it is often wise to 'cover' yourself with any non-standard offer by specifying the duration of availability. I would counsel you though, if you're dealing with a financial service, to beware of the Financial Service Act which prohibits 'artificial' closing dates. But you may lose quite a profitable 'tail' of business if you don't get your timings right. Too short loses business. Not everybody wants to reply to suit your schedule and you must respect that. Too long and it won't have the desired 'hurry up' effect. Indeed people may actually delay responding because you've told them you'll give them 12 weeks to do it. And once they've put you on one side, whatever their intentions at the time, you will have your likelihood of response reduced to about one tenth.

What has become known as 'the early bird' is one answer to this problem and usefully leaves the door ajar for those who want to reply in their own good time. An 'early bird' is an extra offer for acting within the timeframe. But you make it abundantly clear that it's the extra offer that closes on the chosen date, the proposition is acceptable any time.

Another, rather obvious (but still overlooked by many), way of asking for order or response is to provide the means for it to happen. And indeed to explain how they achieve it. Hence:

Clarify

There are two things to clarify. You need to be absolutely certain that you have made your proposition, offer and terms clear to them. The best way to do this is to run through it *totally* again. Don't worry about repeating yourself. But it will need to be kept interesting. So use different words to do it. You also need to be certain that the response methods and procedures are clear to them. The blatant way to do this is

most successful. That's why you see this headline so often —
'How to apply'.

Again this is easy to convert to other situations.

'Please complete and return the enclosed application promptly.
You'll find a reply envelope enclosed and no stamp or addressing
is needed. Please also be sure to sign and date the . . .'

Or the executive version!

'Please ask your secretary to fax your acceptance within the next
48 hours. She will need to complete the five questions relating to
your current financial policy, and naturally we guarantee
absolute confidentiality. However, I must point out that places
will be given on a strictly "first come" basis. Since I feel your
presence is particularly important, and to assure your
registration, please ask your secretary to provide your American
Express, Diners Club, Access or Visa number and expiry date.'

As you draw to the close of your message it's quite possible to
find ways of weaving the last three together — that is
organising an opportune opportunity, asking for the order and
clarifying why and how they should respond.

And last, in the creative APPROACH.

Help

The more you can do to help, the better. This extends from
helping them to afford your product or service, to helping
them get answers to questions (a telephone hotline?) or just
helping them to respond by providing the wherewithal, advice
and convenience.

Five great problem-solvers

I believe any one of these formulae can help you. Take your
pick from my three — Now Buy, Golden or Approach, or use
AIDA or Bob Stone's Seven Key Points. You'll probably find
that you 'bed down' with one. But here's the important part.
When you've completed your work (or you've had it presented
to you by your supplier) use two of the others and score the
proposed mailing on all three.

Sure, the formulae are all headed in the same direction.
That's OK, so are you! But their perspective and emphasis is
different. So you're judging from different angles!

Now let's start to take a look at those ten things with
creativity in mind!

We'll start with the most significant aspect of creativity.
The one which is so important it must influence and lead your
problem-solving, solution-finding steps in all the other nine
creative issues of which you must be mindful. I suggest that

every decision you make, every action you take, and every thought you have should be made . . .

The best advice I have ever given anybody, and that includes myself, was first crystallised while writing some years ago for the first printing of the *Post Office Direct Mail Handbook*.

It is this:

WRITE WHAT THE READER WANTS TO READ
NOT
WHAT THE WRITER WANTS TO WRITE

Depending on your level of personal modesty you will find the next statement anywhere between easy or hard to take!

People are *always* more interested in themselves than they are in you. That applies to even the most deserving charitable cause.

So we're back to what's in it for them. The biggest mistake when analysing or appraising this statement is to assume that you should take it as advice which can only be answered on a material level. And, that it is black and white. Neither is true. However, it can be followed in many, many ways. But at the end of it all, it should tell the recipient what they want to hear (or read). It should explain how their life will benefit, be enriched or improved through accepting what you have to offer. As opposed to explaining how great you are.

Start out from their view of you. Remember the McGraw-Hill ad?

I don't know who you are.
I don't know your company.
I don't know your company's product.
I don't know what your company stands for.
I don't know your company's customers.
I don't know your company's record.
I don't know your company's reputation.
Now — what was it you wanted to sell me?

Now, extreme as that is, why should they want to hear about you? They don't. So in order to get them interested in you, we need to make you interesting. The best way is to explain just what you can do for them.

Take this tip seriously and use it to question every decision. I remember working with one account manager who was debating with a client the rights and wrongs of something that the client wanted to do. Flatly, the account manager refused. The client asked him why. His reply was:

'Fred won't like it!'

Naturally, the client enquired about the identity of the hitherto unheard of Fred. Obviously, since his opinion mattered more than the client's, he was a rather important person.

'Fred,' said the account manager, 'is the poor bugger that's got to reply to this. And I'm his representative here today.'

Call up a Rent-a-Fred. Have your own. Carry him with you everywhere. The reader's representative. And every time somebody asks, or suggests, or decides, go through the mental discipline of asking Fred how he feels about it. Fred has only a two-word vocabulary. 'Good' and 'Bad'.

Seeing things from the readers' point of view, putting them first, will never do you any harm. It will always serve you in the end. So extend this simple philosophy way beyond the copy. To the graphics. To the development of the proposition. To the format. Throughout!

With **copy** in mind

The largest single difference between ordinary advertising copy and direct response advertising copy is that ours *sells*. What it sells is the proposition. Whether that proposition is that the reader should buy, enquire, or visit a store or exhibition. You name it, we'll sell it!

In direct mail creativity, copy is far, far more important than art. Pictures don't sell. Design doesn't sell. Pictures might explain, demonstrate or illustrate. Those things help a sale. They don't make one. Pictures certainly grab attention, as we'll discuss later. It is the use — with copy — that you make of the attention that is more important.

Design doesn't sell. Not in direct mail. It positions. It supports copy. It displays your wares. It humanises, creates mood, eases the task of reading. But it doesn't sell. It certainly contributes, you might say it smooths the way to the sale. But it doesn't sell.

Copy sells for you

Direct mail is a words medium. You will be amazed at the word-power that is available to you. And just how many words you can get people to read. Very few good mailings (or for that matter press ads and other kindred manifestations of the direct marketing way) feature anything near good writing. We chuck away the grammar textbooks. We ignore convention. We use punctuation in ways that would make our old English masters cringe. It is possible to achieve both, but it cannot be coincidence that talented writers and talented direct marketing writers are two different things. My feeling is that most of the truly talented writers in direct marketing only ever get halfway up the ladder. That's probably because there are two more important attributes in our copy writing league. You must have a headful of ideas. And you must be able to sell.

All you have to do that is any different to any other sales situation, is to use these ideas to sell on paper.

Since I cannot write your copy for you, I propose now to give you a short checklist of advice I have been given, thoughts I have developed, and experiences I have gained.

Whether you are facing what might seem the daunting prospect of writing a mailing, deciding which presentation to accept, or trying to assess some work you've been given, this list will help you.

Seventeen do's. Plus ten don'ts. That's 27 ways to make copy irresistible. Just for you!

To start with, let's check out some 'do's'.

1 *Do plan what you want to say*   Develop a rationale that would convince *you* to accept the offer. Then work on it. But be flexible. Often you will stumble on a better, stronger or more appealing idea half-way through what you have already started. Write both. And then choose.

2 *Do develop a flowing style*   Not smooth or bland, but pleasant and charming. In letters be conversational and personal without being impertinent or cheeky.

3 *Do write long and edit back if you need to*   NEVER the other way round. If your copy runs short but you feel you did the job, the designer will be delighted! And the reader won't mind either.

4 *Do make yourself easy to read and understand*   The easiest sentences to understand are just eight words long. At 32 words they've lost you.

5 *Do concentrate on communicating well*   Forget about grammar. Worry more about flow, being understood and communicating well. One acid test is to read copy aloud, or better, to get someone else to. Where this reader trips up, so will others.

6   *Do be warm and sunny-natured*   Then let yourself shine
     through. It's infectious. Just as tele-sales people are
     advised to 'smile' on the phone!
7   *Do avoid the crescendo*   Crescendo letters arrive on my
     desk every other day. They look a bit like this:

> Dear Managing Director,
> We were founded over 20 years ago and have now
> become the world's leading supplier of gringing
> machinery.
>
> We have 75 staff at our Warrington headquarters
> which, when it was built, was the most modern
> gringing machinery plant in Europe. It is conveniently
> situated near the M62.
>
> In order to extend our reputation into allied areas of
> gringing, we recently opened a new gringing pipework
> cleansing facility a few miles further south on the
> motorway.
>
> Here we have achieved notable success and received
> much acclaim for our pioneering pipe flocking
> processes.
>
> I am pleased to enclose our latest brochure which
> tells you more about our gringing success story. If you
> would like further information please return the
> enclosed card and we will tell you the full gringing
> story.
>
> FOR AND ON BEHALF OF
> Premier Gringing Ltd
>   (Signature)
> Managing Director
>
> PS   A display of our gringing equipment and pipework
> will be at Olympia for International GRINGEX 2000.
> We have taken a stand this year for the first time to tell
> more people about our gringing. Will you visit us?

OK, it's a slight exaggeration! But you can see what I
mean. First, it's written from the wrong side. Second,
the crescendo gradually builds up to what has to be the
main event. An invitation to an exhibition.

In 99 cases out of 100, this kind of letter should be stood
on its head. People do not start out interested. They start
out indifferent. We have to earn their attention. They
start out looking for excuses to bin us. So the strongest
way to come out fighting is to hit them with the biggest
benefit. That provides — or should do — your trump card.

In one go it answers what's in it for them and earns you time to explain, justify, give more REASONS TO READ.

The best reasons to read are benefits. There are others. Curiosity. News value. Scandal even! But one Reason to Read is never enough. Jo Sugarmann described this process as the 'greased chute'. I have also heard it described as the 'string of pearls'. Each sentence has two objectives: to make its point, and buy readership of the next sentence.

8 *Do use link-words and phrases* They help to 'grease the chute'. Start paragraphs with these: And, But, Also, What's more, For example. You may have had problems with this style at school — but school's out! And use punctuation and text marks too. There are all manner of devices . . .

. . . which just tell the reader to keep going!

9 *Do use simple language* And simple construction. This kind of thing. It's so easy to handle.

Especially in comparison with the much longer and, from a constructional aspect, markedly more complex style of sentences that barely give the unfortunate individual trying to cope with them a chance to breathe and which become, therefore, asphyxiating in more ways than one!

10 *Do humanise wherever possible* Bring in personalities and names. Do away with 'Our sales department can . . .'. Use 'Jenny Pearce, your personal Customer Service Manager, can . . .'.

11 *Do snuggle up with the reader!* Do away with 'It's got many features . . .'. Use 'Let's run through the features together . . .'.

12 *Do use active words* Tick. Send. Act. Claim. Take. Grab. Select. Slash.

13 *Do sprinkle the evergreen 'turn-on's' plentifully around* YOU. NEW. NOW. FREE. INTRODUCING. ANNOUNCING. SAVE.

Use unique very carefully. It is an evergreen. But with severe leaf mould!

14 *Do picture your reader* Hold imaginary sales chats with them. Fantasise the sale in your head. And then write about it.

15 *Paint word pictures* Try to find words that are evocative and inspiring. Which do you want your policy to be, the one that pays 'a regular monthly benefit' or 'a fountain of money, placing hard cash in your hands each and every month'?

16 *Do be ruthless* Strip out waffle or padding. But don't take out chute grease. And be careful not to dehumanise, cool or get in the way of the flowing style. The yardstick: Is it of benefit? Is it interesting? Does it convince? Does it hold them? Is it there to lubricate? If it doesn't do one of these, it doesn't deserve to get printed.

You can often strike out whole paragraphs measuring against this yardstick. Interestingly, with amateur or classic ad writers' work, they are mostly to be found at the beginning. Funny that!

17 *Do ensure the copy works on all three levels* This you should do with the layout artist/designer (see Human Nature).

If you're not sure whether it succeeds use the 'snatch test'. Give it to someone. Count five seconds. Then snatch it back. If they can't tell you what it's about, you've failed!

And here come the don'ts

18 *Don't use incredible or uncaring words or phrases* Avoid the time-weary as opposed to the time-honoured. Do you honestly want to do business with people who offer

- THIS WORLD-BEATING COTTONWOOL BALL (Reagan's secret weapon?)
- THE MOST DYNAMIC GARDEN PIECE YOU'LL EVER OWN (what's a garden piece?)
- ONE TASTE WHISKS YOU TO PALM-FRINGED, SUN-SOAKED LAGOONS (I can only handle one lagoon at a time)
- THE BANK ACCOUNT THAT'S LIKE A PERMANENT FRIEND (a high interest friend, yet?)
- IT'S THE DOG FOOD BREEDERS PREFER (Yeah! But how do the muts feel about it?)

19 *Don't use word-play, puns or be clever* It doesn't work. Nuff said!

20 *Don't use too many 'me words'* I, MY, WE, OUR. It's supposed to be all about *them*. The readers! So by all means use enough of these to be personal, but don't go overboard. YOU and YOURS is fine! They can be used as much as you like — especially at the beginning of paragraphs, a place where ME words should only rarely be found.

21 *Don't use negative words* Change the aspect from which you are writing round to the positive.

22 *Don't use abstract or needlessly complex words and*

descriptions   Do you really mean 'seating arrangements' — or chairs?

23 *Don't use etc.*   It's fine in books! But in a mailing it means you've left something unsaid, partially explained, or worse, you've left the reader something to work out for themselves.

24 *Don't forget. You'll lose more readers in the first 50 words than you will in the rest*   So turn up the heat. Put plenty of thought and effort into headlines.

One professional letter writer tells the story of a client who asked him to write six letters and mail one of the letters to one sixth of his total list so that six equal parts of the list were mailed different letters. If we give the poorest pulling letter a score of 100, the others worked out at 132 (32 per cent better than the poorest) 174, 156, 300 and 136.

One of those letters out-pulled the poorest by three to one. When the client asked the writer about the differences between these letters he confessed that essentially the difference was in the openings.

They all had the same business proposition, benefits, etc. He knew that one of the tasks of the beginning is to pull the interest of the person reading and move them on into the balance of the selling copy. The writer said he gave all six letters an equal portion of blood, sweat and tears, yet the best out-pulled the worst by 300 per cent.

Either Mr Ogilvy himself, or someone else of Ogilverian disposition, once explained that: 'When you've written the headline you've spent 70 per cent of the client's budget.' This does not indicate the tariff of the agency. It's to demonstrate how important these details are.

25 *Don't worry about length of copy*   Worry more about whether it's interesting, paced and easy to read.

Almost a decade ago, German direct mail expert Siegfried Vögele presented a 'Readability Index' which he uses in his seminars in Germany and which was passed on to him many years ago by a teacher of copywriting who is, I believe, now dead.

Try it out. See how you score.

How to check your copy for readability

(a) Determine the average number of words per sentence in your copy.

(b) Calculate the average number of syllables per 100 words.

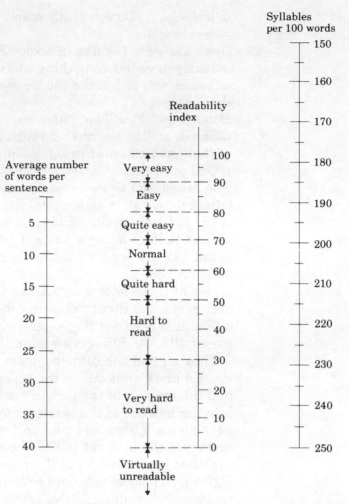

Figure 10.1
Readability index

(c) Plot the points on the left- and right-hand columns respectively, and draw a line between them.

(d) Read off the answer where your line cuts through the centre scale.

A good objective, says Siegfried, is: full-stop every 12 words — so no more than 30 syllables per sentence!

26 *Don't leave questions unanswered* To the direct mail copywriter a 'Question and Answer' routine is like a favourite old pair of shoes. We'll slip into 'em at first excuse.

But also, you should ensure throughout that you are provoking questions in the reader's head. One of the best ways to retain their attention and interest is to pose or manipulate a question to which they need an answer. The secret is not to withhold all the answers to the end! The secret is to make sure that in every answer, you carefully plant the next question.

There are some questions that will occur to the reader anyway. They are suggested by the very structure of your mailing, perhaps the components, its shape, format, design, or function.

Courtesy of Siegfried Vögele again, here's a useful checklist, presented component by component, of the questions that will quite naturally occur to the reader.

Envelope

1   Is this for me?
2   Who is it from? (You may choose to answer this later!)

And your *existing* customers —

3(a) What's it all about today?
4(a) Am I interested in this?

And *cold* prospects —

3(b) What's in this envelope?
4(b) More important — what's in it for me?

Letter

1   Why are they writing to me?
2   What's so interesting about this? (i.e. put your main benefit first)
3   Who signed this letter?
4   Shall I go on reading?
5   Do I need this?
6   Again — what's in it for me?
7   Can they prove it? Where's the evidence?
8   What am I supposed to do?

Leaflet

1   How did I get along without this up to now?
2   Why will this make things better tomorrow?
3   What's in it for me?
4   And who says so?
5   And who can prove it?
6   Is it exactly what I need?
7   Should I react?
8   Is this urgent?
9   How do I respond?

Reponse device

1   What must I do with this? (All the way through your package you should talk about response as if it is expected.)

2 How much .. what's the price?
3 Must I sign?
4 What is the risk once I sign? (You'll say none, of course!)
5 What happens next?
6 Do I have to make any decisions? (Preferably not.)
7 Must I fill in, or just check my address?
8 Must I pay postage?
9 Is it urgent? (Yes, yes, yes!!!)

27 *Don't make a monkey out of yourself* (or, why so many copywriters have long arms!)   People are very nice sometimes. Even the people you're going to write to. They'll do just as you say. Follow you lemming-like. So when, in paragraph three of your letter, you casually invite them to 'take a look at the stunning new villas in this year's exciting brochure enclosed . . .', they will.

More often than not, most of them, right there, right then.

It's usually the very last thing you want them to do. Having spent a great deal of time and effort getting them into the letter, you would much rather they carried on with that. Because the trouble is, they won't come back to it. And you, knowing that the brochure was going to 300 000 new prospects as well as the 50 491 customers from the previous two years, only mentioned the special offer for past customers in the letter. And now they'll never get to know.

Think about it. A simple rearrangement of your copy will make sure you give them the right advice. Be sure to build into copy and design the visual and verbal signposts that will help the majority of readers to get the whole story. Build in as many as possible, in the most logical, convincing sequence. Otherwise, they'll miss loads of good reasons to respond!

Lastly, if you write a fair amount of copy, you might like to get hold of a little paperback gem called *Words that Sell*. It's the brainchild of an American copywriter called Richard Bayan. You'll find details in the Bibliography. And probably your fastest way to get a copy would be via our old friends Hoke Communications who take all major credit cards. And telephone orders! From the UK the number is 010 1 516 746 6700 and the time difference is around five hours. I'm not on commission! It's just a jolly useful 'thesaurus-style' moneymaker of a book. For you and him!

With **design** in mind

Copywriters, that is direct marketing copywriters anyway, are pretty brutal with designers. Which, for many years, has kept most of the really talented designers out of direct mail in particular. They felt it was dull, stylised and boring.

They were right. However, three things have happened that are decidedly good news and showing all the signs of proving that design has a valuable, indeed vital, part to play in the world of direct mail — even if it is a supporting role. These changes haven't altered the fact that it's a double act. The copy is Holmes. The graphics, Watson. The copy is Margaret and the design is Dennis. the copy is gin and the design is tonic.

The changes that are slowly improving the level and quality of design in direct mail and, in fact, direct marketing as a whole, are these:

- More young people, often very talented, are coming into direct marketing
- Some of the better classical advertising art directors and their teams have been bitten by the 'direct' bug
- As the 'establishment' advertising names — clients and agencies — move into 'direct' they will not tolerate what they perceive as the inferior graphic standards of direct advertising.

For years, especially when the influence of creative was so vastly overrated, the dominant copyists (make that domineering copyists) insisted that the pretty and the neat, tidy, smarter, more aesthetic didn't sell so well. That it actually got in the way of copy.

There remains truth in this. And therefore I place the credit for this surge in graphic standards at the feet of all those designers who manage to find ways to work within the often artistically constraining walls of direct mail, but still demonstrate their freshness, flair and ingenuity.

Long may it continue. But never in the cause of good design. Always in the cause of a good response!

Let's look at the function of the design element of a direct mail package — as a part of the total sales effort. Then we'll look at a design checklist, to go with the copy checklist you've just seen.

For a number of years now I have identified the functions of design in direct mail thus:

- To get the words read
- To enhance, illustrate, dramatise and emphasise the proposition

- To illustrate, clarify and endorse the text
- To show the reader the why to go, and how to deal with the various pieces
- To indicate and encourage the desired response

There are others, of course. But we are essentially dealing with a very practical approach to design, followed by a highly informed and aware typographic mentality. Then followed by 'how it looks' which is to man 'lay' people what they think is meant by design. A good looking piece is well designed. And an ugly piece is badly designed.

I can't agree with this. The classical advertising business is the living example. Most of the design is pretty. Or nice looking. But at least 50 per cent so appalling as, in my view, to constitute professional negligence. I mean purely as examples of design in its wider sense.

That's why it is so rewarding to watch the more skilled and talented designers now working down a path that says it does not have to be a conflict.

It is possible to meet the demanding requirements of the direct marketing world. And satisfy the noble and refined aesthetic desires of the artier factions of design.

Perhaps it is unfortunate that the last few design trends have all seemed to veer away from the user or audience to indulge the creator.

Typefaces went crazy. Then the wave of 'broken theme' design — slabs of colour here and there. A mass of different typefaces — all over the place. For no useful or apparent reason.

The pastel era. Everything went so soft that you could barely read the copy in light grey, bath-tile powder blues and soft pinks and beiges.

And then the year of the squiggle. When some half-wit seems to have gone round all the new restaurants and 'design-conscious' establishments squiggling frantically over a portion of their name in a colour or two. Not content with that they've squiggled all over corporate brochures, trendy annual reports, Marks and Spencers bill stuffers, and the letterheads and business cards of several hundred thousand small businesses up and down Europe.

Will the next fad sign in please.

Direct marketing design, the more tasteful quality end anyway, tends to settle rather more easily with the classical approach. That does'nt mean it should be stuffy. It does mean it should generally make looking at it a pleasant experience. It should look inviting and attractive. It should work with the materials to aid the product/service/corporate positioning.

To achieve our objectives, all a designer, typographer or artist has to do is think. Not about their own desires or purposes. About the reader's.

And probably the most compromising factor of all of these is that the design should not be so striking as to distract the reader, get in the way of the copy. We don't want to hear, 'what a lovely brochure', we want to hear, 'what a lovely hotel'. Or holiday. Or nest of tables. Or headscarf. That's all!

At last it seems that it is not too much to ask. There are designers who can do it. Most of them are ridiculously young. But then they haven't hardened to a school yet. If you've been a rebel, or convention fighter, or devil-may-care genius for 20 years, I suppose it gets to be a habit. For some reason the design world is full of such ageing twits.

If you overlay this on to my LCD factor, the past settles perfectly in perspective. In direct marketing, we were going through that era of over-obsession with rolled-up-sleeve creative, absolute infatuation with the position of the full stop and apostrophe. The design element had been forced into near submission. So it was found to make less difference when you tinkered with design, than copy. They were operating in a subterranean tunnel of blandness and mediocrity. We direct copywriters, who are after all the barrow boys of the advertising business, were more than happy to chase the maximum response. And it always worked. The louder, brasher and more blatant we got, the more response went up. It was a vicious spiral downwards from quality. Never mind the quality, feel this great stack of reply cards.

Despite all this progress in the design and art side, I cannot say that I feel copy skills moving so distinctly in any direction. Other perhaps, than to be grappling with the technological breakthroughs.

Yet I cannot get away from this fundamental. And it seems to those who know anything about direct mail, from Claude Hopkins in 1923, to Ogilvy in his time, to me and my contemporaries now.

In direct mail it is inescapable. The copy has to sell. Design has to join in and help. But then I'm the kind of believer in sexual equality that likes to open doors for ladies!

Number 1 on the checklist is much along the same path.

Designer do's and don'ts

1   *Do use the 'reward' psychology*   Conventional advertising and marketing design operates largely on the psychology of approval. The nicer we look, and the prettier we are, the

more they will like us. If they like us they will admire us greatly and do as we ask.

Result: 'What a lovely brochure.'

Direct marketing operates more on the reward psychology. 'Hey look! If you do this, you'll get this.' It's very much more basic. In design terms it translates principally as action-based formats. And those rather less than subtle headline styles and forceful, powerful layouts.

Let's look at an example. A classical designer wants to make sure that something looks as nice as possible when it arrives. He or she will design into the brochure (often as the last fold of an A4 concertina leaflet, for example) a reply card. To make it come together as a piece of design they have created a layout that runs across the entire spread. Perhaps a tint or illustration softened into the background. Or maybe the copy is carefully ranged around a colour pic of your building, or the massed bands of the product range. You know the sort of thing. The design encompasses the whole spread.

This psychology is wrong because the action you want, the card ripped off and returned, is at complete loggerheads with the designer's achievement. So the reader has to spoil or mutilate the work to do what is necessary. And to compound the felony, the better the job the designer does, the worse the conflict. The less likely it is that people will want to mutilate it or spoil it.

That is one of the contributory factors to my advice to keep reply cards separate. Nobody has to spoil anything to take the action. Plus some other reasons we'll come to.

But designers can move one step further. You must have seen all those leaflets and inserts where the reply card hangs off, flapping about like that cartoon of the last leaf on the autumn tree.

They beg to be torn off. In fact, if the design is right, people will tear 'em off anyway. Even if they're not responding. Why? Because they don't look right. They look awkward and out of place. In fact, if you were just to tear that last bit off it would actually look better.

Bullseye!

Right into the deepest mire of what we were looking at a few moments ago. At the very heart of this piece of advice is the need for the designer to create a piece that looks awkward and clumsy, and unwieldy. So that when the reader looks at it, the blossoming conscious desire to respond is egged on by the subliminal desire to improve the shape and design of the piece. The two are in concert.

Take the action. Reward. You move nearer to the offer. Reward. Suddenly you've made that thing look better. Now what will you do with that enquiry card you're holding in your left hand?

Did I hear a cry from the back? A still, small voice suggesting that no hard-headed, right-minded person — consumer or business — is going to spend money just to make a leaflet look better and because they couldn't think what to do with a reply card in their left hand. Correct. My point is what are you giving them? A magical mystery tour or an assault course?

2 *Do make your packages readable*   I won't go back through my squiggly line trauma. I won't even mention fine typefaces, reversed white out of 'thin' four colour process. Promise!

No. This 'do' is all about using simple, clear typefaces, preferably serif which everybody (according to Graeme McCorkell, everybody apart from the Swiss) finds easier to read. Nothing less than 8 point if typeset, 10 point if typewritten. And working to reasonable column widths. That's why newspapers and magazines do it. So should you! Use distinct colours for type. No fancy stuff. Don't ever make copy blend into the design.

3 *Do use shape and folds and construction to 'present' the rationale for you*   In copy 'do's' we learned to develop a rationale. In other words, to orchestrate our sales story. To lead readers down a natural Path of Persuasion. Designers can do a fantastic job here, developing formats and paper-folds so that as the paper unfolds, so too does the sales story.

4 *Do establish the role of each component*   Think about the tasks and objectives of each individual component. Is it to inform, to entertain, to involve, to announce, to celebrate, to invite, to impress? Use design and choice of materials to make this role clear. Make the fun elements look like fun. The technical pieces look technical.

Above all else, appreciate that mailings have a character. That the various components should all work together even though each may perform a different individual task.

Remember too that when people hold the mailing in their hands, they should feel your company. That's about positioning, image, style, tone-of-voice and personality. Whether the letter comes from the chairman or the area sales manager should make a difference.

5 *Do use illustration and photography to score points, not just*

for imagery The sales story will benefit from illustration — photographic or otherwise — to add understanding. Remember that the picture will get looked at well in advance of most of the copy. Photographs generally work better than illustration as such. To waste either in 'theme-ing' or 'mood-ing' will be bad for you. Use them carefully when and where they will add maximum emphasis to the story.

Remember the dual role. Photos and illustrations tend to get looked at twice at least. Once very early on, then more but by smaller quantities of people who are, none the less of greater significance when the copy is being read seriously.

They must work to the objectives of both situations. Theme-ing and mood-ing can be dealt with quite well by backgrounds, choice of models, props, and all the details that are so important.

6 *Don't leave out the human race* People warm up print. They attract the eye. They convince.

Who wants to eat in a restaurant with nobody in it? Who wants to sail on a boat that nobody else sails on? Who wants to drive a car that nobody else seems to want? Who wants to fly on a plane that nobody else seems to want to fly on? Get some People Power!

There are six design pointers. Much more for the design-conscious momentarily!

With **human nature** in mind

Confession. One of my conference routines was stolen from California's Ray Jutkins. To make a point Ray asks the audience to think, instantaneously, of four things.

He gives them subject-headers, they have to write the first thing that comes into their head.

'Gimme a colour!' asks Ray.

'OK. Now give me a flower.'

'Next, a piece of furniture.'

And so on.

Most people — never all, but the majority — choose the same. Red. Rose. Chair.

Some things just are so. We react naturally to certain stimuli. Just as we always have. They're just human nature. Some of them go back through centuries.

I said earlier that I'd tell you about Siegfried Vögele. Now is the time.

Vögele is a technician in creative strategies. Particularly in direct mail. And he's quite brilliant. He's also very aware of his second skill. He's a great communicator. Siegfried and I spend more time nodding and smiling at each other than anything else. He wishes me a good session as I go into the one I'm leading. I reciprocate. Whenever I get the chance to spend even ten minutes in any of his sessions it would take more than wild horses to keep me away. If you ever get the chance yourself, don't miss him.

So for the next few minutes I'd like to run through a blend of our two ideas. But a great deal of the hard evidence of what I'm going to show you is courtesy of Siegfried Vögele. Or rather, in particular his scientific approach to studying how people handle and read their direct mail and other forms of direct marketing.

I'd like to address human nature from two aspects. First, the mainly visual, then the mainly verbal.

The concept of eye track management

There are some things I just can't resist. Stealing the top strawberry in a bowl. A good glimpse of female cleavage is another. Making light of a difficult situation. And any opportunity to swim. I like to do a couple of kilometres most days, so it needs to be warm. 'Cos something else I can't resist are creature comforts!

How about you? I expect you can think of some things you can't resist.

There are probably going to be some things that neither of us can resist. Because one of the things we've got in common is that we're both human beings. So we respond to those things in a particular (in fact a predictable) way. Because it's just human nature to do so.

And these reflexes stretch across all boundaries. Geographic. Ethnic. And social.

The point is that they can be manipulated in our favour. We want to manipulate them to get the reader moving in the right direction We want to ensure that they go where we want them to go. Or that we are sitting waiting for them when they go places they're going to go whether we like it or not.

To discover where and what these places are, Siegfried has carried out some ingenious experiments with an eye movement recorder.

A memorable experience for me was a live demonstration organised at the Montreux Symposium one year. In front of an audience of about 200, Siegfried subjected a Swiss lady to the test.

Blissfully unaware of what she was supposed to do — and with four close-circuit TV cameras, one showing the eye movements related to the pages she looked at — she went through piles of magazines and mailings demonstrating with innocent Swiss precision what Siegfreid wished her to demonstrate.

I'll take you through some of it now. Then you'll realise, perhaps, just how ignorant most advertising layouts are, and how you can in future improve the work you do or use.

Our objective will be to make sure that the readers' attention — where their eye goes — is, or is made to be, in harmony with our sales rationale. Enabling us to achieve, as was suggested earlier, our aim to lead the reader logically along our path to persuasion.

Glance, Scan, Read

In the early glancing process, Siegfried has identified fixing points. His name for those places where the reader's eye will alight momentarily to absorb information — be it verbal or visual. This is a horrendously fast event. It should frighten copywriters to the very core.

The eye rests on each fixing point for just two-tenths of a second. The tolerance level per A4 spread is about ten fixing points. Your work lives or dies in just two seconds!

With an A3 spread the tolerance level goes up to about 15. So you've got three seconds. Good luck!

Then, with the speed of light, the glancer's brain makes a decision.

Go again or quit? With Germanic logic, Siegfried attributes the decision-making to a count. More than five out of ten your A4 sheet gets upgraded to a scan. Less, and you die. I suspect that it is not quite that clear-cut. I believe it more likely that one very strong success out of ten can buy you a reprieve.

The second trip round — the scan — gives you more time. But not that much! The scan is also about gathering hard evidence to justify a read. It will include much more copy. The glance was picking up odd words, maybe a full phrase but not much else other than feeding the visual sense. Here you'll get whole headlines read, photocaptions, sub-heads and so on.

How you fare from here on is down to you. With some you'll get the in-depth read. Some will still not decide without a pre-read. Then they'll go for the body copy and diagrams and more complicated pictures and illustrations.

You need to use 'eyecatchers' to get the highest score! Here are eleven

This isn't all news. But it's a valuable confirmation nonetheless. Let's look at a list of eyecatchers and discuss some of them.

1 *Big pictures beat* small pictures.   We all know *that*. Sure we do. All except the agency that gives us an ad with a small black and white picture and places it in a magazine notorious for lavish big colour spreads. And we paid extra for a right-hand page!
2 *Colour pictures beat* black and white.
3 *Warm colours beat* cool colours.
4 *Pictures of humans beat* pictures of products.   Memo: in the same shot, if the product doesn't *really* stand out they may only see the human *not* the product!
5 *Pictures of lots of people beat* pictures of a few.   Suggestion: Get a football team to endorse the product. *And* remember what I said about empty planes and restaurants!
6 *Portraits beat* whole-body pictures.   Because we can see faces, particularly eyes.
7 *Solids beat* copy.   What to do: Use headlines reversed out of solids.
8 *Vertical shapes beat* horizontal.   Apparently this goes back to the fact that once upon a time we reckoned anything standing was a threat. Anything lying down was not.
9 *Circles beat* rectangles.   This one, I am told, is a sexual preference. Don't worry, it was your forefathers' fault!
10 *Short headlines beat* long headlines.   Now here's an interesting one! Because most direct marketing know-alls (like me) will tell you that longer headlines work best.

Let's play with this one a little.

We're discussing eye-pulling power here, not response-pulling power. Thus, you can still stack up a high success rate on the fixing point test while at the same time ignoring one or more of them.

Try to imagine this. You have a full-page A4 in front of you. Across the top left to a width of two-thirds you have a longish headline, say three lines deep.

Ranged with it in depth, to the right, you have a picture, in colour, of a group of people. The headline is printed black against white, but with the last two words of the middle line emphasised in bright red. They are 'YOURS FREE'. The photo has a short caption '£1 million! You could join these 17 lucky winners.'

What's going to happen? Answer: your long headline isn't going to get fully read until second time round. But the number of successful fixing points will get more people to go round the second time!

These 'eyecatchers' are not arranged in any order. The list is not definitive.

We'll talk some more on eye track management when we discuss letters.

Now let's look at some more human nature.

Some of your best friends are human . . .

Always remember not to get over-involved with your actual product or service. Remember the person you're writing to is *a person* and, as such, is susceptible to all the traditional weaknesses and needs. Think beyond the immediate benefits that you have to offer and consider how these will relate to their character and personality.

Here is a brief checklist of what most human beings like in life . . .

Money. Status. Comfort. Sex. Toys and games. Possessions. Visible evidence of their ability to acquire things and culture.

People like knowledge, new information, practical and DIY skills, intellectual enjoyment and satisfaction.

People like security, protection, being prepared, having reserves or safety devices, feeling safe; avoiding discomfort, embarassment, risk and worry.

People like to feel fulfilled, creative, individual, happy and self-confident. They like to get away, to escape, to avoid pressures or sometimes even decisions. To be free.

People like to be accepted, popular, to receive praise, to be stylish, fashionable or up-to-date; they like to receive status and authority and respectability — sometimes even unrespectability or notoriety! They like to be seen to be helping others. They like to help themselves.

People like to be one-up; to be sensible, organised, well-equipped, faster — to have got a better deal, to be better prepared, to be warned in advance or to know about something before others. They like to feel cosy, smug and satisfied. They like to please their peers, to be seen as efficient and smart.

And despite all this, they like to be liked!

Getting ideas is a problem for some people. Too many is a problem for others. One of the great assets of direct marketing is the ability to test lots of ideas to establish which really are the good ones.

I may as well be blunt. I find ideas happen in particular places. I commuted daily across one particular level crossing on the Brighton/Portsmouth line. It was always, always closed. Well, nine times out of ten. At first it irritated me. Then I got resigned to it. Later I loved it. It became one of my great idea places. There are others. Two are the bath and the loo!

There are also idea times. My two favourites are last thing at night (well, nearly last thing!). I nearly always end the day with a scotch. We Capricorns love routine. As my mind empties the day, it starts to generate ideas like crazy. Another time is early morning. Sometimes they are so strong they literally wake me up. Or seem to. I always forget these because I drift back to sleep. So a scrap-pad and pencil by the bed is a 'good idea'!

Also just as I wake. These stay with me. I guess they are the result of a night's mental data processing.

Sometimes, however, the loo, the level crossing and my late night 'quiet moment' fail me. Or the timing doesn't suit. Or perhaps it's other people's ideas that are required. Particularly if the idea I'm seeking is to do with something I'm very much involved in.

Personally, I've always found my best ideas work better for other people than they do for me. One of my most expensive ideas — I lost a lot of money! — was in the mid-sixties trying to sell fashion wigs by mail order. One friend told me it was a hair-brained scheme. On both counts I was forced to agree.

Other people's idea can be great problem-solvers. So here's an idea to generate ideas when you're too close to . . .

See the wood from the trees

Use this particularly when you are closely involved with whatever it is that you are selling or promoting. It will pay you to examine carefully the many different aspects that your products or services have from the point of view of the buyer. It is always very different to the seller.

One of the best ways to examine new opportunities, new angles and new strategies for promotion is the brainstorming technique. Gather together your creative team, your production team, your client service people — even a few customers if you're feeling adventurous — and take another look at what you're trying to promote. Turn it upside down. Inside out.

Here are a few triggers for brainstorming sessions.

Increase it!

Make it bigger; give it more value; add to it; multiply it; make it more frequent; give it more strength; make it higher; make it wider, longer or fatter!

Decrease it!

Omit something; halve it; make it smaller; divide it into pieces or parts; make it more compact; condense it; understate it!

All-in-one?

Put your ideas together; put all the elements together; put all the separate bits and pieces together; sell as a complete piece!

Modify it?

Add a new twist or flavour; give it new form, design or shape; change its new appeal to the eye, the ear, taste, smell or feel!

Change it round?

Can you put something else first? Can you change the sequence or order? Can you change the frequency or timing?

Try a substitute!

What else can you use instead? Or who else? Or where else? What other element can be included or left out?

How about a different angle?

Don't accept the obvious; try the absolute opposite; turn it upside down; turn it inside out. How about backwards? Turn it around; try the unexpected or even sometimes the unacceptable.

Make sure you've asked these!

Why? When? Where? Who? What? How? What about? What if? What else?

In order to make a brainstorming session work well, you should select your participants carefully. You must describe your problems to them clearly. You must create an informal atmosphere and get your participants relaxed before the session gets under way.

It is not necessarily a bad idea to provide drinks and start with a joke session or a few anecdotes.

Make sure everyone is encouraged to speak. Compliment them. And react positively. Never make negative comments.

Encourage innovation and effort. Encourage building on other people's ideas and suggestions. Make notes unobtrusively rather than record or video the session. Never come to conclusions during the session. Lock out senior management!

With a **proposition** in mind

I'm not going to spend a great deal more time on propositions. I am going to give you a little lecture — in the emphatic tone of voice that mothers use when they are explaining to children how to cross the road.

Not a bad analogy really since the life of your mailing is at stake. So look left (list and/or database!), look right (proposition/offer!) and go if it's clear (package!).

Here's about all that matters:

1 Think a great deal about constructing a proposition that people will want to accept. The more you can do to relate that proposition to your audience (or segments of audience) the better it will work.
2 Consider what you can do to enhance it with an offer that will attract action and have a clearly established link with either the product/service that you are selling, or the people you are selling to. Why not both?
3 Develop a clear and explicit rationale for both proposition and offer.
4 Sell it. Sell the proposition harder than the product or service. Sell it in front. Sell it first. Sell it fast. And sell it thoroughly.

With **letters** in mind

Letters are undoubtedly, undisputedly and consistently the single strongest weapon in the creative armoury. A good letter is a joy to read. Or at the very least a pleasure. It is so formidable for a number of reasons:

1 People's natural instinct is to head for the letter first, often shunning more than casual glances of your other items in favour of it.

This is simply the conditioning of time. We expect letters in the post. We know they'll explain what it's about. So if there's any news, or anything significant, or anything important, it'll be in there.

2 Letters often look the easiest to cope with, the least threatening or blatantly trying to 'sell'. Not always.

But there is a 'comfort' factor to a letter which, once we've established that it's good news not bad, we enjoy and attracts us.

3 This is enhanced and forwarded by the fact that letters come from people. Leaflets are issued by companies. Letters are sent by an individual, even if they are obviously mass-produced. They have signatures. They talk in a light (sometimes chatty) style. So there's obviously a person there. A person behind it. A person involved.

Logically, of course, this is true of all the other items too! They just don't show it so engagingly!

Let's look at some more of Siegfried Vögele's evidence. Because there's no doubt that eye track management on this item is of huge importance. For so many readers it will be where positive or negative decisions for the Glance–Scan–Read process will be made.

One of the big differences with letters as opposed to other printed or published items is the number of historically conditioned (I call them *involuntary*) fixing points. They are there anyway. For example:

- The recipient's name and address block
- Your name and address
- The signature
- The name and title of the signatory
- A PS

You can create other fixing points (I call these *voluntary* fixing points). For example:

- Indented paragraphs
- Underlining
- Capital letters
- Handwritten margin notes
- All those **<!!>?@-ing things around the keyboard
- A Johnson box

```
* * * * * * * * * * * * * * * * * * * *   *
*                                          *
*                                          *
*                                          *
*    that's one of these . . .             *
*                                          *
*                                          *
*    often used for highlighting,          *
*                                          *
*                                          *
*    particularly at the beginning         *
*                                          *
*                                          *
*    of a letter                           *
*                                          *
*                                          *
*                                          *
*                                          *
* * * * * * * * * * * * * * * * * * * *   *
```

We also know the eye start positions — where the eye will come in. And where it will go out. If it's left to its own devices.

Creating a natural eye path

So you see, taking A4 as an example, it is possible to manage an eye track in order to boost our score with the reader and move them along the glance–scan–read path.

The numbers will dive — no, plummet — during these first seconds whatever you do. So saving just the odd extra reader or two is important. Don't be disheartened by the number of cop-outs — that's the way it is. As long as you have done everything you can to retain the ones you want.

Here are two layouts showing a simple use of this information. 'Before' (Fig. 10.3) shows a typical single page letter format that many (including a lot of professionals) would turn out. 'After', with the most likely eye tracks superimposed, shows a better way (Figs 10.4 and 10.5).

Lastly, may I urge you to spend lots and lots and lots of creative time on the letter. It'll *pay* you back handsomely.

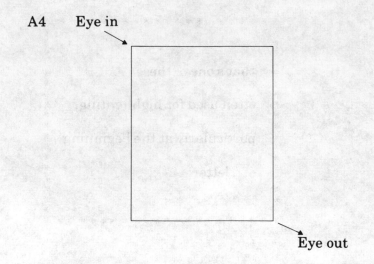

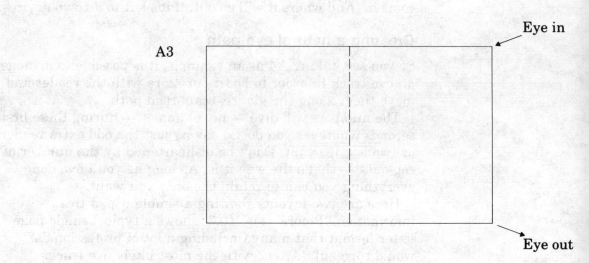

Figure 10.2
The natural eye path

CHOOSE YOUR <u>FREE</u> GIFT <u>NOW</u>

Figure 10.3
An innocently designed letter-style page ignoring eye-path principles

OWN THIS <u>PERSONALISED</u> <u>DIRECT MARKETING LIBRARY</u> FOR JUST <u>£99.95.</u> <u>SAVE</u> OVER £25.00, CLAIM <u>TODAY.</u>

Dear Marketer

BONUS FREE!

EVERY ASPECT OF DIRECT MARKETING EXPERTLY AND COMPREHENSIVELY REVEALED..

★DIRECT MAIL

★DATABASE

★TELEMARKETING

★OFF-THE-PAGE

★ELECTRONIC MEDIA

RETURN YOUR BONUS OFFER CLAIM NOW

SAVE £25.00 PLUS!

Figure 10.4
A layout which follows the eye management concept

EYE IN

OWN THIS PERSONALISED
DIRECT MARKETING LIBRARY
FOR JUST £99.95.
SAVE OVER £25.00. CLAIM TODAY.

Dear Marketer

BONUS FREE!

EVERY ASPECT OF
DIRECT
MARKETING
EXPERTLY AND
COMPREHENSIVELY
REVEALED..

★DIRECT MAIL

★DATABASE

★TELEMARKETING

★OFF-THE-PAGE

★ELECTRONIC
MEDIA

RETURN YOUR
BONUS OFFER
CLAIM NOW

SAVE
£25.00
PLUS!

EYE OUT

Figure 10.5
So a typical 'glance' might follow this easy path for the eye. (But note just how disruptive the salutation might prove to the first glance eye path)

With **personalisation** in mind

I once came out with this immortal line . . .

'I had forgotten how bad my memory is!'

What I'm building up to here is yet another acronym. I find they help me to carry thoughts in my head.

Since I have yet another circulating the whispering gallery that is my cerebellum right now and it's for personalisation, we may as well verbalise it.

The MIGHT of personalisation

Match-in **I**ndividualise **G**rab attention **H**elp response **T**ransmit information

So that is the basic 'menu'. What creative have to do is to decide with you which of these, often more than one, are required.

Certain choices — Individualise, for example — can achieve a bucketful of Grab Attention at the same time.

But creative will obviously make a more proficient job of presenting the personalisation, if they have a clear idea of why it is being used. For instance, if you've picked T — Transmit information — and you're going to announce the price increase of a subscription it will need to be handled differently in comparison to someone who is going to declare a record dividend on a savings plan or unit trust.

Personalisation needs to complement all manner of things. Style, tone of voice, positioning, image are a few. It needs to be influenced by the list or database, the character of the audience, the nature of the proposition and the personality of the package.

It is one of the major development areas for creativity in direct marketing and endorses the need for a new breed of practical, ingenious, technically detail-conscious creative mind that wants to enjoy the benefits of new technology. That is precisely why I invented the phrase 'techno-creativity'.

It describes the future of creativity in direct marketing. And no more so than in direct mail.

With the **package** in mind

With some occasional exceptions a 'package' should be a cohesive sales machine. Or enquiry generator. Each component performing a task.

Envelopes intrigue, lead the reader in, or introduce.

Letters announce. Explain. Invite. Encourage action.

Leaflets tell. Describe. Expand. Give detail. Illustrate and stimulate.

Flyers and other devices emphasise. Highlight. Carry urgent Stop Press. Provide extra fine detail. Or a last push for response.

Reply devices re-sell. Take orders. Encourage a dialogue. Re-illustrate offers. Reassure responders.

Reply envelopes bring replies, money and sensitive data.

But they all have to pull together. If you have been able to identify one clear offer/proposition they should all work together, gradually moving the reader's mind nearer to a decision — the decision to respond to that proposition.

When establishing the functions of the various pieces one must be clear that, for example, a flyer being used to emphasise a point does not overpower the leaflet or letter so that, in effect, the point becomes greater than the reason for making it.

Endeavour to make each item in your package a stand-alone item, meaning simply that whichever one is picked up, looked at first, come back to after a telephone call, catches the eye when emptying the wastepaper basket (*never* give up!), the reader can still grasp the proposition, find out where and how to get it.

If you build in a whole heap of eye-catchers, they will go on catching eyes until they reach the rubbish dump or incinerator.

In my early years in the business as a cub salesman, one of the leads I was given to follow up turned out to be from a mailing that was 13 years old. The returns address on it was two 'moves' out of date. All credit to the postmen of London who tracked us down. The responder became a profitable client for some two or three years.

Over a pie and pint (mange-tout hadn't been invented) I asked the young client — who, like me, obviously hadn't been at work thirteen years — how he had come to respond. He was, he explained, throwing out old files when the offer illustrated on the card (a list of lists called MAILWAY) had caught his eye.

This is especially important to achieve on the reply device. In fact, there really is a lot to think about with reply cards, coupons and other, often quite complex response items. So let's consider what we have to do.

The response device needs to ask for the order. It needs to close the sale. It needs to stand alone. It needs to perform its task with the minimum of fuss or effort by the responder. And lastly (meaning literally *lastly* — give it final priority), it needs to be economically and conveniently processed by you when it gets back.

Here's a checklist of ideas to help you achieve those objectives.

Response device checklist

1 *Keep it nice. Keep it clean* Design is all-important here. Yet a lot of designers rush out the response piece, either because they get bored with it, because it's no fun designing forms, or because they think it's a fairly trivial piece of detail.

   Wrong. It needs to look just as attractive, logical, open and inviting as the other items. Bearing in mind all it has to do, that's often a real designer's challenge.

2 *Keep it simple* It needs to look happy, colourful and friendly but not confusing. So use colour in the twin roles of making it cheerful and also making it easier to understand and follow.

3 *Give sufficient space* Responders should not be forced to cramp or abbreviate their name and address details or their order or response requests.

   Don't lose orders for items because you didn't allow enough lines. Ask them to write in BLOCK CAPITALS.

4 *Identify it* Make sure the response item stands out and is clearly headed. Avoid the word form if you can. Slip, coupon, request, claim, application are all more positive, less formal and inviting.

5 *Make sure they don't miss bits* You can use emphatic arrows to highlight important bits like signatures or postal codes, or place tinted crosses like your accountant or solicitor does in pencil to show you where to sign.

   You can achieve a great deal with background tints. For example, leaving all the sections they have to fill in as white sections out of a light background. This has the added advantage of making a large piece look less than it does as a whole. One only notices the white spaces!

6 *Give clear instructions or advice* If you have something that requires difficult, time-consuming or hard-to-find information, be helpful.

Nothing beats a step-by-step guide, the 1–2–3 of how to apply. If necessary give additional tips and hints alongside trick bits. Such as '. . . your bank sort code is the six digit code, top right of your cheques'.

Then make sure the space you leave for them to fill in looks like this:

☐ ☐ – ☐ ☐ – ☐ ☐
not like
☐ ☐ ☐ ☐ ☐
or even this!
☐────────────☐

7 *Put on their name and address together with a fast-find computer code for response handling*   You'll boost response by filling in the basic details for them. If you can design the document so the name and address block then shows through an envelope window you'll do yourself another favour.

But find some discreet place to print a code which will speed up your access of their record when you need to.

8 *Remember the keycodes you need*   This is definitely the place for codes. But don't make people feel like you used to work at the Inland Revenue, or for that matter, that they are just a set of numbers to you.

9 *Code incoming responses for a fast handling stream*   If you use reply envelopes for other things, or you want to apply different priorities to response handling, code the outer envelopes or return address sides for your mail handling staff.

This can be achieved by a simple change of colour. A side stripe or corner flash, and so on. Or a changed department name in the address!

10 *Encourage the personal contact*   Be sure to give them a named individual to ring. And a number!

You will have spent some time humanising the package, don't stop at the reply device. Print a name for them to return it to. One person sent them the letter. Let them reply to one person too. If they can be the same, that's great.

11 *Tell them how to pay*   Make payment easy. Accept credit cards (and telephone orders!). Additionally, do test 'Send no money now' if it's feasible or appropriate. Bad debt certainly goes up. But so does response. See if one outweighs the other.

12 *Go for extra or bigger sales*   Offer de-luxe versions, or even — just like they do by the checkouts at your local

store — tempt with an impulse purchase. Even if it's only 'Gift Wrapped' or 'Express Delivery'. Both at a good profit for you, of course.

Much better to go for 'real' extras. You'll be surprised how this can bump up order values. An order slip is a very 'hot' SALES area.

13 *Remember their worries*   Keep re-assuring. This document, at one level or another, is often a commitment from them to you. Repeat the guarantee here, for sure.

14 *Remember the common courtesies*   Say 'thank you'. Tell them how quickly you will deliver or respond. Ask for their day/early evening phone numbers, if appropriate.

15 *Ask for further information — but not intrusively, or if you've already got a lot*   Name of a friend. Forthcoming or recent address change. And so on.

JFR's box of tricks

- *Don't forget materials*   Your paper merchant can become a friend. One great way to make impact is the vast array of different textures and weights and colours available to you. But remember my earlier advice. When they hold your mailing in their hands they hold your company representative. If they don't know you, the materials (not just paper, but typography too) will be a major piece of evidence.

- *Be up-front!*   Someone with the unfortunate name of Joseph Krotch is on record as saying 'Cats seem to go all out on the principle that it never does any harm to ask for what you want.' I agree. Be positive. Ask for what you want. Justify your request. And ye shall receive.

- *Use layout for emphasis*   Have you ever noticed how many direct mail letters use indented paragraphs?

They work well both as fixing points but also to add emphasis to the importance of particular passages.

I've always worked to three paragraph widths which have the added benefit of adding shape and interest to the layout of a letter. As do indented paragraph openings. Generally the more tidied up copy looks the more boring and solid and heavy it looks — so justify left but 'ragged right'!

Here is my paragraph grid:

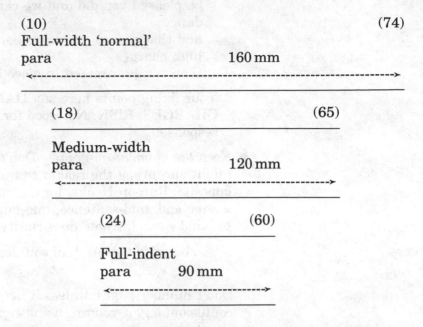

(10)   (74)

Full-width 'normal'
para   160 mm

<--->

(18)   (65)

Medium-width
para   120 mm

<--->

(24)   (60)

Full-indent
para   90 mm

<-------------------------------->

Notes
1   Minimum type size 10 point.
2   Use a serif type face.
3   Minimum left- and right-hand margins 25 mm (i.e. 10
      spaces in on 10 point).
4   Figures in brackets show spaces in from left edge
5   Layout on 'centred' format.

- *Avoid standard company letterheadings* So often their design gets in the way of eye track management. Often your logo and name will do just as much for you as the whole lot. Relegate boring address information, telephone numbers, and your registered address and incorporation number to the bottom.

  Who needs your address and phone number unless you've given them a reason to contact you anyway?

  Clear them away! Now you've got a great big hole. Fill it up with a great big benefit-laden headline!!
- *Beware the DANGER fixing points!* These are the unintentional ones. The most common are those paragraphs that run on to a new line which is just one word long. No problem if the word's a good one but, unless you are careful, even the apparently positive will work against you.

For example,

- be pleased you did and we can help you to avoid danger.
- and that means one more benefit. You won't pay our high charges.
- then it's guaranteed that we take out all the risk.

Your fixing points here say DANGER. HIGH CHARGES. RISK. Not good for building readership or response!

- *Keep the momentum going* Don't do anything which might encourage the reader to quit. In fact try to do the opposite. Run-on Hooks, for example. That's breaking at a page-end, mid-sentence, mid-paragraph. If possible try to build some intrigue or curiosity into the 'hook' too.

'. . . benefits too. And, of course, you could win . . .

/over please

Don't number pages, unless it helps to clarify or avoid confusion, e.g. if you are using separate sheets.

- *Don't worry about repeating yourself* The fact that the leaflet tells them the same as the letter already did (preferably two or three times!) doesn't matter, as long as you find alternative phraseology. Leaflets are generally best written in the third person anyway — so that's one difference!
- *Lift letters* Now and again you can steal the dynamic readership levels of the letter and spread it around a little with a second letter. And you'll grab the same if not more. This is a technique pioneered by the publishing fraternity with the now famous 'Only read this if you've decided not to buy . . .'

The rules are: (1) Don't confuse the reader (2) Reassure the reader (guarantee?);
(3) Remind the reader (main benefit — ONE *MORE* TIME!!).

11 There's only **one** kind of direct mail—

And that's . . .

yours

Now don't get cross. I haven't changed my mind about the last nine chapters! It's just that I want to say a word or two more about *your* direct mail. Because it will be that. *Yours*.

You'll get excited. Caught up. Involved. And constantly invigorated with direct mail, probably more than with any other medium. It is quite the most fascinating advertising there is. But more, it's fun and interesting too.

Originally, like all good direct marketers, I wanted to give you a money-back guarantee. Sadly, because of the way this book is to be published and marketed, it isn't technically possible. So instead, I'll extend an invitation to you. If you get problems, get in touch.

At the time of writing, my 24-hour home fax number in Britain is

0243 827932

If that fails, call one of the trade associations in Part Three. They *always* know what I'm up to!

I *love* direct mail. I hope you have come to realise that. And that includes *yours*. Which is really what this book has been about.

In Parts Three and Four, you'll find lots of useful information together with a Glossary of Direct Mail/Marketing Speak! But with the closing of Part Two we come to the end of the Why, When, Where and What. You are the proud owner of my *Secrets of Effective Direct Mail*.

So I'd like to wish you just one thing which is *not* luck. I'd like to wish you what I wish myself. What else?

Money. And success.

► PART THREE ◄

Assistance, Contacts, the Law, and Standards. Language, and where you can read some more

This section is to help you further. And to ensure that you don't lose all that money and success out the back door by failing to comply with the law or meet the standards required by the industry.

It's also to enable you to get in touch with new friends and contacts with whom you can share our experiences — and learn and grow. And maybe join a good 'club' or two.

Then, you'll find a Bibliography, a Glossary and an Index.

I must point out that this information is, to the best of my knowledge, correct at time of writing. Further, with regard to the legislation and standards, I have produced a general set of guidelines rather than an interpretation of the originals. You should only use my commentary as an indication of the potential danger-points and thus use them to flag the topics about which you should learn more or seek specialist help. The responsibility is entirely yours!

12 Contacts and associations

There are four principal publishers whose publications I would commend to you.

1 HOKE COMMUNICATIONS INC.
224 Seventh Street
Garden City
New York NY 11530
Tel: 516-746-6700

Monthly magazine and books.

2 DIRECT MARKETING WORLD (UK)
Charterhouse Communications
Boundary House
91–93 Charterhouse Street
London EC1M 6HR
Tel: (01) 250 0646
Fax: (01) 250 0637

Monthly magazine and conferences.

3 DIRECT RESPONSE MAGAZINE LTD
4 Market Place
Hertford SG14 1EB
Tel: (0992) 501177
Fax: (0992) 500387

Monthly magazine and conferences.

4 PRECISION MARKETING
Centaur Communications
St Giles House
50 Poland Street
London W1V 4AX
Tel: (01) 439 4222
Fax: (01) 439 8065

And I also said I'd give you the details of the Annual Symposium in Montreux. It's as follows:

Montreux Marketing Symposium for Direct Marketing Communication, Bahnhofstrasse 17, CH 8702-Zollikon-Station, Switzerland.

See also the European Direct Marketing Association (page 356, under Worldwide Associations), who hold conferences in their own right and in partnership with the (US) Direct Marketing Association.

Associations

Association of Mail Order Publishers

Address: 1 New Burlington Street
           LONDON
           W1X 1FD

Telephone: (01) 437 0706

How and when it started

AMOP started in 1970, as the result of a feeling shared by many of the leading companies of the mail order publishing industry that none of the larger associations met their specific needs.

Its role

As the industry association of companies and agencies involved in direct selling of books, magazines, music and video products, AMOP's role is to protect and further the interests of its members.

Help to members

AMOP acts as a strong voice for its members within the direct marketing industry and in discussions with government departments, statutory and other bodies. This involvement includes contributing to draft legislation. AMOP members all undertake to follow a voluntary code which set standards of procedure. A separate body, the Mail Order Publishers Authority, administers and supervises this Code of Practice.

The Authority receives, investigates and adjudicates in cases of complaint from the public about treatment they have received from a member. The Mail Order Publishers Authority makes an annual report to the Director General of Fair Trading.

The Mail Order Traders Association

Address: 25 Castle Street
           LIVERPOOL
           L2 4TD

Telephone: (051) 236 7581
           (051) 227 4181

How and when it started

The Mail Order Traders Association was formed in 1940 as the industry association, representing the large general catalogue mail order companies.

Its role

The Association has a dual role: representing and protecting its members in matters which relate to mail order trade by catalogue, while simultaneously representing and protecting the interests of the general public who order goods from mail order catalogues.

Help to members

The Mail Order Traders Association advises and represents its members in all matters relating to the mail order catalogue business, frequently negotiating with government departments, consumer organisations and European institutions. The Association is represented on many organisations, such as the Council of the Retail Consortium, the Non-Food Wages Council, the EC European and Social Committee.

The Association has a code to which its members adhere. Although much of it is required by law, the code does fully define the ethics and standards which it seeks to forward. The code covers the pricing, advertising, postage, packing and delivery of goods, together with sales promotions and goods supply. Other guidelines include customer information, assembling goods, safety standards, delivery dates, etc. A complaints procedure to be followed by the public when dealing in disputes with members is also laid down in the Association's code.

The Advertising Association

Address: Abford House
            15 Wilton Road
            LONDON
            SW1W OBS
Telephone: (01) 828 2771

How and when it started

The Advertising Association was founded 1926. It was set up as the professional body to represent all those in the advertising business as it was at the time. The business of advertising was very much smaller, and mainly limited to the published media, outdoor advertising and some direct mail.

Its role

With the massive growth in advertising the Association has expanded enormously and comprises a 'federation' of 29 trade associations and professional bodies. As such, its membership varies from advertisers, agencies and media and support services. The principal purpose of the Association is therefore those tasks which have a bearing on all of its membership, serving all interests equally.

Help to members

The Association lobbies legislative proposals at a national and international level. It campaigns for the freedom to advertise and to improve public attitudes to advertising.

It is concerned with the process of training and development within the advertising industry. The Advertising Association publishes advertising statistics for both the UK and Europe, and instigates research projects on advertising issues.

The Association also organises seminars and training courses for those involved in the advertising and media fields. Advertising Association members also benefit from the comprehensive library facilities in the Advertising Association Information Centre, which contains one of the most impressive collections of literature on advertising in Europe.

The Direct Mail Producers Association

Address: 34 Grand Avenue
LONDON
N10 3BP
Telephone: (01) 883 7229

How and when it started

The DMPA was formed in 1962 starting as an offshoot of the Direct Mail House Committee of the BDMA, when it became apparent that member interests would be better served in a separate association.

Its role

The association represents the interest of companies mainly engaged in the production of direct mail (i.e. those that perform direct mail services for their clients). It sees its most important role as promoting high ethical and professional standards in the direct mail industry which is evidenced by the rigorous entry requirements for those who wish to join.

Help to members

The DMPA holds regular meetings and discussions with other trade associations, e.g. the AA, and other advertising bodies, the BDMA, AMOP, MUA, BLBA and other direct marketing related associations.

The DMPA has engaged in negotiations particularly with the Post Office (which resulted in the introduction of new services and incentives to direct mail advertisers) and the DMSSB in view of the increasing volume of legislation affecting member interests.

The DMPA also operates an enquiry service for those companies and individuals wishing to use direct mail and locate potential suppliers. Many list enquiries are handled, and this service brings substantial new business for members.

The British Direct Marketing Association

Address: Grosvenor Gardens House
            35 Grosvenor Gardens
            LONDON
            SW1W 0BS
Telephone: (01) 630 7322

How and when it started

The BDMA goes back in some form to the twenties, but in its present form it started in the late sixties.

Its role

Its role, as the major British association for the direct marketing industry, is to further the interests of both clients using direct marketing, and agencies servicing these companies.

Help to members

The BDMA gives its members direct marketing contacts, information and advice. All BDMA members must adhere to a code of practice although many of its stipulations are anyway contained in both current legislation and other codes.

Their code covers all aspects of direct marketing and by every available media. The BDMA represents direct marketing interests in the political forum, as well as to the press.

For company members who wish to use direct marketing, the BDMA give advice on how to start, suggest who might be best able to serve their needs, and give any other information available, free of charge. For agency members, the BDMA adds credibility and support.

The BDMA sends each member bi-monthly newsletters, monthly bulletins and regular mailings. Books and publications can be bought direct from the BDMA booklist at discounted prices. Direct marketing information and statistics are freely available to members by phone.

The BDMA Diploma in Direct Marketing is a recognised asset in the industry, which until recent years had little recognised training or educational courses.

The Mail Users Association

Address: 6 Whitgift Street
              CROYDON
              Surrey
              CR0 1DH
Telephone: (01) 681 7196

How and when it started

The Mail Users Association was established by businessmen in 1976 for commercial users of the postal service.

Its role

It is the only organisation dedicated to postal affairs and is primarily a pressure group. The main objective of the Mail Users Association is to achieve a healthy and vigorous Post Office, vital to the business interests of its members.

The Mail Users Association influences the Post Office and the government. It is sometimes seen as an outspoken association, but is also widely recognised for its strong and authoritative arguments, together with constructive criticism.

The Mail Users Association frequently carry out research into the quality of the Post Office service. It recommends actions as to marketing, productivity, service, quality, price as well as management style.

Help to members

The Mail Users Association does not specialise in direct mail, although some of its members do. The Association represents any business/commercial organisations which use the postal services.

Members can seek advice on postal problems through the Association office, and receive a regular newsletter, which gives the latest information on postal affairs.

The Institute of Practitioners in Advertising

Address: 44 Belgrave Square
LONDON
SW1X 8QS
Telephone: (01) 235 7020

How and when it started

The IPA was established in 1927, as a professional body for UK advertising agencies.

Its role

The IPA has two main roles:
1   A voice for the collective views of agencies, the media and other trade associations
2   An advisory, training and informative service

Help to members

The IPA is a representative for agencies with media, market research, broadcast, press advertisement, print and production bodies. The IPA also maintains a close relationship with the press and government departments. It provides advice for advertising agency members on legislation and voluntary codes of practice. Surveys are carried out on a regular basis covering topics of interest to managers in the advertising field (e.g. annual survey of agency credentials) and projects of interest (e.g. new technology). The IPA administers and services three employers associations, in order to improve employee relations within their profession.

The IPA run intensive training courses, designed to improve professional skills of agency staff and has an information centre, which houses several databases and major research tracts. All this information can be accessed by IPA members free of charge.

However, there are stringent requirements which have to be satisfied before membership to this Association can be granted.

The British List Brokers Association

Address: Springfield House
Princess Street
BEDMINSTER
Bristol
BS3 4EF
Telephone: (0272) 666 900

How and when it started

The BLBA was established in May 1983 by a few leading companies in the list business who felt that the list industry needed a trade association, in addition and separate to the mainstream direct marketing associations.

Its role

The BLBA aims to draw all reputable list brokers in Great Britain together, to maintain the highest possible standards. This is important in view of the growth of the use of direct mail, and the once precarious ethics in the use of lists.

Help to members

The BLBA has laid down a trading practice guide to which member brokers, owners and list managers, must adhere as their proper conduct. The guide also lays down a complaints procedure, for which the BLBA arbitrates.

The BLBA, along with five other trade associations and the Post Office have all contributed to sponsoring the Mailing Preference Service. This service has a natural affinity with the BLBA, since it operates the cleaning of mailing lists, enabling consumer names and addresses to be excluded from (or added to) mailing lists.

This facility benefits BLBA members by reducing wastage and improves the image of the industry in the eyes of the public.

The Direct Mail Sales Bureau

Address: 14 Floral Street
          Covent Garden
          LONDON
          WC2E 9RR
Telephone: (01) 379 7531

How and when it started

The DMSB was set up jointly by the Post Office and direct mail industry in 1982.

Its role

Its purpose is to attract business for the direct mail industry from 'new' markets, especially to encourage advertising agencies to use the medium more knowledgeably.

Help to members

The DMSB assists the industry as a whole, by encouraging

more advertisers to experiment with using direct mail in consort with mainstream advertising. The DMSB's development of the Consumer Location System has been crucial to this. The CLS is a targeting system, which specifies markets, provides rationale for media selection, and access to accurate names and addresses of potential purchasers within the identified markets.

The CLS has demonstrated to many advertisers that direct mail can be the most appropriate media to use in a campaign.

The Direct Mail Services and Standards Board

Address: 26 Eccleston Street
                LONDON
                SW1 1PY
Telephone: (01) 824 8651

How and when it started
The DMSSB was launched in 1983. It was created to counter the suspicions or doubts of large advertisers. Although it stands as a separate association in its own right, the initial launch was finance by the Post Office.

Its role
To operate a recognition scheme to assure clients of the standing and integrity of the direct marketing agencies and kindred suppliers that they can approach.

Help to members
The Board encourages membership applications from all direct marketing agencies. If the Board accepts an application, that company receives a 1 per cent discount (variable each year) on its annual postage bill.

The Advertising Standards Authority

Address: Brook House
                2–16 Torrington Place
                LONDON
                WC1E 7HN
Telephone: (01) 580 5555

How and when it started
The ASA was formed in 1963, in order to set standards in advertising, in line with other trade associations for other forms of media.

Its role

Is to set standards for advertisements transmitted by all forms of media, except television and radio.

Help to members

It administers two self-regulatory codes of practice on behalf of its members — the British Code of Advertising Standards and the British Code for Sales Promotion.

It handles formal complaints raised by members of the public about an advertisement or a promotion by one of its members, and monitors such advertisements and promotions.

Worldwide Associations

Australia

Terry Murphy,
National Director,
AUSTRALIAN DIRECT MARKETING ASSOCIATION,
10F, 52–58 Clarence Street,
Sydney,
NSW 2000,
AUSTRALIA

Belgium

Guy Oliver,
GROUPEMENT DE LA VENTE PAR CORRESPONDANCE,
Rue de la Science, 3,
1040 Brussels,
BELGIUM

Brazil

Antonio Silvio Lefevre,
President,
ASSOCIACAO BRASILEIRA DE MARKETING DIRETO,
Avenida Paulista 2202,
São Paulo,
SP CEP 01310
BRAZIL

Canada

Terence Belgue,
President,
CANADIAN DIRECT MARKETING ASSOCIATION,
1 Concorde Gate,
Don Mills,
Ontario M3C 3N6
CANADA

Denmark

John Brauer,
Chairman,
THE DANISH DIRECT MARKETING ASSOCIATION,
Store Kongensgade 69,
1264 Copenhagen, K,
DENMARK

Finland

Harry Soderholm,
Chairman of the Board,
FINNISH DIRECT MARKETING ASSOCIATION,
Fredrikinkatu 58 A4,
SF–00100 Helsinki
FINLAND

France

Bernard Siouffi,
Délégué Général,
UNION FRANÇAISE DE LA PUBLICITÉ DIRECTE,
60 rue La Boétie,
5008 Paris,
FRANCE

Hong Kong

Mario A. Freude,
Chairman,
HONG KONG DIRECT MAIL & MARKETING
ASSOCIATION,
GPO Box 7416
HONG KONG

Italy

Graziano Fiorelli,
President,
ASSOCIAZIONE NATIONALE FRA AZIENDE
DI VENDITA PER CORRISPONDENZA,
Via Melchiore Gioia 70,
20125 Milano
ITALY

Dr Pietro Sanfelice de Monteforte,
President,
AIDIM (ASSOCIAZIONE ITALIANA PER IL DIRECT
MARKETING),
Corso Venezia, 16,
20121 Milano,
ITALY

Japan

Shigeru Kawakami,
Managing Director,
JAPAN DIRECT MAIL ASSOCIATION (JDMA),
Dai Hachi Kojimachi Bldg. 3F,
4–5 Kojimachi, Chiyoda-ku,
Tokyo 102,
JAPAN

Kaoru Nomiyama,
Managing Director,
JAPAN DIRECT MARKETING ASSOCIATION (JADMA),
32 Mori Bldg., 3–4–30 Shiba-Koen,
Minato-ku,
Tokyo 105,
JAPAN

Buichi Kurozumi,
Chairman,
NIHON DIRECT MARKETING ASSOCIATION (NDMA),
2–2–15 Minai Aoyama,
Wion Aoyama 337,
Minato-ku,
Tokyo 107
JAPAN

Mexico

McNeely Kroupensky,
Vice President,
ASSOCIATION MEXICANA DE MERCADOTECNIA
POR CORREO DIRECTO, A.C. (AMMCD),
c/o Panamerican Ogily & Mather SA,
Bahia de Santa Barbara 143 11300
MEXICO

The Netherlands

F.H. Van Dorst,
Managing Director,
DIRECT MARKETING INSTITUUT NEDERLAND,
Weerdestein 96,
1083GG Amsterdam,
THE NETHERLANDS

Aad Weening,
Secretary,
NEDERLANDSE POSTORDERBOND,
Lange Voorhout 86,
2514 EJ Den Haag,
THE NETHERLANDS

New Zealand

Keith W. Norris,
President,
NEW ZEALAND DIRECT MARKETING ASSOCIATION,
146 Hinemoa Street,
Birkenhead,
Auckland,
NEW ZEALAND

Singapore

Charlie In Nany Sing,
Chairman,
DIRECT MAIL & MARKETING ASSOCIATION OF
SINGAPORE,
Waterloo Centre,
Block 261,
Waterloo Street, 03–26
SINGAPORE 0718

South Africa

Maryna van Jaarsveld,
Executive Director,
THE SOUTH AFRICAN DIRECT MARKETING
ASSOCIATION,
PO Box 85370,
Emmerentia 2029,
REP. OF SOUTH AFRICA

Spain

Juan Menal,
President,
ASOCIACION DE VENTA POR CORREO Y MARKETING DIRECTO,
Provenza, 238,
Barcelona 08008
SPAIN

Sweden

Tom Ekelund,
President,
SWEDISH DIRECT MARKETING ASSOCIATION,
PO Box 45110,
104–30 Stockholm
SWEDEN

Switzerland

Ernst Siegenthaler,
Secretary General,
EUROPEAN DIRECT MARKETING ASSOCIATION,
4 Rue de la Scie,
CH-1207 Geneva,
SWITZERLAND
Telephone: 022 86 33 86

USA

Angela Draper-Singh,
Director, International Operations,
THE DIRECT MARKETING ASSOCIATION, INC.,
6 East 43rd Street,
New York,
NY 10017
USA
Telephone: (010) 212 689 4977

West Germany

Hasso Herbst,
Geschäftsführer,
DDV-DEUTSCHER DIREKT MARKETING VERBAND e.v.,
Schiersteiner Strasse 29,
D-6200 Wiesbaden,
WEST GERMANY

13 Legislation and standards

The subject of legislation and industry standards are often considered to be intricate, dry, and for the businessman both potentially tedious and time-consuming. However, disregarding either can result in graver problems than restrictions to the design of mailing packages and time-loss. A court case can cause enormous problems and embarrassment to a company, whether an offence be deliberate or unintentional.

Direct mail is, in some respects, difficult, detailed and dangerous. Activities at nearly every stage of the mailing process have both legal and self-regulatory guidelines controlling them, as this section will show. However, I hope to encourage you to view both legislation and standards as being beneficial to all rather than restrictive. It is only when high standards are upheld, that the image of direct mail as an honest and likeable medium is maintained.

As the industry develops, becoming more sophisticated and expansive, there will no doubt be still more regulation, not less.

There are only two types of regulation:

1 *Legislation* Law enacted by Parliament.
2 *Self-regulation* Voluntarily agreed by a body or institution set up by or within the industry.

Let's look at how the various stages of a direct mail campaign are affected, with both types of regulation in mind.

Lists

Legislation

The Data Protection Act is the main law to affect the list industry. This Act has a widespread impact for the majority of businesses, since it was passed to regulate computer activities. The rapid advance and intricate development of computer storage systems during the late seventies and

357

eighties, led to similar advances in information processing. The British Data Protection Act was instigated as a result of the need for Britain to fall in line with the Council of Europe Convention on Data Protection.

Originally there were fears that the principles laid down by the European Convention would be so strictly adhered to, that it might have forced list brokers out of business altogether, since the use of data, obtained for one purpose would not have been permitted to be used for any other.

When the Data Protection Act was passed in 1984, many people in the list industry were able to breathe a sigh of relief, for the final Act was not as restrictive as the White Paper had been when it was issued in 1982. But this could still be an issue.

Three definitions from the Act affecting the direct mail industry

'Data subject': 'an individual who is the subject of personal data', i.e., the customer on a list whose personal details can consist of a name and address together with other details such as recency of purchase, income and family data.

'Data User': 'a person who holds data'. Those who store and control the content of data intended for processing. In direct mail terms this could include the list owner, the list broker and the list manager.

'Computer Bureau': 'a person carries on a Computer Bureau if he provides other persons with services in respect of data'. The definition continues to explain that this could be either as an agent, or by allowing others the use of equipment for processing data. For example, list brokers, computer bureaux and printers, and mailing houses.

The Data Protection Act requirements

1   All those holding computerised information which specifically refers to named individuals must apply to register with the Data Protection Registrar, who oversees the imposition of the Act, more details of which are given below. Those who register become bound to operate within the terms of registration.
2   For those data users and computer bureaux involved in the list industry, this means a licence for all data activities has to be obtained for each individual company (rather than every list having to be registered separately, as was first imagined).
3   The Data Protection Act only requires registration from those companies processing personal data held on

computer. Information held on a manual or card system does not require registration.

4   Harm caused through the disclosure or destruction of data, by these processing data, to the data subject, was made an offence under the Act. The courts were given the power to enforce the correction of harmful or faulty information, with the payment of compensation to the data user where applicable.

5   Data subjects are able to view any information held about themselves by a specific data user or computer bureau, on payment of an administrative charge. Under the Act this information is required to be given.

How to register

Data users must apply to the Data Protection Registrar at the following address:

Office of the Data Protection Registrar,
Springfield House,
Water Lane,
Wilmslow,
Cheshire
SK9 5AX

When registering the following information must be given:

1   Details of the personal data being held.
2   The purpose for which the data user intends use.
3   The sources of the data.
4   Those to whom the data will be disclosed.
5   The countries outside the UK to which the data may be transferred.

An entry fee is charged for registration, which is renewable. Refusal of registration can be made where:

1   Insufficient information in the particulars are given.
2   The applicant is considered likely to contravene the principle of the Act.
3   Insufficient information leads to the possibility that an application could contravene the Act.

Four areas of difficulty

1   It may be, in certain circumstances, worthwhile for the data users to register each list on which a name reoccurs so that an enquirer is forced to pay several fees, rather than just a single one.
2   The source of a data subject's name must also be disclosed

to the data subject at their request. However, if the source of a name is an individual, not a company, the user can refuse to reveal it.

3 Data users should ensure that a print-out of information is a complete file. It is customary for print-outs of portions of the file to be taken.

4 Data users must establish that enquirers are genuinely who they claim to be. This is especially difficult for those who only deal with customers through the post. Thus, for instance, it would be prudent that copies of information should therefore only be sent to known addresses, unless a genuine change of address can be established.

Offences under the Data Protection Act

The data user can fall foul of the law, committing a criminal offence, when he knowingly does one of the following:

1 'holds such data of any description other than that which he has registered.

2 holds or uses any such data for other than a registered purpose.

3 obtains such data, or information to be contained in them, from any source which he has not described in his entry in the register.

4 discloses such data to any person not described in his entry.

5 directly or indirectly transfers such data to any place outside the UK which is not named in his entry.'
(quoted from *Direct Response Magazine*)

Further reading

The eight data protection principles, together with other practical guidelines, are contained in eight, allegedly clear and readable booklets written by the Data Protection Registrar. These can be obtained from the address given above and are available free of charge.

The Lindop Report (HMSO, Cmnd 7341) written in 1978, details background to the Data Protection Act. Apart from Chapter 17, 'Direct Marketing' (page 139), other relevant sections include Chapter 28 'Data Handling Bureaux' (page 252), Chapters 18 and 19 on the regulation of the Act (page 149ff) and Chapter 2 on 'Privacy and Data Protection' (page 9).

The Data Protection Act is explained in detail in Sizer and Newman's book entitled the *Data Protection Act: A practical guide* (Gower, ISBN 0-566-02445-4).

Self-regulation

The industry has itself reacted to the Data Protection Act, by bringing about a code of practice in the form of the Mailing Preference Service In the words of the Data Protection Registrar:

> The Service offers a facility for individuals to suppress the receipt of unwanted mail which I feel accords well with the requirement of fair processing of personal data contained in the First Data Protection Principle.

The Mailing Preference Service has three fundamental principles:

1 To delete names of those who do not wish to be on non-customer mailing lists, so that they no longer receive unwanted mail. MPS exclusion can be carried out on both non-customer mailing lists and, by direct removal requests, from both in-house and outside lists.
2 To add names of those who wish to be included on our lists, so that they receive more mail.
3 All members of the scheme are encouraged to recommend others in the industry to comply with the scheme.

This benefits the direct mail industry by:

1 Helping to improve the image of direct mail. Those aware of the scheme are impressed by the concern of the industry to adapt to people's needs.
2 Reducing wasted mail, by avoiding the cost of sending mailing packages to those who do not wish to receive them and who are therefore less likely to respond.
3 Attracting new names who enjoy receiving direct mail, and as such are more likely to respond.

How the scheme operates

Members of the public contact the service direct to be included in the scheme. Those companies who subscribe to the service are sent updated copies of the file (either held on computer tape or printed onto a hard copy as required), on a quarterly basis. Names remaim on the file for three years. Change of addresses are the responsibility of the member of the public, as explained to them on entry to the scheme.

Registration

Everyone involved in direct marketing is encouraged to join the service. Membership is renewable annually, the fee is based on the scale of operations, calculated by the quantity of items mailed in a year. A separate fixed fee is set for those members who derive no direct benefits from the scheme (e.g. list owners, and computer bureaux, etc.).

An application form to register with the Mailing Preference Service, together with further details are obtainable from:

The Mailing Preference Service,
1 New Burlington Street,
LONDON
W1X 1FD
Telephone: (01) 437 070

Legislation

The copyright laws

Current law regulating copyright mainly dates back to the Copyright Act 1956. The reason for this legislation is to protect those who engage in creative activity, whose value is derived from the ideas, skill and labour to produce a unique object. The nature of work which can be viewed as creative, varies widely. It could be a drawing, a record, a video or musical cassette, a computer program, or an architectural plan. All of which may or may not have been published. Copyright laws affect those creating direct mail packages in two ways:

1   Mailings can contravene copyright if material is included which is the copyright of another party. This can be:

 (i) Testimonials
 (ii) Photographs or other illustrative material
 (iii) Written material

2   Mailings themselves have a copyright in their own right as company literature.

Who owns copyright?   The author of the work is the first owner of a copyright. The author is not necessarily an individual, in the case of company literature the author is deemed to be the company, rather than the employee who undertook the work.

How long does it last?   Copyright generally lasts for the lifetime of, and for 50 years from the death of, the author. In the event that the work is published after the death of the author, copyright lasts for 50 years from the date when the work is published. The exception to this is those industrial designs which are considered appealing to the eye, for which copyright currently lasts for 15 years only. Future legislation is likely to bring these into line with the other works.

How does one obtain copyright?   Copyright arises automatically. There is no need to register a copyright. The idea or principle behind a creative work cannot constitute a copyright. It is the work itself which is protected. A mark on the product is not necessary for copyright to be enforced. However, such a mark does act as a warning to those who might be in danger of infringing copyright.

How does one prevent an infringement on another person's copyright?   Those who wish to use a piece of work which might infringe copyright, must obtain the permission of the author (be it an individual, or a company). The process of finding the author may not be straightforward, but is essential to avoid infringement.

The degree of infringement   Infringement can be either to a primary or secondary degree. Primary infringement is where an author's work is reproduced exactly, or in a recognisable form without prior permission being obtained. However, if it can be proved that the second piece of work was arrived at independently, this does not constitute infringement.

Secondary infringement occurs when selling or importing copies of the infringing product is carried out (something that mail order traders may be in danger of doing). People are only liable if this infringement is committed knowingly.

In cases when the act of copyright infringement is of urgent concern, a court may issue an order to restrain the infringer, or to seize the goods which are causing this infringement.

FURTHER READING
An excellent booklet which explains copyright is available free of charge from Pinset & Co. at the following address:

Pinset & Co.,
Post & Mail House,
26 Colmore Circus,
Birmingham
B4 6BH
Telephone: (021) 200 1050

OTHER USEFUL PUBLICATIONS
Copyright, W. A. Copinger and E. P. Skone James, Sweet & Maxwell.
The Visual Artists' Copyright Handbook, Henry Lydiate Publications.
Layman's Guide to the Copyright, Designs and Patents Bill, Department of Trade and Industry, October 1987.

Government introduces Bill to reform Copyright, Designs and Patents Law, Press Notice, Department of Trade and Industry, 30 October 1987.

Libel

Libel and slander both amount to defamation of someone's good reputation, to which everyone is naturally entitled. Libel occurs when someone publishes something which damages a third party's reputation. In direct mail, libel can occur when either a picture, photograph, name or words used in a mailing is, albeit unknown to the publisher, libellous.

For libel to be upheld:

1 The statement complained of must be brought by the person to whom it refers.
2 The statement must be false, though this can be by implication.
3 The statement must be published so that a third person can read it and can interpret the statement as defamatory.

The degree of defamation need not be large, but it does have to cause ridicule, lower the reputation and image of the person or cause hatred to them. There are cases where libel is caused unwittingly. However, this is still an offence in law, and a person's innocence will only have an effect as to the degree of punishment for the offence.

In Direct Mail libel can occur if someone's photograph is used in a way that defames him. For example if the picture is touched up to cause the individual ridicule or harm. Similarly, copy which mentions a named individual can be deemed libellous, if defamatory.

The Financial Services Act

For those who have to create a mailing to do with a financial service, the Financial Services Act will obviously carry the most dramatic impact. Financial companies will be aware of various specialist aspects of legislation which affect their business. For further information, a good source is *Marketing Insurance: A Practical Guide*, N. Dyer and R. Anderson, pages 380–405. Also of interest is *Insurance Direct Marketing*, Tony Martin, pages 249–258.

The ramifications of the Financial Services Act for advertisers using direct mail   The Financial Services Act covers 'dealing in, arranging deals in, managing or advising on those things which are classified in the Act as investments'.

For those 'carrying out investment businesses' in Great Britain, namely the client company, there are two points of interest:

1 The activity of advising on investments. In cases where a joint affinity or cooperative mailing includes lierature for a financial service, whilst the financial company is likely to be aware of the ramifications of the Act, the company sharing the mailing may also have to be authorised under the FSA, if their literature can be seen as endorsing that of the financial company.

2 The activity of arranging deals which require special explanation. In cases where an outside company database is used to select likely prospects for the investment business, this collaboration might be seen as 'arranging deals'.

The ramifications of the Financial Services Act for direct marketing agencies   Direct marketing agencies are affected by the clause which states that 'a person who issues, or causes to be issued, an investment advertisement' must be authorised under the Act. An agency has a responsibility to ensure that a mailing package has been approved by the client, and also that the person who has given this approval is authorised under the Act. This second point requires an agency to consult a register of authorised businesses from the board.

If a knowingly false or dishonest statement is included in a mailing, in order to induce people to buy or sell their investments, a criminal offence has been committed which could result in a two-year sentence.

The Act also prohibits artificial closing dates for investments or for the terms for which they are available to be given.

The Medicine Act 1968

This Act, which made new provisions for medicinal products and their associated uses, also made provisions for advertising that would have an impact on the design and content of direct mail packages.

Under the Act

1 Any person with commercial interests in the sale of medicines, or related products, who issues a false or misleading advertisement relating to medicinal products is guilty of an offence.

2 Any person who holds a licence authorising him or her as

being able to recommend such a product, and who falsely recommends such a product due to commercial self-interest, is also guilty of an offence.

Defence of the above two charges is given to those who acted unknowingly.

3 Advertisements and direct mail packages can be prohibited or regulated by appropriate government ministers. This ensures that sufficient information is supplied about the medicinal product, that this information is not misleading, and that the safety of such products is preserved.

4 The Act also stipulates that a 'data sheet' (a standard sheet providing a breakdown of the contents of the medical products as for prescription) must be supplied along with any direct mail advertisement sent directly to a practitioner in the medical field. The exception to this is when such a sheet has been sent to the same practitioner within 15 months prior to the advertisement being sent.

There must be a consistency between the particulars contained with the advertisement and data sheet. The licensing authority holds the power to require to see copies of advertisements, together with their relevant data sheets.

Competitions

A competition or other form of prize-winning event offered as an incentive in a mailing must comply with the two pieces of legislation which follow:

The Gaming Act 1968

Section 42 of this Act prohibits advertisements (or mailings) which inform, or invite queries from the public about premises where gaming is currently taking place, or which will take place in future.

Likewise, those advertisements which invite the public to subscribe money to be used for the purposes of gaming, either in this country or abroad, are prohibited.

The Lotteries and Amusements Act 1976

This prevents the sale of lottery tickets through the post. The Act also stipulates that it is unlawful to conduct prize competitions, unless some exercise of skill is required of the recipients. Amusements with prizes must be devoted to purposes other than private gain.

The British Code of Advertising Standards

Background

In 1961 the first British Code of Advertising was drawn up by the Advertising Association in order to bring printed advertising into line with television advertising, which had recently drawn up its own code.

Today's code remains much the same as the very first BCAP code. It is administered by the CAP Committee under the general umbrella of the Advertising Standards Association. The responsibility for upholding the code lies with the advertiser.

What the code covers

The code voluntarily regulates advertising of all types except those transmitted by radio and television. The IBA has it own code for broadcast advertising. Thus, not only direct response advertisers, but also other advertisers adhere to these guidelines.

What are the aims of the code?

It is in the interests of all those who advertise to uphold standards of belief and trust, for otherwise advertising will not be deemed credible by the very same public it is designed to convince. If an advertisement is offensive, then the image of the advertising industry itself is in effect tarnished. The code seeks to ensure that the content of each advertisement meets standards, rather than judging each advertisement for its artistic appeal, or success according to any other criteria.

What happens when the code is contravened?

An advertiser comes under scrutiny as a result of either a formal complaint made by a member of the public, or as a result of the monitoring process which is carried out on a continual basis by the Advertising Standards Authority.

Contraventions of the code result in a formal request made to the advertiser to alter his practices immediately. In certain cases, compensation must be paid to affected parties.

What does the code lay down?

The code requires that an advertisement:

1   adheres to British law
2   is decent
3   is honest
4   is truthful

The fourth of these points is discussed in some depth. Truthfulness is crucial to political advertisements, advertisements where prices are quoted, those which use the word 'free', testimonials used within advertisements and for guarantees.

The code also states that an advertisement must be recognisable as such. An advertiser must be sure that the product or service is available as it was advertised.

Advertisements must be responsible to both the consumer and to society in general. For example, violence should not be encouraged, special rules must be adhered to in the cases of health-related products, cosmetics, cigarette and alcohol advertisements, and other sensitive areas.

The Acts which affect advertisers include the following:

1 Consumer Safety Act 1978 (adherence to given standards must be kept)
2 Hallmarking Act 1973 (the quantity of metal used in a product must be stated by the advertiser). Goods must conform to their description/or to sample supplied. Size/ weight must be clearly stated within an advertisement. Goods sent on approval, if returned by the consumer, must have postage paid by the latter.
3 Post Office Act 1953 (Section II) not all goods are suitable for offer by mail order, e.g. unsafe items. The address of an advertiser must be clearly stated in the body of the advertisement.
4 Mail Order Transactions (Information) Order Act 1976.
5 The European Communities Act 1972.

The code contains a special section for mail order and direct response advertising. Mailing and packaging must be carefully considered as to their design (children have access to packages delivered at home). In cases where cash with order is chosen as the method of payment, mail order advertisers are obliged to return all advanced payments where the unwanted goods are returned by the consumer within seven days of fulfilment.

Repayment must also be met by the advertiser in cases where a consumer wishes to be reimbursed due to a delay in fulfilment, or when a product does not match its description in the advertisement.

All orders must be fulfilled within 28 days of the order being placed. Exceptions to this must clearly state the terms of despatch.

A refund should be offered to a consumer as soon as an advertiser is aware that fulfilment will be delayed.

Financial services and products, advertisements offering either employment or business opportunities, limited editions, and advertisements concerning children are all other areas for special consideration, and detailed in the code itelf.

Further information

The Code of Advertising Practice Committee,
Brook House,
2–16 Torrington Place,
LONDON
WC1E 7HN

The British Code of Sales Promotion Practice

The first edition of the current code was published in 1980. The code is based on the principles of the International Code of Sales Promotion Practice.

What happens when the code is contravened?

This code is administered by the Advertising Association. The monitoring of promotions and dealing with public complaints similarly result in the termination of malpractice, and compensation being met where necessary.

What are the aims of the code?

The code protects the consumer from malpractice of those marketing techniques which give, usually on a limited basis, offers and incentives including premiums, vouchers, coupons, samples, and all types of prize promotions, etc.

The fundamental principles are similar to the Code of Advertising Practice. All promotions should be legal, decent, honest and truthful. A consumer must be able to understand the terms of the promotion fully and easily. No disappointment should be caused by it. The guidelines of the code stipulate that:

1 The consumer's right to privacy be protected, e.g.:

   (i) precision must be ensured in the compilation of the list
   (ii) written permission must be sought from competition winners, before they can be used as a part of any company publicity.

2 Those under 16 be protected in particular, since this age-

group are more susceptible and easily taken advantage of.

3   All consumers be protected from safety risks.

4   Promotions should not mislead consumers by their presentation, or publicity, e.g. the terms under which the promotion operates must be both clear and complete.

5   Promotional products must meet satisfactory standards of durability, and should not cause offence to their recipients.

6   Over-exaggerated claims about the product, e.g. its quality, must not be made.

7   Claims of 'savings' made by the consumer must comply with the following Acts:

The Price Marking (Bargain Offers) Order 1979
Trade Descriptions Act 1968, section II

8   The availability of a promotional product must be given, where limited. Where a delay occurs, consumers must be informed immediately.

9   Faulty or damaged goods must either be replaced, or a refund made.

10   It is only acceptable to call an offer 'free' when there is no cost to the consumer, other than possibly postal or incidental expense incurred in claiming the free offer. Such charges cannot be raised deliberately to recoup the cost of the free offer.

11   Entry and judging conditions should be clearly stated, prizewinners must be notified individually, and a complete list of prizewinners must later be made available for anyone wanting to see this information. A closing date should be clearly stated in the rules of entry, and prizewinners, unless otherwise stated, must receive their prize within six weeks of the closing date. All promotions with prizes should conform with:

  (i) The Lotteries and Amusement Act 1976
 (ii) The Prevention of Corruption Acts 1889–1916
(iii) The Income and Corporation Taxes Act 1970

12   Sales promotions should allow for a free decision to be made, and should not be unfair to competitors. Business incentives should not come between the employee and his duty to his employer.

Further information

A copy of this code is available from the CAP Committee at the address given on page 369. As well as giving further

detail, the code also lists government legislation which should
be adhered to in the context of promotions.

Mail order legislation

Throughout the sixties and seventies, a series of Acts were
passed to protect consumers. Many of these Acts have a direct
effect on the type of mail order transaction that can be offered.
Most of these particular laws are based on the fact that the
consumer needs certain information to assist him or her in the
decision whether or not to purchase goods.

When the consumer buys at a retail outlet, legislation
requires that such goods be marked with, or be accompanied
by, such relevant information. In the case of buying direct,
however, the advertisement or direct mailing acts as a
substitute point of sale.

The measures that protect the mail order buyer are
numerous. Just to indicate their extent, the following section
sets out the major Acts, their dates, together with associated
implications for the mailer.

The Trading Stamps Act 1964

Under this Act, promoters of trading stamp schemes were
restricted to companies or industrial and provident societies.
Other groups or individuals were prohibited from promoting
such schemes.

Thus a mail order company could still promote a scheme
under this Act, so long as the following clauses of the Act were
also adhered to:

(i) The company is registered.
(ii) A statement of its value in relation to current currency
must be clearly indicated on a stamp.
(iii) The holder of trading stamps of a value of under 50p
has the right to demand to exchange the stamps with
the promoter for their aggregate cash value.
(iv) There is an implied warranty on the part of the
promoter of such a scheme, that goods can be given in
exchange for the stamps, and that their quality will be
assured, etc.
(v) Catalogues and stamp books must include the name
and address of the promoter.
(vi) Advertisements, by any media, which refer to the
value of trading stamps are prohibited.

The Advertisements (Hire-purchase) Act 1967

Under this Act information regarding the total number of instalments payable, the length of the time-period before each instalment is to be paid, and the number of instalments payable before goods are delivered, must all be clearly displayed in the advertisement.

Where a deposit is not payable, this must also be shown. Where specific sums payable are expressed in the advertisement, the proportion that the deposit and interest rates represent of the total must also be shown. No terms used should be misleading.

The Act also covers 'credit sales' (where total payment is made in fixed instalments). Where alternative methods of purchase are possible, there is no requirement on the advertiser to display each of the possibilities, but if he chooses to, one must not be displayed in disproportion to any other.

Any terms quoted in any advertisement, must be upheld.

The Trades Descriptions Act 1968

Under the Acts those who

(i) give a false trade description to goods, or
(ii) supply or offer to supply any goods to which a false trade description is applied will be guilty of an offence.

A trade description can be any indication made about a 'good' or part of a 'good'. This can include quantity, size or other measurement, method of manufacture or production, composition, strength, performance, results of tests or approvals, place or date of manufacture, and any other relevant history. A false trade description is one that is misleading.

A trade description can be applied to goods directly, e.g. by their markings, or indirectly (e.g. an oral statement which clearly refers to such goods).

Under section 5, an advertisement which includes a false trade description constitutes an offence under the Act, whether or not the goods to which it relates have yet been manufactured.

Under section 8 of the Act, where necessary or helpful to consumers, instructions or trade descriptions are to be attached to goods. Section 9 extends this to advertisements. The Board of Trade is given the right to make an order to require this type of information to be given.

False or misleading indications as to the price of goods is also an offence under this Act. Prices cannot be more than indicated, similarly prices cannot be lowered unless they have been offered at a higher price for at least 28 days.

A recommended price is strictly the price suggested by the manufacturer.

Other offences include false representations about:

(i) Royal approval or award, etc.
(ii) the supply of goods or services
(iii) services offered, ie giving false or misleading statements about these.

The import of goods with either infringing trademarks or false indication of origin, is prohibited under the Act. The Act is enforced by local Weights and Measures Authorities reporting to the Board of Trade. The local authority inspector has the right to seize goods and make test purchases in order to oversee the Act.

Unsolicited Goods and Services Act 1971

This Act stipulates that the recipient of unsolicited goods (where the recipient has no prior anticipation of such goods), has the right to do as he wishes with them, on the following conditions:

(i) that the recipient notifies the sender of their arrival within six months of their receipt.
(ii) that the sender does not use his right to collect the goods within the 30 days after he receives the sender's notification.

The sender of unsolicited goods commits an offence when he demands or threatens the recipient for payment for the goods.

Unsolicited books, or other publications which describe illustrated human sexual techniques, were also made an offence under this Act.

Trade Descriptions Act 1972

This Act requires imported goods to be marked with, or accompanied by an indication of origin. An offence is committed if a person or company supplies or offers goods without such information.

The 1972 Act was followed by further Trade Descriptions Orders in 1981 (see page 376).

Textile Products (Indication of Fibre Content) 1973

Article 4 of these regulations requires full details of the fibre content of goods in the case of a textile advertisement to be given.

Consumer Credit Act 1974

This Act aimed to 'establish for the protection of consumers a new system, . . . of licensing and other control of traders concerned with the provision of credit, or the supply of goods on hire or hire-purchase, and their transactions . . .'

The Act requires a consumer credit business or consumer hire business to obtain a licence from the Director General of Fair Trading (newly appointed under this Act). Such a licence is mainly given on an individual, rather than a group basis.

A licence will not be granted to anyone who has committed unfair practices, e.g. fraud, sexual or racial discrimination, and the terms of a licence can be changed or a licence be removed altogether if an offence against the Act is committed.

An offence is committed when credit practices are carried out either without a licence at all, or under another name, or alternatively when the Director General is not informed of changes in the particulars of such a business.

Section 43 stipulates that any advertisements which indicate that the advertisers are willing to provide credit or hire-purchase agreements, must be regulated as to their form and content.

Specific information must be included, while other information is excluded and the advertisement must be balanced so as not to mislead the reader.

Under this Act an advertiser commits an offence if he is only prepared to enter a credit agreement, rather than being prepared to accept cash for the sale of the goods or services.

The deliberate conveyance of false or misleading information in an advertisement is an offence against this Act, both by the advertiser and the publisher of the advertisement.

Section 50 makes it an offence to send a minor any literature inviting the minor to borrow money, obtain goods on credit or hire, obtain services on credit, or even apply for information on borrowing money or obtaining credit, or hiring goods. A credit or hire-purchase agreement must conform to the form and content set out by the Secretary of State so that the hirer is aware of the rights and duties imposed by the agreement, the amount and rate of credit charged, and the protection available under this Act.

An agreement must be signed by both the hirer/debtor and owner/creditor. The owner/creditor is also obliged to supply a copy of the agreement, give notice of the cancellation of any rights, give information to the creditor about the return of goods or credit terms which come into force in the event of the death of the debtor or hirer.

The local Weights and Measures Authority enforces this Act.

The Mail Order Transactions (Information) Order 1976

This Order protects only consumers, not those who purchase in their business capacity. It stipulates that any advertisement or direct mail solicitation, inviting payment to be made with order, must give the advertiser's true name (either surname, or corporate name), or registered business name, and the address where the business is managed.

The Consumer's Transactions (Restrictions on Statements) Order 1976

This Order ensures advertisements state that a consumer's statutory rights are not affected where other terms and conditions are either made to or for the consumer. Where a wholesaler or manufacturer expects to sell goods direct, they too are included under the above terms of the Order.

The Unfair Contract Terms Act 1977

This Act stipulates that certain terms and conditions are prohibited from being included in a contract.

Article 5 covers the sale and supply of goods. No manufacturer or distributor is permitted to write into a contract that they are not responsible for those goods that prove defective while in consumer use, as a result of their own negligence.

Any written assurance or promise that defects will be made good either by repair or replacement, constitutes a binding guarantee.

Any liability under the 1893 Sale of Goods Act or the 1973 Hire-purchase Act cannot be avoided by any contract term.

The Consumer Safety Act 1978

This Act requires that goods be safe, and that appropriate information be provided, and inappropriate information excluded in respect of goods. These regulations cover:

(i) The composition, contents, design, construction and finishing of goods
(ii) The approved standards of goods and the manner in which information is given
(iii) The tests which form these standards
(iv) The instructions or warning that goods do not meet the required standards. The supply and sale of dangerous

goods or components. This Act is enforced by the Weights and Measures Authority.

The Price Marking (Bargain Offers) Order 1979

This Order regulates the practice of promoting products or services at a lower price than their market value. A price can only be expressed as 'lower' when it correlates with either a past price, or an intended future charge. Alternatively, if the terms of sale have changed, the quality of the goods has altered, or when goods are offered in different combinations.

The Trade Descriptions (Sealskin Goods) (Information) Order 1980

This Order requires sealskin goods to be clearly marked as such and the country given in which they were killed.

Trade Descriptions (Origin Marking Order) 1981

This Order prohibits the supply, or offering to supply, new goods (specifically clothing and textiles, domestic and electrical appliances, footwear and cutlery) without a mark or other indication of origin. Where such goods are sold by mail, under this Order the indication of origin must be given on the advertisement, unless the advertisement states that goods are returnable if the customer is not satisfied, and such goods are marked with, or accompanied by their country of origin.

Trade Description (Country of Origin) (Cutlery) Order 1981

This Order clarifies that the country of origin which should be indicated for cutlery is where the initial manufacture took place, rather than where any subsequent silver-plating or other ancillary process occurred.

Fulfilment

As well as ensuring mail order transactions provided sufficient information, safety and conditions of hire-purchase and other credit arrangements, consumer legislation also makes provision for the fulfilment and supply of the goods and services.

Sale of Goods Act 1979

This Act brought in measures on the contract of the sale of goods — both actual sales and agreements to future sales.

Under this Act a sales contract becomes:

(i) Void when unbeknown to a seller his goods have perished in transit.

(ii) Under warranty when a seller has not fulfilled a condition in a sales contract.

All charges must be disclosed to the buyer before the contract is made.

Goods must correspond to their description, and samples must correspond with the goods they represent.

There is an implied condition that goods will be of a merchantable quality, except when defects have been pointed out to a buyer, prior to their purchase.

Unless otherwise agreed, the goods remain the seller's risk until the property is transferred to the buyer, but once this has occurred, the buyer has responsibility for the property, whether delivery has been made or not.

Delivery for goods, unless otherwise agreed, must be concurrent with the payment for them.

If a seller sends goods to a buyer, this fulfilment must occur within a reasonable time-limit. Unless otherwise agreed, the seller pays for delivery. In the event of the wrong quantity or goods of the wrong description being delivered, the buyer holds the right of refusal, but if he accepts the goods, he must pay for them at the agreed rate.

A buyer also holds the right of refusal on goods sent in instalments, when this method of fulfilment has not been agreed by him. Any instalment that is not delivered or not paid for can constitute a breach of contract.

When a seller sends goods to a buyer in a distant place, the buyer bears the risk of damage in transit. The buyer is only deemed to have purchased goods after he or she has had a reasonable opportunity of examination, and he or she informs the seller otherwise.

Unless otherwise agreed, the buyer is not required to return goods he or she is dissatisfied with, but must notify the seller if refusing to accept them for any deterioration of the goods between their delivery date and their return, the seller is liable.

When a buyer does not pay, the seller has a right either to seize the goods or to stop their transit, and action can be taken. A buyer can take action against the seller for non-delivery and breach of warranty.

The Supply of Goods and Services Act 1982

This Act brings the hire of goods and all methods of payment for services into line with the Sale of Goods Act 1979.

In the case of the supply of a service, there is an implied degree of care and skill contained, and an implied time for the service to be carried out.

Print and production

Print legislation and industry standards are often ignored in discussion of existing guidelines for direct mail generally.

While there are as yet no industry guidelines laid down by the British Printing Industries Federation, legislation has set out standards which are commonly in use by printers.

Legislation

Libel

A printer is responsible, jointly with the publisher and the author, for all libels which are printed by him. He makes a profit from such printing, and he is bound to make himself acquainted with what he is printing.

There is more information to do with libel in the section on legislation affecting creative work.

The Children and Young Persons (Harmful Publications) Act 1955

It is an offence to print or publish any work which includes pictures portraying:

(i) the committing of a crime
(ii) acts of cruelty or violence
(iii) repulsive or horrifying incidents.

An offence under this Act can lead to a fine up to £400 and or alternatively four months' imprisonment.

The Obscene Publications Act 1959 and 1964

It is an offence to distribute, sell, let on hire or to keep in possession an obscene matter for publication or the purpose of any gain to an individual.

A defence against the Act can only be proven in the instance that the material is in the interests of the public good, e.g. for subjects such as science, literature, art or learning.

The Public Order Act 1936 and amendment of the Race Relations Act 1976

It is an offence to publish or distribute any material which is either threatening, abusive or insulting and likely to stir up feelings of racial hatred against any group.

The use of emblems and pictures of the Royal Family in advertising

It is an offence to use the emblem of the Red Cross and certain other emblems without permission from the Army Council.

Pictures of the Royal Family may not be used for advertising in any medium, except for the promotion of a book, newspaper or magazine or television broadcast specifically about a member of the Royal Family.

Stamps and postmarks

All postage stamps and postmarks must be authorised by the Post Office, before they can be reproduced. A fee is usually levied on the reproduction of stamps and postmarks for commercial use. Applications for such permissions should be made in writing to the following address:

Royal Mail, Stamps and Philately,
22–25 Finsbury Square,
LONDON, EC2A 1PH

Stamps will be authorised in most cases, including advertising and decorative purposes. There are no colour restrictions to the printing of stamps, but reproductions of existing stamps must either be considerably smaller or larger than the original, or alternatively be marked across by a defacement or the reproduction of a postmark.

The Weights and Measures Act 1963

This Act sets out the general regulations to which units and other standards of measurement have to conform. For direct mail this has set a standard size for envelopes, and paper, etc.

The Act requires goods for trade to have a clear indication of their quantity and that such weights and measurements are accurate.

Certain transactions are also required by this Act to have relevant quantities stated in writing, and procedures laid down for cases of short weight, etc.

Imprint

Legislation, culminating in the Printer's Imprint Act 1961, enforces a printer to give his name and address on the first and/or last leaf of every book or magazine he prints. For the direct mail printer, this would include any booklets written by a company to be sent to prospects or existing customers.

However, exemption from imprinting is given on all company literature, including catalogues of goods or services for sale, price lists and business cards. Thus a printer is not required to give his name and address in the majority of literature contained in enquiry fulfilment packs.

A fine of up to £50 is liable as a penalty for not giving a name and address as required.

Origin marking of exported print

The origin marking of goods is discussed elsewhere in this chapter. For printed matter destined abroad, a printer must ensure that the correct marking of the country of origin must be given where necessary.

Further information can be obtained from the Overseas Trade Divisions of the Department of Trade and Industry.

The Health and Safety Acts

All businesses have to comply with certain legislation which controls their in-house operations. The Health and Safety Act is one such Act, which protects the safety of personnel while at work. Printing businesses have to be particularly aware of such legislation, because of dangerous machinery and chemicals.

Standard conditions of contract

The BPIF drew up standard conditions of contract in conjunction with the Office of Fair Trading. The first stipulation is that standard BPIF conditions are included on the back of a contract, and that they are brought to the attention of the customer, in a way that a customer cannot possibly claim he did not see the terms.

If a firm wishes to use its own special conditions it may do so, but must indicate these on the front of a contract. An unconditional acceptance of a printer's contract by a buyer is legally binding. A buyer can either provisionally accept contract terms, or alternatively amend the standard contract. In these cases a contract is not binding in the eyes of the law.

The standard contract conditions stipulate the following:

(i) That prices are subject to the current costs, and that amendments can occur at any time.

(ii) The printer can charge VAT whether or not it is printed on an estimate or invoice.

(iii) A customer can be charged for any experimental work made at his request, and can also incur the extra costs for changes made to copy.

Prices

Estimated prices are subject to amendment either up or down.

VAT is chargeable, whether or not this is stated on invoices on estimates. Extra charges can be incurred by a print buyer on copy changes and any experimental work undertaken on request.

Delivery

When the printer delivers the work (free of charge, unless stated otherwise) ownership passes to the customer and a charge is payable. If delivery is delayed by the customer, the printer is entitled to payment on goods bought or ordered for the job, as well as a charge for the additional costs incurred such as storage.

Quantity

While attempts are generally made to deliver the exact quantity required, conditional margins of 5 per cent for one-colour work and 10 per cent for other work are allowable. (For orders over 50 000, these margin percentages are 4 per cent and 8 per cent, respectively.)

Liability

Advice of damage occurring in transit must be made within three days of the delivery date, followed by a claim in writing. Other claims must be made in writing within 28 days.

Property

Materials which are owned by the printer, used for a job remain his property and type and other equipment set up for a articular job can be effaced once the order has been filled.

Customers can supply their own materials, where the printer deems these acceptable for the job. The customer remains liable for this, and should insure against damage.

Insolvency

In the event of the buyer becoming insolvent, the printer has the right to stop the work, and charge for any work carried out on his behalf, whether it has been completed or not. Goods and property belonging to the customer can be sold to pay some or all outstanding debts.

Printing matter

A printer cannot print any matter which is illegal or libellous or which would infringe on the rights of another, e.g. copyright laws.

Force majeure

The printer is not liable for not carrying out a contract in circumstances beyond his control. These might include flood, power failure, etc., or a strike by the workforce.

PART FOUR

Bibliography and glossary

Bibliography

Books

Advertiser's Desk Book, Business Publications Ltd, London, 1963

Andrews, Les (ed.), *The Royal Mail Direct Mail Handbook,* 2nd edn, Exley, Watford, 1988

Baier, Martin, *Elements of Direct Marketing,* McGraw-Hill, New York, 1983

Bayan, Richard, *Words That Sell: A Thesaurus to Help Promote Your Products, Services, and Ideas,* Asher-Gallant Press, New York, 1984

Bird, Drayton, *Commonsense Direct Marketing,* The Printed Shop, London, 1982

Brann, Christian, *Cost-effective Direct Marketing by Mail, Telephone and Direct Response Advertising,* Collectors' Books Ltd, Cirencester, 1984

Caples, John, *How to Make Your Advertising Make Money,* Prentice-Hall, New Jersey, 1983

Caples, John, *Tested Advertising Methods,* Prentice-Hall, New Jersey, 1974

Cohen, William, *Building a Mail-Order Business,* John Wiley and Sons, New York, 1982

Corby, Michael and Robin Fairlie, *The Mail Users' Handbook, or How to Really Get the Most from your Post,* C. H. W. Roles & Associates Ltd, Kingston-upon-Thames, 1984

Crompton, Alastair, *The Craft of Copywriting,* Business Books Ltd, London, 1979

Data Protection Act 1984, HMSO, London, 1984

Dillon, John, *Handboook of International Direct Marketing,* McGraw-Hill, Maidenhead, 1976

Dyer, Nigel and Roger Anderson (eds.), *Marketing Insurance,* Kluwer, 1986

Effective Ways to Merchandise Advertising, Report no. 19, The Marketing Communications Research Centre, Princeton, 1968

Fairlie, Robin, *Direct Mail: Principles and Practice,* Kogan Page, 1979

Forrester, Martyn, *Everything you always suspected was true about advertising . . . but were too legal, decent and honest to ask,* Roger Houghton, London, 1987

Goodwin, Leslie, *Direct Mail Databook,* Gower, Aldershot, 1984

Harper, Rose, *Mailing List Strategies: A Guide to Direct Mail Success,* McGraw-Hill, New York, 1986

Hill, Lawson Traphagen, *How to Build a Multi-Million Dollar Catalogue Mail Order Business by Someone who Did,* Prentice-Hall, New Jersey, 1984.

Hodgeson, Dick, *Direct Mail and Mail Order Handbook*, Dartnell Press, Chicago, 1980

Hoge Sr, Cecil C., *Mail Order Moonlighting*, Business Studies, Inc., New York, 1976

Hopkins, Claude, *Scientific Advertising: The Classic Book on the Fundamentals of Advertising*, MacGibbon & Kee, London, 1968

How to Co-ordinate Industrial Sales and Advertising, Industrial Advertising Research Institute, Princeton, 1958

How to Improve Results from Business Direct Mail. Report No. 14, Marketing Communications Research Centre, Princeton, 1973

Jenkins, Vin, *Direct Mail Advertising in Australia, A Handbook in 6 Volumes*, Australia Post HQ, Victoria, 1981

Jenkins, Vin, *The Concept of Direct Marketing*, Australia Post HQ, Victoria, 1984

Lewis, Herschell Gordon, *How to Make Your Advertising Twice as Effective at Half the Cost*, Prentice-Hall, New Jersey, 1986

Lewis, Herschell Gordon, *More than you ever wanted to know about Mail Order Advertising*, Prentice-Hall, New Jersey, 1983

Lewis, Hershell Gordon, *Direct Mail Copy that Sells*, Prentice-Hall, New Jersey, 1984

McIntosh, Dorothy and Alastair McIntosh, *Marketing: A Guide for Charities*, The Directory of Social Change, London, 1984

McLean, Ed, *The Basics of Copy, A Monograph on Direct Marketing*, Ryan Gilmore, New York, 1977

McLean, Ed, *The Basics of Testing, A Monograph on Direct Marketing*, Ryan Gilmore, New York, 1978

Martin, Tony, *Insurance Direct Marketing*, Financial Marketing Ltd, Ascot, 1988

Mitchell, Jeremy, *Marketing and the Consumer Movement*, McGraw-Hill, New York, 1978

Montague, Joy, *The A to Z of Shopping by Post*, Exley, Watford, 1979

Myers, James, *Marketing*, McGraw-Hill, New York, 1986

Nash, Edward, *Direct Marketing: Strategy, Planning, Execution*, McGraw-Hill, New York, 1982

Nash, Edward, *The Direct Marketing Handbook*, McGraw-Hill, New York, 1984.

Peacock, J., M. Barnard and C. Berill, *The Print and Production Manual*, Blueprint, London, 1987

Pocket Pal: A Graphic Arts Production Handbook, International Paper Co., New York, 1983

Posch, Robert, *The Direct Marketer's Legal Adviser*, McGraw-Hill, New York, 1983

Raphel, Murray and Ken Erdman, *The Do-it-yourself Direct Mail Handbook*, The Marketers Bookshelf, Philadelphia, 1986

Raphel, Murray and Ray Considine. *The Great Brain Robbery*, Business Tips, Pasadena, 1981

Raphel, Murray, *But Would Saks Fifth Avenue Do It?* Murray Raphel/Advertising, New Jersey, 1981

Rapp, Stan and Tom Collins, *MaxiMarketing*, McGraw-Hill, New York, 1987

Ries, Al and Jack Trout, *Marketing Warfare*, McGraw-Hill, New York, 1986

Ries, Al and Jack Trout, *Positioning the Battle for your Mind*, McGraw-Hill, New York, 1986

Simon, Julian, *Getting into the Mail Order Business,* McGraw-Hill, New York, 1984

Simon, Julian, *How to Start and Operate a Mail-Order Business,* McGraw-Hill, New York, 1981

Sizer, Richard and Philip Newman, *The Data Protection Act: A practical guide,* Gower, Aldershot, 1984

Stanton, William and Charles Futrell, *Fundamentals of Marketing,* McGraw-Hill, New York, 1987

Stephenson, George, *Graphic Arts Encyclopedia,* McGraw-Hill, New York, 1979

Stone, Bob, *Successful Direct Marketing Methods,* Crain Books, Chicago, 1979

Booklets

31 Tips to Improve Your Order Form, Webcraft, 500 Chesham House, 150 Regent St, London W1R 5FA

Andrews, F., *Fundraising — Marketing for Human Needs,* Direct Marketing Association Inc., New York, 1976

Benn's Direct Marketing Services: Industrial Lists Directory 1987, Benn's Business Information Services Ltd, PO Box 20, Sovereign Way, Tonbridge, Kent TN9 1RQ

The British Code of Advertising Practice, 1985, Code of Advertising Practice Committee, Brook House, 2–16 Torrington Place, London WC1E 7HN

The British Code of Sales Promotion Practice, 1986, Code of Advertising Practice Committee, Brook House, 2–16 Torrington Place, London WC1E 7HN

Business/Industrial Direct Marketing: Monograph Vol. 5, Direct Mail/Marketing Assoc., New York, 1982

Changing the Advertising Budget?, Billet & Co., 55/57 Gt Marlborough St, London W1V 1DD

Code of Practice: covering the use of personal data for advertising and DM purposes, 1987, The Advertising Association, Abford House, 15 Wilton Road, London SW1V 1NJ

Consumer Credit, Report of the Committee (Chairman Lord Crowther), Cmnd 4596, HMSO, London, 1971

The Data Protection Act 1984, Infolink, Coombe Cross, 2–4 South End, Croydon CR9 1DL

The Data Protection Act 1984: Introduction and Guide to the Act, The Data Protection Registrar, Springfield House, Water Lane, Wilmslow, Cheshire SK9 5AX

Direct Marketing Industry Statistics, 1987, British Direct Marketing Assoc., 35 Grosvenor Gardens, London SW1W 0BS

Get Results from your Mailshot, IPCD Direct Mail Services, Quadrant House, The Quadrant, Surrey SM2 5AS

Guideline: Data Protection Act 1984, 1987, The Data Protection Registrar, Springfield House, Water Lane, Wilmslow, Cheshire SK9 5AX (Eight booklets: 1. The Data Protection Registrar; 2. The Definitions; 3. The Register and Registration; 4. The

Data Protection Principles; 5. Individual Rights; 6. The Exemptions; 7. Enforcement and Appeals; 8. Summary for Computer Bureaux.)

Henley, Mike, *The Marketer's Guide to Computer Printing,* Christian Brann Ltd, Cirencester, 1985

How to Generate a More Cost Efficient Response from Direct Consumer Marketing, Billett & Co., 55/57 Gt Marlborough St, London W1V 1DD

How to Get your Sums Right: price strategy in direct marketing, British Direct Marketing Assoc., 35 Grosvenor Gardens, London SW1W 0BS

How to Select, Purchase and Use Advertising Premiums Successfully, Innovative Marketing International Ltd, 21 Dorset Sq., London NW1 6QG

How to Work with Mailing Lists, Direct Mail/Marketing Association, Inc., New York, 1976

How to Write Successful Direct Mail Letter Copy, Direct Marketing Association, New York, 1976

Introduction to Fulfilment Operations in Direct Marketing, Monograph Vol. 4, Direct Marketing Association, New York, 1981

The Mail Marketing File, 1982, Mail Marketing (Bristol) Ltd, Springfield House, Mill Ave, Queen Sq., Bristol BS1 4SA

Mail Order Marketing Checklist, 1975, Institute of Practitioners in Advertising, 44 Belgrave Sq., London SW1X 8QS

The Mail Preference Service, 1984, Mailing Preference Service, 1 New Burlington St, London W1X 1FD

Mailing Lists: A Practical Guide, Monograph Vol. 8, Direct Marketing Association, New York, 1984

Making the Most of Direct Mail, British Direct Marketing Assoc., 35 Grosvenor Gdns, London SW1W 0BS

Measuring the Effectiveness of Industrial Direct Mail, IARI Report No. 14, 1965, Industrial Advertising Research Inst., 15 Chambers Street, Princeton, New Jersey, USA

The Planner's Guide to Direct Mail, 1984, The Direct Mail Sales Bureau, 12–13 Henrietta St, London WC2E 8BR

Precision Marketing, 1985, Direct Mail Sales Bureau, 14 Floral St, Covent Garden, London WC2E 9RR

Precision Marketing: The Media Perspective, Billet & Co., 55/57 Gt Marlborough St, London W1V 1DD

Pricing Survey 1985, Direct Mail Producers Assoc., 34 Grand Ave, London N10 3BP

Report of the Committee on Data Protection, Cmnd 7341, HMSO, London, 1978

Sell More!: 101 hints for effective direct mail and higher sales, 1975, Scriptomatic S.A., 35 rue des Jeunes, 1211 Geneva 26, Switzerland

The Systems of Control of Advertising Standards: Report of the Committee of Inquiry, 1987, The Advertising Assoc., Abford House, 15 Wilson Rd, London SW1V 1NJ

Typefaces, E. G. Willis & Sons, Willow Street, Chingford, Essex

What People Think about Direct Mail, Direct Mail Advertising Assoc., 230 Park Ave, New York NY 10017, USA

Working for Customers, 1983, Confederation of British Industry, Centre Point, 103 New Oxford St, London WC1A 1DU

Royal Mail publications

The following booklets are available, free of charge, from The Customer Care Unit, Room 141, Post Office Headquarters, 33 Grosvenor Place, London SW1X 1PX

The Guide to Effective Direct Mail (1988)
The Mailsort User's Guide (1988)
The Postcode Portfolio (1988)

Glossary

A4 A standard paper size, measuring 210×297 mm.

A/B split A type of two-way test used for two variations of one element of the same mailing package, to determine which version will bring in greater response.

AEL After Event Letter (follow-up).

AIDA Copy-writing formula. An acronym which stands for Attention, Interest, Desire, Action.

AMOP Association of Mail Order Publishers. Trade Association set up for publishers active in selling by mail order.

Above the line An out-of-date piece of jargon which is often misused, and should be avoided where possible. It once described advertising through any of television, radio or published media. Advertising using other media known as 'below the line'.

Accordion fold Parallel folds in paper, which open like an accordion bellows.

Acknowledgement An expression of thanks to a person or group for their contribution to a printed work.

Acorn An acronym for A Classification Of Residential Neighbourhoods. A consumer list selection and targeting system used, as its name suggests, on residential property information in minimum areas of approximately 150 households (an enumeration district).

Acquisition cost The advertisement cost of obtaining a customer or enquiry.

Active buyer/member/subscriber A person on a company list whose last purchase, membership or subscription to a magazine was made within a given period, usually the previous 12 months.

Add-on The sale of a supplement, accessory, replacement part, or a de-luxe version of a product.

Address The identification of a unique location (either place of abode or computer storage location).

Adhesive binding Binding style for catalogues and books. Hot-melt adhesive is applied to the roughened or ground back, to hold the page and cover together.

Advance (early) booking discount rate A discount given for advertising booked in advance, either by a specified number of weeks or by a given date in advance. The reduction is generally given as a fixed percentage off rate-card.

Advertisement A paid-for communication intended to inform and influence, to sell a product or service, or to modify or change people's attitudes.

Advertisement rate card A table of standard advertisement sizes, costs and production particulars, issued by a publisher to an advertiser who wishes to buy space.

Advertising schedule A list of planned or booked advertisements showing details of media, sizes, timing and costs.

Advertising Standards Authority The association which regulates, monitors and handles public complaints of all advertisements (except those transmitted by broadcast media).

Agency fee Remuneration based on a negotiated fee, as opposed to commission.

Airmail Fast postal service for overseas locations or lightweight paper, usually below 40 gsm, used when postage cost is at a premium.

Alignment The arrangement of type or other graphic material to level up at one horizontal or vertical line.

Alphanumeric (A contraction of 'alphabetic' and 'numeric'). Pertaining to a machine character set that contains letters, digits and often other characters, such as punctuation marks, etc.

Analysis The findings of both quantitative and/or qualitative data, put into a form which is both readable and easy to understand.

Aperture Either a lens opening, or an envelope where a window has been cut, but there is no glassine covering.

Art (paper) Paper with a china clay content, giving characteristic smooth finish — eminently suited to half-tone reproduction and four-colour work.

Artwork Material in its final layout, such as type, and illustrations, assembled in preparation for making the printing plate.

Assembly Bringing together several individual items to form a complete product, such as the printing and the collation of the components of a calendar, or the assembly of film, etc.

Attention factors Research-based factors applied to the BARB-reported audience to allow for distractions or breaks in viewing.

Attitude Mode of thinking, attitude or opinion, which predispose people to a certain type of behaviour.

Audience research Research carried out within an audience about an advertised product or service.

Author's corrections Revisions to typesetting made necessary by an advertiser's alterations to the text or layout.

Average contribution The average total gross income per contribution from those responding to a mailing.

Average customer life The average period of time (or number of buying seasons) during which a customer will continue to purchase.

Average issue readership The total average number of readers for a magazine.

Average order cost The total cost of orders, divided by the total number of orders.

Average order value The total volume of orders divided by the total number of orders.

–B–

BDMA British Direct Marketing Association (trade association for direct marketing users, agencies and suppliers).

BRAD *British Rates and Data*—a monthly reference guide of advertising and media information.

BRE Acronym for Business Reply Envelope. A pre-addressed envelope to be returned to the mailer. The mailer pays postage on those envelopes returned.

Back end   Has two meanings. Can be those fulfilment procedures carried out after the receipt of an order to complete a mail order transaction. Also the completion of a campaign or a job. Hence the back-end results or performance includes final figures for paid and unpaid orders.

Back number   Copy of a previous issue of a periodical.

Back test   A 'retest' of 'confirming test', carried out when a sample test was of an acceptable level of success, but not so convincing as to go ahead immediately with full roll-out.

Bangtail   A type of envelope generally referring to those formed (often as part of one-piece mailer or self-mailer formats) with an attached perforated 'tail' used as an order or response coupon.

Banker envelope   An envelope with the flap on the long edge. Often used for machine enclosing.

Bar code   A symbol which can be 'read' by computer, put on the outside of a publication for stock control.

Base artwork   Artwork awaiting the addition of other elements, e.g. half-tone positives, before reproduction.

Base price   The price of one unit of a product at the point of its production or its resale.

Basic rates   The price for television slots bought, according to day and time of transmission.

Bastard size   Non-standard size (of material or format).

Batch   Method of computer processing, where input data or computer programs are collected together (into batches) prior to processing.

Batch control   Controlling documents by putting them together in groups which are counted and logged.

Batch-header   Batch-headers are used in batch control, when document information is standard. The batch-header is a code representing this information, saving repeated keying-in.

Batched job   A job grouped with other jobs on input into the computer, as opposed to a single job entry which is handled on its own.

Behavioural research   The study of human behaviour. Actions as opposed to opinions.

Below the line   Opposite to above the line. Advertising media that used to be considered more as promotional channels, including direct mail, telemarketing, electronic media, displays, leaflets and brochures and sales promotion and other media.

Benefit   The translation of a product's feature into an advantage, or use for a customer. Direct mail copywriters often use the technique of presenting the reader with the benefits they will receive from purchasing a product or service, rather than merely highlighting the characteristics of a product or service.

Benefit segmentation   One criteria for the segmentation of a total market, based on the customers' perceptions of the various benefits provided by a product.

Bill-me-later   One method of payment (charged after the goods have been received).

Bill stuffer   Any type of promotional piece, inserted with an invoice or statement, in order to save postage.

Billing series   Number of invoices and/or statements in a planned programme of mailings.

Bindery The place where books are stitched or glued, and have their jacket covers bound.

Bingo card Otherwise known as reader service card. A reply card bound into a publication, which readers can complete to request literature, samples or general information from those companies that have either advertised or are referred to in the publication.

Black and white Single-colour black originals or reproductions, rather than multi-colour. Otherwise known as monochrome.

Blind test Research where a sample of consumers are asked to indicate their preference between two or more unidentified products.

Blockmaker Someone who uses photogravure to produce blocks for letterpress printing.

Blow-in card A loose card with reply device inserted into a publication for advertising purposes.

Blow-up An enlargement (either a photographic or printing term).

Body copy/matter/type UK: Printed words which form the main part of a work, but which do not include the headlines, etc. USA: body type is the actual type used in a text.

Body matter The text of an advertisement.

Body size Photosetting term for the size of the type.

Bold A **heavier** form of type often used for emphasis, as opposed to light or medium.

Border A decorative design or rule around the text of a page.

Bottom line This term is used in accounting to refer to the final figure on a ledger page. In direct mail it is the cumulative result of test cells (expressed as either a percentage return or revenue quota).

Bounce back A further offer enclosed in the fulfilment package. This is a most effective device to interest the buyer at a psychologically strategic time.

Brand A device that identifies the product or service with the seller, by name, term, symbol and/or special design.

Brand mark A symbol, picture or design element of a brand.

Brand name The element of a brand that can be vocalised, i.e. words and numbers.

Breakeven The level at which expenditure is equalled by financial return.

Breakeven point The level where revenue gained recovers the total outgoings (e.g. the production costs of the product and the mailing).

British Direct Marketing Association See BDMA.

Broadsheets Publications which measure a maximum of 56 cm wide, and a minimum of 36 cm deep. Often used generally to describe large leaflets folded several times to a small finished size.

Broadside An old-fashioned term meaning paper printed on one side only.

Brochure A printed pamphlet which contains fewer pages than a book. (Derived from the French word *brocher* meaning to stitch.)

Broker An independent intermediary who brings buyer and seller together and provides specialised market information.

Bromide A photographic print (on bromide paper).

Bubble-pack   A type of packaging made of plastic bubbles to protect a product.

Buck slip   A 'dollar-bill'-sized enclosure. it is generally used to announce a premium or discounted offer for early reply.

–C–

CAP   Code of Advertising Practice.

CHADD   Change of address.

CPE   Cost per enquiry. Total cost of a mailing divided by the number of resultant inquiries received.

CPO   Cost per order. Total cost of a mailing divided by the number of resultant orders received.

Calligraphy   Artistic handwriting.

Camera-ready   A term given to artwork, copy or paste-up which is ready for reproduction, prior to platemaking.

Camera-ready artwork   As above.

Camera-ready copy   As above.

Campaign   A term given to either advertising, promotions or sales. It describes a coordinated series of efforts built around a theme and designed to reach an identified goal.

Campaigning charity   A charity which sees its major role as to lobby and canvass on a particular subject.

Cancel   Has two meanings. To remove a leaf in a book and replace it with another. Also those sheets used to replace cancelled leaves.

Cancellation   Notice to cancel bookings, e.g. press advertisement space.

Cancellation notice   Notice given by a mail order buyer to a mail order company to cancel an order for merchandise.

Caps   Short for capital or upper case letters.

Caps and smalls   Type consisting of capitals for initials and smaller capitals in place of lower case letters.

Caption   Written material (copy) to describe a picture or illustration.

Card code   A combination of punched holes that represent a certain key code.

Card-deck   See Postcard deck.

Card rates   The costs for buying advertisement space as set out on the advertisement rate card.

Carriage   A part of either a typewriter or printing machine on which the type lies. Also, another word for delivery, e.g. carriage costs.

Case history   An actual example of past activity acting as an illustration for future practice.

Cash buyer   A mail order buyer who encloses a cheque or postal order with his order.

Cash discount   A deduction from the listed price often for payment within a given time-period.

Cash up-front   Where a product or service is charged for in advance (also known as pro forma).

Cash with order   As above.

Catalogue   A printed book or pamphlet which lists and describes merchandise for sale.

Catalogue buyer A person who has bought one or more products from a catalogue.

Catalogue request Has two meanings. Those who have asked for a catalogue. The request of a catalogue.

Census The enumeration of all people or groups involved in a survey.

Census tract. An American term for a small geographical area, of approximately 1200 households, containing a population of relatively similar economic and social characteristics.

Centre fold The centre opening of a section (two pages) where one plate may be used to print two facing pages (with consecutive page numbers).

Centre spread As above.

Centred Type which lies exactly central across the width of a page.

Chalking The disfiguration of a printed image. It is a powdery effect caused by the ink failing to adhere to the paper.

Change of address The alteration of address particulars on files or lists upon notification by the customer.

Channel of distribution The means of transferral of goods or services from the buyer to the seller (which may or may not involve intermediaries).

Chapter head The title, or number, given to each chapter.

Character A letter, figure or other type symbol.

Character count The total number of both spaces and type in a piece of copy.

Charge card buyer A buyer who gives a charge card number, from which a seller receives payment.

Check digit A digit used for carrying out a check, e.g. an additional digit to verify the accuracy of a sequence or customer number.

Checking copy A copy of a publication sent to an advertiser or advertising agency in order to verify the position and reproduction of an advertisement prior to printing.

Cheshire One make of labelling machine. It cuts continuous stationery to label size and fixes it to material.

Cheshire label. A label produced by a Cheshire machine. Cheshire labels are printed in a continuous form in a special format (generally 4 labels across and 11 down).

Chroma Purity of colour.

Chroma copy A colour print made without a negative.

Circulars Notice or advertisement of any form to be distributed by post. An out-of-date description frowned upon by the direct marketing fraternity.

Circulation Has two meanings. The distribution of a publication. The number of copies sold per issue of a publication.

Clasp envelope A type of envelope which is sealed by means of a metal clip.

Classified As below.

Classified ads Newspaper or magazine advertisements which appear under specific headings, sold mostly at a rate per line and which have no accompanying illustration.

Closing date The last day on which space for a couponed ad may be ordered. Also, the final date on which offers used in a mailing as incentives can be taken up.

Closing out The final (or closing) results of either a mailing or a direct response advertisement, e.g. it closed out at a 2 per cent response.

Cluster Grouping of people or items with an affinity.

Cluster analysis A mathematical technique for grouping data into clusters with similar characteristics.

Cluster selection A selection routine based on taking a regular sample of group of names in a series, e.g. the first ten names of every 100 on a list.

Cluster theory The marketing theory which states that households sharing demographic or other characteristics are likely also to share buying preferences.

Coarse screen Half-tone screen used on newspapers or other newsprint publications.

Coated paper Paper covered in substance to give it a smooth surface for half-tone reproduction (e.g. china clay).

Coating Has two meanings. Light-sensitive surface applied to litho plate. Clear protective varnish applied to printed surface for protection.

Coding An identification reference given to material (numeric and/or alpha).

Coin rub A type of involvement device. A special type of coating is applied to areas of the mailing or advertisement that have already been pre-printed with a phrase or design underneath. By rubbing a coin over the area, the underlying image can be made to appear.

Cold list(s) List(s) of people with whom the advertiser has had no prior transaction or contact of any description.

Cold mailing Mailing to a list of people with whom the advertiser has had no prior transaction or contact.

Collate Gather and arrange material in a specific order, e.g. paper.

Collating marks Indication marks put on backfolds of paper in order to verify the order sequence of a publication.

Collectable An object, or more commonly a series of objects, sold as limited editions through mail order.

Collection series A series of 'reminder' letters or cards sent to mail order buyers who have not paid outstanding invoices.

Colour Sensation produced upon the eye caused by the effects of light rays. Different colours can stimulate different emotional moods in the individual, which can be harnessed in direct mail.

Colour bars A strip of sample colours printed on the edge of a proof as a guide to the colour strengths.

Colour cast An excess of one shade or hue in a subject for reproduction or printing.

Colour chart Chart used in colour printing to standardise, select and match coloured inks or tints used.

Colour correction The adjustment of colour tints in reproduction to obtain a correct image.

Colour guide The colour guide is a set of small marginal marks placed on each of the negatives used for colour printing, so that the printer can superimpose them in register when building up the picture.

Colour key A process for reproducing coloured line drawings. A line block is made from the original drawing and reproduced in light blue ink. Colours are drawn onto this, a separate sheet being produced for each printing.

Colour positives A set of screened positive colour separations.

Colour separations Separating full colour into (generally) the four 'process' colours by means of filters, resulting in four films used to make printing plates.

Colour transparency A full colour photographic positive on film.

Column Columns divide text into vertical sections. They set parameters, between which text lies across a page.

Column inch (centimetre) A newspaper measure of text space, one column wide and one inch (centimetre) deep.

Comb binding A method of binding loose sheets together. Slots are punched into the left-hand edge of the collated pages, and a rolled plastic spine inserted into place.

Comparative advertising Advertisements that compare the advertiser's product with those of specifically named competitors.

Competitors Companies whose business is to sell the same, or a similar or alternative product or service.

Compiled lists Lists built up through the research of directories and other published data, as opposed to lists generated as a by-product of direct marketing activity.

Compiler A researcher who prepares compiled lists.

Composite artwork Artwork combining a number of different elements.

Computer bureau A company that provides data processing services. These can be of a wide range of specialisation.

Computer graphics The use of computer to create a graphic image, e.g. a picture, diagram or map.

Computer language A generic term for the codes used to give computers their instructions.

Computer letter A computer-printed letter that includes personalised fill-in information from a source file, in predesignated positions in the letter.

Computer personalisation The process of tailoring each piece of correspondence to the needs of the recipient, by filling name, address or other information relating to the recipient into predesignated positions within the correspondence (see above).

Computer program A series of instructions keyed into the computer in order to achieve a preconceived objective for a variety of data input or output.

Computer record All the information collected about an individual, company or transaction stored on a computer disk or tape.

Computer service bureau As above.

Computer typesetting As below.

Computerised composition/computer typesetting The use of computers to control various aspects of photocomposition such as character assembly. The computer can be programmed with details of format, tabulation, rules of punctuation, type sizes, measure, etc.

Concept testing Pre-testing the idea of a new product. (After which pre-testing the product and market can be carried out).

Concertina fold A type of fold which opens out like the bellows of a concertina.

Condensed (type)   A typeface which is narrowed to occupy less space than a standard face.

Confidence level   The number of times, out of 100 attempts, that the results' predictions must be correct. This degree of confidence is expressed in terms of the number of standard deviations.

Configuration   The arrangement of peripherals into a computer system.

Consultant   A professional who gives independent advice and direction. For direct mail this might include strategy, lists, offers, copy and design, computer skills and result analysis.

Consumer   A buyer, potential buyer, or end-user of a product or service — often referring to a non-business product or service.

Consumer behaviour   The study of consumer buying actions used in marketing research. This type of research is used to determine why consumers either buy or do not buy, and is usually carried out by using qualitative methods: conducted by personal and telephone interviews.

Consumer goods   Articles or services which are intended to be used outside the work environment.

Consumer list   A list of individuals' names and home addresses.

Consumer location system   A market identification system which gives marketers an indication as to the most suitable areas to target.

Consumer profile   The combined characteristics of those who buy or use a given product or service, e.g. their sex, age, class, etc.

Consumer research   Research into the numbers, preferences and behaviours of consumers.

Continuation   The next step after an initial list test. If a test mailing has been responsive within predetermined financial parameters, the list is ordered again in quantities relating to response.

Continuity programme   See Continuity series.

Continuity series   *A marketing technique whereby a customer is sold a series of similar products over an extended period.*

Continuous form   Paper designed for computer printing. It is folded, may be perforated at the edges, and may be a variety of formats: letters, forms, cards or invoices.

Continuous research   Research carried out on an on-going basis, in order to monitor trends, etc.

Contributor list   A mailing list made up of names who have made donations in the past to a fund-raising mailing. Otherwise known as donor list.

Control   A component in a direct mail package which has been tested before, and was at that time the most successful of two or more packages. The control is used in testing as a true measure against which the effectiveness of new components are gauged. The component can be either the whole package, or elements of a package such as the copy, offer and premiums

Control package   As above.

Control tape   Computer tape containing control information, rather than data.

Controlled circulation   The distribution of publication to a list of exclusive, often invited, readers.

Conversion   Has two meanings: The act or process of upgrading an enquirer (suspect) to a customer. The process of changing from one method of data processing or system to another.

Conversion pack The material sent out to an enquirer by the advertiser, in the hope of converting the enquiry into a sale.

Conversion rate The number of those who actually buy or subscribe to a service, out of the total number of enquiries received as the result of advertising, expressed as a percentage.

Conversion systems A printing term given to systems which convert type or plates into film, prior to printing using a different method.

Cooling-off laws See Cooling-off period.

Cooling-off period A period of days or weeks during which the seller must give notification of the buyer's right to cancel within a specified number of days.

Co-op See Co-op mailing.

Co-op mailing Two or more products or services (usually non-competitive) mailed in the same envelope to prospects.

Copy Written material intended for publication.

Copy block Block of typesetting treated as one unit.

Copy control Copy restrictions laid down by the IBA.

Copy date The submission date by which the copy must reach the publisher or author.

Copy segmentation Adapting the advertising message to the unique needs of each market segment.

Copy test A test of an advertisement's copy which aims to discover the reactions of prospects, either prior to or after an advertisement has been published.

Copyboard A frame used to hold material, while it is photographed for reproduction.

Copyfitting The determination of the typographical specification which is required to be set in order to fill a given amount of space.

Copyprep Short for copy preparation. The instructions put on a manuscript to ensure that the copy is published as intended.

Copyright The legal right given to a work that protects it from being unfairly stolen by a second party.

Copywriting A term given specifically to writing copy for advertising purposes.

Corporate identity/housestyle Distinguishing design or phrases, which give a company a consistent image or 'personality'.

Correction overlay A transparent sheet attached to artwork on which corrections are made.

Correlation A statistical term which is used to show a degree of relationships between factors. A correlation of 1.0 is perfect correlation, 0.0 shows no correlation, and -0.1 is perfect disagreement. A correlation factor of over 0.8 shows close agreement.

Correlation analysis A market-factor method of forecasting sales.

Cost of goods sold A section in an operating statement, showing calculations to work out the cost of products sold over the period covered by the statement, usually in total and per unit.

Cost per enquiry (CPE) Total cost of obtaining enquiries divided by the number of enquiries.

Cost per order (CPO) Total cost of obtaining sales divided by the number of sales.

Cost per sale   The total cost of obtaining one sale as above.

Cost per thousand   The total cost of reaching 1000 customers or prospects

Cost plus pricing   A popular method of determining the price of a product. A given product is priced as the cost of production plus the level of desired profit.

Cost/rank order   The ranking of publications, according to both the cost of advertising space and readership.

Coupon   That portion of an advertisement or a mailing to be filled in by an enquirer or customer, and returned to the advertiser to request a follow-up or fulfilment.

Coupon clipper   One who habitually responds to offers without any serious intentions of buying.

Coupon offer   A voucher which entitles the consumer to an offer on goods or services, as indicated.

Couponed ad   A display advertisement in a publication that the reader can reply to by mail using the coupon provided. Often a telephone order alternative is given.

Cover   The number of times an advertisement is seen or heard.

Cover date   The date of a publication.

Coverage   Also known as net coverage, or reach. The number of people in a particular target group who have the opportunity to see or hear an advertisement at least once.

Covering envelope   Those outer envelopes which are sent by the mailer, as opposed to enclosure envelopes for use by the consumer to the mailer. Also outer envelope.

Crease   To impress an indented line across a sheet of paper or cardboard.

Creative   An original thought or idea. Also the department of an agency which carries out design and copywriting functions.

Credit   To extend or relax terms of payment on merchandise. Credit offers widen the market for a particular product, by lowering the immediate price barrier.

Credit buyer   Someone who pays for mail order goods after they are delivered.

Cromalin   A substitute proof for a four-colour proof which does not require machine plates to be made.

Cross folds   Folds which lie perpendicular to the direction of machine feed.

Crown   British imperial paper size measuring 384×504 mm.

Cumulative index   An index combining several other preceding indices.

Cumulative quantity discount   A reduction on a sliding-scale basis. Higher discount rates are given on larger quantities.

Customer base   Shortened term for customer database. A facility (generally computerised) that records customer information (name, address, lifestyle particulars, transactions, etc.)

Customer file   A list of customers

Customer profile   The key characteristics of a customer.

Customer replacement   The process of acquiring additional customers to replace those lost through attrition.

Cut marks   Marks on artwork that indicate where cuts are to be made.

Cut off Another term for closing date or period end (e.g. limited period on an offer).

Cyan One of the printing primary colours, a shade close to light blue.

Cycle time The length of time a computer process takes relating to a storage location.

–D–

DID Delay in Delivery.

DMA Direct Marketing Association. The major American trade association for direct marketers.

DMA Mail Preference Service The American arrangement whereby a name can either be added to or deleted from mailing lists by notifying the DMA.

DMMA The old name for the American Direct Marketing Association (short for Direct Mail Marketing Association). The name changed in 1982 in order to reflect the increasing use of direct marketing media other than direct mail.

DMPA The Direct Mail Producers Association. The trade association for those who produce direct mail packages.

DMSB The Direct Mail Sales Bureau. A plc set up by the Post Office and industry in order to promote the idea of using direct mail to advertisers and leading agencies.

DMSSB Direct Mail Services Standards Board. A board set up to uphold standards within the industry.

Daisy wheel A flat disc with characters on stalks used within a printing machine.

Data capture Information taken and stored on a computer.

Data card A card containing information about a specific mailing list, which is sent to mailers by a list broker or manager.

Data entry The conversion of data into machine-readable code.

Data processing The execution of a series of systematic operations performed on data.

Data sheet Leaflet setting out factual information about a product or service.

Database An organised collection of information held on computer, from which sections can be accessed easily.

Datapost A Post Office service which guarantees next day or same day delivery.

Dealer Synonymous with retailer.

Dealer incentive A direct marketing incentive aimed specifically at the retailer. Sometimes known as the 'dealer loader'.

Decoding The process whereby the computer interprets instruction codes.

De-collage To separate continuous sheets.

Decoy A unique name inserted into a mailing list in order to verify list usage.

Dedicated An item of equipment or electronics, used for one type of application or one programme.

De-dupe The process of identifying and eliminating duplicate names from two or more mailing lists, in order to prevent repeat mailing an individual's address.

De-dupe data Information identified as duplicated from two or more mailing lists.

Definition   The degree of detail and sharpness in a reproduction.

Degradation   The result of overloading a computer system to the extent that the terminal operations are affected.

Delivery date   The specified date on which an ordered list is to be received by the list user, from the list owner.

Delivery point   A description of an address or other location of where a delivery will take place, used both as a postal and general term.

Demographic segmentation   Selecting targets on the basis of statistical information such as age, income, sex or lifestyle criteria.

Demographics   A statistical description of a group based on common patterns, e.g. geography, socio-economic factors or buying patterns.

Demography   The statistical study of human population and its distribution characteristics.

Density   The number of characters contained in a specific area of magnetic tape.

Depth interview   Unstructured informal interview to ascertain attitudes and motivation.

Depth of product line   The make-up of a product line.

Descriptive label   A label giving either descriptive or instructive information.

Design   The style and layout of the elements of a mailing, advertisement or other publication.

Designation marks   Identification letters which confirm the sequence of a book, prior to its make-up.

Desk research   Research carried out by examining published material.

Desktop publishing   A custom-made, graphics-oriented microcomputer linked to a laser printer to produce high-quality documents with both copy and/or illustration.

Diary   A record of transactions or other behaviour.

Die cutter   A cutter which is specially shaped to punch out paper or card.

Die-stamping   A type of printing where the characters arc set in relief.

Digest-sized   A catalogue size which measures approximately 140 mm×215 mm.

Dimension marks   Indication marks on camera-copy showing areas to be either enlarged or reduced.

Dimensional mailing   A high-quality mailing which often includes a high-cost attention-getting device, e.g. including a free gift or sample.

Direct access   Use of a storage medium which can access information without sequential searching, e.g. a disc as opposed to a cassette.

Direct mail   Unsolicited mail, usually sent either to advertise or to sell goods or services. It is delivered by the Post Office.

Direct mail advertising   Advertising through the post.

Direct Mail Producers Association   See above, DMPA.

Direct Mail Sales Bureau   See above, DMSB.

Direct Mail Services Standards Board   See above, DMSSB.

Direct mail shot   Sending out a collection of direct mailing packages to those on a mailing list at one time.

Direct response   Advertising or selling through any medium inviting the consumer to respond to the advertiser.

Direct response list   A list of known responders to direct marketing solicitations. This list may include those who have responded, but are not known mail order buyers.

Direct selling   Selling directly from producer to consumer without any intermediary.

Discount in pricing   A reduction from the list price, usually offered to those purchasing in bulk, or paying cash with order.

Discount retailing   Selling below the list, or regularly advertised price.

Discretionary buying power   The amount of disposable income a person has left, after paying for fixed expenses and household needs.

Disk   Computer storage device for holding information.

Display ads   Advertising matter designed to a distinctive size or quality to attract instant attention from the reader.

Display advertisement   As above.

Display face   A larger typeface designed for display size advertisements.

Display matter   Typography which is set apart from the text, e.g. headings.

Display size   Type which is 14 pt and over.

Display type   As above.

Distribution   Has two meanings. The process and structure by which goods are transferred from the seller to the buyer (which may or may not include intermediaries). A shortened statistical term for frequency distribution, describing the spread of data along a scale of a parameter.

Distribution centre   A technique used in warehouses enabling a company to keep an inventory and location control.

Distribution channel   The route taken by a product as it passes from a seller to a buyer.

Diversification   Moving into a new market sector, either by acquiring a new business or by dealing with a new product/service.

Donor list   A list of people who have donated to a charity.

Door-to-door   A type of service, where direct marketing offers are delivered to the target recipients by hand, rather than being stamped or franked and sent through the post.

Dot   The individual element of print from which a half-tone reproduction is made up, e.g. the dots which make up newsprint.

Dot matrix printer   A type of computer printer. It produces the required image by making a pattern of dots.

Dot spread   An accidental unacceptably enlarged dot size formation which occurs during printing.

Double column   Two columns of continuous text.

Double page spread   Print which continues over two facing pages, as if they were one page.

Downtime   A term to describe the period(s) when a machine is not in productive use.

Drop   The date(s) on which the Post Office, or private distribution company, will deliver the prepared packs.

Drop date   As above.

Drop shipper   A person who sells merchandise to a customer and then arranges for the manufacturer to deliver it directly to the buyer.

Dry mounting A type of photographic mounting which uses heat-sensitive adhesives.

Dry test A test used to ensure that there will be a demand for the product (a frequent practice among publishers). Consumers are asked to order before the product has been manufactured. The manufacture only goes ahead in cases where the response will guarantee a desired profit level. Where this level is not met and the product never manufactured, compensation is given.

Drying time The time taken for ink on a sheet to dry, so that other processes can be carried out on the sheet (e.g. further printing, binding, etc.).

Dual distribution Using two channels to market a product.

Dummy A mock-up (sometimes plain) to check either pagination (for a publication), function, thickness and weight for a mailing.

Dummy name A unique name inserted into a mailing list to track list usage. (See also Decoy).

Dump Transfer of a computer file either in or out of storage.

Dump letter A mailing to a book or record company subscriber which offers all units in a series at a discount.

Dumping Selling products in another country, at a lower price than in home markets.

Dunning cycle The duration between each consecutive reminder letter sent out to prompt consumers to settle their bill.

Dunning letters A series of reminder letters requesting consumers to settle their bill.

Dupe An abbreviation for duplication.

Dupe elimination A computer process run to eliminate all but one record, when a number of lists are to be used for a mailing.

Duplex A line-casting matrix with two character moulds.

Duplex printing Both sides of the sheet (computer printing).

Duplication Two or more names and address records which are found to be for the same potential recipient when two or more lists are run against each other.

–E–

E13B A type of magnetic ink font used on cheques.

EAN European Article Number.

EDMA European Direct Marketing Association.

Early payment discount A reduction offered for payment on an invoice being settled within a specified period.

Edit Check, rearrange or correct data or copy before production.

Editing rules Specific guidelines laid down for preparing text or records, so that all elements are treated in the same way at all times.

Editorial The contents of a publication, apart from paid advertising space.

Editorial mention A paragraph or two of editorial copy which is included in a publication (often a way of rewarding regular advertisers).

Effective cost per thousand The cost of the medium for advertising divided by the number of people in the target audience it reaches.

Electoral roll confirmation (verification)   The use of the electoral roll to ensure a list contains correct addresses, or that the individual is listed (for credit scoring).

Electronic mail   The transmission of messages from one person to another via electronic media.

Electronic publishing   The publication and circulation of information in an electronic form.

Elite   Small size of typewriter type.

Embossed finish   Letters printed in relief.

Embossing   The process of printing with a relief finish.

Emulsion   A mixture of light-sensitive silver salts suspended in gelatine or a similar mixture, for coating photographic plates and films.

Enclosure   Anything included in a direct mail package besides a letter.

Encode   To give a code to a group of characters.

Encoding   To identify information by means of codes given to groups of characters.

End fold   A fold or saddle-stitching in a booklet which lies along the short side.

End leaf   Extra-strong paper used to hold the body of a book to its jacket.

Endorsement   Where approval from one company is given to another unrelated company. In direct mail this is often a recommendation from a company a customer knows, of a second, non-competitive company with which the customer has had no previous dealings.

Endpaper   See End leaf above.

Engraving   The etched printing plate for use in a litho press. Also, the print made from such a plate.

Enquirers   Those responding to a direct response advertisement or selling device for further information, rather than placing an order.

Enquiry   A response to a direct marketing solicitation requesting further information about a company or their products, rather than placing an actual order.

Enquiry file   A file of those people who have requested further information from a company, but who have not (yet) placed an order.

Enumeration district   A geographical area of about 150 households, which correlates with the Census breakdown of Great Britain, which can be used for market or list segmentation purposes.

Envelope   The outer carrier of a letter or other carrier of material to be posted.

Envelope stuffer   Promotional material enclosed in an envelope already containing either business letters, invoices or statements.

Environment   The macro-environment is outside conditions, over which a company has no control. The micro-environment is the internal conditions within which a company operates (e.g. management, staffing, etc.).

Erase   To rub out or overwrite data, e.g. on magnetic tape or disk.

Ertma   The name of European inserting systems (both gravity/suction-fed systems).

Estimate   The calculation of the cost of work for an order.

European Community Those European countries which have signed an agreement to operate a Common Market system of trading.

European Free Trade Association An economic union of six European nations.

Evaluation The analysis of the results of a test or operation which gives a directive for future work.

Every-other-name A test where alternate names receive a control and test mailing or advertisement, sometimes known as an A/B split.

Exclusive dealing A practice where a manufacturer prohibits its retailers from selling other products which would act as competition to their own.

Exclusive distribution The practice where a manufacturer uses only one retailer or wholesaler in a given market.

Exclusive territories The practice by which an intermediary is required by the manufacturer to sell only within an assigned area.

Exhibition lists The list of names collected of visitors to an exhibition.

Expected (actual) per cent of response The number of times, expressed in percentage terms, that a response will be positive. The difference between this positive response and the total quantity mailed describes the percentage of non-response.

Expected price The price that a customer consciously or unconsciously expects to have to pay for a product. (See Perceived value.)

Expected response rate The percentage of people approached who are expected to respond to a solicitation in a required manner.

Expiration date A closing date given in direct mail copy to motivate the reader to respond to an offer.

Expire A term for a former subscriber (e.g. to a magazine series).

Exploded view A drawing of an object which shows the individual parts, but in a way that indicates their relationship, so that the complete object can be understood.

Exposure The process where light sensitive materials (plates and films) are subjected to light.

Extended type Typeface with characters wider than the normal roman type.

Extract A passage which is a quote. It is often indented and reproduced in smaller type.

Eyeball To look over a rented mailing list to ensure that the names are genuine/satisfactory/as described.

–F–

FAW Finished artwork.

FD Finished drawing.

FIFO First in, first out.

FILO First in, last out.

FOC Free of charge.

Face The printing surface of a piece of type, or a style of type (typeface).

Facing matter An advertisement position facing an editorial page.

Facing pages Pages tha face ech other in a magazine or book.

Facsimile   An exact reproduction of a document or document part.

Factor analysis   A mathematical procedure for reducing data used in attitude research, as a forecasting tool.

Fair copy   A copy of a document with no correction marks.

Fair sample   A term often used when asking for a list sample from a broker or owner. (More useful is to request a specific sample.)

Fair-trade laws   Laws which existed until 1975 which enabled manufacturers to set a retail price for their products.

Fan fold   A type of fold, also known as a concertina fold, which opens in the same way as a hand-held fan.

Fan-out   Moisture-filled edges on a sheet which create a waviness in paper.

Fashion cycle   The market waves (trends) in the popularity of a fashion style.

Fax   An abbreviation of facsimile transmission. This process enables a document to be reproduced at a separate location, by means of the telephone system carrying a message. Compatible machines are required at both ends.

Feature   A distinctive element advantageous to the user of a product or service.

Feed edge   The leading edge of a sheet of paper, as it is presented to the printing machine.

Feed holes   Holes placed at regular intervals in the edges of tape or paper to guide the feed of the paper smoothly.

Feedback   Information telling the sender whether and how the message was received.

Feeder   A mechanism on a press that separates and lifts sheets into the preprinting position.

File   A collection of data, in direct mail usually grouped as a list of customers, enquirers, etc.

File layout   The structure and arrangement of data lying within a file (including the data's size and sequence).

File maintenance   List cleaning by correcting addresses and errors, and adding those names who wish to be excluded from, and included on, the list.

Fill-in   Words, personalised to the recipient of the mailing, that are added to spaces within the body of the copy, either by hand or by machine.

Filler   An extra illustration or piece of copy, put into a newspaper or magazine, in order to fill up empty space.

Filler advertisement   An advertisement not booked for insertion, but included to fill up redundant space.

Film coating   A very light paper coating.

Film mechanical   Camera-ready material prepared on film, rather than on paper.

Film positive   Photographic print on transparent film taken from artwork for use by the printer.

Film processor   A machine that automatically develops, fixes, washes and dries exposed film.

Finish   Has two meanings. The type of surface a material has (e.g. matt, or gloss, etc.). Also, the processes a printed sheet may go through before it is incorporated into a book, magazine, newspaper or other publication.

Finished artwork   Artwork from which print can be produced.

Finished rough   Material which is the neat mock-up of a proposed advertisement, often produced by an agency or studio for a client's approval.

Finishing   The printing term given for the process between printing and completion (ie. binding, stitching and folding).

First class discount   The reduction given to pre-sorted mailings, but which receive the same treatment as standard first class mail. (Mailsort 1.)

First class letter contracts   As for First class discount.

First class mail   Post which should be delivered the following day, if posted by the last collection the previous evening.

First colour down   The first colour printed on a sheet, where more than one is required.

First day cover   A decorative envelope and stamp, issued in conjunction with the Post Office commissioning a new set of commemorative stamps.

First generation   An early model of machine or product.

First proof   The earliest proof used for checking by proof readers.

First-time buyer   A person who is buying a company's product or service for the first time.

Fixed cost   A constant cost, regardless of whether or not goods or services are sold.

Fixed field   An area on a computer into which a variety of information can be input although the space and position relative to other fields do not vary.

Fixed line address   An address which is forced into a pre-set number of lines.

Flag   To give an indicator against chosen addresses, in order to treat them differently at a later stage (e.g. by selection, or segmentation).

Flagging   To apply a flag as above.

Flap   The lip or overlap which is used to seal an envelope or bag.

Flat   Unprinted paper, or printed paper prior to folding.

Flat artwork   Material prepared on to board, ready for camera.

Flat rate   A set rate for advertising space or time, not subject to discount for either volume or frequency.

Flat stitch   A method of stapling a book together, performed while the book is spread flat.

Flat wrapping   Wrapping a newspaper or magazine without folding it, with either a film or paper covering.

Folding, right-angle   A method of folding a sheet, with folds perpendicular to one another.

Follow-up mailing   A subsequent mailing, sometimes a repeat of the first, sent to those who were non-responders to an original mailing.

Font   American spelling of fount.

Foolscap   A paper size (330×200 mm) which used to be regarded as standard, but now replaced by A4 (297×210 mm).

Format   The physical specification for a mailing piece, book or other publication.

Former buyer   A person who has not purchased from a company within the past twelve months.

Formula   A well-known principle, to be applied to new situations.

Forward dating   A sales method whereby a customer buys goods or services in an off-season, but only has to pay later, when the season starts.

Fount A complete set of type for a given typeface.

Four-colour process A method of full-colour printing using each of the four-colour plates in separation.

Flip-flop An electronic term given to an electronic circuit which represents the binary values either 0 or 1, by being in one of these states.

Floppy disk A plastic disk capable of storing information, for use in microcomputers.

Flowchart A diagram that shows sequence in a series of steps (e.g. in a computer program).

Flush left/right The alignment of type with respective margins.

Focus group A group of consumers led by a researcher in discussion, in order to collect opinion about a product or other market attitudes.

Focus group interview See above.

Fold A paper turned and creased intentionally. In direct mail the succession of folds is designed to lead the reader through the mailing, following the sales message through to responding to the offer.

Fold-out A folded sheet in a text which folds out to extend the normal page size.

Folding guide Printed marks on stationery which indicate where folds should be placed.

Folding, parallel A method of folding a sheet, with folds parallel to one another

Four-up A galley of mailing labels, arranged four-across.

Fourth generation Photosetters using lasers to expose characters.

Fragrance mailing A mailing in which one element has had a fragrance or simulated fragrance applied to it.

Franking The process of marking an envelope or a postcard with a postage-paid impression. These machines normally work on a meter system, operated on a pre-payment basis to the Post Office.

Frankly, I'm puzzled letter Also known as a publisher's or lift letter. A separate piece (usually of a smaller size) within a mailing which is designed to dispel any doubts that a recipient of a mailing may have about responding to an offer.

Free Completely without cost.

Free flier An additional small insert in a mailing, included as a 'last-minute' offer of a free gift.

Free-keeper A modest gift, given as an incentive in return for placing an order by mail, that can be kept even if the buyer returns the goods ordered.

Free-ride A mailing device with another offer which is inserted into another mailing, often administrative or procedural, in order to capitalise on postage costs.

Free-standing stuffer (insert) A promotional piece inserted loose into a newspaper or magazing. Also known as free-fall.

Free trial A sample of goods or services, either for a limited period or in a limited quantity.

Freefone A British Telecom service. A firm offering a freefone number pays for any call received on the freefone line.

Freelancer An independent supplier who undertakes project work on a fee basis.

Freepost A Royal Mail service. A firm offering a freepost address pays postage on all mail received at the freepost address.

Frequency The number of times a person has ordered from a company within a given period. This word is often used in conjunction with recency and monetary, in order to forecast future sales potential.

Friend-of-a-friend The recommendation made by one person to an advertiser to put a friend on their mailing list.

Front end General term for the devices which control a computerised photosetting machine (e.g. keypad, screens and editing facilities).

Front end costs The costs of all procedures undertaken in creating an advertisement or a mailing, before orders are received as a result.

Fulfilment The process of dealing with an order or enquiry, from its receipt to delivery. This includes opening, processing, administration, packing and transport.

Fulfilment package The package containing the goods or the details of the arrangement of the service, which fulfil the order. Or containing requested details in response to an enquiry.

Full colour Four-colour printing process.

Full postcode. A code which depicts a unique geographical location.

Full run rate The lower price rate given for those printing jobs carried out in large quantities (e.g. mailing roll-out).

Function codes Codes that control the functions of a machine, rather than the generation of characters.

Functional costs The grouping of operation expenses into various categories.

Fund raising list A list of people who have responded to requests for donations.

–G–

GAF Get a Friend. Similar to member get a member, but there is no requirement of membership.

GND Goods not Delivered.

GNO Goods not Ordered.

GSM Grammes per Square Metre.

Galley A long shallow tray in which type is kept. Also the common usage for galley proof: the form in which copy is returned from the typesetter for proof reading, prior to being arranged into pages.

Galley proof As above.

Gang printing Running more than one job on the same sheet.

Gap analysis The study of the difference between the position an organisation holds currently, and where it would like to be.

Gatefold A fold that turns in on itself from both edges towards the centre.

Gaevert proof A proof produced photographically to simulate the finished job in four colours.

Generic coding Coding of the structure of a document rather than its typographical make-up.

Generic product A product which has no element of advertising incorporated in its packaging, i.e. it is sold with no brand name, but instead merely under the name of whatever the good is, e.g. tomatoes.

Generic use of brand names   When a product becomes known as one brand name, e.g. 'Sellotape' and 'Hoover'.

Geo code   Symbols used to identify geographical areas, e.g. post-codes.

Geographic   Method of segmenting a list according to geographic criteria, e.g. town, country, TV area, etc.

Ghosting   A printing term meaning an accidentally feint printed image.

Gift buyer   A person who buys a good or service for another.

Gifts   Given by suppliers of products or services to either customers or prospects. Unlike premiums they are not usually imprinted, e.g. with a company logo or other embellishment.

Gimmick   Any device, apart from the copy which aims to attract attention or build involvement into a mailer's offer.

Gimmick stamps   Adhesive-backed stamps for the respondent to apply to forms or envelopes, devised to increase involvement in a mailer's offer.

Give-away   A low-cost free gift given to a prospect or customer without any obligation.

Glassine   A type of transparent paper, often used for window envelopes.

Gloss art   Hardcoated artpaper, as opposed to matt.

Glossary   An alphabetically arranged list of specialised terms, and their definitions.

Gone aways   A term given for those mailings sent to an individual at an address where he or she no longer resides.

Grain   The lie of paper fibres. Papermaking is carried out in liquids. The grain is determined by the direction of the liquid flow. The long fibres should lie parallel to the long edge.

Grant   A device used by artists and typographers to enlarge or reduce images.

Grant-making charity   A charity whose principal role is to raise money and redistribute it in the form of grants to other charity organisations.

Graphic design   Design that is a two-dimensional process, e.g. illustration, typography, photography and print.

Graphic display terminal   A VDU screen able to display both line and tone.

Graphics   Illustrations, pictures and photographs in printed work.

Gravity feed   The use of gravity to feed a machine (e.g. with a sloping horizontal plate, possibly assisted by a rotating friction wheel).

Gravure   A type of printing technique. The surface to be printed is etched below the non-printing areas of a printing plate. The surface is flooded with ink, wiped clean, leaving the indents filled with ink. Paper is pressed against the plate and the ink transferred.

Grip   Margin required at the feed edge of a piece of paper to allow the grippers to hold onto the sheet.

Gross costs   The total costs, before deductions have been accounted for.

Gross income The total income, before deductions have been accounted for.

Gross margin Net sales minus the cost of goods sold. (Also called gross profit.)

Group discussion A research technique where a researcher leads a discussion with a group of consumers about their habits, attitudes and opinions concerning a product.

Growth stage (of the product life cycle) The stage where sales continue to increase, and profits increase, prior to the peak and decline.

Guarantee A warranty made by a seller to a buyer to refund or replace goods that do not meet their satisfaction.

Guardbook A book that contains essential information of all an advertiser's advertising activities, and a book that contains copies of all advertisements published for a client.

Guideline Line on artwork which indicates the area to be printed.

Guillotine A machine which cuts paper, by means of a sharp blade descending onto a flat surface.

Gummed paper Paper coated with adhesive on one side.

Gumming The application of adhesive to paper.

Gutter A binding margin in a book or on a sheet.

–H–

HDS Household Delivery Service. The Royal Mail delivery service of unaddressed promotional literature.

Hairline A very fine line in typeset matter.

Half-and-half letter A letter written only on one half of a page, either vertically or horizontally. This type of letter is used to collect payment for outstanding accounts, as well as for renewing subscriptions.

Half-tone Illustration or photography created by the use of dots, which give the effect of continuous tone (a 'complete' picture).

Handling house A company which checks, packs and mails premiums.

Hard copy A printed copy of computer output.

Hard sell An aggressive approach to selling, which asks for an immediate response to a solicitation.

Hard-bound A hard outside covering to a book or other literature.

Hardware A computer term applied to equipment, rather than computer programs.

Head margin The white space above copy and illustration on a page.

Head to head A position for laying copy which is to be printed using the 'work and tumble method'. A term given to testing when a direct comparison is to be made.

Header record A record which contains common or unique information identifying a group of records.

Heading A line of type which is displayed at the head, before a piece of text.

Headline As above.

Heat sealing The process used to close plastic bags, by semi-melting techniques.

Heat transfer addressing A process by which a name and address are applied to an envelope.

Heat-set One stage in the web-offset printing process for non-absorbent papers, where ink is dried in a heated chamber.

Hologram A three-dimensional image created by lasers.

Holograph As above.

Homeworkers Those who undertake work at home.

Horizontal industrial market A demand for a product or service across a large number of industries.

Horizontal information flow A theory that suggests people follow views and opinions which are held by leaders within their own social class.

Horizontal trade journals Journals written for executives of similar positions across a broad spread of different industries.

Hot line The most recent names on a mail order buyer or enquirer list. Also a rapid telephone order or enquiry service.

Hot line list As above.

Hot metal A term given to the machines from which individual pieces of type are cast.

Hotline buyers Those people who have bought a product or service most recently.

House advertisement An advertisement included in a publication, often to fill empty space, which advertises the publication itself or other services offered by the publisher.

House list A mailer's own list of people who are either former or current customers or prospects.

House mailing A mailing to your own house list.

House offer An advertisement or co-op insert which is usually charged internally at the cost of production only.

House style An illustration or copy which is a distinctive production of the company who produced it.

House to house The delivery of unaddressed promotional literature to households.

House-list duplicate A name and address record which appears on both the mailer's own list and one or more lists rented for a particular mailing.

—I—

IBM The largest computer system manufacturer worldwide.

IBM 3800 laser A high speed laser printer, with a continuous stationery feed. One of the most popular types of laser printer.

IBM 6670 laser High-quality, slow-speed laser printer.

ISBA Incorporated Society of British Advertisers. An association which voices the collective opinion of advertisers.

ISBN International Standard Book Number.

ISO sizes International range of paper and envelope sizes, which replaced the term 'Din sizes'.

Idea bank A pool of ideas, collected on an on-going basis for use in the future, e.g. copy ideas, premiums and pricings.

Illustrated letter A letter that contains illustrations and/or photographs, as well as copy.

Illustration Any type of pictorial image that helps explain written copy. This may be a photograph, drawing or diagram.

Impact printer Printing machine using a printing element hammered onto the paper through a ribbon, in a similar manner to a typewriter.

Impression The pressure of plates in contact with either the blanket or paper at the moment of printing. Also the image left after printing has taken place.

Imprint Details of the printer, publisher and other general details about a book.

Impulse buying Unpredicted purchasing.

Inactive buyer A person who has bought from a company, but not within a specified period.

Incentive An inducement to purchase or respond. Unlike a gift or premium, which can be sent gratis, an inducement requires a prospect to act in some way to receive the offer in return.

Indent To leave a space at the beginning of a line of copy, e.g. at the start of each paragraph, or set in from a main margin.

Index An alphabetical list of topics covered in a book, with their appropriate page references.

Indicia A mark or frank used in place of a postage stamp. It is printed onto material to be posted, and permits the item to be mailed.

Industrial buying process The steps that an industrial buyer goes through in deciding whether or not to buy a product.

Industrial marketing The marketing of industrial goods to industrial users.

Industrial products Products intended for use in the business sphere.

Industrial users People who buy products for use within their company's business.

In-fill A word or phrase added to predetermined positions within the main body copy after this has been printed (e.g. in order to personalise a mailing).

Information processing The process, usually computer-aided, of translating raw data into usable information.

Information retrieval The process of recovering specific information from stored data.

In-house Carried out within a company, rather than being bought in from outside firms.

In-house facility The resources, of staff, equipment and time, to carry out a job within a company, rather than being bought in from outside.

Ink jet A type of printing process. Tiny ink droplets are sprayed from a jet. This process is of a lower quality than laser printing, but can be carried out at high speed.

Ink piling A build-up of ink on a printing blanket.

Inner Common usage for inner envelope. This envelope is included in a mailing for the recipient's use to respond to an offer, as opposed to an outer envelope.

Inner forme The imposed forme which appears on the inside of a sheet when folded.

Input To key in raw data into computer storage.

Inquiries Response to direct marketing solicitations offering further information or other literature, which generally contains the selling message.

Inquiry names A list of those people who requested information to be sent to them, as a result of a direct marketing solicitation, but who did not generally make a purchase.

Insert   An alternative method of advertising using the published media. A paid-for promotional piece which is placed loose or bound-in to each edition of a magazine issue, or other publication.

Inset   A paid-for promotional piece which is bound into a magazine or other publication.

Insetting   Placing and fixing one section inside another.

Instalment buyer   A person who pays for goods or services in two or more periodic payments.

Institutional advertising   Advertising that aims to create a favourable image for a company, rather than to achieve sales for a specific product or service.

Intelpost   A Royal Mail service that is created around a worldwide facsimile transmission network.

Interactive   A two-way information system, whereby the information receiver can communicate directly with the information supplier.

Interface   The link between different parts of the computer.

Interleaves   Sheets of paper put between wet printed sheets, to ensure true setting. Also different types of paper put in between the text pages of a book.

Inter-list duplicate   Duplication of a name and address record on two or more mailing lists that have been rented for the same mailing (i.e. other than a house-list).

Internal data   Operational data, e.g. the monitoring of sales figures, company performance, etc.

Internal (house) list   The advertiser's own list of current or past customers or prospects.

International Standards Organisation (ISO)   The association that draws up internationally recognised standards, particularly size and measures.

Inter-neg   An intermediate negative for a colour plate.

Intra-list duplicate   A duplication of a name and address record within a given list.

Invalid record   A record that is either technically unacceptable to a processing device, or which does not conform to the list owner's or list user's requirements or specifications.

Invoice cancellation   A marketing technique, often used by publishers. A trial magazine or several magazine issues are sent, followed by an invoice. The recipient only pays if what has been received is satisfactory.

Issue date/cover date   The official date for the sale of a magazine or other publication, which can differ from the date when it is actually available on sale in retail outlets.

Italic   A typeface, used for emphasis, with letters that *slope forwards*.

Ivoryboard   Fine board that is manufactured by laminating two high-quality sheets together.

–J–

Job title   A title assigned on a mailing list or database to describe a person's position at work.

Jobbing   A term for general printing.

Johnson box   A phrase, sentence or short passage, highlighted by being enclosed in a box, generally formed of asterisks, at the head of a piece of copy.

Joint venture A partnership formed by two or more different collaborators in order for one to use the pre-established marketing systems of the other. A recognised way of expanding into new territories.

Jumbo envelope An envelope 324 mm×229 mm (more commonly known as a C4 envelope).

Junk mail A term, offensive to direct mailers, used by the media which means unsolicited mail.

Justify Typesetting aligned to margins adjusted to be spaced into the predetermined measure.

–K–

KISS Short for Keep It Simple, Stupid. A formula used in copy writing.

Key Or keycode. A reference code (either letters, numbers or other symbols) which enables an advertiser to identify the source of an enquiry from any type of direct response advertising.

Key code analysis The analysis of results obtained from monitoring response by key.

Key lines Lines on artwork which indicate where tints should be laid, or where solids are to be printed up.

Key number A code put on a reply device enabling response to be monitored.

Keyboard The array of keys that control a machine, representing data and commands.

Keystroke One key depression, often used as a measure of an operator's production.

Knife folder A type of folding machine which uses a blade edge to fold paper.

Knock and drop Another term, used incorrectly, for the delivery of unaddressed, unsolicited mail. It is the more exact term used in conjunction with sample distributions.

Knocking up To align up edges of a pile of paper.

–L–

LHE Left-hand edge.

LHS Left-hand side.

LIFO Last in, first out. (Stock that is issued as early as possible, regardless of similar stock which is already held.)

LILO Last in, last out. (Stock that is issued in rotation according to the date it is received.)

Label A slip of paper which bears the information, either about a product itself, or details of the manufacturer, advertiser or consumer. Or an address label, being an affixable address carrier.

Label paper Paper gummed one side, the other for name, address or other particulars.

Laid paper A high-quality paper, identified by what appear to be watermarking lines running in parallel.

Laminate The application of plastic to paper or card, to give either protection or a glossy surface.

Landing date The date on which the mailer targets the mailing package to reach the consumer.

Landscape An image whose width across is greater than its height.

Language   Computer communication which uses words that translate into machine code.

Large post   Standard imperial paper size measuring 419×533 mm.

Laser   A shortened word which stands for Light Amplification by Stimulated Emission of Radiation. Concentrated light beam of narrow width, used for creating images, engravings, etc.

Laser personalisation   A method of computer printing usually incorporating file data in pre-planned positions. (A computer attachment to the laser printer supplies personal data about each record.)

Last colour   The final colour to be printed in colour work.

Latin alphabet   Western European alphabet (such as our own).

Launch   The first campaign to promote a new product or service.

Lay down   Impose a job.

Layout   The arrangement for production, as it is planned.

Lead generation   Mailings inviting enquiries for sales follow-up.

Lead sentence   The first sentence in a piece of copy (crucial to gain reader attention).

Lead-in   A phrase or sentence that precedes a headline in a direct response advertisement, or mailing.

Leading   Space inserted between type.

Leading edge   The edge of a sheet of paper or plate where printing begins.

Leads   Enquiries for sales follow-up and conversion to sale.

Leaf   A single sheet which makes up two pages.

Legal-sized envelope   A term used in the US, Canada and Australia, for the most common direct mail envelope used in mailings to businesses.

Legend   A caption.

Legibility   The ease with which text can be read.

Letraset   A brand name which is commonly used for rub-down transfer lettering and graphics for artwork.

Letter   In direct mail the bearer of the sales proposition.

Letterhead   Printing on a letter which identifies the sender, usually giving a contact address and telephone number.

Letterhead enquiry   A solicited sales enquiry that comes in on a company's letterheaded paper, rather than on a reply device, or through any other media.

Letterpress   Printing from raised surfaces of either metal or plastic.

Letterset   A printing method where the image transfers from a relief plate, first onto a blanket, and then from the blanket onto paper. It is sometimes known as dry offset, offset letterpress and indirect letterpress.

Lettershop   A company which offers to handle production stages of a mailing for an advertiser, e.g. addressing and enclosing.

Library shot/pic   A picture or illustration taken from an existing source, known as a photo or picture library.

Lifestyle   A person's way of life, which has a direct influence on the type of products or services they buy or require.

Lifetime value   The full-term value of a customer to a company. Using direct marketing techniques a customer will often provide a company with sales on a long-term basis. In such cases, the calculation of a customer's lifetime value can be essential to evaluate what initial cost can be spent acquiring a new customer.

Lift letter A marketing technique to increase the response to a direct mail letter. Often a second letter from an authoritative individual who endorses the product or service.

Lift memo As above, produced in the style of a memo.

Limited edition Products of which a restricted number are produced or available. This increases their perceived value. Such products are successfully marketed by mail order.

Line and half-tone An illustration process in which line and half-tone negatives are combined, then printed onto a plate and etched.

Linotype A brand name of machines which cast lines of metal type.

List The collection of people's names and addresses.

List broker Someone who works for a list user (an advertiser who wishes to rent another company's list) to advise, select and arrange the rental of outside lists.

List buyer Someone who buys a list from a company for their permanent use. In common usage, this term also includes those who rent a company list.

List catalogue A list of mailing lists that are available for rental.

List cleaning The process of correcting, or removing incorrect entries from a mailing list.

List code The code to a list, when lists or list segments are being monitored during a test. The list code is printed somewhere on the reply device.

List compiler A researcher who builds lists from directories and other published sources.

List conversion Changing one magnetic tape format to another.

List count The quantity breakdown given to elements of rented list for comparison when an analysis of the success of different lists used in the same mailing is made.

List data card A card which gives full details of a list for rental.

List exchange An agreement drawn up by two organisations, in which the lists are mutually exchanged.

List maintenance The process of correcting, removing and/or adding a record on a list.

List manager The agent retained by list owners, to maintain and/or market their list(s)

List owner An individual or organisation who has built or gathered their own list, generally through trading or compilation.

List price The cost of a list.

List rental An arrangement where a list owner or manager supplies a list to a mailer, in return for a rental fee.

List sample A group of names taken at random or in line with an intended selection from a list, in order to evaluate its qualities and assess its value.

List segment Portions of a list which have been selected against specific criteria, e.g. geographic area, lifestyle, gender, age, etc. The purpose of segmenting a list is to improve response by more accurately targeting a mailing and reducing wastage.

List segmentation The process of sorting and selecting names from a list into list segments.

List selection The process of choosing both a mailing list(s) and segments within lists, for names to be included in a final name and address file.

List sequence   The order in which names and addresses are kept in a file, e.g. alphabetically or in 'town and county order'.

List sort   The process of putting a list into a specific order (either from an existing sequence or none at all).

List source   The media from which names for a list are obtained.

List test   A test carried out by mailing a sample taken from two or more list segments and/or entire lists.

List user   A person who uses someone else's list names for their own mailing.

Listing   A computer print-out of data or a file.

Literal   A keyboarding or typesetting error.

Litho   The generic name for offset lithography, and also a smooth printing surface.

Live names   Describes those who are current 'active' customers who have responded recently, and might do so again in future.

Local advertising   Advertising that is placed in local media such as provincial press or local radio.

Local Parcels Delivery Service   The Royal Mail service that delivers parcels to the local area.

Logo   An emblem which a company or organisation uses to establish and project its identity.

Long copy   An approach to letter writing for mailing, generally characterised by a sales story that extends to, for example, four or more pages in a mail order letter or two or more pages in lead generation. It is also used to describe a certain style of off-the-page advertising.

Loose insert   A method of advertising in published media, where a promotional piece is placed between the pages of a magazine, or other publication.

Loose leaf   A method of binding, employing metal binders in a file to hold loose sheets together by means of holes punched into the left-hand edge of the paper.

Loss leaders   A temporary price-cut, usually in order to attract increased store traffic or a first purchase.

Lottery   A sales promotion device which requires a contest containing the elements of chance consideration and prizes.

Lower case   Type consists of upper and lower case letters. Upper case describes the capitals, lower case the remainder.

Lower-middle class   An arbitrary term used to classify white-collar workers, e.g. office workers, teachers, etc.

Lower-upper class   An arbitrary term used to classify the socially prominent, and *nouveaux riches*.

Loyalty   A measure of brand allegiance, determined by consumer panels or attitude research.

–M–

MG   Machine Glazed. Paper having a smooth appearance on one side, by being passed under a hot roller.

MGM   Member Get Member. A marketing technique where current customers are offered an incentive to enlist a new member.

MPS   See Mailing Preference Service.

MUA Mailers Users Association. An organisation whose role is to protect the interests of members using the postal services.

Machine proof A proof that has been prepared for a print machine plate, or blocks as for the run.

Machinable envelope An envelope which is designed to be run on an enclosing machine, characterised by a wide 'mouth' and long rectangular gum-flap.

Magalog A catalogue which has a sufficient element of editorial so that its recipients perceive it as a magazine.

Magenta One of the primary printing four-colour process colours.

Magnetic tape A medium for storing computer data. Commonly used for list storage and processing.

Magtape As above.

Mail date See Mailing date.

Mail date protection Interval of agreed time that a list is not used for mailing, e.g. a week before or after a list is used by a mailer, in order not to vie with other promotions.

Mail house A company which offers all aspects of a direct mail service, prior to its despatch (from idea, printing, packing, through to mailing).

Mail interview A questionnaire survey sent to a consumer, completed by them and returned to the mailer.

Mail list A list of people to mail to.

Mail order A buying/selling transaction carried out by mail. Strictly speaking, both the order should be placed and fulfilment should be carried out by mail. However, often the order is placed via other media (e.g. by telephone) and order delivery by other means too!

Mail order buyer A person who made a mail order purchase.

Mail order product A product more suitable for mail order than by retail.

Mailer The organisation on whose behalf the mailing is being carried out.

Mailing date The date direct mail pieces are put into the post (and the date any rented list owner has agreed for his list to be used).

Mailing Preference Service An organisation which supervises and administers a service, by which members of the public can have their name added to or removed from suitably screened lists, on request.

Mailshop A combined poster and display leaflet dispenser sited in post offices, which can be rented to advertisers of products and services to generate additional letter or parcel business in the UK.

Mailsort (1, 2, 3) Generic name for pre-sorted mailings for which the Royal Mail offer discounts. There are three service standards: first class, second class and slower bulk rate.

Make-ready The preparatory running up of printing machines so that both heavy and light areas print with their respective correct impressions.

Make-up The positioning of type and illustration to conform to a layout. More usually called a paste-up.

Manilla A tough brown or yellow paper which was originally made from manilla hemp. Often used for envelopes.

Manuscript copy The text of a book before it is published.

Marginal analysis A method used to establish a base selling price. Market demand and product costs are balanced to establish the best price to maximise profit.

Marginal cost The cost of producing one additional unit (i.e. the cost of the last unit produced or sold).

Margins Areas of white space around the text matter on a page.

Mark-up As goods and services are traded from the seller to the buyer each of those involved in the transaction adds their required handling and profit levels or 'mark-up'. It is commonly expressed as a percentage, although unit or total monetary values are also used. Alternatively, the details of the size and style or type to be used. Also known as type specification.

Marked proof The proof on which the *printer's* reader has made corrections and queries, etc.

Market People or organisations deemed to have the desire or need to buy a product or service, and the potential capacity and willingness to do so.

Market aggregation A marketing strategy in which an organisation treats its entire market as if it is homogeneous.

Market analysis The study of a market to discover what its various characteristics are.

Market-based pricing A pricing strategy whereby a product is priced only in relation to the competitive market price, rather than the price being influenced by company or provisionary costs.

Market expansion The strategy of seeking additional buyers by expanding promotional efforts into new areas.

Market factor An item that is related to the demand for a product.

Market factor analysis A sales forecasting method based on assumptions that future demand for a product is consistent with the behaviour of certain market factors.

Market index A numeric expression of a market factor (see above) related to a base figure.

Market potential Total expected sales for a product in a given market over a certain time-period.

Market research A type of research which seeks and analyses information from the market, as a basis for decision-making about a product or service directed at that market.

Market segmentation The process of dividing a market into portions or groups which have distinctive characteristics. Or strategy which involves the seller developing multiple marketing strategies, each aimed to have the maximum effect on their respective segments.

Market share One company's percentage share of the total industry sales within a given market.

Marketing All activities that are associated with the identification, communication and satisfaction of the market.

Marketing (macro-societal dimension) Any sale or exchange that satisfies a human want or need.

Marketing cost analysis A detailed study of the operational expenses in an assessment of a company's profit and loss situation.

Marketing information system An on-going, organised system for gathering and processing information to assist with marketing decisions.

Marketing mix   A combination of the four elements that make up the core of an organisation's marketing system: product, price, distribution and promotion.

Marketing plan   A strategy for a set future time-period.

Marketing strategy   The plan of action for marketing a product or service.

Marketing system   The total series of ideas and subsequent inter-related actions by which marketing occurs.

Mask   An overlay which masks out unwanted areas in a photograph or on a piece of artwork (usually opaque).

Masking   Photomechanical control of colour contrast and detail on separation negatives.

Masking paper   Opaque orange paper on which film is assembled for platemaking.

Master   A plate for a duplicating machine.

Master file   A file that is either a permanent or authoritative file, or a file that contains several sub-files.

Masthead   A graphic device which displays a newspaper's name on the front page.

Match code   A numerical and/or alpha reference code generated by computer to form a unique identifying code.

Matching-in   The process of inserting a name, address or other phrase into pre-positioned spaces within a pre-printed piece of text so as to be as nearly indistinguishable as possible, one from the other.

Matrix printer   A printer which creates each character from a set of dots, usually character by character, but also can be produced as a line at once.

Matt   A dull soft finish, as opposed to glossy.

Matter   Copy or manuscript to be printed.

Mechanical data   Information supplied about a publication by publishers to prospective advertisers, e.g. page length, column width, etc.

Mechanicals   The material supplied in its final form to a publication for the reproduction of an advertisement, e.g. headlines, pictures, text, etc.

Media   Any vehicle for the transmission of a communication, e.g. television, radio, direct mail.

Media data form   Established format for presenting comparative data in a publication.

Media independent   An organisation which specialises in buying media time and space, in the same role as the media department of a large advertising agency.

Media inserts   An alternative method of advertising in a publication, by placing a pre-paid printed piece, either loose or bound-in, between the pages of each edition of a magazine or other publication.

Media owner   A company which owns and operates commercially a media organisation, e.g. television, radio station, or a newspaper, etc.

Media plan   A plan prepared by an agency which shows a client through which media it proposes the budget should be spent, and the rationale behind this.

Media schedule   A record of space or other bookings planned and made for a campaign.

Media systems   A comprehensive system for recording bookings, transmissions, and the invoicing of advertisers by computer.

Megabyte   One million computer bytes (loosely termed one million characters).

Member   One who has paid a fee for the right to belong to a group or receive information, and/or goods or services under specific conditions.

Member get member   A marketing technique whereby a member is offered an incentive to get a friend also to join as a member.

Menu-driven   Software program laid out so that the operator has to answer questions in order to action the program.

Merchandising   A part of marketing that is concerned with maximising product movement most usually used in reference to retail level.

Merge   The process of combining two or more mailing lists in order to build one larger one.

Merge and purge   The process of combining two or more mailing lists in order to build one larger one, but including the removal of duplication.

Mini-catalogue   A mailing which contains single-sheet advertisements, each with a reply coupon. Or a folder featuring a selection of merchandise, rather than a full line of products in a regular catalogue.

Minimum   The minimum quantity of names a list owner will rent for a test of his or her list.

Misprint   Typographical error.

Misregister   One or more colours printed out of alignment with other colours.

Mock-up   A layout or rough of artwork. Also called a visual.

Modem   Short for Modulator/Demodulator device, which converts communications (e.g. telephone transmissions) into a digital form, and vice versa.

Monetary value   One of the criteria for judging the potential value of a person on a mailing list.

Monochrome   One colour.

Monotype   A brand name for a 'hot-metal' type-casting machine, which assembles characters individually, rather than line-by-line.

Montage   Several images assembled into one piece of artwork.

Motivation research   A type of research which aims to establish the relationship between people's behaviour and their underlying motives, desires and other emotions.

Multi-buyers   Those people who have bought more than once from a mailer or advertiser.

Multicode   A key which generates several commands at once.

Multilith   Proprietary name of a small offset press.

Multi-mailer   A mailing that contains a number of loose single-page promotional sheets.

Multi-media   A campaign using more than one medium of advertising or selling.

Multiple packaging   A sales strategy. Several units of a product are packaged as one, in order to increase the volume of sales of the lower level products by strapping them to higher volume performers.

Multiple regression A statistical technique used to measure the relationship between response and lists or list segments.

–N–

Name acquisition Technique used to prompt a response in order to generate new names for a mailing list.

Name addressing The use of a person's name in addressing from a mailing list, rather than using their title or other means of identification.

Name removal request A request made to have a name removed from a mailing list.

Negative A photographic image on film, in which black values in the original are transparent, and white values opaque.

Negative option A buying arrangement in which a customer or member agrees to accept a proposition unless they formally notify the seller to cancel, often within the specified time-period.

Negative sell A copy approach which leads off on a perceived drawback or disadvantage of the product or service.

Negs A shortened photographic term describing negative film, being that used with positive plates to create an image.

Neighbourhood mailing Mailing the neighbours who live nextdoor to or nearby a person who has responded to a mailing in the past.

Nesting Placing one insertion inside another, before inserting into an outer envelope.

Net cost The cost to the advertiser of reaching the target audience.

Net disposable income This term is used to describe the amount of earnings a person has left after tax, bills and other essential outgoings have been deducted.

Net name arrangement The terms of an agreement between list owners and users. Lists are run together to find duplicate records. The list owner receives payment for the number of new names, or the number of names as percentage of the whole, whichever is the greater. There is generally a specified minimum percentage.

Net names The number of names used for a mailing, after duplicate names have been eliminated.

Net sales The total number of sales made, after returns and sales allowances have been deducted.

Netting down The process of merging several lists or list segments in order to find and eliminate duplicate records.

Newsprint Paper made from mechanical pulp for the printing of newspapers.

Niche A small, tightly targeted segment of a market to whom a particular product, variation of a product or presentation of a product may appeal.

Nixie The direct mail package returned to a mailer because of an incorrect address.

Nominal data Data which are made up of elements which can be counted in terms of frequencies (e.g. number of responses, etc.).

Nominal weight An American system of specifying the basis weight of paper.

North/south strip A term describing a specific type of sheeting for labels. (Labels on a reel as opposed to labels on a rectangular or square sheet.)

Nth name   A method of selecting names to make a sample for list testing. The total list quantity is divided by the quantity of names to be tested, i.e. 10 000 names selected from 100 000 would mean that every 10th name would be selected.

—O—

OCR   Optical Character Recognition. The interpretation of characters by a computer which scans the text and stores or reads or translates data.

OFT   Office of Fair Trading. An association which regulates trading matters in the UK, in order to protect the consumer.

OMR   Optical Mark Reading. Use of marks such as dots or bars, which, when positioned on a sheet of paper, break a light contact and indicates a certain function to the machine.

Oblique   Roman characters which are slanted.

Oblong   Refers to a book's shape. The binding is at the shorter side.

Observational method   The method of gathering information from primary sources by observing the respondents in person, rather than interviewing them.

Occupant addressing   Using the words 'The Occupier' instead of a name in an address.

Off line   A computer term meaning the entry of information away from the processor, either by tape or by floppy disk. There is no direct access to the computer memory and the processor is not used.

Off-the-page   The acquisition of a lead or sale directly from a press ad, without follow-up by any other media.

Off-the-page-advertising   Advertising using page media, e.g. in magazines and newspapers.

Off-peak   Rates for advertising, when audiences would normally be at their lowest.

Offer   The terms under which a product or service is promoted.

Offset   A method of printing from etched plates using ink and water, whereby the image is transferred from these plates onto a rubber mat, which is then transferred to the paper.

On line   A computing term where the entry of information is directly linked to a processor which allows immediate interaction.

On-pack   A free sample or free gift or offer which is promoted on the product or its packaging.

On-sale date   The date on which a publication goes on sale. This is often different from the cover date, for example with monthly magazines.

Once only   An intrinsic part of a list agreement, whereby it is understood that the mailer will only use names on a rented list once, unless prior approval of the list owner is sought.

One-off   Short for one-off rental. See above, Once only.

One shot   A solus mailing, promoting usually one product at a time.

One-stage   Short for one-stage sell. A promotion which is designed to sell directly, without any follow-up process.

One-time buyer   A buyer who has only made one order for a company's product(s) or service.

One-time usage   See above, Once only.

Opacity The density of a material which minimises the reflection or transmission of light, so that the image on one side cannot be seen through from the other.

Open account A customer record that reflects an unpaid balance for goods.

Optical A trick effect achieved mechanically by the combination of two or more film pictures into one composition.

Optical Character Recognition See OCR above.

Optical scanner A machine which reads a line of printed characters and converts these into a usable form for processing.

Order card The reply card which a person fills out and returns to order a product or service.

Order form A printed form on which a recipient can initiate an order by mail, usually designed to be posted in an envelope.

Order processing All activities involved in the handling of an order for goods or services up to the point of despatch, e.g. the handling of monies received, the production of despatch notes, etc., as well as the despatch of the order.

Original Any printed matter or image which is intended for reproduction.

Out of register Printing where the images of different colours are not in true alignment, so that reproduction is inaccurate.

Outdoor advertising All forms of advertising that appear outside, e.g. posters, facias, signs, etc.

Outer The container for a mailing piece, e.g. envelope, plastic or wrapper made from other material.

Outer envelope The envelope used to carry a direct mail package to the prospect or customer.

Outline A typeface which contains no 'solid' area, merely an outline form.

Output Data or other forms of communication which come as a result of computer processing.

Output data The final data after computer processing, which are transferred from the computer's memory to another device, e.g. printer or magnetic tape.

Outward postcode The first half of a postcode identifying the general area for delivery (the first two letters, followed by a number). The remainder of a postcode, called the inward code, identifies the exact location for delivery.

Outwork Operations given to another company, either for specialism or capacity.

Outworker A person who undertakes finishing work for direct mail producers.

Over-runs Copies printed over the specified printing quantity.

Overlay The transparent cover over artwork which contains instructions for the underlying artwork.

Overprint To run a previously printed piece through the printing presses a second time in order to add further material in required positions.

Overs Any unused material left once a job has been finished. Often print is ordered plus 'overs', to allow for spoilage while printing.

Ozalid A form of copying process used to proof film (a blueprint).

PC Short for personal computer.

PI deals Payment by results. The number of sales or enquiries generated are paid in accordance with a pre-agreed rate of charge.

PIN Short for Pinpoint Identified Neighbourhoods. A Census-based classification index, used to segment the population and to market products in the most relevant way to each segment.

PMS A colour-matching system by Pantone enabling specification of a range of colours.

PMT Short for Photo-Mechanical Transfer. A mechanical method which quickly produces a photoprint from flat originals for use as artwork paste-ups.

POP Short for Post Office Preferred. Describes those envelope sizes which conform to assist with the processing through automated sorting offices.

PPI Printed Postage Impression. The printing of a Royal Mail licensed mark, together with a special number, on the face of either an envelope or other material, e.g. plastic wrapping, which is to be handled by the Post Office in bulk. This avoids the Post Office having to frank the mail in their sorting office.

PS Postscript. A 'last-minute', additional message, appearing usually at the end of a letter, which in direct mail is often used to re-emphasise a major part of the selling message.

PSR Postal Service Representative. Each major post office has a representative who liaises with clients over postal matters. In effect, Royal Mail's salesforce.

Package All of the components which make up a single direct mail shot.

Package insert A promotional piece which is included in the fulfilment package (i.e. with the shipment of the product, or along with the details of the ordered service).

Package test A test between one complete mailing piece and another, varying in offer, or creative approach or both.

Packaging The presentation of the product service, or appeal in a manner appropriate to the needs, and interests of the target market.

Packing The paper placed next to the plate or blanket in litho, or next to the impression cylinder in letterpress, to adjust printing pressure.

Page One side of a leaf.

Page make-up The process of assembling a page ready for printing. Also, a display showing copy as it will appear on a page in photocomposition.

Page one break A break in mid-sentence at the end of the first page of a direct mail letter, which is designed to encourage the reader to continue reading onto the next page. Also known as a run-on-hook.

Page proof The proof of a page before it is printed.

Page pull test The test to determine the strength of a binding of an adhesive bound book.

Pagination The page numbering.

Paid cancel Someone who completes a basic buying commitment before cancelling that commitment.

Paid circulation The subscribers to a publication who have paid for their subscription to it.

Pallet A wooden base suitable for mechanical handling on which paper or books are stored.

Pamphlet A small publication which has more than one page (a leaflet), but fewer pages than a booklet.

Panel A sample of shops or people used for regular or periodic research, used to monitor performance, etc.

Pantone A brand name of an international colour matching system for printing/art products, which has a common usage. (See PMS.)

Paper tape A paper strip which records data as a series of punched holes, arranged in channels or 'tracks' across the width.

Paragraph opener A symbol which marks the start of a paragraph for emphasis, e.g. *

Parenthesis A round bracket, e.g. (.

Pareto's Law The 80/20 rule. The general tendency for the majority of revenue to come from the minority sources.

Partwork A publication which is issued in a number of parts, for separate purchase, but which combine to make one whole.

Pass-along Those readers of a publication which they neither subscribed to nor purchased.

Passive file A file of those customers who have bought from a company, but have not undertaken a recent transaction.

Past buyer A person who has bought from a company before, but not within the previous twelve months.

Paste-up The process by which an artist puts typesetting and photographs together into artwork.

Pasteboard Board made from the lamination of several thinner sheets.

Patterned interview A standard list of questions asked of interviewees in order to compare like with like.

Pebble finish A textured surface to paper.

Peel-offs Self-adhesive labels, which are stored on greaseproof paper, and often used for address-labelling items for posting.

Penetration A measure of the uptake of a product in consumer research, i.e. the proportion of homes or the number of individuals who have either bought or used a product.

Penetration pricing A pricing policy, whereby a product is given a low price initially, in order immediately to reach a large mass-market.

Perceived value The notional valuation a buyer attaches to an item for sale when he first sees it.

Perf Short for perforation.

Perfect binding Adhesive binding commonly used for paperback books. Glue is applied to the roughened back edges of sections to hold them together and to the cover.

Perfect register Colour advertisements which appear in the press or other publications without their design being cut.

Perfecting The printing process, whereby both sides of a sheet of paper are printed in one pass.

Perforating The process of punching holes into paper or card either as a code, or in order to facilitate tearing off a part.

Perforator A keyboard which produces punched paper type.

Perfume application An especially formulated solution containing micro-encapsulated particles of perfume, which when rubbed, release a fragrance.

Periodical A publication which is issued at regular intervals (usually either weekly or monthly), e.g. a newspaper or magazine.

Personal interview Gathering data from a survey using face-to-face methods.

Personalisation The addition of personal information (e.g. name, address or other personal details about a prospect or customer) incorporated into the copy, usually via computer.

Phillipsburg A make of automatic inserting machine which collates and inserts mailing pieces into envelopes and seals them ready for posting.

Photoset Headlines and text composed photographically, instead of using metal letters.

Photocopy A duplicate of a document reproduced on a copying machine.

Photogravure The process of printing from a photomechanically prepared surface (a negative image is transferred to the metal plate and an image etched into it). Ink is held in the recessed cells, from which the final print is created.

Photomontage The use of images from different photographs in combination to provide a new composite image.

Photosetting The process of composing headlines and text photographically.

Photostat See Photocopy above.

Pica Has two meanings. A unit of measurement used in printing which is equal to 12 points (4.21 mm). Also the size of type commonly used on typewriters.

Picking The lifting of areas of the paper surface during printing, when the ink tack is stronger than the surface strength.

Picture captions A phrase or sentence or two of descriptive copy either beneath or alongside an illustration chart or photograph.

Piggyback The enclosure of an additional promotional effort into a company's own or a second company's mailing package.

Pigment Fine solid particles used to give either colour, body or opacity to printing inks.

Pin feed The method of feeding continuous stationery by lining up pins on the machines with a series of small holes in the mould ejector pin.

Pin marks The indentations on the side of typefounders' characters caused by the mould ejector pin.

Pinholes Small holes in the surface of paper or small holes of transparency in black film emulsion.

Pitch The measurement of the number of characters per horizontal inch in typewriter faces.

Pitney Bowes The brand name of a range of mailing machinery.

Planer A wooden block used to tap letterpress type into place, on the surface of stone.

Planned obsolescence An intentional change in the superficial characteristics of a product, so that the new model is easily differentiated from the old one, in order intentionally to make people dissatisfied with the old one.

Planner The person who prepares the media plan for presentation to the client.

Planning All the processes involved in getting ready for plate-making.

Plastic wrapping Polythene outer coverings used for mailing magazines, etc., usually made by machine.

Plate A separate illustration, often on a different type of paper. A printing surface, made from one piece, rather than from assembled type.

Plate making The process whereby artwork is converted into letterpress or litho printing plates.

Pocket envelope A term given to describe those envelopes which have the flap along the short edge. These envelopes cannot usually be passed through inserting equipment.

Point size The measure used to describe type sizes.

Point-of-sale display Display material used in a retail outlet to draw attention to a product or offer.

Poly-lope A brand name of a polythene mailing bag sealed by a gummed flap.

Polythene wrapping An outer covering for a mailing made from polythene.

Pop-up A printed piece which is constructed so that when it is opened it 'pops up' to form a three dimensional image.

Population (or universe or sampling frame) The total domain or group of people being considered.

Portrait A picture or page with vertical dimensions which are greater than the horizontal ones.

Positive An image made photographically on paper or film which corresponds to the original copy (the reverse of a negative).

Positive option A method of distributing products or services, whereby the order is shipped and a person is billed until he or she formally cancels this order.

Postcard deck A loose deck of postcards, each with a separate offer and reply device. Generally the person who arranges this type of co-op mailing is the owner of the list to which the mailing is going. The participants pay a fee, plus cost of the printing of the card. Also Card-deck.

Postcode An identification code used to facilitate postal delivery to an address.

Postcode sort The sorting and bagging of a mailing into postcode sequence.

Postscript See PS above.

Premium An item offered to a buyer, usually free or at a nominal price, as an inducement to purchase or to obtain a product or service on trial.

Premium buyer A person who buys a product or service in order to receive a second product or service (usually free or at a special price), or who responds to an offer of a special product (premium) on the package or label (or sometimes in the advertising) of another product.

Pre-paid A mail order shipment for which there is no additional charge for postage, packing, shipping or handling. These costs have already been included in the purchase price. Or a response device requiring no postage to be paid by the responder.

Pre-printed Part of the copy which has been printed before receiving additional printed material to it.

Presentation visual Also known as a finished rough. Material prepared as a sample of the proposed appearance of a printed work.

Press costs The cost associated with printing and manufacturing a job from the manufacturing of the plates onwards.

Press date The date on which a publication goes on the press for printing.

Press proof The last proof to be read before printing is agreed.

Press run The total number of copies produced in one printing.

Pressure-sensitive label A type of label that is attached to a backing sheet to make it easier for the recipient to peel off.

Prestel British Telecom's information service which is available on screen via a telephone link.

Pre-testing Research carried out to test advertising before a campaign is carried out.

Price point The price people will pay for a product or service, or a level at which it becomes sensitive.

Price test A direct mail test to compare two or more prices for the same or similar product or service.

Primary (subtractive) colours Pure colours from which all other colours can be mixed. In printing colour mixing is a subtractive process. The primary printing colours are magenta, cyan and yellow.

Print image The form of data representation from which print lines can be logically drawn by a printer, with no intermediate format required.

Print origination A printing term given to preparatory work completed prior to proofing.

Print run The number of copies printed or the process of printing a particular job.

Printed Postage Impression See PPI above.

Printer's error Often known as PE. Most frequently a literal or typesetting error.

Prize draw Numbers are drawn at random to provide a 'chance' winner of a prize. This technique is popular in direct mail to boost response, often announcing that the draw has already been made.

Probability tables A set of statistical estimates which tabulate the confidence levels which can be achieved.

Process printing The printing of colours 'over' (in fact, alongside) each other to produce different tints and hues.

Product What a company manufactures, or the service or appeal it can offer.

Product information cards Business reply cards in a booklet, or a deck of loose cards.

Product lifecycle The idea that most products pass through a predictable cycle which is an introductory phase followed by rapid growth, maturity and peak, and lastly decline.

Product line The range and diversity of products or service which a company manufactures.

Product manager An executive who is responsible for planning the entire marketing plan for a product or group of products.

Product mix The complete list of products or services offered for sale by a company.

Product planning All activities that enable a company to decide what products it will market.

Product positioning Those activities which develop the intended image (in the customer's mind) for a product in relation to competitive products.

Product stuffer A promotional piece which is enclosed with the fulfilment package. It often illustrates other ancillary items which can be bought.

Profile The common format description or picture of a customer typical to a company.

Program The set of instructions which instruct and control a computer in the performance of a task.

Programme schedule A schedule of programme plans issued by a TV contractor, which the buyer can consult when deciding which spots to book.

Programming The design, writing and testing of a computer program.

Promotion The presentation of material to inform and persuade the market as to a company's product or service.

Promotional mix The promotional elements contained in a company's marketing mix.

Proof An impression taken of camera-ready copy or artwork in order to check for errors and make amendments prior to printing.

Proof-of-purchase A token, or other symbol, removed from a product's packaging in order to qualify wholly or partially for a premium.

Proof reader Someone who reads a proof in order to correct and amend copy or artwork prior to printing.

Proof reader's marks Standard marks used by proof readers to indicate revisions to copy and artwork on printers' proofs.

Proof reading Checking both copy and artwork for inaccuracies and revisions before printing.

Proofs A printed sheet or copy made before production, for checking purposes.

Proposition Synonymous with offer or deal.

Prospect A person who has either expressed an interest in a company or its product, or whose profile suggests they would be likely potential customers.

Prospect list A list of people considered to be prospects as defined above.

Prospect universe All those (individuals or companies) making the mailer's potential customers, subscribers or contributors.

Prospecting Mailings whose purpose is to generate leads rather than to make direct sales.

Psychographics The study of consumers in terms of characteristics and qualities which denote their attitudes and lifestyle.

Public relations A planned effort by a company to influence attitudes towards their organisation through a variety of means and media.

Public service advertising Advertising that urges the public to support a cause or campaign.

Publicity Promotion that is generally not paid for by the organisation benefiting from it.

Publicity cost Any expense that contributes to sales promotion. In direct mail this cost would include list production costs and postage, etc.

Publisher's letter A second letter which is included in a mailing package in order to stress the selling points contained in the first.

Pull Has three meanings. A proof. A single print for subsequent photo-litho production. The percentage response obtained from an offer.

Pull-out section A part of a publication that can be pulled out in its entirety for separate use.

Punched tape Paper tape in which holes are punched, whose pattern represents data for inputting.

Purchase order A signed agreement to accept and pay for a particular item.

Purge The process of eliminating duplicate or unwanted records from a mailing list.

Pyramiding A method used to test lists whereby a small quantity of names is tested to begin with. If positive indications are received from this initial test, further tests are carried out on larger and larger quantities of names.

–Q–

Qualified enquirer A person who has acted in such a way as to indicate that he or she is a serious prospect for goods or services.

Qualitative data Data which measure intangible or objective data, such as people's attitudes and opinions.

Qualitative research Research that examines qualitative data.

Quality control Control checks built into a system to ensure a quality standard is achieved.

Quantitative data Data which are measurable or quantifiable, such as length, weight, etc.

Quantitative research Research which is measurable or quantifiable, such as length, weight, etc.

Quota sample A sample specifically chosen as a being a cross-section of individuals, from which an interviewer can obtain information. The people selected as part of such a sample are directly proportional to the age, sex, class, etc. of the total market they represent. This avoids the more complex sampling process of random sampling.

–R–

Random access A method of directly accessing an address on a computer file without any subsequent processing.

Random sample A sample which is selected in such a way that every unit has an equal chance of being chosen.

Random sampling The process of selecting respondents at random for market research purposes, so that every person has an equal chance of being chosen.

Random selection A method of selecting one list sample from an entire list for testing purposes, so that every other possible sample has the same probability that it could be chosen.

Range left/right Justification of type or line matter to form a vertical either to the left or right.

Ranking A research term given to the act of placing items in order of preference.

Rate card A document or card which sets out the costs for advertisement space, together with production details and copy dates.

Rate of return curve A graph which records the percentage response from a mailing. This chart allows mailers to determine the point in time when percentage response correlates with the accurate forecast of total response.

Raw data Data before they are processed or prepared.

Re-run A repeat of a machine-run, usually because of a correction, interruption or false start.

Reader Short for proofreader. Or a device that can read from magnetic machines or from typescript.

Reader benefit The features of a product translated into the benefits a reader will enjoy if they take up an offer.

Reader enquiry service A service run by a publisher which enables the reader to obtain further details of featured products and services from suppliers/advertisers.

Reader's proof The first proof of the printed material or copy for the printer's reader.

Readership The total number of readers of a publication as distinct from its circulation.

Readership test A research measure to gauge the effectiveness of an advertisement by estimating the number of people who read or saw it.

Real time A method of computing, in which operations performed on data are simultaneous with input and output.

Reason-why copy A copy approach which gives a presentation of features and uses for a product or service, with a point-by-point discussion of how the reader will benefit from these.

Rebate post The Royal Mail Service that preceded Mailsort 3. A postal discount given to second class letters posted in bulk, provided that they were sorted, bundled and bagged in accordance with requirements. The amount of rebate was calculated on a sliding scale based on the number sent.

Recall Memory or the act of remembering. A term often used in research as in spontaneous or prompted recall. Also the calling of a computer file from a backing store into memory.

Recall test A test to measure the effectiveness of an ad. It determines how many people can identify a particular advertisement.

Recency The time which has elapsed since a customer either bought from or entered into another transaction with a mailer.

Record A block of computer data.

Record format or layout The shape and nature of the contents of a record, i.e. what the various fields included in a record are.

Record-keeping The continual maintenance and monitoring of data, e.g. on costs, test and regular mailings, refunds, keys, conversions, etc.

Reduced price offer An incentive made in order to attract a would-be purchaser to buy a particular brand, by offering a genuine reduction on either an established price or a price which is to be the established one in future.

Reel-fed Machinery which can accept paper or plastic for printing or processing straight from the reels onto which they were originally manufactured.

Referral name The name of a person obtained by referral from a current customer. This is usually a member get a member scheme whereby a member is offered a free gift in return for the name(s) and address(es) of a friend who they believe would also be interested in purchasing the goods or service.

Register The specific position that an image appears on a page. True register is vital when laying colour sheets together to form full-colour reproduction.

Register marks Marks or devices used in printing to align different colour sheets.

Regression A mathematical technique which produces a functional relationship between two or more correlated variables. It is often used to predict values of one variable when the other values are known.

Rejection Information that has not been accepted by the computer, either at the point of input, or on updating the file.

Renewal The process of re-subscribing to a series of publications or to a service.

Rental agreement See List rental. An agreement made where one party hires either a segment or an entire customer list that belongs to a second for a one-time use, in return either for a set charge or another form of recompense.

Re-order lead time A mail order term for the period between the day inventory requirements are assessed, and the day the resulting merchandise arrives and is ready to fill orders.

Re-order period The time-period required to sell a commitment for merchandise. This is the sum of the re-order lead time (see above) and the time required to sell the stock held as safety.

Repeat business letter A sales letter created to sell more to existing customers.

Repeat buyer A person who has bought from a company more than once within a specified time limit.

Repeat mailing A second mailing to follow up a first, to the same list of names.

Repetition of ads In tests coupon ads often maximise their cost efficiency when run consistently.

Reply card A card included in a mailing which is return-addressed to facilitate a response from a prospect or customer. The reply card may or may not require the recipient to pay postage.

Reply-involvement Various techniques used to involve the recipient of a direct mail shot in replying to a direct mail offer (such as using stickers, rub-down patches, etc.).

Reply-o-letter A type of direct mail letter format which carries its own reply device in a paper pocket behind the top of the letter, once popular, particularly for lead generation.

Reprint A new version of a previously printed work.

Repro Short for reproduction proof. It is a high quality pre-press artwork proof.

Residence list A list of address records with no names. Direct mailshots are addressed to 'The Resident' or 'The Occupant' instead.

Resolution The efficiency of a photomechanical or computer graphics system in reproducing fine detail.

Respondent The person being interviewed or who replies positively to a mail shot.

Responder list A list of those people who have responded to a mailing.

Response curve The graph produced by plotting the daily intake of responses as a result of a direct response advertisement. This curve can be used to predict the future pull of promotions, as most curves make a similar pattern.

Response rate The percentage of orders or enquiries received of the total number of people who received the promotion.

Response time The time taken before a computer command is displayed on a VDU screen.

Retailer An organisation whose business is primarily to sell products to consumers and/or users.

Retest The verification of the results of a test mailing (both favourable and unfavourable) whereby a further test sample is taken from the same list and the test repeated.

Retouching Correcting, improving or altering a photographic print or transparency before reproduction.

Return address The return address to which a mailing should be returned if it cannot be delivered.

Return envelope An envelope included in mailing which is self-addressed by the mailer, as distinct from Business Reply or Freepost envelopes which obviate a postage payment by the responder.

Return on investment A measure of the performance and success of a company or project.

Reverse b to w An instruction given to the printer to reverse black and white on an image.

Reverse flap The flap that closes a side-seam envelope.

Reverse out See Reverse type.

Reverse type Type that is produced by printing a solid surround leaving the type white out. A colour can be printed into the area to give the 'colour reversed out'.

Reversed out See Reverse type.

Revise Short for a revised proof required for subsequent reading.

Right reading Film that views from left to right from the emulsion side. Opposite 'wrong-reading'.

Right-angle folds Folds that are at 90 degrees to one another.

River A term describing an undesirable visual effect caused when word spaces coincidentally form a long white space vertically ribboning down the page.

Roll fold A folding method. Material is rolled around itself at each fold.

Roll out Mailing to an entire list (or the remainder of the list), usually following a test sample of the list has been proved successful.

Roll wrapping A method of parcelling a magazine for mailing. The magazine is rolled and the outer wrapper put round it, rather than folding the magazine before sending it.

Roman type Refers to two typeface characteristics. Those typefaces that are upright, rather than italic. Those typefaces that are light, rather than bold.

Rotary knife A knife mounted to a rotating shaft which cuts to a fixed length.

Rotary press A press for printing newspapers or magazines which uses a cylindrical printing surface. This type of press can generally also deliver, fold and count finished articles, ready for despatch.

Rotogravure Gravure printing on a rotary press.

Rough A sketch showing a proposed design concept. Also known as a scamp or visual.

Run The number of sheets printed at one time, as opposed to the number of finished articles. Thus if a sheet contains four images (4-up) of the same piece, a 200 000 printing will be a 50 000 run.

Run of paper A paid-for advertisement placed at the discretion of the media owner at the standard rate.

Run on To continue copy on the same line, rather than starting a new line. Or the production of additional sheets printed over the original requirement.

Run on hook A break in mid- sentence at the end of the first page of a direct mail letter, which is designed to encourage the reader to continue reading onto the next page.

Run-on price The cost of producing additional sheets printed over the original requirement (Run-on prices do not include origination or machine make-ready).

–S–

SA Short for Self-Adhesive.

SC Short for Self-Coloured. A term given to paper which has not been overprinted, but which is coloured as a result of its manufacturing process.

Saddle stitching The binding of a book or magazine with wire staples through the middle fold of its sheets.

Sales leads The name and address volunteered by an individual in response to a mailing, advertisement or promotion, in order to receive more information about a certain product or service, and which is intended for follow-up by a salesperson or telephone call.

Sales promotion Any materials or activities designed to support, prompt or create sales.

Sales-results test A method of measuring advertising's effectiveness by monitoring the amount of sales volume created directly from an advertisement or a campaign.

Sales-volume analysis A detailed study of a company's sales volumes over a given time period.

Salt name Names and addresses inserted into a mailing list as known decoys (or seeds), to ascertain whether proper usage of the list has been maintained, or to measure speed of delivery, etc.

Salting The process of placing names into a mailing list, as above.

Salutation The introductory line of a letter, e.g. 'Dear Mr Smith'.

Sample A limited or trial portion of a whole or greater quantity. In direct marketing the quantity and character of the test portion selected from a larger mailing list. Or a free trial of a product included in a promotion.

Sample buyer A person who orders a sample of a product, either for a small charge, or free.

Sample mailing A copy or a specimen mail package.

Sample size The number of observations in an experiment. In direct mail the number of individual packages sent out in a test from which ultimately the percentage of response is assessed.

Sampling error The difference between the test results (of a sample) and the population parameter.

Sampling method The means of obtaining the sample from the entire total (population).

Sans serif Those typefaces which have no serifs, these being the small end tips which occur on certain typefaces as the ends of ascenders, descenders and strokes of letters.

Scamp An idea which has been drawn up roughly. Also known as a rough or first visual.

Scanner Electronic equipment which can read the various copy densities to make colour separations.

Scatter proof An illustration proof, where the various — generally colour — subjects are all arrayed on one proof, not as seen in their final position.

Schedule The details of advertising which is proposed, or booked, e.g. media, type and size of space, dates and costs, etc.

Score The crease or indentation which facilitates paper folding.

'Scratch 'n' sniff' The application of perfumed printing inks which release their fragrance when scratched or scored.

Screen The dotformation which enables photographs, tints or tones to be incorporated into a printed work.

Screen printing A printing process whereby ink is forced through fine material, e.g. silk, on which a design (usually a stencil) has been imposed.

Screens A series of dots or lines superimposed onto a transparency negative or positive, through which the image of the photograph is broken down. The image can then be converted for transposition to a printing plate or block.

Script A typeface which gives the appearance of being hand-written.

Seasonal discount A discount given to a customer for buying a product or service in a seller's specified season.

Seasonality The influence (such as the time of year when sales are made) of the season which can be either positive or negative.

Second colour Any colour other than the primary.

Second reply device An extra reply item provided in order to gain a further response.

Seed To insert names and addresses into a list as decoys to ensure that it is not misused, or to monitor its use.

Seed names Those names and addresses inserted into a mailing list, for monitoring purposes. See Salt name.

Segment To divide into specific or identified parts. To divide data on a list into smaller entities. Or the part so identified.

Segmentation The process of division into specific parts. As above.

Selection criteria Characteristics on which segments or selections are based, e.g. sex, age, class, first-time buyer or a multi-buyer, etc.

Self-cover A cover for a leaflet or brochure of the same material as the inside pages.

Self-liquidator Any incentive or premium whose costs (including handling and postage) are covered by charging the potential customer.

Self-mailer A direct mail piece that does not require an outer envelope.

Separation artwork Artwork in which a separate layer for each colour to be printed is created by means of a translucent overlay.

Series discount A discount given to advertisers for booking a series of advertisements.

Series rate See Series discount.

Serif The small terminal stroke on the end of a main stroke of a letter, which appears on certain typefaces.

Set-off The unintentional transfer of wet ink to a following sheet.

Setting Short for typesetting.

Shared mailing A mailing that promotes the products of two or more companies, whose participants share the mailing and incurred expenses.

Sheet The flat size of cut paper for printing, before it is folded and cut or trimmed.

Sheet-fed Printing by separate sheets, rather than from a reel.

Sheet size The size of the sheet for printing.

Shelflife The saleable life of a material or product.

Shipping date The date on which the list owner 'ships' the names to the mailer.

Silk screen printing A printing method where ink is forced through a fine material screen onto which a stencil has been placed.

Sleeper An unidentifiable and indistinguishable name and address placed as a 'seed' on a list.

Small-order Individual sales or orders that are so small as to be unprofitable relative to the cost of filling them.

Social grades Also known as socio-economic grades. An out-dated means of defining social class (A–E), usually determined by the occupation of the head of the household.

Socio-economic groups See Social grades.

Solus mailing A single mailing from which the whole sales objective must be achieved.

Solus position The position of an advertisement on a page where there is no other advertising matter.

Sort A computer program which rearranges a file into a sequence logically, according to a given parameter.

Source code A unique identification distinguishing one list or media source from another.

Space buyer A person who has made at least his initial purchase by responding to an advertisement in a magazine or newspaper. Or the buyer of advertisement space.

Special position A place in a publication which is pre-designated by the advertiser for his advertisement.

Specimen A sample page which is set to show the typography. Also, in direct mail, a complete finished make-up of a mailing prepared for checking prior to despatch to the post.

Spiral binding A method of binding, whereby loose pages have a series of holes punched on one edge, into which a binding coil is inserted.

Split run A test where one element of a promotion is tested against another or a control by having alternate copies of the same issue of the same publication. These are also known as A/B splits in the press, and a 'head to head' in direct mail.

Split test A test in which two or more samples from the same list, considered to be representative, are tested against one another, either to test the more successful or to test the homogeneity of the audience.

Spoilage The waste incurred during either the printing, mailing or finishing processes.

Sponsorship The financing of sports or cultural activities, usually by commercial companies, for public relations or promotional benefit.

Spot A booking or transmission of a television or radio commercial.

Spot colour Single additional colour printed in a block working.

Spot gumming The application of a spot of adhesive which lightly attaches one piece of material to another, often in order to facilitate its later removal.

Spot rate A rate quoted for an individual booking, as opposed to packages of airtime.

Spread Facing pages across which matter is continued as if the pages were one.

Square serif Typeface whose serifs are heavier than their strokes.

Stacking This term is given to the method in which names on a reel of magnetic tape are sequenced.

Stamping A method of binding, where an impression is made into a book cover, which is often filled with metal foil or another similar material. Or the affixing of stamps to an item to be mailed.

Stamping die A plate used for blocking.

Stand-alone A self-contained system of hardware which needs no other machine assistance to function.

Statement stuffer An advertisement which is included in an statement mailing.

Stereotype A duplicate printing plate that is cast in a mould taken from the original. This is sometimes abbreviated to stereo.

Stet A proof reader's instruction which means to ignore marked correction, i.e. let the text stand as it was originally.

Stitch To sew, or bind, by means of either a thread or staple.

Stock The liquid pulp prior to being made into paper, or the flat paper to be used by the printer for a printing.

Storage Computer memory or a magnetic storage medium which can hold data.

Store traffic The number of people, not necessarily customers who pass through a retail store.

Strategic marketing planning The process of setting marketing goals, selecting target markets and designing a marketing promotional and sales mix to achieve the set goals.

Strategic planning A management task to align resources and strengths to match the market opportunities available.

Strategy An underlying plan or philosophy to achieve given goals.

Stuffer Advertising material which is placed in other media, e.g. as inserts in a publication, in a shared mailing with other products and with an invoice or product despatch, etc.

Style of the house The typographic and linguistic rules of a publishing house. A company can also be said to have a house style, which is the consistent image it projects to the marketplace.

Styling The mailing industry description of a designation, title or position above the address, e.g. The Managing Director.

Subhead Copy set apart from the body of the text, under the main headline, usually to explain or add detail to the headline's statement. Or throughout the body copy to lead the reader through the subject matter or identify portions of it.

Subscriber A person who has placed an order to receive a publication or other series of products on a regular basis.

Subscriber list A list of those people who have ordered and are currently receiving a publication on a regular paid for basis.

Subscription series The continuity programme in which the buyer agrees to acquire the products in this series at regular intervals.

Suction feed The process of feeding material through a machine by using suction which is switched on and off by using a CAM drive.

Superprofiles A Census-based classification index which indicates geographical areas most likely to respond to a mailing, and can be used for consumer profiling and targeting.

Supplement An extra section distributed with a publication.

Suppression The removal of name and address records during computer processing in order to avoid inaccuracies such as mailing previously mailed prospects, mailing a prospect twice, or mailing those records which are out-of-date, or which have requested omission.

Suppression file The file containing those name and address records that are not to be mailed.

Swash letter An ornamental character, usually an italic capital.

Swatch A set of colour specimens printed on paper or a set of material samples.

Sweepstakes A method designed to increase sales by offering prizes to participants. Unlike competitions, sweepstakes generally require no skill. Consumers only need to return their name and address, or other particulars to be entered into a draw. Although no purchase is necessary, this device has the effect of increasing response.

Syndicated mailings Mailings or catalogues prepared and sold for the use of more than one advertiser. Usually each participant involved in a syndicated mailing has their name and address particulars printed on these, so that the campaign appears to be from them.

Synthetic papers Synthetic materials that have similar properties to paper, and can be used in printing.

Systems analyst A person whose specialism in computing is the analysis of the needs of a particular project, to determine the most efficient system, using existing software and/or writing new programs.

TAN   British Telecom telephone answering service.

TGI   Target Group Index. An aid to media and sales planning. A service which provides information on the purchasing and other behaviour of individual consumer segments.

TRHC/TRHE   Abbreviations for Top Right-Hand Corner and Top Right-Hand Edge.

TVR   Television Rating. A unit of measurement which indicates the level of audience viewing a particular spot.

Tab-pull envelope   An envelope which is opened by means of pulling a tab which tears open along perforation lines.

Table look-up   A machine procedure used to determine whether to accept or delete a record based on its accuracy and completeness, or to insert related data in a computer prepared text. E.g. insurance rates taken from a table when the computer gives the age of the customer.

Tabloid   A newspaper with small pages, e.g. *Daily Mirror* (half the size of a broadsheet).

Tag   The marking of a record with given criteria, which allows for subsequent suppression or selection.

Tail-piece   An ornamental typographical device at the end of a chapter or book.

Take   An amount of copy for typesetting given to one operator. Part of a newspaper story divided up for quicker setting

Take one   Leaflets displayed at point-of-sale or dispensers placed in areas where potential customers gather.

Tandem working   Using more than one printing machine in-line.

Tape   Used to operate a machine. Holes in tape fed into a computer or machine represent commands or data that are understood and interpreted.

Tape conversion   The change of data from one format to another.

Tape density   The number of bytes that are included in each unit of magnetic tape.

Tape drive   An input/output device which moves magnetic tape past sensing/recording mechanisms to transfer or record data to/from a processing unit.

Tape dump   A print-out of typical record data which is held on magnetic tape, in order to check for its suitability, readability, format, correctness and accuracy.

Tape editing   The alteration of data held on a magnetic tape, which usually necessitates a second or next-generation such tape being created.

Tape format layout   A map of the specific or relative location of data within each record.

Tape library   A collection of magnetic tapes which is available to a computer, generally held in a security area.

Tape merging   The combination of a master tape with a correction tape to produce a third, error-free tape, or new master.

Target audience   Those broad segments of a population identified by a marketer as suited or suitable business prospects.

Target Group Index   See TGI above.

Target market   Those people who are most likely to buy a product or service.

Targeting   The process of identifying audiences or markets or specific sections or clusters of them to match known or assessed profiles or characteristics of the buyers of a product or service.

Tear sheet A page or item torn from a periodical and filed as reference material. In certain cases this can be an advertisement either as a proof or instead of a complete copy of the publication.

Tear test A test which determines either the strength or the grain direction in paper, by assessing its ease of tearing.

Teaser A device (either a phrase or an illustration) intended to entice a reader to open an envelope and read its contents.

Tele-answering A professional answering service which is constantly manned and undertakes work for clients.

Telecommunications Communications of any kind over the telephone line.

Telecopier A means of facsimile of typed matter and layout transmitted and received by telephone, mostly used to describe the early methods of what is now known as fax or facsimile transmission.

Telemarketing The use of the telephone as a marketing medium for any activity such as list building, lead generation or selling.

Telephone marketing See Telemarketing.

Telephone response The method of responding to a direct marketing solicitation by telephone, rather than by mail or other method.

Telephone selling The use of the telephone to sell, rather than to receive enquiries.

Telephone survey or interview A research method for collecting information by interviewing people over the telephone.

Tele-sales Those involved in, or the department or group responsible for, telephone selling.

Teletext Systems where data messages and graphics can be received and decoded by a TV set generally allowing the viewer to choose pages with a keypad.

Template A shape or sheet of cut-outs which is used as a drawing aid.

Terminal A device which receives information from and/or sends information to a computer, e.g. a VDU or a printer, either of which is linked to the computer by cable or telephone.

Test In direct mail a trial of two or more variants (lists, packages, offers, etc.) the results of which determine future activities.

Test market A defined area which has characteristics representative of the entire market, which make it suitable for testing a product or campaign. Or the activity of testing as described.

Test package A mailing package used in a test.

Test panel A term given to the group of selected names used in testing.

Test tape A selection of records within a mailing list which enables a list user or bureau to reformat or convert the list to a more efficient form for the user, or to prove the feasibility of the required future function.

Testimonial A favourable comment made by a customer or a known personality. It is made to reassure the reader or to add emphasis or credibility to the product or proposition.

Testing The process of trying new ideas, lists or copy approaches by testing one against a second or more and comparing results of one against another and/or against previous results.

Text pages The principal matter in a book or publication, as opposed to the index or other adjuncts.

Text paper Good quality paper for printed publicity work. Or the body of a book, rather than its cover stock.

Thank you letter Acknowledgement letter following a response, sale or donation.

Theme The central idea behind a campaign or focal point in a promotion.

Third generation Phototypesetting equipment which uses cathode ray tubes to generate the typographical images.

Third party letter A letter which is signed by someone other than the mailer or company employee, endorsing the subject of the promotion. This procedure is frequently used for mailings to the membership or customer list of the third party.

Thumbnails Small sketches or graphic impressions.

Tie-breaker A device used in competitions to ensure that only a certain number of people win prizes. This usually involves a quasi-skill activity composing a slogan, completing a sentence, or demonstrating knowledge about the subject production or service.

Til forbid A method of ordering which continues until the customer specifically cancels it.

Time buyer The person who buys airtime from contractors. In some agencies the buyer is also the planner.

Time limit The date on which an offer expires.

Tint A light colour which is usually solid, used for backgrounds and achieved by a dot or tone value of a colour.

Tip in An insert which is placed loose between the pages of a publication.

Tip on An item glued to a printed piece.

Title A designation given to explain an individual's status or position, e.g. Miss, Mr (prefixes) or Director of Sales or Managing Director.

Title addressing A form of addressing on a direct mail letter in which a person uses a job title (or styling), rather than a name.

Title page The page of a publication which carries the title and often the author's and publisher's names.

Titling Type fount in full-faced caps.

Tolerance The degree of acceptable difference between the test results and the actual mail shot.

Topping and tailing Hand-written salutations and signatures applied to typed letters.

Track To follow the subsequent transactions of a new customer after their first purchase.

Tracking The grouping of colours of similar values in the same printing area of a sheet or web which ensures a consistent printing result. Or the use of layout and design to lead a reader a particular way.

Trade-up premium A more expensive premium offered either to prompt increased spending or as a secondary incentive to a completed sale.

Traffic builder Direct mail whose purpose is to increase store traffic (in a retail outlet).

Trailer record A special record which summarises pertinent data about a group of records.

Trannie (or tranny) Short for transparency, meaning film that can be used to make prints or from which colour separations can be made.

Transparency See Trannie.

Trend analysis A method of forecasting future sales from projections of past sale trends.

Trial buyer A person who buys a short-term supply of a product, or who buys a product with the understanding that it can be used or examined and be returned or paid for as wished after a given period.

Trial close A technique used in copy in which the writer asks for the order, and points the reader to completing the order form early in the sales copy. This technique is sometimes used on every page of a direct mail letter.

Trial subscriber A person who orders a service or product on a conditional basis. The condition may be the buyer's right to cancel, or delay a payment, or a special introductory price.

Trial subscription A method of selling newspapers or magazines by enabling readers to see a representative number of issues at a free or lower introductory rate before deciding whether or not to become a regular subscriber.

Trim The area which, after printing, is cut off as waste round the finished paper size. This area allows for bleed, grip, etc.

Trim to bleed See above.

Tube cards Advertisements which are displayed in carriages on the Underground system.

Turnaround The time between the submission of a job and the return of the results.

Two-colour press A printing machine which can print two colours on a sheet in one pass.

Two-stage sell A selling technique which uses two steps to sell a product or service. The first is designed to invite an enquiry, the second to convert this enquiry into a sale.

Two-up The number of copies to be printed from one sheet of paper. Two-up indicates the sheet will be cut in half to print two finished articles (similarly three-up, four-up, etc.).

Type The raised image of a character cast onto a rectangular piece of metal, used for letterpress printing.

Type area The area occupied by text on a page.

Type family The versions of one style of typeface, e.g. roman, italic or bold.

Type mark-up Instructions marked by a typographer which indicate size, typeface, etc.

Type specification See Type mark-up.

Typesetting The assembly of printing text and line matter by means of handpicking, keyboarding and/or casting or photosetting.

Typographic errors Sometimes shortened to typos. Typesetting errors in copy caused or repeated in the assembly to type.

Typography The art, appearance and general design of printed matter using type.

Underkill A term applied to the process of eliminating duplicate names from different lists or list segments, when only those names that are positively identified as being duplicates are extracted, leaving possible duplicates included within the final mailing list.

Underlay An effect laid under artwork, photograph or illustration, e.g. a colour, tone or pattern.

Unique names Those names that appear only once in a mailing list, after duplicate names have been eliminated.

Unique selling proposition The single most saleable feature of a product used in advertising to distinguish a particular product benefit/feature which competitive products cannot promise.

Unit pricing A consumer aid to assist customers with the comparison of prices per unit volume. Alongside the cost of a product, the price of a product is given for a standard weight, e.g. price per kg or some other standard measure.

Unit value The number of units in a character for typesetting. A unit is a subdivision of the em measurement, the size of which varies with the system.

Universe The total quantity of a complete selection of mailing lists. Also the total quantity of a market.

Untrimmed size The dimensions of a sheet or printed piece before it is trimmed down.

Up-market A description given to a product, generally of high quality and expensively priced, that appeals to those in the higher income or status groups.

Update To bring up-to-date. A term given to the input of the latest information into a list, e.g. latest transactions, additions and deletions.

Upgrading Those techniques to sell a more expensive product or to sell further products to existing customers.

Upper/lower case Typographical terms used to distinguish between CAPITAL LETTERS (upper) and normal letters (lower).

VDU/VDT Short for visual display unit/terminal. A device which displays information from the computer and commands from a keyboard on a screen.

Value Lightness or darkness of tone.

Variable cost A cost that varies in accordance with the number of units sold or produced.

Variable field A method of conserving space on magnetic tape or disk. List information is assigned specific sequence, but not without specific positions to its layout or format.

Variable format See Variable field.

Variable space Space inserted between words in order to justify a line.

Variable-price policy A pricing strategy whereby a company sells its goods or services in similar quantities to similar buyers, but at different prices, set usually as a result of bargaining.

Variance The relative importance or priority of differing market factors, determined by a statistical process.

Vertical market A market confined to specific industries or segments — i.e. light engineering or farming — as distinct from horizontal markets such as chief creatives or business travellers who will be found right across the vertical markets.

Vertical marketing system A system of distribution, the stages of which are treated as one integral unit.

Viewdata Any system which links a central computer to TV screens, via telephone lines or satellite, on which a user can call up data, and send messages.

Visual A sketched piece of artwork or design idea.

Visual display unit/terminal See VDU/VDT.

Visualiser A trained artist whose specialism is the production of visuals.

Volume discount A reduced unit price offered to those who buy products or services in bulk.

Voucher copy A copy of a publication given by publishers to advertisers for proof that an advertisement appeared as agreed.

—W—

W/S Short for wire-stitched. A binding method which staples the leaves of a publication together.

Wallet A type of envelope whose flap lies on the long edge. This type of envelope is more usually suitable for inserting machines.

Warm colours Red and yellow shades.

Warm donors People who have previously supported a charity, and thus are considered to be more likely sources for future donations.

Warranty A promise or an agreement made by a mailer to a prospect, the breach of which entitles the buyer to make claims for replacement, compensation or repair against the warrantor.

Watermark A semi-transparent design which is impressed into paper when it is being made.

We miss you letter A letter which is sent to former or dormant customers or subscribers, to try to win back their custom, usually with an incentive.

Web A continuous sheet of paper on a roll or reel, rather than a series of cut sheets.

Web offset An offset printing process that uses continuous paper fed from a reel.

Web press A printing press that uses continuous feed paper rather than sheets.

Weight The degree of boldness of a typeface style, e.g. light, medium, etc.

Weight steps The tariff bands charged for mail, according to the weight of what is being mailed.

Weighting The process of assigning different values to data in accordance with its judged importance.

White mail A phrase which describes those letters received by mail order firms which result in extra administrative work. These include letters from prospects and customers which are either complaints, enquiries or testimonials.

White out A method of printing so that an image or word appears white, against surrounding colour. In fact, achieved by preventing areas of the white paper from being printed. And the elimination of the background to a print by the application of process white.

White space   The blank area without illustration or type around an advertisement or printed item. Also called air.

Window envelope   An aperture cut into an envelope, so that this area shows the part of a letter lying underneath from the outside. A window is usually covered by either glassine or plastic, and is most frequently used to display the recipient's name and address.

Wire binding   A method of binding which uses a double loop of wire to run through slots in the back of a book.

Wire stitching   See W/S.

With the grain   A method of folding paper in parallel with the grain.

Word-break   The division of a word at the end of a line.

Wordspace   The space between words that can be varied so that lines are justified.

Work and tumble   A printing technique whereby paper is printed on both sides, achieved by turning it over from the gripper to the back and using the same printing plate.

Work and turn   A printing technique whereby paper is printed on both sides, achieved by using the same gripper edge and turning the sheet by its side to pass the plate for a second time.

Wraparound   A second outside cover for a mail order catalogue, which may contain another order form or special announcement, etc.

Wrapping   The insertion of magazines or other publications into wrappers for posting.

Wrong-reading   The reverse of right-reading. Film which reads correctly from the reverse side when viewed from the emulsion side (i.e. from right to left).

–X–

X date   Has two meanings. For subscriptions, the date a member or subscriber 'expires'. In direct mail, the date a particular offer will terminate.

Xerography   An electrostatic copying process whereby 'toner' adheres to charged paper to produce an image.

–Y–

Yankee dryer   A steam-heated cylinder which dries paper in a way that gives it a glazed finish.

Yapp   Binding material edges which overlap the caseboards of a book to give a fringed effect.

Yellow   One of the specific primary colours used for printing.

Yes/no envelope   A device designed to improve response, by requesting readers to reply regardless of whether they intend to take up an offer or not. The 'no' proves that they are responsive and are then used for different product approaches in the future. This can be an economical method of 'lifting' the maximum in names from rented lists avoiding future charges.

Yes/no stamp   A stamp designed to attach to a card or coupon for a similar purpose to the yes/no envelope above.

Z fold A fold that resembles the letter Z. To make a Z fold paper is folded into three equal parts, so that the central third forms the 'diagonal' in the letter Z.

Zip envelopes Envelopes that open by pulling a tag which opens the envelope along perforation lines.

Index